Twelfth Night or What You Will

Texts and Contexts

OTHER BEDFORD/ST. MARTIN'S TITLES OF INTEREST

William Shakespeare, *The First Part of King Henry the Fourth: Texts and Contexts*
(The Bedford Shakespeare Series)
EDITED BY BARBARA HODGDON,
DRAKE UNIVERSITY

William Shakespeare, *Hamlet*
(Case Studies in Contemporary Criticism)
EDITED BY SUSANNE L. WOFFORD,
UNIVERSITY OF WISCONSIN — MADISON

William Shakespeare, *Macbeth: Texts and Contexts*
(The Bedford Shakespeare Series)
EDITED BY WILLIAM C. CARROLL,
BOSTON UNIVERSITY

William Shakespeare,
A Midsummer Night's Dream: Texts and Contexts
(The Bedford Shakespeare Series)
EDITED BY GAIL KERN PASTER,
GEORGE WASHINGTON UNIVERSITY
AND
SKILES HOWARD,
RUTGERS UNIVERSITY AT NEW BRUNSWICK

William Shakespeare, *The Taming of the Shrew: Texts and Contexts*
(The Bedford Shakespeare Series)
EDITED BY FRANCES E. DOLAN,
MIAMI UNIVERSITY

William Shakespeare, *The Tempest*
(Case Studies in Critical Controversy)
EDITED BY GERALD GRAFF,
UNIVERSITY OF ILLINOIS AT CHICAGO
AND
JAMES PHELAN,
OHIO STATE UNIVERSITY

The Bedford Companion to Shakespeare: An Introduction with Documents, Second Edition
BY RUSS MCDONALD,
UNIVERSITY OF NORTH CAROLINA AT GREENSBORO

WILLIAM SHAKESPEARE

Twelfth Night or What You Will

Texts and Contexts

Edited by

BRUCE R. SMITH

Georgetown University

Bedford/St. Martin's BOSTON ◆ NEW YORK

For Bedford/St. Martin's

Editorial Assistants: Caroline Thompson, Maria Teresa Burwell
Senior Production Supervisor: Joe Ford
Project Management: Publisher's Studio/Stratford Publishing Services, Inc.
Marketing Manager: Richard Cadman
Text Design: Claire Seng-Niemoeller
Cover Design: Claire Jarvis
Cover Art: Dining Scene from the Time of James I; Morris Dancers. By the permission of the Folger Shakespeare Library.
Composition: Stratford Publishing Services, Inc.
Printing and Binding: Haddon Craftsmen, an R. R. Donnelley & Sons Company

President: Charles H. Christensen
Editorial Director: Joan E. Feinberg
Editor in Chief: Karen S. Henry
Director of Marketing: Karen R. Melton
Director of Editing, Design, and Production: Marcia Cohen
Manager, Publishing Services: Emily Berleth

Library of Congress Control Number: 00-108533

Manufactured in the United States of America.

6 5 4 3 2 1
f e d c b a

For information, write: Bedford/St. Martin's, 75 Arlington Street, Boston, MA 02116 (617-399-4000)

ISBN: 0–312–20219–9 (paperback)
0–312–23712–X (hardcover)

Published and distributed outside North America by

PALGRAVE
Houndmills, Basingstoke, Hampshire RG21 2XS and London
Companies and representatives throughout the world.
PALGRAVE is the new global academic imprint of St. Martin's Press LLC Scholarly and Reference Division and Palgrave Publishers Ltd. (formerly Macmillan Press Ltd.).

ISBN: 0-333-94714-2

A catalog record for this book is available from the British Library.

Acknowledgments and copyrights can be found at the back of the book on pages 411–413, which constitute an extension of the copyright page.

For Kendall Reed Smith,
a natural mocker

About the Series

Shakespeare wrote his plays in a culture unlike, though related to, the culture of the emerging twenty-first century. The Bedford Shakespeare Series resituates Shakespeare within the sometimes alien context of the sixteenth and seventeenth centuries while inviting students to explore ways in which Shakespeare, as text and as cultural icon, continues to be part of contemporary life. Each volume frames a Shakespearean play with a wide range of written and visual material from the early modern period, such as homilies, polemical literature, emblem books, facsimiles of early modern documents, maps, woodcut prints, court records, other plays, medical tracts, ballads, chronicle histories, and travel narratives. Selected to reveal the many ways in which Shakespeare's plays were connected to the events, discourses, and social structures of his time, these documents and illustrations also show the contradictions and the social divisions in Shakespeare's culture and in the plays he wrote. Engaging critical introductions and headnotes to the primary materials help students identify some of the issues they can explore by reading these texts with and against one another, setting up a two-way traffic between the Shakespearean text and the social world these documents help to construct.

Jean E. Howard
Columbia University
Series Editor

About This Volume

Bodies, space, time, and sound are the elements out of which all fictions are made, but in dramatic performance those elements are physically present. A printed book can offer no more than a poor substitute for the real thing. This edition of *Twelfth Night* is designed to overcome those limitations. Think of it as a conjuring trick. A rare, first-hand account of one of the play's earliest performances, in February 1602, gives us unusually intimate access to some of the things that were on the minds of that early audience. In the introduction we leaf through the diary of John Manningham, the young law student who was present at the performance, and take stock of the day-by-day entries that Manningham made in the weeks just before and just after he saw *Twelfth Night.* Then comes the script of the play itself. Manningham's preoccupations — with romance, music, sexuality, clothing and disguise, household economies, Puritan probity, and laughter and clowning — form the basis for the seven chapters that follow. As it happens, the seven contexts are very much concerned with bodies, space, time, and sound. The texts and images on offer in Part Two of this volume have been chosen to bring those concerns to dramatic life here and now, but with full appreciation of the cultural differences that separate our perceptions from those of Shakespeare and his contemporaries. With the exception of Barnaby Rich's tale of Apolonius and Silla, which gave Shakespeare the idea for the play's plot, none of the texts here can be regarded as direct sources of *Twelfth Night.* Rather, they should be read as items found in an old scrapbook. Interesting to consider individually, they may offer, taken altogether, a sense of the past that is greater than the sum of the parts.

A NOTE ON EDITING AND GLOSSING

The text of *Twelfth Night* reproduced here is that edited by David Bevington in *The Complete Works of Shakespeare,* fourth edition (New York: Addison Wesley Longman, 1997), complete with Bevington's notes and glosses, with one or two additional stage directions and a few minor changes in lineation. Texts reproduced in the seven chapters that come after the play fall into two categories. Some are reprinted from modern editions, in which case they include glosses provided by the editor of the text in question, with the occasional addition of glosses provided by the editor of the present volume. Other texts have been specially edited for this edition. In general, the spelling in this second group of texts has been modernized, but punctuation has been left as close to the original as modern reading conventions will allow. Glosses to all the texts have been supplied to facilitate easy reading in connection with *Twelfth Night* and are not intended to be exhaustive.

ACKNOWLEDGMENTS

Any production of *Twelfth Night,* on stage, on screen, on video, requires the collaboration of many people. So, too, has this edition of the play. I want especially to thank Jean Howard, the series editor, for inviting me to prepare the edition and Karen Henry, Boston Editor in Chief of Bedford / St. Martin's, for her encouragement, counsel, and patience. The reviewers of the original proposal—Ivo Camps, University of Mississippi; Susan Frye, University of Wyoming; Theodora Jankowski, Washington State University; Laurie Osborne, Colby College; and Michael Schoenfeldt, University of Michigan—will recognize more than a few of their suggestions here. For recommendations of texts to be included I am grateful to Nora Johnson, Margaret Rose Jaster, and Peter Stallybrass. Expert help in transcribing and modernizing the texts was provided by Jennifer Margiotta. Anne Loomis Roberts genially offered advice about translations from ancient Greek. Staff members at several libraries showed extraordinary generosity in answering my requests for help, in some cases at long distance: Susan Harris at the Bodleian Library, Beatrice Franklin at the Egan Library of the University of Alaska Southeast, Georgianna Ziegler and Lori Johnson at the Folger Shakespeare Library, Stephen Tabor and Lisa Libby at the Huntington Library,

Judy McManus at Lauinger Library of Georgetown University, Miriam Mandelbaum and A. Teodoro at the New York Public Library, and Joy Allison at the Phillips Library of Mount St. Mary's College. For assistance in securing illustrations I am grateful to Joan Pong Linton at Indiana University, and Mike Spain, Deputy Under Treasurer, and Leslie Whitelaw, Archivist, with the Honorable Society of the Middle Temple in London. Andrew Gurr obliged with information at a crucial juncture when needed books were out of reach. For tactical support in London I am much indebted to Judy Hill and Patricia Tatspaugh. The logistics of turning twenty-nine illustrations, extracts from sixty different sources, and my own text into a uniform book were managed with professional aplomb by Emily Berleth, Manager of Publishing Services at Bedford/St. Martin's; Kate Cohen, copy editor; and Leslie Connor, Project Manager at Publisher's Studio/Stratford Publishing. The offices of the Dean of the Graduate School and the Dean of Georgetown College at Georgetown University provided financial support for illustrations and permissions fees. To all these individuals and institutions I give hearty thanks.

Bruce R. Smith
Georgetown University

Contents

Illustrations

Introduction

Most unusually among Shakespeare's plays, the text of *Twelfth Night* comes down to today's readers framed within the context of one of its earliest performances. John Manningham, in his late twenties, was a little over halfway through his seven-year course of legal studies at the Middle Temple in London when he joined his fellow students, their masters, and some distinguished alumni to celebrate one of the academic household's two great holidays, Candlemas, on February 2, 1602. (The other great communal celebration occurred on All Saints' Day, November 1.) The Inns of Court, as the Middle Temple and its allied centers of legal activity were called, sometimes hired professional actors for holiday celebrations, just as the court of the realm did. It was probably Shakespeare's company, for example, that had put on "a comedy of errors (like to Plautus his *Menaechmus*)" at Gray's Inn during the Christmas revels of 1594.[1] In his diary Manningham devotes about a hundred words to describing the 1602 performance of *Twelfth Night* — the same number of words he allots to most other events in his life:

[1] An account of the performance is included in the souvenir pamphlet of the occasion, *Gesta Grayorum,* ed. Desmond Bland, 31–32.

> At our feast we had a play called "~~Mid~~ Twelve Night, or What You Will," much like "The Comedy of Errors" or "Menaechmi" in Plautus, but most like and near to that in Italian called "Inganni."
>
> A good practice in it to make the steward believe his lady-widow was in love with him, by counterfeiting a letter as from his lady, in general terms telling him what she liked best in him and prescribing his gesture in smiling, his apparel, etc. and then, when he came to practice, making him believe they took him to be mad.

Manningham's description bears the hallmarks of a young man of his time and place. He displays a Cambridge man's learning by citing Latin and Italian precedents for Shakespeare's plot involving twins who keep getting mistaken for one another. (Manningham had graduated from Magdalene College, Cambridge, before he took up his legal studies in London.) But the part of the play Manningham singles out for special comment, the duping of Olivia's household steward Malvolio, "a kind of puritan" (2.3.115), shows an interest in affairs closer to home than plays from Italy. Manningham's knowing reference to *The Comedy of Errors* reveals that he, like other inns-of-court men, made up a recognizable part of audiences in the public playhouses where Shakespeare and his troupe usually performed. Perhaps Manningham's knowledge of Shakespeare's work extended beyond these two plays. Does the crossed out "Mid" before "Night" represent a mistake for "Midnight" (the reveling hour favored by Sir Toby Belch and his crew) or for *A Midsummer Night's Dream*?

The site of the 1602 performance of *Twelfth Night,* the Middle Temple's great hall, still stands in London (see Figure 1). We can enter that *physical* context by getting ourselves to London, finding our way to Fleet Street, and taking a turn into Middle Temple Lane. To enter the *psychological* context of *Twelfth Night* in 1602 presents a greater challenge. Fortunately, Manningham offers himself as a guide. Taken altogether, the things Manningham chose to write down in his diary during January and February 1602, just before and just after his description of *Twelfth Night* at Candlemas, reveal the hopes and fears, desires and anxieties that might have preoccupied the play's earliest audiences. Sampling some of Manningham's diary entries may help us to appreciate *Twelfth Night*'s original appeal.

Many of these entries record gossip about other young men's fortunes as they make their way in the world. Take, for example, the notes Manningham made to himself on January 11, three weeks before he was to see *Twelfth Night,* concerning a young man in the country near his foster father's place in Kent, where Manningham spent the Christmas holidays:

FIGURE 1 *Middle Temple Hall (built 1562–70).*

> Mr. Francis Vane, a young gentleman of great hope and forwardness, very well affected in the country already, insomuch that [at] the last parliament the country gave him the place of knight before Sir H. Newell. His possibility of living by his wife very much, she being daughter and heir to Sir Anthony Mildmay. And thought her mother will give her all her inheritance also. The father worth £3,000 per annum, the mother's [inheritance], £1,200. (Manningham 43)

Manningham's concern with religious controversy may have primed him to appreciate the gulling of Malvolio. Manningham records, with disapproval, his foster father's wife's praise of a Puritan neighbor who delighted in out-arguing established church authorities:

> My cousin she speaking lavishly in commendations of one Lovell of Cranbrook, a good honest poor silly Puritan, "Oh," said she, "he goes to the ground when he talks in divinity with a preacher." "True," said I, "'Tis very likely a man shall go to the ground when he will either venture to take upon him a matter that is too weighty for him or meddle with with such as are more than his match." (44)

A related entry:

> "I put him down i'faith," said one, when he had outtalked a wiser than himself. "Just," said I, "as a drummer puts down sweet still music, not as better but as more sounding." (44–45)

Drumming versus "sweet still music": Manningham shows an appreciation of music as a metaphor. For all his disdain for the "good honest poor silly Puritan" Lovell, Manningham can still quote with approval one of his friend's remarks about reserving Sunday afternoons, as well as Sunday mornings, for religious activities. Stealing time on Sundays is like chipping gold and silver off coins: "The spending of the afternoons on Sundays either idly or about temporal affairs is like clipping the Queen's coin: this treason to the prince, that prophanation and robbing God of his own" (45). Within a few days, however, he is taking the side of merrymaking servants and poking fun at spoilsports during holidays:

> Certain in the country this last Christmas chose a jury to find the churl of their parish, and when they came to give their verdict, they named one whose friend, being present, began to be very choleric [angry] with the boys for abusing them. "Hold you content, gaffer," said one of them. "If your boy had not been one of the jury, *you* had been found to have been the churl." (46)

Several days and several lines later Manningham is upbraiding the haughtiness of William, first Baron Paget, who conveniently forgot his own humble origins but liked to remind other people of theirs. Paget's interlocutor in this anecdote was the son of a cloth merchant who prospered at his father's trade and went on to found Merchant Taylor's School in London and St. John's College, Oxford:

> The Lord Paget upon a time thinking to have goaded Sir Thomas White (an alderman of London) in a great assembly, asked him what he thought of that cloth, showing him a garment in present. "Truly, my lord," said he, "it seems to be a very good cloth, but I remember when I was a young beginner I sold your father a far better to make him a gown when he was Sergeant to the Lord Mayor. Truly he was a very honest sergeant!" None so ready to carp at other men's mean beginnings as such as were themselves no better. (46)

Clothing — who wears what and how much it costs — figures here as a highly visible index of social status. How the story about Lord Paget's hypocrisy is to be reconciled with Manningham's envy of socially ambitious young men like Francis Vane is left unexplored.

Not least among the things that interest John Manningham are jokes. A week before he saw *Twelfth Night* he records this one about the stage clown Richard Tarlton, who rails against the stinginess of William Cecil, Lord Burghley, Queen Elizabeth's lord treasurer and chief minister: "Tarlton called Burghley House Gate in the Strand towards the Savoy 'the Lord Treasurer's Alms Gate,' because it was seldom or never opened" (46). Later in his diary Manningham records a fellow law student's joke about none other than William Shakespeare, who outsmarted the company's chief actor, Richard Burbage:

> Upon a time when Burbage played Richard III there was a citizen grew so far in liking with him that before she went from the play she appointed him to come that night unto her by the name of "Richard III." Shakespeare, overhearing their conclusion, went before, was entertained, and at his game ere Burbage came. Then message being brought that "Richard III" was at the door, Shakespeare caused return to be made that "William the Conqueror" was before "Richard III." Shakespeare's name [is] William. (75)

The immediate foils to Manningham's description of *Twelfth Night* are especially suggestive about what was on the minds of the audience in February 1602. The first of these foils is an observation about con artists who seize the license of the season and try to pass themselves off as gentlemen: "This last Christmas the cony-catchers would call themselves country gentlemen at dice" (47). Next comes one of the bawdy jokes in which Manningham delights. It turns on the promise of a fellow law student many years before to have a certain gentlewoman act as godparent to his son:

> When a gentlewoman told Mr. Lancaster [probably Thomas Lancaster of Gray's Inn] he had not been so good as his word, because he promised she should be gossip to his first child (glancing at the bastard on his laundress), "Tut," said he, "you shall be *mother* to my next, if you will." (47)

Then comes an anagram on a lady who was famous for her wordplay: "Margaret Westphaling / My greatest welfaring" (48). And then, cryptic indeed, another anagram: "Davis Advis Iudas (Martin)" (48). What Manningham is doing here is turning the name of the poet John Davies, via the made-up Latin word *advis* (from *advertere,* to turn against), into Judas the betrayer of Christ. In doing so he is remembering an event that had happened at the Middle Temple four years earlier, just before Manningham joined the community, when Davies strode into the great hall with a cudgel and brutually attacked his sometime friend Richard Martin. Martin had been chosen over Davies to preside over the Christmas revels of 1597–98 as "Le Prince d'Amour," the Prince of Love, and Davies was aggrieved. The chivalric romance the students had played out during the Christmas revels ended, a week after Candlemas, in a bloody fracas. Then comes Manningham's description of *this* year's Candlemas, complete with a performance of "a play called '~~Mid~~ Twelve Night, or What You Will.'"

The entries that follow continue to reflect Manningham's interests in advantageous marriages, young men who get on in the world, good laughs, religious controversy, word games, and gossip about the all-male household of which he is a member (44–49). One of the entries adds an element of trickery and perhaps disguise to Manningham's interest in marriage: "Cousin Norton told me that one Mr. Cokayne of Hertfordshire got his brother H. Norton by a wile to his house and there married him upon a push to a kinswoman of his, and made a serving man serve the purpose instead of a priest" (49). In all their variety, the entries in Manningham's diary suggest some of the contexts in which we might place the text of *Twelfth Night* to understand what it meant to watchers and listeners like John Manningham and his peers. Let us consider those contexts one by one.

Romance

The elaborate fiction sustained over days and weeks during the reign of "Le Prince d'Amour" shows that the original audiences of *Twelfth Night* liked to project themselves into a world of romance. A contemporary description of the Middle Temple revels of 1597–98, over which Richard Martin presided, was printed in 1660 as a piece of nostalgia for the bygone golden days before the Civil Wars, when men of public affairs could still imagine themselves as chivalric knights. Excerpts from the pamphlet *Le Prince d'Amour* are included in Chapter 1. What makes such a fiction appealing — indeed, what makes it possible in the first place — is *distance.* The revelers of 1597–98 were no less distanced in time from the Age of Chivalry than the readers of 1660 were from the Elizabethan world of "Le Prince d'Amour." The first scenes of *Twelfth Night* seem calculated to create a similar sense of distance in both time and space. "If music be the food of love . . ." (1.1.1): Orsino's opening line wafts the audience to a world where love — falling in love, falling out of love, pursuing love, fleeing love, extolling love, and making sport of love — seems to be life's main occupation. The second scene marks the distance between *there* and *here* via a shipwreck. Furthermore, it gives Orsino's desire a local habitation and a name:

VIOLA: What country, friends, is this?
CAPTAIN: This is Illyria, lady. (1.2.1–2)

Illyria, as we shall see in Chapter 1, could be found on a map, on the Adriatic coast of modern-day Croatia. Two references in *Twelfth Night* (2.5.177 and 3.4.280) to "the Sophy," the Safavid shah of Persia, serve to associate Illyria with the East more generally. Tales of the sophy's wealth and splendor had reached England from Sir Robert Shirley (1581?–1628), an adventurer who ingratiated himself with the shah and was serving as the shah's ambassador to Christendom. A published account of Sir Robert's exploits and those of his two brothers Anthony and Thomas, printed in 1607, begins with the woodcut image of a ship, as if inviting the reader on board for the passage east (see Figure 2). Contemplating that destination was likely to fill men like John Manningham with both delight and dread. On the one hand, the East was a kind of utopia, a no-place where the rules constraining everyday life in

FIGURE 2 *Sailing Eastward, from Anthony Nixon,* The Three English Brothers.

England could be forgotten and a hero like Sir Robert Shirley could find a scope for action impossible at home. On the other hand, it was a dystopia, the domain of infidels, a place of tyranny, cruelty, and sexual depravity.

As the title *Twelfth Night* makes clear, time in Illyria is no less extraordinary than place: it is holiday time. The Feast of the Epiphany on the twelfth day after Christmas (January 6) marked a climax to the days and nights of continuous revelry that had begun with Christmas itself. The biblical event celebrated on January 6 was the visit to the Christ child of "wise men from the east" (Matthew 2.1), trailing behind them the mysteries of the Orient. The very word *epiphany* means an appearance or a revelation and suggests that on that special day celebrants could expect something visionary, a miracle, a manifestation of divinity. Occasion for one final burst of celebration came on the fortieth day after Christmas, at Candlemas, on the Feast of the Purification.

The *candle* in Candlemas refers to the candles that once had been brought to church to be blessed on this day, just as the Virgin Mary had been brought to the temple to be purified forty days after giving birth to Christ. Protestant theologians may have put an end to what they considered the superstitious practice of blessing candles, but Candlemas in 1602 remained a welcome island of light amid the gloom of early February. Candles were a relatively expensive commodity in Shakespeare's England: a single wax candle cost as much as three pence — three times the price of a standing place at the Globe. A hall full of candlelight against the dark night outside was a rare and luxurious sight.[2] What *Twelfth Night* offered John Manningham and his friends was a perfect entertainment for such a splendid occasion: a few golden hours of respite from the gray world of winter. It gave them time out in a place apart, and they were not about to let a "churl" like the old "gaffer" in Kent — or Malvolio in the play — spoil their fun. The topsy-turvydom of traditional Christmas celebrations at the Middle Temple had once been embodied in a "Lord of Misrule," an individual elected among the students to exercise, during the festivities, the sort of authority that usually belonged to the masters. After the masters had banned the practice in 1584 there were periodic protests, including one in 1591 that involved John Davies and Richard Martin, then fast friends (Manningham 262, 311). "Le Prince d'Amour" in 1602 could trace his lineage to these earlier Lords of Misrule.

The fact that John Davies and Richard Martin came to blows over "Le Prince d'Amour" demonstrates, however, that faraway fictions might be

[2] On Candlemas as a festival see Hutton, 139–45. In 1602 the royal Office of Works was paying three shillings, six pence per dozen-pound of candles. See Beveridge, 468. The extant account books of the royal Revels Office include substantial payments in the 1570s to the chandler Bernard Fabian, for example, fifty-seven shillings for Candlemas 1574. See Feuillerat, 208–09.

more than escapist fantasies. From the beginning, the genre of romance combined the exotic and the familiar, the "matter of Rome" with the language of home. True to form, events in Illyria engage anxieties that, for the original audiences, were pressingly immediate. Manningham's concerns with making his way in the world, with sexual desire, with marriage, with precedence and hierarchy find resonances in Shakespeare's tale of twins who must negotiate the labyrinth of desire in Illyria. The son of a yeoman farmer, Manningham enrolled in the Middle Temple with the support of a wealthy relative in 1598, married his roommate's sister in 1607, and claimed the coat of arms of a gentleman in 1619.

In his *Description of England* (1577), William Harrison describes four "sorts" or "degrees" of men below the rank of titled artistocrats: (1) gentlemen, (2) merchants and professional men, (3) yeomen farmers, and (4) servants and laborers. The lower three of these four ranks had to work for a living; gentlemen shared with aristocrats the advantage of living off inherited wealth, generally in the form of land. The mobility among these categories can be witnessed in the life of William Shakespeare himself. According to the letter of the law, he and the other actors in his company were servants, first to the lord chamberlain and later to King James. In terms of income and lifestyle, he was a merchant or professional man. By aspiration he was a gentleman, and he became one legally when he secured a gentleman's coat of arms for his merchant father.

Seven years of legal study in one of the Inns of Court was more secure than playwrighting or acting as a means of securing status as a gentleman. In the years just after Manningham left the Middle Temple, 90 percent of the entrants were either aristocrats or gentlemen, but many of the gentlemen were younger sons who would not, under English custom, inherit their fathers' estates, which went to first-born sons. For the remaining 10 percent of the entrants between 1610 and 1639, the Inns of Court could be a passport from merchant status into the gentry. As an only child, adopted by a rich relative and poised to inherit that relative's property, Manningham may have been atypical, but the entries in his diary about how much money goes with which position — and with which marriage — suggest a certain social anxiety that allies him with his peers (Wrightson 189). Part of the romance of *Twelfth Night* is the vision it offers of social mobility. The social prospects of Viola and Sebastian in *Twelfth Night* are quite as unsettled as the social prospects of many of the students who followed the twins' adventures in Middle Temple Hall. When Olivia asks the disguised Viola, "What is your parentage?" Viola as "Cesario" replies, "Above my fortunes, yet my state is well: / I am a gentleman" (1.5.223–24). Viola ends the play, however, higher up the social scale than that, as a titled aristocrat, as the wife of a duke.

Sebastian, for his part, marries Lady Olivia, herself of rank sufficiently high to have engaged the duke's serious consideration as a wife. How much Duke Orsino and Lady Olivia may have been worth in pounds per annum is left to Manningham's imagination.

Music

Prominent among the features of Illyria that establish it as a place apart is music. The contrast John Manningham draws between loud drumming and soft, sweet music draws our attention to the difference between the brash, percussive sounds of Shakespeare's history plays and tragedies and the harmonious, consorted sounds of *Twelfth Night.* The play begins with music and ends with music. "Play on," *keep* playing: Orsino's command indicates that music is floating through the air before a single word of speech is sounded. Surprisingly for the festive occasion announced in the play's title, the music that the audience first hears is sad: it has a "dying fall" (1.1.1, 4). Quite possibly what the original audience heard was music in the languid idiom of John Dowland (1563?–1626?), whose lute songs were, in 1602, at the very height of their popularity. Collections of Dowland's songs had been published in 1597 and 1600; a third set was to appear in 1603. *Semper Dowland, semper dolens,* (ever Dowland, ever doleful) — a contemporary tag catches the fashionably melancholy nature of Dowland's music, which could be performed without words by a consort of viols or other instruments as well as by a singer with a lute, as suggested in Figure 3.[3] As sad music begins the play, so sad music closes the play, in the form of Feste's song "When that I was and a little tiny boy." In between, in act 2, scene 3, comes more varied fare: Feste's performances of "O mistress mine" and "Come away, death," the "catch" or round he sings with Sir Toby and Sir Andrew, and the tags of old songs the revelers trade among themselves until Malvolio bursts on the scene to silence them, not to mention the snatches Feste sings of "Hey Robin, jolly Robin" later in the play (4.2.55–62). In a theater without illusionistic scenery, Illyria is more a *sound*scape than a landscape, and music forms a prominent feature within the play's acoustic horizons. Indeed, the very name of the place, Il*lyr*ia, incorporates the name of the ancient stringed instrument of Apollo, the lyre.

[3] John Dowland's professional career included a stint at the court of Denmark and concluded, back in England, with his service as lutenist to Charles I. See Poulton.

FIGURE 3 *Concocting the Food of Love, from Adrien LeRoy,* A Brief and Easy Instruction to Learn the Tablature . . . unto the Lute.

The appeal of music, in Orsino's description, is synaesthetic. It engages multiple senses all at once:

> That strain again! It had a dying fall;
> O, it came o'er my ear like the sweet sound
> That breathes upon a bank of violets,
> Stealing and giving odor. (1.1.4–7)

Music fuses the sense of hearing ("it came o'er my ear") with the senses of taste ("like the sweet sound"), touch ("that breathes"), sight ("upon a bank of violets"), and smell ("stealing and giving odor"). It challenges the categorical boundaries of language that would keep the senses separate and the world in order. Hence, at bottom, Malvolio's objections to music-making at odd hours. In imagining a bank of violets Orsino anticipates the name of the woman he is about to meet and marry. *Viola* is a type of violet; it is also a stringed instrument played with a bow.

The music in *Twelfth Night* is not just to hear but to think about. Renaissance theorists recognized two kinds of music: "contemplative" and "practical." Formal education had always emphasized the former. Music, along with arithmetic, geometry, and astronomy, belonged to the quadrivium, the higher division of the seven liberal arts. In its numerosity, in its ordering of elements in time, music was allied with these other scientific disciplines. "Practical" music, heard with the ears, was taken to be the sense-accessible equivalent of "contemplative" music, thought about with the mind: "contemplative" music belonged to Plato's realm of Being, "practical" music to the realm of Becoming. The discovery of music, in both classical tradition and Christian tradition, involved making a connection between the two realms. Iamblichus credits Pythagoras with passing a blacksmith's shop, hearing the different pitches of the hammers, and hitting upon the idea of weighting different lengths of wire with the hammers to produce a seven-note scale. When he measured the lengths of wire, Pythagoras discovered that they corresponded to the relative distances between the planets. Christian tradition attributes the same discovery to Jubal, brother of the blacksmith Tubalcain.[4] Both versions of the story establish the alliance of music with arithmetic, geometry, and astronomy. "The music of the spheres" could be seen with a telescope as well as heard through the ears. Indeed, music of the right sort could make a listener experience cosmic harmony without benefit of a telescope. What was needed was a stringed instrument and a human voice to sing words in precisely ordered rhythm and in precisely ordered sequences of pitch. Music heard in time thus replicates music measured in space.

Ovid's two accounts of the musical contest between Apollo and Marsyas (*Fasti* 6.697–710 and *Metamorphoses* 6.382–400) turn on a contrast between Apollo's word-imbued songs to the lyre versus Marsyas's sensual music on a pipe that has been cast aside by Minerva, the goddess of wisdom. (The accounts figure in Chapter 2.) *Twelfth Night* gives its listeners music of both kinds: Feste, likely singing to lute accompaniment, and Sir Toby and

[4] Iamblichus, *Life of Pythagoras,* trans. Thomas Taylor (London: Watkins, 1926), 62, tells the classical version of the story. The description of Jubal in Genesis 4.21 as "the father of all that play on the harp and organ" inspired Christian commentators to apply the story to him. See Strunk, 117, 246–47.

friends bellowing away in the midnight air. In more ways than one, it is Feste's music that carries the day — or rather the night. Viola expresses a faith in "contemplative" music when, putting on a eunuch's disguise, she declares, "What else may hap to time I will commit" (1.2.60). Music is, after all, an artful ordering of time. Heard music harmonizes one tune with the next, even as "the music of the spheres" proportions one planet's movements to another. Both sorts of music unfold in time, according to regular rhythms. Reeling with the confusions of her disguise later in the play, Viola declares, "O time, thou must untangle this, not I. / It is too hard a knot for me t'untie" (2.2.35–36). And so time does. The marriages at the end will take place when "golden time *convents*" (5.1.359, emphasis added), that is to say, when golden time *brings things together.* The song that Feste sings as an epilogue, "When that I was and a little tiny boy," brings the play full circle to its musical beginning even as it brings a man's life full circle by recounting Aristotle's four ages of man: boy, young man, husband, old man.

Sexuality

"What You Will": Manningham is careful to note the subtitle of the play he saw at Candlemas 1602. The pleasures invited by that subtitle may well be specifically sexual pleasures. As a noun at least, the word *will* in 1602 might mean "carnal desire or appetite" (*Oxford English Dictionary* 1.2) or "that which one desires" (*OED* 1.3), as well as "expressing natural disposition to do something, and hence habitual action" (*OED* 1.8). The valences of the word are wittily pressed to their limits in Shakespeare's sonnets 135 ("Whoever hath her wish, thou hast thy will") and 136 ("If thy soul check thee that I come so near, / Swear to thy blind soul that I was thy Will"), where *will* can be taken to mean volition, the auxiliary verb *will,* lust, penis, vagina, and the nickname Will, sometimes all at the same time. Thomas Wright's treatise on *The Passions of the Mind* (1604) helps us to understand the place of will in early modern understandings of sensation, desire, and action, particularly the conflict between sense experience and reason. (Sonnets 135 and 138 and an excerpt from Wright's treatise appear in Chapter 3.) When it comes to will, *Twelfth Night* seems almost as audacious as sonnets 135 and 136. For someone like Manningham, a collector of bawdy jokes, the play offers plenty of choices as to what one would: in sequential order a member of the audience gets to witness Orsino's passion for Olivia, Sir Andrew's mercenary pursuit of Olivia, Sir Toby's knowing ways with Maria, Orsino's familiarity with "Cesario," Olivia's flirtation with "Cesario," Antonio's declaration of love for Sebastian, Malvolio's wanton daydreams about Olivia, even the thriftless marriage of Feste's final song.

What really animates the love play's love-play, however, is the presence of two erotic objects who look and sound alike: the twins Sebastian and Viola. Separated from each other by shipwreck at the start of the play, they are reunited at the end. Manningham compares them to the twin brothers in Plautus's *Menaechmi,* as if Sebastian and Viola's difference in sex didn't really matter. Near the start Sebastian confirms as much: he testifies "it was said she much resembled me" and apologizes for being "yet so near the manners of my mother" as to shed tears (2.1.18, 29). Toward the end everyone onstage is astonished at the twins' likeness. Orsino speaks for all: "One face, one voice, one habit, and two persons" (5.1.200). *Habit* here carries its early modern sense as clothing; *person,* its early modern sense as body.

As alike as they may appear in habit, Sebastian and Viola *are* different in person: they have different genitalia — at least within the fiction. In anatomical fact, of course, the actors playing both parts were males. The play is designed to make their difference in gender seem as inconsequential as possible. "Conceal me what I am," Viola asks the Captain in act 1, scene 2. When she disguises herself as "Cesario" — or rather when the boy actor playing Viola disguises himself/herself as "Cesario" — the situation gives Shakespeare opportunity to play up the androgyny of the body in question. In doing so he gives shape and voice to ideas about the human body going back to the physician Galen in the first century C.E. According to Galen, female genitalia *inside* the body are merely the inverse of male genitalia *outside* the body — implying that early modern men and women saw one sex where we today see two.[5] Scientific anatomy was calling the concept into question, but even an authority like Helkiah Crooke gives the "one-sex" model serious consideration in his encyclopedic *Microcosmographia: A Description of the Body of Man* (1618), a chapter of which is reprinted in Part 2.

It is the interchangeability of Viola and Sebastian that sparks the play's erotic confusions. In choosing a male disguise and taking service with Orsino ("Thou shalt present me as an eunuch to him" [1.2.56]) — Viola imagines she is making herself sex-neutral. "Be you his eunuch," the Captain replies, "and your mute I'll be" (1.2.62). His mouth and her sexual organs are set in alliance: as a mute can't speak, so a eunuch can't be sexually active. The fallacy (so to speak) of that proposition becomes apparent just as soon as "Cesario" has presented himself/herself/himself to Orsino and Olivia. Both refer to him/her/him as a "youth" — who could be male or fe-

[5]Thomas Laqueur has studied the currency of this idea in the sixteenth and seventeenth centuries in *Making Sex: Body and Gender from the Greeks to Freud.*

male (*OED* 6) — and both fall in love with him/her/him in that uncertain guise. Viola/"Cesario" strikes both suitors as fetchingly androgynous. Orsino is sure "Cesario" will make an effective emissary to Olivia precisely because of his feminine appearance:

> Diana's lip
> Is not more smooth and rubious; thy small pipe
> Is as the maiden's organ, shrill and sound,
> And all is semblative a woman's part. (1.4.29–32)

Orsino's prophecy proves true: Olivia succumbs to "this youth's perfections" and offers a "five-fold blazon" of the seeming Diana's tongue, face, limbs, action, and spirit in just the way a male poet might celebrate the beauty of his lady (1.5.237–38). Sebastian, who by his own testimony looks and sounds like his sister, not only takes up with Olivia where Viola/"Cesario" left off but inspires in Antonio a passion that is unabashedly homoerotic. After Sebastian has left the stage in act 2, scene 1, Antonio says to the vanished image, "But come what may, I do adore thee so / That danger shall seem sport, and I will go" (2.1.35–36). The next time the two encounter one another, in act 3, scene 3, Antonio's declaration of desire exceeds even the warmest degree of male friendship: "My desire, / More sharp than filèd steel, did spur me forth" (3.3.4–5). Orsino calls Antonio a "notable pirate" (5.1.57), and pirates, on seventeenth-century seas as in the pages of romance, were notorious sodomites. Amid the pairings of the play's last scene Orsino is no less forthright in maintaining homoerotic affections. He persists in calling Viola "Cesario": "For so you shall be while you are a man; / But when in other habits you are seen, / Orsino's mistress and his fancy's queen" (5.1.364–65). *Habits,* in this case, may be not just modes of dress but modes of sexual behavior.

Desire of male for female (Orsino for Olivia, Sebastian for Olivia), of female for male (Olivia for "Cesario," Viola for Orsino), of male for male (Antonio for Sebastian, Orsino for "Cesario"), of female for female (Olivia for Viola), of male for either, of female for either, of either for either: the love plots in *Twelfth Night* truly offer "what you will." The selections in Chapter 3 take stock of early modern ideas about eroticism, focusing in particular on the fantasy of making love to both sexes at once.

Clothing and Disguise

When Viola tells the Captain who has saved her from drowning, "I will believe thou hast a mind that suits / With this thy fair and outward character" (1.2.50–51), she calls attention to the often dubious relation that personal appearance bears to personal identity in *Twelfth Night.* Clothing is fetishized from start to finish: it is invested with transformative powers. Olivia appears in black mourning; Orsino likely affects the melancholic's black "suits of woe" along with his punning humor; Malvolio cuts a sober figure until he is tricked into owning feelings not at all suited to his dress; Viola disguises herself as "an eunuch"; Sebastian causes confusion by appearing identical to his disguised sister in habit as well as in face and voice; Feste dons a gown and false beard to become Sir Topas; Viola remains, in Orsino's eyes at least, "Cesario" to the very end. *Habits,* to use the early modern word for clothing, constitute a major context for viewing *Twelfth Night.*

"Of Excess of Apparel" in *The Second Tome of Homilies* (1563), appointed to be read aloud in churches, attempts to establish carefully regulated correspondences between dress and social class, dress and religious conformity, dress and gender. (An excerpt figures in Chapter 4.) The relationship between dress and social class was particularly important to the well-placed people who ruled the realm. Laws dating back to the reigns of Henry VIII (1533 and 1542) and Philip and Mary (1555) tried to regulate dress by dividing the people of England into precisely defined ranks (twelve such ranks are specified in the law of 1533) and legislating the fabrics, yardage, colors, and adornments that each rank could wear. There were periodic attempts to bring the laws up to date, as exemplified during the reign of Elizabeth by numerous royal proclamations, such as that issued on July 6, 1597 (included in Chapter 4). The sort of material one could wear, the yardage in the sleeves, the kind of lace in the collars, the number of cutouts in the bulbous trousers or "hose" that men wore, the trimmings on one's hat, the length of the weapons one could carry: all of these things were regulated by royal decree. The fact that such regulations had to be issued again and again, each time making allowances for ever more extravagant yardage and ever higher prices, suggests how often such decrees must have been ignored.[6]

Chief among the offenders were actors, whose most expensive props were the clothes they purchased as costumes, clothes that in many cases had actually been worn by the aristocrats the actors pretended to be onstage. Sometimes the actors would buy the clothes from the servants who had inherited the garments on their masters' deaths; sometimes the actors would

[6] On the so-called sumptuary laws of the sixteenth century, see Hooper, "The Tudor Sumptuary Laws," and Young, *The Proclamations of the Tudor Queens,* 161–70. A brilliant cultural analysis of sixteenth- and seventeenth-century clothing practices is provided by Anne Jones and Peter Stallybrass, *Renaissance Clothing and the Materials of Memory.*

rent out the clothes for weddings and other special occasions.[7] The actors' consciousness of the political implications of their practices is suggested by the title of a now-lost script, *Cloth Britches and Velvet Hose,* among the plays Shakespeare's company acted in the 1599–1600 season. Inspiration for the script must have come from Robert Greene's satiric pamphlet *A Quip for an Upstart Courtier* (1592), which pits an upstart apologist for fashion, Velvet Britches, against a defender of traditional English dress, Cloth Britches. You'll find some of their dialogue in Chapter 4. Cloth Britches agrees with the proclamation of 1597 in associating plain dress with true English values and new fashions with instability and foreign corruption. The Italianate world of *Twelfth Night* is very much Velvet Britches' milieu. In a society where everyone seemed intent on dressing upscale and outlandishly, Puritans were remarkable for the modesty of their dress. Conduct books aimed at Puritan readers (books bearing improbably romantic titles like *The Haven of Pleasure* [1596] and *The Golden Grove* [1600]), suggest that Malvolio's attire in *Twelfth Night* — at least until he reads the forged letter from Olivia — must have been sober, probably as dark-hued as his temperament. When he appears in the yellow stockings and cross garters that the forged letter recommends, Malvolio strides right into one of the great social controversies of early modern London. Puritans have their say in excerpts from these books in Part 2.

Even more upsetting to traditionalists like Cloth Britches were fashions that confused the difference between the male and female persons beneath the fabric. Pamphlets like *Hic Mulier* (1620) and *Haec-Vir* (1620) suggest that cross-dressed men and women were to be seen on the streets of London. If not on the streets of London, such figures were certainly at home in romance narratives, as witness Sir Philip Sidney's *Arcadia* (begun 1580), in which Musidorus comes upon his friend Pyrocles disguised as the maiden Zelmane, finds himself strangely attracted, and (when he has discovered "Zelmane's" true identity) proceeds to argue against cross-gender disguise in terms that Puritan critics would appreciate, while later in the narrative the heroine Philoclea finds *herself* strangely attracted to "Zelmane" even though, to all appearances, "Zelmane" is a woman. The key passage appears in Chapter 4. *Twelfth Night* plays out versions of these romantic adventures in Orsino's and Olivia's attractions to Viola/"Cesario."

With respect to gender as well as to social class, theaters were at the heart of controversy over dress. In flagrant violation of the teachings of Deuteronomy 22.5, boy actors on the early modern stage assumed the dress of women.

[7] Testimony to the practice of the actors' buying noblemen's apparel is provided by a Swiss traveler, Thomas Platter, who saw a performance of *Julius Caesar* in 1599, almost certainly at the Globe. See Gurr, 194.

When the boy actor playing Viola sets aside his woman's weeds and dons the garb of a gentleman (eunuch though he be), he upsets the simple binary of real-life boy and fictional woman that allowed Puritans to fulminate; instead, actor/Viola/"Cesario" introduces a third entity: fictional boy. The result was calculated to make the literal-minded lose their bearings. Selections in Chapter 4 survey the variety of reactions that eyewitnesses at the time recorded to the spectacle of boys playing women's parts. The range of responses is broad indeed: from "homosexual panic" in Stubbes's *Anatomy of Abuses* (1583) and John Rainolds's *The Overthrow of Stage Plays* (1599) to uncomplicated acceptance of custom in Thomas Platter's casual remarks on the jig that followed *Julius Caesar* at the Globe (*Travels in England* [1599]) and Thomas Heywood's insistence that no one mistakes boys for women in *An Apology for Actors* (1608) to Henry Jackson's declension of Desdemona as "she" in his Latin account of the King's Men's performance of *Othello* at Oxford in 1610 to Thomas Coryate's mild surprise at women onstage in Venice in *Coryate's Crudities* (1611) to George Sandys's aesthetic objection to Sicilian actresses in *A Relation of a Journey* (1615) to Lady Mary Wroth's patronizing references to "play boys" in *The Countess of Montgomery's Urania* (1621). From such a wide range of responses one thing is certain: We should never speak of "*the* early-modern viewer" — especially when it comes to boys playing women's parts. With its insistence on the interchangeability of Viola and Sebastian, *Twelfth Night* raises the issue of gender and dress with particular immediacy.

Concern with dress is ultimately a concern with *decorum,* with what is proper, suitable, seemly, becoming, fit (*OED* 1). The application of that term in everyday life is derived from its use as a specifically theatrical concept, as appropriateness to a certain personage, place, or time in a play (*OED* 1a). The principles laid down by Horace dictate that noble persons be represented in noble surroundings, behaving in noble ways, according to the occasion at hand. Shakespeare's fellow playwright Ben Jonson praised himself for observing decorum in the Prologue to his comedy *Volpone* (published 1607): "The laws of time, place, persons he observeth, / From no needful rule he swerveth" (*Volpone,* Prologue 31–32). By playing with decorum onstage, *Twelfth Night* calls into question the naturalness of decorum in the world outside the theater.

Household Economies

In multiple ways *Twelfth Night* is a play about households and about the management of households. In Middle Temple Hall in February 1602, six households were present. Within the fiction there were Orsino's household and Olivia's household; in social fact, the Middle Temple and the Lord Chamberlain's Men; and by implication, the "household" of Illyria and the "household" of Britain. Today we think of *economy* as a specifically monetary concept, but the original meaning of the word applied to the management of a household (*OED* 1.1). "Home economics" survives as an example. The senses of *economy* as administration of the concerns of a larger community, indeed of a whole society, come later, more than a generation after Shakespeare's death (*OED* 1.2). Richard Martin, John Davies, and John Manningham belonged to the household economy of the Middle Temple in just the way that Sir Toby, Maria, Fabian, Malvolio, Feste, and Sir Andrew belong to the household economy of Olivia's estate. So, too, did Shakespeare and his fellow actors constitute a household economy: the boys who played Olivia, Viola, and possibly Maria (an old tradition in academic drama called for the adult male masters to play comic women's parts like Maria) lived with the adult actors in just the way that apprentices in every trade boarded with their masters.

According to the principle of correspondences in early modern thinking, the multiple households in *Twelfth Night* are homologous institutions: they line up, one above the other, in a great cosmic scheme of order. What goes on in one has implications for what goes in the others (see Tillyard 83–100). The economy of Olivia's household, for example, has direct implications for the economy of Britain; the economy of Orsino's household, for the economy of the Lord Chamberlain's Men. Within *Twelfth Night* the situation is complicated by the presence of *competing* ideas of household economy. On the one hand, the play celebrates the traditional hospitality of feudal England, which calls for the generous entertainment of guests like Sir Andrew and bounteous celebration of holidays like Twelfth Night and Candlemas.[8] Pictures of traditional hospitality are drawn in Ben Jonson's country house poem "To Penshurst" (1616), in the anonymous pamphlet *Grevious Groans for the Poor* (1621), and in Donald Lupton's satire *London and the Country Carbonadoed and Quartered* (1632), excerpts from which are included in Chapter 5.

In dress and in attitude Malvolio stands for an alternative idea of household economy. Malvolio is Olivia's steward. He controls the domestic affairs of the household, managing Olivia's material possessions, directing the servants, regulating household expenditures. As such, he tries to control the household's people in the same way he controls the household's material

[8] Daryl W. Palmer, *Hospitable Performances: Dramatic Genre and Cultural Practices in Early Modern England,* provides an extended study of the controversy over declining standards of hospitality.

goods. When he upbraids Sir Toby, Sir Andrew, Maria, and Feste for their noisy singing, he speaks the language of traditional decorum. Persons, time, and place all figure in his diatribe:

> My masters, are you mad? Or what are you? Have you no wit, manners, nor honesty, but to gabble like tinkers at this time of night? Do ye make an alehouse of my lady's house, that ye squeak out your coziers' catches without any mitigation or remorse of voice? Is there no respect of place, persons, nor time in you? (2.3.73–77)

In such speeches Malvolio gives voice to Puritan ideas of economy, as set forth in *The Haven of Pleasure* (1596) , William Vaughan's *The Golden Grove* (1600), and William Perkins's *Christian Economy* (1608), parts of which are reprinted in Chapter 5. The gulling of Malvolio would seem to affirm the economy of largess over the economy of frugality, and yet the play does not end with the expected gesture toward feasting and dancing that marks the ends of *Much Ado About Nothing* and *As You Like It.* It ends instead with Feste's lonely song about the ages of man, quite outside all the households that the play invokes.

Puritan Probity

The seventy-five years before 1602 had witnessed two large-scale revolutions that bear on *Twelfth Night:* a change throughout Western Europe in the relationship between popular culture and elite culture and a schism in religion. The first change concerns how communities confirmed their identities in celebrations of seasonal rites like Christmas. Among the multiple dislocations occasioned by a gradual shift from a feudal economy to a capitalist economy was a gradual separation between what Peter Burke has called "the little tradition" and "the great tradition." Once noble and commoner, master and servant, the learned and the ignorant had come together to mark the major rites of passage from season to season and from one life stage to another among the people in their midst; by the early seventeenth century the upper classes were increasingly withdrawing from such celebrations (Burke 58–64, 270–81). For many people in 1602 the merry mood of Sir Toby, Sir Andrew, and Maria in *Twelfth Night* was indecorous behavior for gentle folk. A contributing factor in the withdrawal of the upper classes, in northern countries at least, was the Protestant Reformation, which condemned many traditional festivities as vestiges of Catholicism, if not of pre-Catholic paganism. It is in this spirit of religious scepticism that Henry

Bourne takes stock of local Twelfth Night customs in his book *Antiquitates Vulgares, or Common Antiquities* (1725), excerpts from which are included in Chapter 1. Bourne was a local priest in the Church of England who genuinely wanted to preserve popular pastimes — as long as those pastimes were not vestiges of pagan rites.

Other religious authorities, especially those outside the official church, were harsher. Philip Stubbes, for example, devotes his utopian satire *The Anatomy of Abuses in Ailgna* (1583) to describing in lurid detail all the things he, through his spokesman Philoponus, disapproves of in Ailgna (*alias* Anglia): among them dancing, gambling, face-painting, stage plays, traditional holiday pastimes, and Lords of Misrule. To hear Stubbes at his fulminating best, turn to Chapter 6. When authorities at the Middle Temple banned Lords of Misrule in 1584, they were following a trend that had begun with the disestablishment of the Catholic Church in England in 1534. Stubbes was a self-proclaimed Puritan, who wished to "purify" the Church of England of the superstitious rites and ethical laxity it had supposedly preserved from Catholicism.

The ambivalent entries in Manningham's diary — on the one hand he makes fun of his foster father's disputatious Puritan neighbor, on the other he piously records his disapproval of Sabbath-breaking and takes notes on sermons by Puritan preachers — suggest the general ambivalence that Puritans were provoking in English society, at least in 1602. They lived circumspect lives and were noted for their business acumen, but their insistence on following the Bible's teachings to the letter — and condemning everyone who did not do the same — made less strict sorts of people distinctly uncomfortable. Malvolio's myopic letter-by-letter attention to Olivia's supposed *billet doux* shapes up as a satire of what many people regarded as a Puritan habit of twisting the letter of Scripture to fit what they wanted it to say.[9] In the England of John Manningham and William Shakespeare, "merry" and "mirth" were politically charged words. "Merry old England" was rapidly ceasing to exist. "The politics of mirth," as Leah Marcus has termed the falling out between Puritans and more moderate folk, became a major issue in the 1620s and 1630s as Puritans attempted to abolish May-games and other traditional pastimes through local edicts and the laws of the realm. The so-called King's Book of Sports (included in Chapter 6), issued by James I in 1618 and reissued by Charles I in 1633, proved to be one of the major controversies leading to Charles's overthrow, as local priests refused to read the royal proclamation that dancing and other pastimes were lawful on Sunday afternoons and at holiday times. Spoilsport, social climber, literalist

[9] Simmons (181–201) has catalogued Malvolio's Puritan traits.

interpreter of the word, victim of a cruel joke: Malvolio catches something of the ambivalent position that Puritans occupied in England at the turn of the seventeenth century. The readings in Chapter 6 have been chosen to present positive as well as negative views of Malvolio's real-life counterparts.

Laughter and Clowning

For all its concern with perplexities of sexuality, religion, and economy, the last word in *Twelfth Night* is Feste's. At the Middle Temple, the last word was Robert Armin's. Armin joined the Lord Chamberlain's Men during the 1599–1600 season, and Shakespeare seems to have lost no time in devising clown roles that capitalized on Armin's sardonic humor, his knack for mimicking, and his ability to sing. Feste was likely Armin's second role, after Touchstone in *As You Like It,* and just before his appearances as Thersites in *Troilus and Cressida* and as the Fool in *King Lear.*[10] As Lear's Fool, Armin got to sing a brief reprise of the song that closes *Twelfth Night,* "When that I was and a little tiny boy" (compare *Twelfth Night* 5.1.336–85 and *King Lear* 3.2.74–77). Armin was perhaps alluding to his own dwarfish stature and dog-like body when Feste says to the audience, as he dons Sir Topas's gown and false beard, "I am not tall enough to become the function well, nor lean enough to be thought a good student" (4.2.5–6). The title page of Armin's play *The Two Maids of Moreclack* carries a woodcut that may be a portrait of the author (see Figure 4). Certainly Feste's way with clever questions and answers — "A sentence is but a cheveril glove to a good wit, how quickly the wrong side may be turned outward" (3.1.8–9) — was Armin's own stock in trade, as witness one of the jest books attributed to him, *Quips upon Questions* (1600). Other printed versions of Armin's clowning, like *Fool upon Fool* (1605), demonstrate how adept Armin was at adopting various voices and demeanors in the same set piece. (Excerpts from both books appear in Part 2.) Feste's gulling of Malvolio in the guise of Sir Topas seems ideally suited to Armin's talents. Armin's status as a professional clown, a man who plays the fool for pay, is perhaps registered in Feste's constant attempts to cajole his listeners into giving him a coin or two. Take, for example, Viola's encounter with Feste when she comes to woo Olivia on Orsino's behalf. Feste perhaps takes occasion to let Viola/"Cesario" know that he suspects her true gender when he calls attention to her beardlessness — and uses that knowledge as a bribe:

[10] Wiles, 136–63, provides a full account of Armin's talents and his career with Shakespeare's company.

FIGURE 4 *A Natural Fool, from Robert Armin,* The Two Maids of Moreclack.

VIOLA: Hold, there's expenses for thee. [*She gives a coin.*]
FESTE: Now Jove, in his next commodity of hair, send thee a beard.
VIOLA: By my troth I'll tell thee, I am almost sick for one — [*aside*] though I would not have it grow on my chin. — Is thy lady within?
FESTE: Would not a pair of these have bred, sir? [*He holds up the coin.*]
VIOLA: Yes, being kept together and put to use.
FESTE: I would play the Lord Pandarus of Phrygia, sir, to bring a Cressida to this Troilus.
VIOLA: I understand you, sir. 'Tis well begged. [*She gives another coin.*]
FESTE: The matter I hope is not great, sir, begging but a beggar; Cressida was a beggar. My lady is within, sir. I will conster to them whence you come. Who you are and what you would are out of my welkin — I might say "element," but the word is overworn. (3.1.33–46)

All in all, Armin's humor, the way he plays fast and loose with both words and body parts — and gets good money for doing so — seems calculated to amuse the likes of John Manningham, who loves to add good jokes to his diary, including the one about the legendary comedian Richard Tarlton, quoted on page 5.

It is laughter from the belly, not just smiling with the lips, that *Twelfth Night* seems designed to provoke. To laugh is not the same thing as to smile. To smile, in *Twelfth Night* at least, is to assume a pose, to adopt a certain decorum of person. Malvolio's ridiculous attempt to smile constantly while strutting about in a lover's yellow stockings has its melancholy counterpart in Viola's projection of her own hidden love for Orsino onto a fictional sister: "She sat like Patience on a monument, / Smiling at grief" (2.4.111–12). To laugh is to *lose* decorum, and in that respect laughter poses a threat to self-possession. Early modern ambivalence about laughter was just as strong as early modern ambivalence about music. On the one hand we have the critical success of scripts like *Twelfth Night* with spectators like Manningham, not to mention the play's presumed commercial success at the Globe; on the other hand we have strictures against laughter that go back to Plato. The different forms that these strictures take each implies a different *theory* of laughter. Quintilian in his guide to public speaking, the *Institutio Oratoria,* remarks just how hard it is to define laughter and to talk about it discursively: "I do not think that anybody can give an adequate explanation, though many have attempted to do so, of the cause of laughter, which is excited not merely by words or deeds, but sometimes even by touch" (6.3.7). Chapter 7 includes examples of the different theories of laughter that were current among Shakespeare's actors and audiences.

First among the implied theories, and the most pervasive in early modern ethics, is the idea that laughter is derision at the follies of others and hence an affirmation of the laugher's own self-worth, what John Morreall in *Taking Laughter Seriously* (1983) calls "the superiority theory" (4–14). Plato speaks to this view in his dialogue *Philebus,* in which he defines the ridiculous as human evil and folly and in the *Republic,* in which he argues that in fictions "men of worth must not be represented as overcome by laughter" — views that Aristotle seconds in his *Rhetoric* and *Nicomachean Ethics.* Malvolio in his opposition to mirth carries Plato's advice to neurotic extremes, even as he becomes the butt of a joke that makes *us* feel superior to *him.* Malvolio becomes an object of others' laughter precisely because he won't laugh himself, least of all at Feste's jokes. Malvolio's protest near the beginning of the play — "I marvel your ladyship takes delight in such a barren rascal. . . . Unless you laugh and minister occasion to him, he is gagged" (1.5.65–68) — comes back to haunt him, word for word, in Feste's taunt at the end (5.1.352–53). Olivia's riposte to Malvolio says it all:

> To be generous, guiltless, and of free disposition is to take those things for birdbolts that you deem cannon bullets. There is no slander in an allowed

> fool, though he do nothing but rail; nor no railing in a known discreet man, though he do nothing but reprove. (1.5.71–75)

Generous, guiltless, and of free disposition is what the play asks its audience to be — qualities that Malvolio (literally, *ill will*) conspicuously lacks.

What Morreall calls "the incongruity theory" of laughter is present in Quintilian's instructions on how to raise an audience's expectations by promising them one thing and then surprising them by giving them something else. The Puritan steward who shows up in gaudy garters, the fool who puts on a doctor's gown and beard, the sister who transforms herself into the image of her brother, the brother who looks a lot like his sister: *Twelfth Night* is chock full of incongruities. Finally "the relief theory," the proposition that laughter is a release of tension, finds a brilliant expositor in Laurent Joubert's *Treatise on Laughter* (1579), with its exploration of the physiology of laughing. Joubert proceeds on grounds shared with Rabelais. Laughter, Joubert argues, comes from the heart, not from the brain, and it arises as a physiological response to the simultaneity of two quite opposite emotions, joy and sadness. The first dilates the heart; the second contracts it. The result is spasms of the diaphragm — and the possibility of losing control over one's body. Included in Chapter 7 is Joubert's investigation of "Whence it comes that one pisses, shits, and sweats by dint of laughing" (1.26). Amid these theories of laughter a golden mean of sorts is offered by Sir Philip Sidney in his *Defense of Poesy* (printed 1595), with his distinction between two quite different forms of comedy: the comedy "of laughter" and the comedy "of delight." The former incites ridicule, setting spectator-listeners at a distance from what they see and hear; the latter invites sympathy, drawing them in. The lasting power of *Twelfth Night* across four centuries lies in that fine balance.

Happy reading.

PART ONE

WILLIAM SHAKESPEARE

Twelfth Night or What You Will

Edited by David Bevington

Twelfe Night, Or what you will.

Actus Primus, Scæna Prima.

Enter Orsino Duke of Illyria, Curio, and other Lords.

Duke.

IF Muſicke be the food of Loue, play on,
Giue me exceſſe of it: that ſurfetting,
The appetite may ſicken, and ſo dye.
That ſtraine agen, it had a dying fall:
O, it came ore my eare, like the ſweet ſound
That breathes vpon a banke of Violets;
Stealing, and giuing Odour. Enough, no more,
'Tis not ſo ſweet now, as it was before.
O ſpirit of Loue, how quicke and freſh art thou,
That notwithſtanding thy capacitie,
Receiueth as the Sea. Nought enters there,
Of what validity, and pitch ſo ere,
But falles into abatement, and low price
Euen in a minute; ſo full of ſhapes is fancie,
That it alone, is high fantaſticall.

Cu. Will you go hunt my Lord?

Du. What *Curio*?

Cu. The Hart.

Du. Why ſo I do, the Nobleſt that I haue:
O when mine eyes did ſee *Oliuia* firſt,
Me thought ſhe purg'd the ayre of peſtilence;
That inſtant was I turn'd into a Hart,
And my deſires like fell and cruell hounds,
Ere ſince purſue me. How now what newes from her?

Enter Valentine.

Val. So pleaſe my Lord, I might not be admitted,
But from her handmaid do returne this anſwer:
The Element it ſelfe, till ſeuen yeares heate,
Shall not behold her face at ample view:
But like a Cloyſtreſſe ſhe will vailed walke,
And water once a day her Chamber round
With eye-offending brine: all this to ſeaſon
A brothers dead loue, which ſhe would keepe freſh
And laſting, in her ſad remembrance.

Du. O ſhe that hath a heart of that fine frame
To pay this debt of loue but to a brother,
How will ſhe loue, when the rich golden ſhaft
Hath kill'd the flocke of all affections elſe
That liue in her. When Liuer, Braine, and Heart,
Theſe ſoueraigne thrones, are all ſupply'd and fill'd
Her ſweete perfections with one ſelfe king:
Away before me, to ſweet beds of Flowres,
Loue-thoughts lye rich, when canopy'd with bowres.
Exeunt

Scena Secunda.

Enter Viola, a Captaine, and Saylors.

Vio. What Country (Friends) is this?

Cap. This is Illyria Ladie.

Vio. And what ſhould I do in Illyria?
My brother he is in Elizium,
Perchance he is not drown'd: What thinke you ſaylors?

Cap. It is perchance that you your ſelfe were ſaued.

Vio. O my poore brother, and ſo perchance may he be.

Cap. True Madam, and to comfort you with chance,
Aſſure your ſelfe, after our ſhip did ſplit,
When you, and thoſe poore number ſaued with you,
Hung on our driuing boate: I ſaw your brother
Moſt prouident in perill, binde himſelfe,
(Courage and hope both teaching him the practiſe)
To a ſtrong Maſte, that liu'd vpon the ſea:
Where like *Orion* on the Dolphines backe,
I ſaw him hold acquaintance with the waues,
So long as I could ſee.

Vio. For ſaying ſo, there's Gold:
Mine owne eſcape vnfoldeth to my hope,
Whereto thy ſpeech ſerues for authoritie
The like of him. Know'ſt thou this Countrey?

Cap. I Madam well, for I was bred and borne
Not three houres trauaile from this very place:

Vio. Who gouernes heere?

Cap. A noble Duke in nature, as in name.

Vio. What is his name?

Cap. *Orſino.*

Vio. *Orſino*: I haue heard my father name him.
He was a Batchellor then.

Cap. And ſo is now, or was ſo very late:
For but a month ago I went from hence,
And then 'twas freſh in murmure (as you know
What great ones do, the leſſe will prattle of,)
That he did ſeeke the loue of faire *Oliuia*.

Vio. What's ſhee?

Cap. A vertuous maid, the daughter of a Count
That dide ſome tweluemonth ſince, then leauing her
In the protection of his ſonne, her brother,
Who ſhortly alſo dide: for whoſe deere loue
(They ſay) ſhe hath abiur'd the ſight
And company of men.

Vio. O that I ſeru'd that Lady,
And might not be deliuered to the world

FIGURE 5 *Landing in Illyria: Act One, Scenes One and Two, of* Twelfth Night *in the First Folio (1623).*

Twelfth Night or What You Will

[DRAMATIS PERSONAE

ORSINO, *Duke (or Count) of Illyria*
VALENTINE, *gentleman attending on Orsino*
CURIO, *gentleman attending on Orsino*

VIOLA, *a shipwrecked lady, later disguised as Cesario*
SEBASTIAN, *twin brother of Viola*
ANTONIO, *a sea captain, friend to Sebastian*
CAPTAIN *of the shipwrecked vessel*

OLIVIA, *a rich countess of Illyria*
MARIA, *gentlewoman in Olivia's household*
SIR TOBY BELCH, *Olivia's uncle*
SIR ANDREW AGUECHEEK, *a companion of Sir Toby*
MALVOLIO, *steward of Olivia's household*
FABIAN, *a member of Olivia's household*
FESTE, *a clown, also called* FOOL, *Olivia's jester*

A PRIEST
FIRST OFFICER
SECOND OFFICER

Lords, Sailors, Musicians, and other Attendants

SCENE: *A city in Illyria, and the seacoast near it*]

ACT 1, SCENE 1°

Enter Orsino Duke of Illyria, Curio, and other lords [*with musicians*].°

ORSINO:
If music be the food of love, play on;
Give me excess of it, that surfeiting,
The appetite may sicken and so die.
That strain again! It had a dying fall;°
O, it came o'er my ear like the sweet sound
That breathes upon a bank of violets,
Stealing and giving odor. Enough; no more.
'Tis not so sweet now as it was before.
O spirit of love, how quick and fresh° art thou,
That, notwithstanding thy capacity
Receiveth as the sea, naught enters there,
Of what validity° and pitch° soe'er,
But falls into abatement° and low price
Even in a minute! So full of shapes° is fancy°
That it alone is high fantastical.°

CURIO:
Will you go hunt, my lord?

ORSINO: What, Curio?

CURIO: The hart.

ORSINO:
Why, so I do, the noblest that I have.°
O, when mine eyes did see Olivia first,

ACT 1, SCENE 1. **Location:** Orsino's court. **s.d.** ***Illyria:*** Nominally on the east coast of the Adriatic Sea, but with a suggestion also of "illusion" and "delirium." **4. fall:** cadence. **9. quick and fresh:** keen and hungry. **12. validity:** value. **pitch:** superiority. (Literally, the highest point of a falcon's flight.) **13. abatement:** depreciation. (The lover's brain entertains innumerable fantasies but soon tires of them all.) **14. shapes:** imagined forms. **fancy:** love. **15. it . . . fantastical:** it surpasses everything else in imaginative power. **17. the noblest . . . have:** i.e., my noblest part, my heart (punning on *hart*).

Methought she purged the air of pestilence.
That instant was I turned into a hart,
And my desires, like fell° and cruel hounds,
E'er since pursue me.°

Enter Valentine.

How now, what news from her?

VALENTINE:

So please my lord, I might not be admitted,
But from her handmaid do return this answer:
The element° itself, till seven years' heat,°
Shall not behold her face at ample view;
But like a cloistress° she will veilèd walk,
And water once a day her chamber round
With eye-offending brine — all this to season°
A brother's dead love,° which she would keep fresh
And lasting in her sad remembrance.

ORSINO:

O, she that hath a heart of that fine frame°
To pay this debt of love but to a brother,
How will she love, when the rich golden shaft°
Hath killed the flock of all affections else°
That live in her; when liver, brain, and heart,°
These sovereign thrones, are all supplied,° and filled
Her sweet perfections,° with one self king!°
Away before me to sweet beds of flowers.
Love-thoughts lie rich when canopied with bowers. *Exeunt.*

21. **fell:** fierce. 22. **pursue me:** (Alludes to the story in Ovid of Actaeon, who, having seen Diana bathing, was transformed into a stag and killed by his own hounds.) 25. **element:** sky. **seven years' heat:** seven summers. 27. **cloistress:** nun secluded in a religious community. 29. **season:** keep fresh (playing on the idea of the salt in her tears). 30. **A brother's dead love:** her love for her dead brother and the memory of his love for her. 32. **frame:** construction. 34. **golden shaft:** Cupid's golden-tipped arrow, causing love. (His lead-tipped arrow causes aversion.) 35. **affections else:** other feelings. 36. **liver, brain, and heart:** (In medieval and Elizabethan psychology, these organs were the seats of the passions, of thought, and of feeling.) 37. **supplied:** filled. 37–38. **and . . . perfections:** and her sweet perfections filled. 38. **self king:** single lord (the object of her entire affection).

ACT 1, SCENE 2°

Enter Viola, a Captain, and sailors.

VIOLA: What country, friends, is this?
CAPTAIN: This is Illyria, lady.
VIOLA:
And what should I do in Illyria?
My brother he is in Elysium.°
Perchance he is not drowned. What think you, sailors?
CAPTAIN:
It is perchance° that you yourself were saved.
VIOLA:
O, my poor brother! And so perchance may he be.
CAPTAIN:
True, madam, and to comfort you with chance,°
Assure yourself, after our ship did split,
When you and those poor number saved with you
Hung on our driving° boat, I saw your brother,
Most provident in peril, bind himself,
Courage and hope both teaching him the practice,
To a strong mast that lived° upon the sea;
Where, like Arion° on the dolphin's back,
I saw him hold acquaintance with the waves
So long as I could see.
VIOLA:
For saying so, there's gold: [*She gives money.*]
Mine own escape unfoldeth to my hope,
Whereto thy speech serves for authority,
The like of him.° Know'st thou this country?
CAPTAIN:
Ay, madam, well, for I was bred and born
Not three hours' travel from this very place.
VIOLA: Who governs here?

ACT 1, SCENE 2. **Location:** The seacoast. 4. **Elysium:** classical abode of the blessed dead. 5–6. **Perchance . . . perchance:** perhaps . . . by mere chance. 8. **chance:** i.e., what one may hope that chance will bring about. 11. **driving:** drifting, driven by the seas. 14. **lived:** i.e., kept afloat. 15. **Arion:** a Greek poet who so charmed the dolphins with his lyre that they saved him when he leaped into the sea to escape murderous sailors. 19–21. **unfoldeth . . . him:** offers a hopeful example that he may have escaped similarly, to which hope your speech provides support.

CAPTAIN:
A noble duke, in nature as in name.
VIOLA: What is his name?
CAPTAIN: Orsino.
VIOLA:
Orsino! I have heard my father name him.
He was a bachelor then.
CAPTAIN:
And so is now, or was so very late;
For but a month ago I went from hence,
And then 'twas fresh in murmur° — as, you know,
What great ones do the less° will prattle of —
That he did seek the love of fair Olivia.
VIOLA: What's she?
CAPTAIN:
A virtuous maid, the daughter of a count
That died some twelvemonth since, then leaving her
In the protection of his son, her brother,
Who shortly also died; for whose dear love,
They say, she hath abjured the sight
And company of men.
VIOLA: O, that I served that lady,
And might not be delivered° to the world
Till I had made mine own occasion mellow,°
What my estate° is!
CAPTAIN: That were hard to compass,°
Because she will admit no kind of suit,
No, not° the Duke's.
VIOLA:
There is a fair behavior in thee, Captain;
And though that° nature with a beauteous wall
Doth oft close in pollution, yet of thee
I will believe thou hast a mind that suits
With this thy fair and outward character.°
I prithee, and I'll pay thee bounteously,
Conceal me what I am, and be my aid

32. **murmur:** rumor. 33. **less:** social inferiors. 42. **delivered:** revealed, made known (with suggestion of "born"). 43. **mellow:** ready or convenient (to be made known). 44. **estate:** position in society. **compass:** bring about, encompass. 46. **not:** not even. 48. **though that:** though. 51. **character:** face or features as indicating moral qualities.

For such disguise as haply shall become
The form of my intent.° I'll serve this duke.
Thou shalt present me as an eunuch° to him.
It may be worth thy pains, for I can sing
And speak to him in many sorts of music
That will allow° me very worth his service.
What else may hap, to time I will commit;
Only shape thou thy silence to my wit.°

CAPTAIN:
Be you his eunuch, and your mute° I'll be;
When my tongue blabs, then let mine eyes not see.

VIOLA: I thank thee. Lead me on. *Exeunt.*

Act 1, Scene 3°

Enter Sir Toby [Belch] and Maria.

SIR TOBY: What a plague means my niece to take the death of her brother thus? I am sure care's an enemy to life.

MARIA: By my troth, Sir Toby, you must come in earlier o' nights. Your cousin,° my lady, takes great exceptions to your ill hours.

SIR TOBY: Why, let her except before excepted.°

MARIA: Ay, but you must confine yourself within the modest° limits of order.

SIR TOBY: Confine? I'll confine myself no finer° than I am. These clothes are good enough to drink in, and so be these boots too. An° they be not, let them hang themselves in their own straps.

MARIA: That quaffing and drinking will undo you. I heard my lady talk of it yesterday, and of a foolish knight that you brought in one night here to be her wooer.

SIR TOBY: Who, Sir Andrew Aguecheek?

MARIA: Ay, he.

SIR TOBY: He's as tall° a man as any's in Illyria.

54–55. **as haply . . . intent:** as may suit the nature of my purpose. 56. **eunuch:** castrato, high-voiced singer. 59. **allow:** prove. 61. **wit:** plan, invention. 62. **mute:** silent attendant (sometimes used of nonspeaking actors). **Act 1, Scene 3. Location:** Olivia's house. 4. **cousin:** kinswoman. 5. **let . . . excepted:** i.e., let her take exception to my conduct all she wants; I don't care. (Plays on the legal phrase *exceptis excipiendis,* "with the exceptions before named.") 6. **modest:** moderate. 8. **I'll . . . finer:** (1) I'll constrain myself no more rigorously (2) I'll dress myself no more finely. 9. **An:** if. 16. **tall:** brave. (But Maria pretends to take the word in the common sense.)

MARIA: What's that to the purpose?

SIR TOBY: Why, he has three thousand ducats° a year.

MARIA: Ay, but he'll have but a year in all these ducats.° He's a very fool and a prodigal.

SIR TOBY: Fie, that you'll say so! He plays o' the viol-de-gamboys,° and speaks three or four languages word for word without book,° and hath all the good gifts of nature.

MARIA: He hath indeed, almost natural,° for, besides that he's a fool, he's a great quarreler, and but that he hath the gift° of a coward to allay the gust° he hath in quarreling, 'tis thought among the prudent he would quickly have the gift of a grave.

SIR TOBY: By this hand, they are scoundrels and substractors° that say so of him. Who are they?

MARIA: They that add, moreover, he's drunk nightly in your company.

SIR TOBY: With drinking healths to my niece. I'll drink to her as long as there is a passage in my throat and drink in Illyria. He's a coward and a coistrel° that will not drink to my niece till his brains turn o' the toe like a parish top.° What, wench! *Castiliano vulgo!*° For here comes Sir Andrew Agueface.°

Enter Sir Andrew [Aguecheek].

SIR ANDREW: Sir Toby Belch! How now, Sir Toby Belch?

SIR TOBY: Sweet Sir Andrew!

SIR ANDREW: [*to Maria*] Bless you, fair shrew.°

MARIA: And you too, sir.

SIR TOBY: Accost,° Sir Andrew, accost.

SIR ANDREW: What's that?

SIR TOBY: My niece's chambermaid.°

SIR ANDREW: Good Mistress Accost, I desire better acquaintance.

MARIA: My name is Mary, sir.

SIR ANDREW: Good Mistress Mary Accost —

18. **ducats:** coins worth about four or five shillings. 19. **he'll . . . ducats:** he'll spend all his money within a year. 21. **viol-de-gamboys:** viola da gamba, leg-viol, bass viol. 22. **without book:** by heart. 24. **natural:** (with a play on the sense "born idiot"). 25. **gift:** natural ability. (But shifted to mean "present" in line 27.) 25–26. **allay the gust:** moderate the taste. 28. **substractors:** i.e., detractors. 33. **coistrel:** horse-groom, base fellow. 34. **parish top:** a large top provided by the parish to be spun by whipping, apparently for exercise. ***Castiliano vulgo:*** (Of uncertain meaning. Possibly Sir Toby is saying "Speak of the devil!" Castiliano is the name adopted by a devil in Haughton's *Grim the Collier of Croydon.*) 35. **Agueface:** (Like *Aguecheek,* this name betokens the thin, pale countenance of one suffering from an ague.) 38. **shrew:** i.e., diminutive creature (but with probably unintended suggestion of shewishness). 40. **Accost:** go alongside (a nautical term), i.e., greet her, address her. 42. **chambermaid:** lady-in-waiting (a gentlewoman, not one who would do menial tasks).

SIR TOBY: You mistake, knight. "Accost" is front° her, board° her, woo her, assail her.

SIR ANDREW: By my troth, I would not undertake° her in this company. Is that the meaning of "accost"?

MARIA: Fare you well, gentlemen. [*Going.*]

SIR TOBY: An thou let part° so, Sir Andrew, would thou mightst never draw sword again.

SIR ANDREW: An you part so, mistress, I would I might never draw sword again. Fair lady, do you think you have fools in hand?

MARIA: Sir, I have not you by the hand.°

SIR ANDREW: Marry,° but you shall have; and here's my hand. [*He gives her his hand.*]

MARIA: Now, sir, thought is free.° I pray you, bring your hand to the buttery-bar,° and let it drink.

SIR ANDREW: Wherefore, sweetheart? What's your metaphor?

MARIA: It's dry,° sir.

SIR ANDREW: Why, I think so. I am not such an ass but I can keep my hand dry. But what's your jest?

MARIA: A dry° jest, sir.

SIR ANDREW: Are you full of them?

MARIA: Ay, sir, I have them at my fingers' ends.° Marry, now I let go your hand, I am barren.°

[*She lets go his hand.*] *Exit Maria.*

SIR TOBY: O knight, thou lack'st a cup of canary!° When did I see thee so put down?

SIR ANDREW: Never in your life, I think, unless you see canary put me down.° Methinks sometimes I have no more wit than a Christian or an ordinary man has. But I am a great eater of beef, and I believe that does harm to my wit.

SIR TOBY: No question.

46. **front:** confront, come alongside. **board:** greet, approach (as though preparing to board in a naval encounter). 48. **undertake:** have to do with (here with unintended sexual suggestion, to which Maria mirthfully replies with her jokes about *dry jests, barren,* and *buttery-bar*). 51. **An . . . part:** if you let her leave. 55. **have . . . hand:** i.e., have to deal with fools. (But Maria puns on the literal sense.) 56. **Marry:** i.e., indeed. (Originally, "By the Virgin Mary."). 57. **thought is free:** i.e., I may think what I like. (Proverbial; replying to *do you think . . . in hand,* above.) 58. **buttery-bar:** ledge on top of the half-door to the buttery or the wine cellar. 60. **dry:** thirsty; also dried up, a sign of age and sexual debility. 63. **dry:** (1) ironic (2) dull, barren (referring to Sir Andrew). 65. **at my fingers' ends:** (1) at the ready (2) by the hand. 66. **barren:** i.e., empty of jests and of Sir Andrew's hand. 67. **thou . . . canary:** i.e., you look as if you need a drink. (*Canary* is a sweet wine from the Canary Islands.) 69–70. **put me down:** (1) baffle my wits (2) lay me out flat.

SIR ANDREW: An I thought that, I'd forswear it. I'll ride home tomorrow, Sir Toby.

SIR TOBY: *Pourquoi,*° my dear knight?

SIR ANDREW: What is *"pourquoi"*? Do or not do? I would I had bestowed that time in the tongues° that I have in fencing, dancing, and bearbaiting. O, had I but followed the arts!°

SIR TOBY: Then hadst thou had an excellent head of hair.

SIR ANDREW: Why, would that have mended° my hair?

SIR TOBY: Past question, for thou seest it will not curl by nature.

SIR ANDREW: But it becomes me well enough, does 't not?

SIR TOBY: Excellent. It hangs like flax on a distaff;° and I hope to see a huswife take thee between her legs and spin it off.°

SIR ANDREW: Faith, I'll home tomorrow, Sir Toby. Your niece will not be seen, or if she be, it's four to one she'll none of me. The Count° himself here hard° by woos her.

SIR TOBY: She'll none o' the Count. She'll not match above her degree,° neither in estate,° years, nor wit; I have heard her swear 't. Tut, there's life in 't,° man.

SIR ANDREW: I'll stay a month longer. I am a fellow o' the strangest mind i' the world; I delight in masques and revels sometimes altogether.

SIR TOBY: Art thou good at these kickshawses,° knight?

SIR ANDREW: As any man in Illyria, whatsoever he be, under the degree of my betters,° and yet I will not compare with an old man.°

SIR TOBY: What is thy excellence in a galliard,° knight?

SIR ANDREW: Faith, I can cut a caper.°

SIR TOBY: And I can cut the mutton to 't.

SIR ANDREW: And I think I have the back-trick° simply as strong as any man in Illyria.

SIR TOBY: Wherefore are these things hid? Wherefore have these gifts a curtain before 'em? Are they like to take° dust, like Mistress Mall's

76. *Pourquoi:* why. 78. **tongues:** languages. (Sir Toby then puns on "tongs," curling irons.) 79. **the arts:** the liberal arts, learning. (But Sir Toby plays on the phrase as meaning "artifice," the antithesis of *nature.*) 81. **mended:** improved. 84. **distaff:** a staff for holding the flax, tow, or wool in spinning. 85. **spin it off:** i.e., (1) treat your flaxen hair as though it were flax on a distaff to be spun (2) cause you to lose hair as a result of venereal disease. (*Huswife* suggests "hussy," "whore.") 87. **Count:** i.e., Duke Orsino, sometimes referred to as Count. 88. **hard:** near 89. **degree:** social position. 90. **estate:** fortune, social position. 90–91. **there's life in 't:** i.e., while there's life there's hope. 94. **kickshawses:** delicacies, fancy trifles. (From the French, *quelque chose.*) 95–96. **under . . . betters:** excepting those who are above me. 96. **old man:** i.e., one experienced through age. 97. **galliard:** lively dance in triple time. 98. **cut a caper:** make a lively leap. (But Sir Toby puns on the *caper* used to make a sauce served with mutton. *Mutton,* in turn, suggests "whore.") 100. **back-trick:** backward step in the galliard. 103. **like to take:** likely to collect.

picture?° Why dost thou not go to church in a galliard and come home in a coranto?° My very walk should be a jig; I would not so much as make water but in a sink-a-pace.° What dost thou mean? Is it a world to hide virtues° in? I did think, by the excellent constitution of thy leg, it was formed under the star of a galliard.°

SIR ANDREW: Ay, 'tis strong, and it does indifferent well° in a dun-colored stock.° Shall we set about some revels?

SIR TOBY: What shall we do else? Were we not born under Taurus?°

SIR ANDREW: Taurus? That's sides and heart.

SIR TOBY: No, sir, it is legs and thighs. Let me see thee caper. [*Sir Andrew capers.*] Ha, higher! Ha, ha, excellent! *Exeunt.*

ACT 1, SCENE 4°

Enter Valentine, and Viola in man's attire.

VALENTINE: If the duke continue these favors towards you, Cesario, you are like to be much advanced. He hath known you but three days, and already you are no stranger.

VIOLA: You either fear his humor° or my negligence, that you call in question the continuance of his love. Is he inconstant, sir, in his favors?

VALENTINE: No, believe me.

Enter Duke [Orsino], Curio, and attendants.

VIOLA: I thank you. Here comes the Count.

ORSINO: Who saw Cesario, ho?

VIOLA: On your attendance,° my lord, here.

ORSINO:
Stand you a while aloof. [*The others stand aside.*] Cesario,
Thou know'st no less but all. I have unclasped
To thee the book even of my secret soul.
Therefore, good youth, address thy gait° unto her;
Be not denied access, stand at her doors,

103–04. **Mistress Mall's picture:** i.e., perhaps the portrait of some woman protected from light and dust, as many pictures were, by curtains. 105. **coranto:** lively running dance. 106. **sink-a-pace:** dance like the galliard. (French *cinquepace.*) 107. **virtues:** talents. 108. **under . . . galliard:** i.e., under a star favorable to dancing. 109. **indifferent well:** well enough. (Said complacently.) 109–10. **dun-colored stock:** mouse-colored stocking. 111. **Taurus:** zodiacal sign. (Sir Andrew is mistaken, since Leo governed sides and hearts in medical astrology. Taurus governed legs and thighs, or, more commonly, neck and throat.) **ACT 1, SCENE 4. Location:** Orsino's court. 4. **humor:** changeableness. 9. **On your attendance:** ready to do you service. 13. **address thy gait:** go.

And tell them,° there thy fixèd foot shall grow
Till thou have audience.

VIOLA: Sure, my noble lord,
If she be so abandoned to her sorrow
As it is spoke, she never will admit me.

ORSINO:
Be clamorous and leap all civil bounds°
Rather than make unprofited return.

VIOLA:
Say I do speak with her, my lord, what then?

ORSINO:
O, then unfold the passion of my love,
Surprise° her with discourse of my dear° faith.
It shall become° thee well to act my woes;
She will attend it better in thy youth
Than in a nuncio's° of more grave aspect.

VIOLA:
I think not so, my lord.

ORSINO: Dear lad, believe it;
For they shall yet belie thy happy years
That say thou art a man: Diana's lip
Is not more smooth and rubious;° thy small pipe°
Is as the maiden's organ, shrill and sound,°
And all is semblative° a woman's part.
I know thy constellation° is right apt
For this affair. — Some four or five attend him.
All, if you will, for I myself am best
When least in company. — Prosper well in this,
And thou shalt live as freely as thy lord,
To call his fortunes thine.

VIOLA: I'll do my best
To woo your lady. [*Aside.*] Yet a barful strife!°
Whoe'er I woo, myself would be his wife. *Exeunt.*

15. **them:** i.e., Olivia's servants. 19. **civil bounds:** bounds of civility. 23. **Surprise:** take by storm. (A military term.) **dear:** heartfelt. 24. **become:** suit. 26. **nuncio's:** messenger's. 30. **rubious:** ruby red. **pipe:** voice, throat. 31. **shrill and sound:** high and clear, uncracked. 32. **semblative:** resembling, like. 33. **constellation:** i.e., nature as determined by your horoscope. 39. **barful strife:** endeavor full of impediments.

ACT 1, SCENE 5°

Enter Maria and Clown [*Feste*].

MARIA: Nay, either tell me where thou hast been, or I will not open my lips so wide as a bristle may enter in way of thy excuse. My lady will hang thee for thy absence.

FESTE: Let her hang me. He that is well hanged in this world needs to fear no colors.°

MARIA: Make that good.°

FESTE: He shall see none to fear.°

MARIA: A good Lenten° answer: I can tell thee where that saying was born, of "I fear no colors."

FESTE: Where, good Mistress Mary?

MARIA: In the wars,° and that may you be bold to say in your foolery.°

FESTE: Well, God give them wisdom that have it; and those that are fools, let them use their talents.°

MARIA: Yet you will be hanged for being so long absent; or to be turned away,° is not that as good as a hanging to you?

FESTE: Many a good hanging° prevents a bad marriage; and for° turning away, let summer bear it out.°

MARIA: You are resolute, then?

FESTE: Not so, neither, but I am resolved on two points.°

MARIA: That if one break, the other will hold; or, if both break, your gaskins° fall.

FESTE: Apt, in good faith; very apt. Well, go thy way. If Sir Toby would leave drinking, thou wert as witty a piece of Eve's flesh as any in Illyria.°

MARIA: Peace, you rogue, no more o' that. Here comes my lady. Make your excuse wisely, you were best.° [*Exit.*]

Enter Lady Olivia with Malvolio [*and attendants*].

ACT 1, SCENE 5. **Location:** Olivia's house. **4–5. fear no colors:** i.e., fear no foe, fear nothing (with pun on *colors,* worldly deceptions, and "collars," halters or nooses). **6. Make that good:** explain that. **7. He . . . fear:** i.e., he'll be dead and unable to see anything. **8. Lenten:** meager, scanty (like Lenten fare), and morbid. **11. In the wars:** (where *colors* would mean "military standards, enemy flags" — the literal meaning of the proverb). **that . . . foolery:** that's an answer you may be bold to use in your fool's conundrums. **13. talents:** abilities (also alluding to the parable of the talents, Matthew 25.14–29, and no "talons," claws). **14–15. turned away:** dismissed (possibly also meaning "turned off," "hanged"). **16. good hanging:** (with possible bawdy pun on "being well hung"). **for:** as for. **17. let . . . out:** i.e., let mild weather make dismissal endurable. **19. points:** (Maria plays on the meaning "laces used to hold up hose or breeches.") **21. gaskins:** wide breeches. **23. thou . . . Illyria:** (Feste may be observing ironically that Maria is as likely to prove witty as Sir Toby is to give up drinking; or he may hint at a match between the two.) **25. you were best:** it would be best for you.

FESTE: [*aside*] Wit, an 't° be thy will, put me into good fooling! Those wits that think they have thee do very oft prove fools, and I that am sure I lack thee may pass for a wise man. For what says Quinapalus?° "Better a witty fool than a foolish wit." — God bless thee, lady!

OLIVIA: [*to attendants*] Take the fool away.

FESTE: Do you not hear, fellows? Take away the lady.

OLIVIA: Go to,° you're a dry° fool. I'll no more of you. Besides, you grow dishonest.

FESTE: Two faults, madonna,° that drink and good counsel will amend. For give the dry fool drink, then is the fool not dry. Bid the dishonest man mend himself; if he mend, he is no longer dishonest; if he cannot, let the botcher° mend him. Anything that's mended is but patched;° virtue that transgresses is but patched with sin, and sin that amends is but patched with virtue. If that this simple syllogism will serve, so;° if it will not, what remedy? As there is no true cuckold but calamity, so beauty's a flower.° The lady bade take away the fool; therefore, I say again, take her away.

OLIVIA: Sir, I bade them take away you.

FESTE: Misprision° in the highest degree! Lady, *cucullus non facit monachum;*° that's as much to say as I wear not motley° in my brain. Good madonna, give me leave to prove you a fool.

OLIVIA: Can you do it?

FESTE: Dexterously, good madonna.

OLIVIA: Make your proof.

FESTE: I must catechize you for it, madonna. Good my mouse of virtue,° answer me.

OLIVIA: Well, sir, for want of other idleness,° I'll bide° your proof.

FESTE: Good madonna, why mourn'st thou?

OLIVIA: Good fool, for my brother's death.

FESTE: I think his soul is in hell, madonna.

OLIVIA: I know his soul is in heaven, fool.

FESTE: The more fool, madonna, to mourn for your brother's soul, being in heaven. Take away the fool, gentlemen.

26. **an 't:** if it. 28. **Quinapalus:** (Feste's invented authority.) 32. **Go to:** (An expression of annoyance or expostulation.) **dry:** dull. 34. **madonna:** my lady. 37. **botcher:** mender of old clothes and shoes (playing on two senses of *mend:* "reform" and "repair"). **Anything . . . patched:** i.e., life is patched or parti-colored like the Fool's garment, a mix of good and bad. 39. **so:** well and good. 40. **As . . . flower:** i.e., Olivia has wedded calamity but will not be faithful to it, for the natural course is to seize the moment of youth and beauty before we lose it. 43. **Misprision:** mistake, misunderstanding. (A legal term meaning a wrongful action or misdemeanor.) 43–44. ***cucullus . . . monachum:*** the cowl does not make the monk. 44. **motley:** the many-colored garment of jesters. 49. **Good . . . virtue:** my good, virtuous mouse. (A term of endearment.) 51. **idleness:** pastime. **bide:** endure.

OLIVIA: What think you of this fool, Malvolio? Doth he not mend?°

MALVOLIO: Yes, and shall do till the pangs of death shake him. Infirmity, that decays the wise, doth ever make the better fool.

FESTE: God send you, sir, a speedy infirmity for the better increasing your folly! Sir Toby will be sworn that I am no fox, but he will not pass° his word for twopence that you are no fool.

OLIVIA: How say you to that, Malvolio?

MALVOLIO: I marvel your ladyship takes delight in such a barren rascal. I saw him put down the other day with° an ordinary fool that has no more brain than a stone. Look you now, he's out of his guard° already. Unless you laugh and minister occasion° to him, he is gagged. I protest° I take these wise men that crow° so at these set° kind of fools no better than the fools' zanies.°

OLIVIA: Oh, you are sick of self-love, Malvolio, and taste with a distempered° appetite. To be generous,° guiltless, and of free° disposition is to take those things for bird-bolts° that you deem cannon bullets. There is no slander in an allowed° fool, though he do nothing but rail; nor no railing in a known discreet man, though he do nothing but reprove.°

FESTE: Now Mercury endue thee with leasing,° for thou speak'st well of fools!

Enter Maria.

MARIA: Madam, there is at the gate a young gentleman much desires to speak with you.

OLIVIA: From the Count Orsino, is it?

MARIA: I know not, madam. 'Tis a fair young man, and well attended.

OLIVIA: Who of my people hold him in delay?

MARIA: Sir Toby, madam, your kinsman.

OLIVIA: Fetch him off, I pray you. He speaks nothing but madman.° Fie on him! [*Exit Maria.*] Go you, Malvolio. If it be a suit from the Count, I am sick, or not at home; what you will, to dismiss it. (*Exit Malvolio.*) Now you see, sir, how your fooling grows old, and people dislike it.

58. **mend:** i.e., improve, grow more amusing. (But Malvolio uses the word to mean "grow more like a fool.") 62. **pass:** give. 66. **with:** by. 67. **out of his guard:** defenseless, unprovided with a witty answer. 68. **minister occasion:** provide opportunity (for his fooling). **protest:** avow, declare. 69. **crow:** laugh stridently. **set:** artificial, stereotyped. 70. **zanies:** assistants, aping attendants. 71–72. **distempered:** diseased. 72. **generous:** noble-minded. **free:** magnanimous. 73. **bird-bolts:** blunt arrows for shooting small birds. 74. **allowed:** licensed (to speak freely). 74–75. **nor . . . reprove:** (Olivia gently chides Malvolio for not reproving more civilly, while at the same time tactfully complimenting his sobriety.) 76. **Now . . . leasing:** i.e., may Mercury, the god of deception, make you a skillful liar. 84. **madman:** i.e., the words of madness.

FESTE: Thou hast spoke for us, madonna, as if thy eldest son should be a fool; whose skull Jove cram with brains, for — here he comes —

Enter Sir Toby.

one of thy kin has a most weak *pia mater.*°

OLIVIA: By mine honor, half drunk. What is he at the gate, cousin?

SIR TOBY: A gentleman.

OLIVIA: A gentleman? What gentleman?

SIR TOBY: 'Tis a gentle man here — [*He belches.*] A plague o' these pickle-herring! [*To Feste.*] How now, sot?°

FESTE: Good Sir Toby.

OLIVIA: Cousin,° cousin, how have you come so early by this lethargy?

SIR TOBY: Lechery? I defy lechery. There's one at the gate.

OLIVIA: Ay, marry, what is he?

SIR TOBY: Let him be the devil an he will, I care not. Give me faith,° say I. Well, it's all one.° *Exit.*

OLIVIA: What's a drunken man like, Fool?

FESTE: Like a drowned man, a fool, and a madman. One draft° above heat° makes him a fool, the second mads him, and a third drowns him.

OLIVIA: Go thou and seek the crowner,° and let him sit o' my coz;° for he's in the third degree of drink, he's drowned. Go, look after him.

FESTE: He is but mad yet, madonna; and the fool shall look to the madman. [*Exit.*]

Enter Malvolio.

MALVOLIO: Madam, yond young fellow swears he will speak with you. I told him you were sick; he takes on him to understand so much, and therefore comes to speak with you. I told him you were asleep; he seems to have a foreknowledge of that too, and therefore comes to speak with you. What is to be said to him, lady? He's fortified against any denial.

OLIVIA: Tell him he shall not speak with me.

MALVOLIO: He's been told so; and he says, he'll stand at your door like a sheriff's post,° and be the supporter to a bench, but he'll speak with you.

OLIVIA: What kind o' man is he?

MALVOLIO: Why, of mankind.

90. *pia mater:* i.e., brain (actually the soft membrane enclosing the brain). 95. **sot:** (1) fool (2) drunkard. 97. **Cousin:** kinsman (here, uncle). 100. **Give me faith:** i.e., to resist the devil. 101. **it's all one:** it doesn't matter. 103. **draft:** drinking portion. **above heat:** above the point needed to make him normally warm. 105. **crowner:** coroner. **sit o' my coz:** hold an inquest on my kinsman (Sir Toby). 116. **sheriff's post:** post before the sheriff's door to mark a residence of authority.

OLIVIA: What manner of man?

MALVOLIO: Of very ill manner. He'll speak with you, will you or no.

OLIVIA: Of what personage and years is he?

MALVOLIO: Not yet old enough for a man, nor young enough for a boy; as a squash° is before 'tis a peascod,° or a codling° when 'tis almost an apple. 'Tis with him in standing water° between boy and man. He is very well-favored,° and he speaks very shrewishly.° One would think his mother's milk were scarce out of him.

OLIVIA: Let him approach. Call in my gentlewoman.

MALVOLIO: Gentlewoman, my lady calls. *Exit.*

Enter Maria.

OLIVIA:
Give me my veil. Come, throw it o'er my face.
We'll once more hear Orsino's embassy. [*Olivia veils.*]

Enter Viola.

VIOLA: The honourable lady of the house, which is she?

OLIVIA: Speak to me; I shall answer for her. Your will?

VIOLA: Most radiant, exquisite, and unmatchable beauty — I pray you, tell me if this be the lady of the house, for I never saw her. I would be loath to cast away my speech; for besides that it is excellently well penned, I have taken great pains to con° it. Good beauties, let me sustain no scorn; I am very comptible,° even to the least sinister° usage.

OLIVIA: Whence came you, sir?

VIOLA: I can say little more than I have studied, and that question's out of my part. Good gentle one, give me modest° assurance if you be the lady of the house, that I may proceed in my speech.

OLIVIA: Are you a comedian?°

VIOLA: No, my profound heart;° and yet, by the very fangs of malice, I swear I am not that I play.° Are you the lady of the house?

OLIVIA: If I do not usurp myself,° I am.

VIOLA: Most certain, if you are she, you do usurp yourself;° for what is yours to bestow is not yours to reserve. But this is from° my commission.

123. **squash:** unripe pea pod. **peascod:** pea pod. **codling:** unripe apple. 124. **in standing water:** at the turn of the tide. 125. **well-favored:** good-looking. **shrewishly:** sharply. 136. **con:** learn by heart. 137. **comptible:** susceptible, sensitive. **least sinister:** slightest discourteous. 140. **modest:** reasonable. 142. **comedian:** actor. 143. **my profound heart:** my most wise lady; or, in all sincerity. 143–44. **by . . . I play:** i.e., I swear, whatever people may maliciously suppose, I am not what I impersonate. 145. **do . . . myself:** am not an impostor. 146. **usurp yourself:** i.e., misappropriate yourself, by withholding yourself from love and marriage. 147. **from:** outside of.

I will on with my speech in your praise, and then show you the heart of my message.

OLIVIA: Come to what is important in 't. I forgive you° the praise.

VIOLA: Alas, I took great pains to study it, and 'tis poetical.

OLIVIA: It is the more like to be feigned. I pray you, keep it in. I heard you were saucy at my gates, and allowed your approach rather to wonder at you than to hear you. If you be not mad,° begone; if you have reason,° be brief. 'Tis not that time of moon° with me to make one° in so skipping a dialogue.

MARIA: Will you hoist sail, sir? Here lies your way.

VIOLA: No, good swabber,° I am to hull° here a little longer. — Some mollification for° your giant,° sweet lady. Tell me your mind; I am a messenger.

OLIVIA: Sure you have some hideous matter to deliver, when the courtesy° of it is so fearful. Speak your office.°

VIOLA: It alone concerns your ear. I bring no overture° of war, no taxation° of homage: I hold the olive° in my hand; my words are as full of peace as matter.

OLIVIA: Yet you began rudely.° What are you? What would you?

VIOLA: The rudeness that hath appeared in me have I learned from my entertainment.° What I am, and what I would are as secret as maidenhead — to your ears, divinity;° to any other's, profanation.

OLIVIA: Give us the place alone. We will hear this divinity. [*Exeunt Maria and attendants.*] Now, sir, what is your text?

VIOLA: Most sweet lady —

OLIVIA: A comfortable° doctrine, and much may be said of it. Where lies your text?

VIOLA: In Orsino's bosom.

OLIVIA: In his bosom! In what chapter of his bosom?

VIOLA: To answer by the method,° in the first of his heart.

150. **forgive you:** excuse you from repeating. 154. **If . . . mad:** i.e., if you don't have madness to excuse your saucy behavior, or, if you be not altogether mad(?). Possibly an error for *If . . . but mad*(?). **reason:** sanity. 155. **moon:** (The moon was thought to affect lunatics according to its changing phases.) **make one:** take part. 158. **swabber:** one in charge of washing the decks. (A nautical retort to *hoist sail.*) **hull:** lie with sails furled. 158–59. **Some . . . for:** i.e., please mollify, pacify. 159. **giant:** i.e., the diminutive Maria who, like many giants in medieval romances, is guarding the lady. 160. **courtesy:** i.e., complimentary, "poetical" introduction. (Or Olivia may refer to Cesario's importunate manner at her gate, as reported by Malvolio.) 161. **office:** commission, business. 162. **overture:** declaration. (Literally, opening.) **taxation:** demand for the payment. 163. **olive:** olive-branch (signifying peace). 165. **Yet . . . rudely:** i.e., yet you were saucy at my gates. 167. **entertainment:** reception. 168. **divinity:** sacred discourse. 172. **comfortable:** comforting. 176. **To . . . method:** i.e., to continue the metaphor (of delivering a sermon, begun with *divinity* and *what is your text* and continued in *doctrine, heresy,* etc.).

OLIVIA: O, I have read it. It is heresy. Have you no more to say?

VIOLA: Good madam, let me see your face.

OLIVIA: Have you any commission from your lord to negotiate with my face? You are now out of° your text. But we will draw the curtain and show you the picture. [*Unveiling.*] Look you, sir, such a one I was this present.° Is 't not well done?

VIOLA: Excellently done, if God did all.

OLIVIA: 'Tis in grain,° sir; 'twill endure wind and weather.

VIOLA:
'Tis beauty truly blent,° whose red and white
Nature's own sweet and cunning° hand laid on:
Lady, you are the cruel'st she alive,
If you will lead these graces to the grave
And leave the world no copy.°

OLIVIA: O, sir, I will not be so hardhearted. I will give out divers schedules° of my beauty. It shall be inventoried, and every particle and utensil° labeled° to my will: as, item, two lips, indifferent° red; item, two gray eyes, with lids to them; item, one neck, one chin, and so forth. Were you sent hither to praise° me?

VIOLA:
I see you what you are, you are too proud;
But, if° you were the devil, you are fair.
My lord and master loves you. O, such love
Could be but recompensed, though° you were crown'd
The nonpareil of beauty!

OLIVIA: How does he love me?

VIOLA:
With adorations, fertile° tears,
With groans that thunder love, with sighs of fire.

OLIVIA:
Your lord does know my mind; I cannot love him.
Yet I suppose him virtuous, know him noble,
Of great estate, of fresh and stainless youth,

180. **out of:** straying from. 181–82. **such . . . present:** this is a recent portrait of me. (Since it was customary to hang curtains in front of pictures, Olivia in unveiling speaks as if she were displaying a picture of herself.) 184. **in grain:** fast dyed. 185. **blent:** blended. 186. **cunning:** skillful. 189. **copy:** i.e., a child. (But Olivia uses the word to mean "transcript.") 190. **schedules:** inventories. 191. **utensil:** article, item. 192. **labeled:** added as a codicil. **indifferent:** somewhat. 194. **praise:** (with pun on "appraise"). 196. **if:** even if. 198. **but . . . though:** no more than evenly repaid even though. 200. **fertile:** copious.

In voices well divulged,° free,° learned and valiant,
And in dimension and the shape of nature°
A gracious° person. But yet I cannot love him.
He might have took his answer long ago.

VIOLA:
If I did love you in my master's flame,°
With such a suffering, such a deadly° life,
In your denial I would find no sense;
I would not understand it.

OLIVIA: Why, what would you?

VIOLA:
Make me a willow cabin° at your gate
And call upon my soul° within the house;
Write loyal cantons° of contemnèd° love
And sing them loud even in the dead of night;
Hallow° your name to the reverberate hills,
And make the babbling gossip of the air°
Cry out "Olivia!" O, you should not rest
Between the elements of air and earth,
But you should pity me!

OLIVIA: You might do much.
What is your parentage?

VIOLA:
Above my fortunes, yet my state° is well:
I am a gentleman.

OLIVIA: Get you to your lord.
I cannot love him. Let him send no more —
Unless, perchance, you come to me again
To tell me how he takes it. Fare you well.
I thank you for your pains. Spend this for me. [*She offers a purse.*]

VIOLA:
I am no fee'd post,° lady. Keep your purse.
My master, not myself, lacks recompense.
Love make his heart of flint that you shall love,°

205. **In . . . divulged:** well spoken of. **free:** generous. 206. **in . . . nature:** in his physical form. 207. **gracious:** graceful, attractive. 209. **flame:** passion. 210. **deadly:** deathlike. 213. **willow cabin:** shelter, hut. (Willow was a symbol of unrequited love.) 214. **my soul:** i.e., Olivia. 215. **cantons:** songs. **contemnèd:** rejected. 217. **Hallow:** (1) halloo (2) bless. 218. **babbling . . . air:** echo. 223. **state:** social standing. 229. **fee'd post:** messenger to be tipped. 231. **Love . . . love:** may Love make the heart of the man you love as hard as flint.

And let your fervor, like my master's, be
Placed in contempt! Farewell, fair cruelty. *Exit.*

OLIVIA: "What is your parentage?"
"Above my fortunes, yet my state is well:
I am a gentleman." I'll be sworn thou art!
Thy tongue, thy face, thy limbs, actions, and spirit
Do give thee fivefold blazon.° Not too fast! Soft,° soft!
Unless the master were the man.° How now?
Even so quickly may one catch the plague?
Methinks I feel this youth's perfections
With an invisible and subtle stealth
To creep in at mine eyes. Well, let it be.
What ho, Malvolio!

Enter Malvolio.

MALVOLIO: Here, madam, at your service.

OLIVIA:
Run after that same peevish messenger,
The County's° man. He left this ring behind him, [*giving a ring*]
Would I or not.° Tell him I'll none of it.
Desire him not to flatter with° his lord,
Nor hold him up with hopes; I am not for him.
If that the youth will come this way tomorrow,
I'll give him reasons for 't. Hie thee, Malvolio.

MALVOLIO: Madam, I will. *Exit.*

OLIVIA:
I do I know not what, and fear to find
Mine eye too great a flatterer for my mind.°
Fate, show thy force. Ourselves we do not owe.°
What is decreed must be; and be this so. [*Exit.*]

238. **blazon:** heraldic description. **Soft:** wait a minute. 239. **Unless . . . man:** i.e., unless Cesario and Orsino changed places. 246. **County's:** Count's, i.e., Duke's. 247. **Would I or not:** whether I wanted it or not. 248. **flatter with:** encourage. 254. **Mine . . . mind:** i.e., that my eyes (through which love enters the soul) have betrayed my reason by giving a flattering view of Cesario. 255. **owe:** own, control.

ACT 2, SCENE 1°

Enter Antonio and Sebastian.

ANTONIO: Will you stay no longer? Nor will you not° that I go with you?

SEBASTIAN: By your patience,° no. My stars shine darkly over me. The malignancy° of my fate might perhaps distemper° yours; therefore I shall crave of you your leave that I may bear my evils alone. It were a bad recompense for your love to lay any of them on you.

ANTONIO: Let me yet know of you whither you are bound.

SEBASTIAN: No, sooth,° sir; my determinate° voyage is mere extravagancy.° But I perceive in you so excellent a touch of modesty that you will not extort from me what I am willing to keep in;° therefore it charges me in manners° the rather to express° myself. You must know of me then, Antonio, my name is Sebastian, which I called Roderigo. My father was that Sebastian of Messaline,° whom I know you have heard of. He left behind him myself and a sister, both born in an hour.° If the heavens had been pleased, would we had so ended! But you, sir, altered that, for some hour° before you took me from the breach of the sea° was my sister drowned.

ANTONIO: Alas the day!

SEBASTIAN: A lady, sir, though it was said she much resembled me, was yet of many accounted beautiful. But though I could not with such estimable wonder° overfar believe that, yet thus far I will boldly publish° her: she bore a mind that envy° could not but call fair. She is drowned already, sir, with salt water, though I seem to drown her remembrance again with more.

ANTONIO: Pardon me, sir, your bad entertainment.°

SEBASTIAN: O good Antonio, forgive me your trouble.°

ANTONIO: If you will not murder me for° my love, let me be your servant.

SEBASTIAN: If you will not undo what you have done, that is, kill him whom you have recovered,° desire it not. Fare ye well at once. My bosom

ACT 2, SCENE 1. **Location:** Somewhere in Illyria. 1. **Nor will you not:** do you not wish. 2. **patience:** leave. 3. **malignancy:** malevolence (of the stars; also in a medical sense). **distemper:** infect. 7. **sooth:** truly. **determinate:** intended, determined upon. **extravagancy:** aimless wandering. 9. **am willing . . . in:** wish to keep secret. 9–10. **it . . . manners:** it is incumbent upon me in all courtesy. 10. **express:** reveal. 12. **Messaline:** possibly Messina, or, more likely, Massila (the modern Marseilles). In Plautus' *Menaechmi,* Massilians and Illyrians are mentioned together. 13. **in an hour:** in the same hour. 14–15. **some hour:** about an hour. 15. **breach of the sea:** surf. 19–20. **estimable wonder:** admiring judgment. 20. **publish:** proclaim. 21. **envy:** even malice. 24. **entertainment:** reception, hospitality. 25. **your trouble:** the trouble I put you to. 26. **murder me for:** i.e., be the cause of my death in return for. 28. **recovered:** rescued, restored.

is full of kindness,° and I am yet so near the manners of my mother° that upon the least occasion more mine eyes will tell tales of me. I am bound to the Count Orsino's court. Farewell. *Exit.*

ANTONIO:

The gentleness of all the gods go with thee!
I have many enemies in Orsino's court,
Else would I very shortly see thee there.
But, come what may, I do adore thee so
That danger shall seem sport, and I will go. *Exit.*

ACT 2, SCENE 2°

Enter Viola and Malvolio, at several° doors.

MALVOLIO: Were not you even now with the Countess Olivia?

VIOLA: Even now, sir. On a moderate pace I have since arrived but hither.

MALVOLIO: She returns this ring to you, sir. You might have saved me my pains, to have taken° it away yourself. She adds, moreover, that you should put your lord into a desperate° assurance she will none of him. And one thing more: that you be never so hardy to come° again in his affairs, unless it be to report your lord's taking of this. Receive it so.

VIOLA: She took the ring of me. I'll none of it.°

MALVOLIO: Come, sir, you peevishly threw it to her, and her will is it should be so returned. [*He thows down the ring.*] If it be worth stooping for, there it lies, in your eye;° if not, be it his that finds it. *Exit.*

VIOLA: [*picking up the ring*]

I left no ring with her. What means this lady?
Fortune forbid my outside have not charmed° her!
She made good view of me, indeed so much
That sure methought her eyes had lost° her tongue,
For she did speak in starts, distractedly.
She loves me, sure! The cunning of her passion
Invites me in° this churlish messenger.
None of my lord's ring? Why, he sent her none.
I am the man.° If it be so — as 'tis —
Poor lady, she were better love a dream.

29. **kindness:** tenderness, natural emotion (of grief). **manners of my mother:** i.e., womanly inclination to weep. **ACT 2, SCENE 2. Location:** Outside Olivia's house. **s.d.** *several:* different. 4. **to have taken:** by taking. 5. **desperate:** without hope. 6. **hardy to come:** bold as to come. 8. **She . . . it:** (Viola tells a quick and friendly lie to shield Olivia.) 11. **in your eye:** in plain sight. 13. **charmed:** enchanted. 15. **lost:** caused her to lose. 18. **in:** in the person of. 20. **the man:** the man of her choice.

Disguise, I see, thou art a wickedness
Wherein the pregnant° enemy° does much.
How easy is it for the proper false°
In women's waxen° hearts to set their forms!°
Alas, our frailty is the cause, not we,
For such as we are made of, such we be.°
How will this fadge?° My master loves her dearly;
And I, poor monster,° fond° as much on him;
And she, mistaken, seems to dote on me.
What will become of this? As I am man,
My state is desperate for my master's love;
As I am woman — now alas the day! —
What thriftless° sighs shall poor Olivia breathe!
O Time, thou must untangle this, not I;
It is too hard a knot for me t' untie! [*Exit.*]

ACT 2, SCENE 3°

Enter Sir Toby and Sir Andrew.

SIR TOBY: Approach, Sir Andrew. Not to be abed after midnight is to be up betimes°; and *diluculo surgere,*° thou know'st —

SIR ANDREW: Nay, by my troth, I know not, but I know to be up late is to be up late.

SIR TOBY: A false conclusion. I hate it as an unfilled can.° To be up after midnight and to go to bed then, is early; so that to go to bed after midnight is to go to bed betimes. Does not our lives consist of the four elements?°

SIR ANDREW: Faith, so they say, but I think it rather consists of eating and drinking.

SIR TOBY: Thou'rt a scholar; let us therefore eat and drink. Marian, I say, a stoup° of wine!

Enter Clown [*Feste*].

23. **pregnant:** quick, resourceful. **enemy:** i.e., Satan. 24. **proper false:** men who are handsome and deceitful. 25. **waxen:** i.e., malleable, impressionable. **set their forms:** stamp their images (as of a seal) 27. **such as . . . be:** being made of frail material, we are frail. 28. **fadge:** turn out. 29. **monster:** i.e., being both man and woman. **fond:** dote. 34. **thriftless:** unprofitable. **ACT 2, SCENE 3. Location:** Olivia's house. 2. **betimes:** early. ***diluculo surgere*** [***saluberrimum est***]: to rise early is most healthful. (A sentence from Lilly's *Latin Grammar.*) 5. **can:** tankard. 7–8. **four elements:** i.e., fire, air, water, and earth, the elements that were thought to make up all matter. 12. **stoup:** drinking vessel.

SIR ANDREW: Here comes the Fool, i' faith.

FESTE: How now, my hearts! Did you never see the picture of "we three"?°

SIR TOBY: Welcome, ass. Now let's have a catch.°

SIR ANDREW: By my troth, the Fool has an excellent breast.° I had rather than forty shillings I had such a leg, and so sweet a breath to sing, as the Fool has. In sooth, thou wast in very gracious fooling last night, when thou spok'st of Pigrogromitus, of the Vapians passing the equinoctial of Queubus.° 'Twas very good, i' faith. I sent thee sixpence for thy leman.° Hadst it?

FESTE: I did impeticos thy gratillity;° for Malvolio's nose is no whipstock.° My lady has a white hand,° and the Myrmidons° are no bottle-ale houses.°

SIR ANDREW: Excellent! Why, this is the best fooling, when all is done. Now, a song.

SIR TOBY: Come on, there is sixpence for you. [*He gives money.*] Let's have a song.

SIR ANDREW: There's a testril° of me too. [*He gives money.*] If one knight give a —

FESTE: Would you have a love song, or a song of good life?°

SIR TOBY: A love song, a love song.

SIR ANDREW: Ay, ay, I care not for good life.

FESTE: (*sings*)

O mistress mine, where are you roaming?
O, stay and hear, your true love 's coming,
  That can sing both high and low.
Trip no further, pretty sweeting;
Journeys end in lovers' meeting,
  Every wise man's son doth know.

SIR ANDREW: Excellent good, i' faith.

SIR TOBY: Good, good.

FESTE: [*sings*]

What is love? 'tis not hereafter;
Present mirth hath present laughter;

14. **picture of "we three":** picture of two fools or asses inscribed "we three," the spectator being the third. 15. **catch:** round. 16. **breast:** voice. 19–20. **Pigrogromitus . . . Queubus:** (Feste's mock erudition.) 20. **leman:** sweetheart. 22. **impeticos thy gratillity:** (Suggests "impetticoat, or pocket up, thy gratuity.") **whipstock:** whip handle. (Possibly suggests that Malvolio can't be led by the nose; or, just nonsense.) 23. **has a white hand:** i.e., is ladylike. (But Feste's speech may be mere nonsense.) **Myrmidons:** followers of Achilles. **bottle-ale houses:** (Used contemptuously of taverns because they sold low-class drink.) 28. **testril:** tester, a coin worth sixpence. 30. **good life:** virtuous living. (Or perhaps Feste means simply "life's pleasures," but is misunderstood by Sir Andrew to mean "virtuous living.")

What's to come is still° unsure.
In delay there lies no plenty.
Then come kiss me, sweet and twenty;°
Youth's a stuff will not endure.

SIR ANDREW: A mellifluous voice, as I am true knight.

SIR TOBY: A contagious breath.°

SIR ANDREW: Very sweet and contagious, i' faith.

SIR TOBY: To hear by the nose, it is dulcet in contagion.° But shall we make the welkin dance° indeed? Shall we rouse the night owl in a catch that will draw three souls° out of one weaver?° Shall we do that?

SIR ANDREW: An you love me, let's do 't: I am dog at° a catch.°

FESTE: By 'r Lady,° sir, and some dogs will catch well.

SIR ANDREW: Most certain. Let our catch be "Thou knave."°

FESTE: "Hold thy peace, thou knave," knight? I shall be constrained in 't to call thee knave, knight.

SIR ANDREW: 'Tis not the first time I have constrained one to call me knave. Begin, Fool. It begins "Hold thy peace."

FESTE: I shall never begin if I hold my peace.

SIR ANDREW: Good, i' faith. Come, begin. *Catch sung.*

Enter Maria.

MARIA: What a caterwauling do you keep here! If my lady have not called up her steward Malvolio and bid him turn you out of doors, never trust me.

SIR TOBY: My lady's a Cataian,° we are politicians,° Malvolio's a Peg-o'-Ramsey, and [*he sings*] "Three merry men be we."° Am not I consanguineous?° Am I not of her blood? Tillyvally!° Lady! [*He sings.*] "There dwelt a man in Babylon, lady, lady."°

43. **still:** always. 45. **sweet and twenty:** i.e., sweet and twenty times sweet. 48. **A contagious breath:** (1) a catchy voice (2) an infected or contagious breath. 50. **To . . . contagion:** i.e., if we were to describe hearing in olfactory terms, we could say it is sweet in stench. (Sir Toby may be mocking Sir Andrew's uncritical acceptance of the word *contagious,* missing the pun.) 51. **make . . . dance:** i.e., drink till the sky seems to turn around. 52. **draw three souls:** (Refers to the threefold nature of the soul — vegetal, sensible, and intellectual — or to the three singers of the three-part catch; or, just a comic exaggeration.) **weaver:** (Weavers were often associated with psalm singing.) 53. **dog at:** very clever at. (But Feste uses the word literally.) **catch:** round. (But Feste uses it to mean "seize.") 54. **By 'r Lady:** (An oath, originally, "by the Virgin Mary.") 55. **"Thou knave":** (This popular round is arranged so that the three singers repeatedly sing to one another, "Thou knave." "Knight and knave" is a common antithesis, like "rich and poor.") 64. **Cataian:** Cathayan, i.e., Chinese, a trickster or inscrutable; or, just nonsense. **politicians:** schemers, intriguers. 64–65. **Peg-o'-Ramsey:** character in a popular song. (Used here contemptuously.) 65. **"Three . . . we":** (A snatch of an old song.) 65–66. **consanguineous:** i.e., a blood relative of Olivia. 66. **Tillyvally:** nonsense, fiddle-faddle. 66–67. **"There . . . lady":** (The first line of a ballad, "The Constancy of Susanna," together with the refrain, "Lady, lady.")

FESTE: Beshrew° me, the knight's in admirable fooling.

SIR ANDREW: Ay, he does well enough if he be disposed, and so do I too. He does it with a better grace, but I do it more natural.°

SIR TOBY: [*sings*]
"O' the twelfth day of December,"° —

MARIA: For the love o' God, peace!

Enter Malvolio.

MALVOLIO: My masters, are you mad? Or what are you? Have ye no wit,° manners, nor honesty° but to gabble like tinkers at this time of night? Do ye make an alehouse of my lady's house, that ye squeak out your coziers'° catches without any mitigation or remorse° of voice? Is there no respect of place, persons, nor time in you?

SIR TOBY: We did keep time, sir, in our catches. Sneck up!°

MALVOLIO: Sir Toby, I must be round° with you. My lady bade me tell you that though she harbors you as her kinsman, she's nothing allied to your disorders. If you can separate yourself and your misdemeanors, you are welcome to the house; if not, an it would please you to take leave of her, she is very willing to bid you farewell.

SIR TOBY: [*sings*]
"Farewell, dear heart, since I must needs be gone."°

MARIA: Nay, good Sir Toby.

FESTE: [*sings*]
"His eyes do show his days are almost done."

MALVOLIO: Is 't even so?

SIR TOBY: [*sings*]
"But I will never die."

FESTE:
"Sir Toby, there you lie."

MALVOLIO: This is much credit to you.

SIR TOBY: [*sings*]
"Shall I bid him go?"

FESTE: [*sings*]
"What an if you do?"

68. **Beshrew:** i.e., devil take. (A mild curse.) 70. **natural:** naturally (but unconsciously suggesting idiocy). 71. **"O' . . . December":** (Possibly part of a ballad about the Battle of Musselburgh Field, or Toby's error for the "twelfth day of Christmas," i.e., Twelfth Night.) 73. **wit:** common sense. 74. **honesty:** decency. 75. **coziers':** cobblers'. 76. **mitigation or remorse:** i.e., considerate lowering. 78. **Sneck up:** go hang. 79. **round:** blunt. 84. **"Farewell . . . gone":** (From the ballad "Corydon's Farewell to Phyllis.")

SIR TOBY: [*sings*]
"Shall I bid him go, and spare not?"

FESTE: [*sings*]
"O no, no, no, no, you dare not."

SIR TOBY: Out o' tune,° sir? Ye lie. Art any more than a steward? Dost thou think, because thou art virtuous, there shall be no more cakes and ale?

FESTE: Yes, by Saint Anne,° and ginger° shall be hot i' the mouth, too.

SIR TOBY: Thou'rt i' the right. — Go, sir, rub your chain with crumbs.° — A stoup of wine, Maria!

MALVOLIO: Mistress Mary, if you prized my lady's favor at anything more than contempt, you would not give means° for this uncivil rule.° She shall know of it, by this hand. *Exit.*

MARIA: Go shake your ears.°

SIR ANDREW: 'Twere as good a deed as to drink when a man's a-hungry to challenge him the field° and then to break promise with him and make a fool of him.

SIR TOBY: Do 't, knight: I'll write thee a challenge: or I'll deliver thy indignation to him by word of mouth.

MARIA: Sweet Sir Toby, be patient for tonight. Since the youth of the Count's was today with my lady, she is much out of quiet. For° Monsieur Malvolio, let me alone with him.° If I do not gull° him into a nayword° and make him a common recreation,° do not think I have wit enough to lie straight in my bed. I know I can do it.

SIR TOBY: Possess° us, possess us. Tell us something of him.

MARIA: Marry, sir, sometimes he is a kind of puritan.°

SIR ANDREW: O, if I thought that, I'd beat him like a dog.

SIR TOBY: What, for being a puritan? Thy exquisite reason, dear knight?

SIR ANDREW: I have no exquisite reason for 't, but I have reason good enough.

95. **Out o' tune:** (Perhaps a quibbling reply — "We did too keep time in our tune" — to Malvolio's accusation of having no respect for place or time, line 77. Often emended to *Out o' time,* easily misread in secretary hand.) 97. **Saint Anne:** mother of the Virgin Mary. (Her cult was derided in the Reformation, much as Puritan reformers also derided the tradition of *cakes and ale* at church feasts.) **ginger:** (Commonly used to spice ale.) 98. **Go . . . crumbs:** i.e., scour or polish your steward's chain; attend to your own business and remember your station. 101. **give means:** i.e., supply drink. **rule:** conduct. 103. **your ears:** i.e., your ass's ears. 105. **the field:** i.e., to a duel. 110. **For:** as for. 111. **let . . . him:** leave him to me. **gull:** trick. **nayword:** byword. (His name will be synonymous with "dupe.") 112. **recreation:** sport. 114. **Possess:** inform. 115. **puritan:** (Maria's point is that Malvolio is sometimes a *kind* of Puritan, insofar as he is precise about moral conduct and censorious of others for immoral conduct, but that he is nothing consistently except a time-server. He is not, then, simply a satirical type of the Puritan sect. The extent of the resemblance is left unstated.)

MARIA: The devil a puritan that he is, or anything constantly,° but a time-pleaser;° an affectioned° ass, that cons state without book° and utters it by great swaths;° the best persuaded° of himself, so crammed, as he thinks, with excellencies, that it is his grounds of faith° that all that look on him love him; and on that vice in him will my revenge find notable cause to work.

SIR TOBY: What wilt thou do?

MARIA: I will drop in his way some obscure epistles of love, wherein, by the color of his beard, the shape of his leg, the manner of his gait, the expressure° of his eye, forehead, and complexion,° he shall find himself most feelingly personated.° I can write very like my lady your niece; on a forgotten matter° we can hardly make distinction of our hands.

SIR TOBY: Excellent! I smell a device.

SIR ANDREW: I have 't in my nose too.

SIR TOBY: He shall think, by the letters that thou wilt drop, that they come from my niece, and that she's in love with him.

MARIA: My purpose is indeed a horse of that color.

SIR ANDREW: And your horse now would make him an ass.

MARIA: Ass, I° doubt not.

SIR ANDREW: O, 'twill be admirable!

MARIA: Sport royal, I warrant you. I know my physic° will work with him. I will plant you two, and let the Fool make a third, where he shall find the letter. Observe his construction° of it. For this night, to bed, and dream on the event.° Farewell. *Exit.*

SIR TOBY: Good night, Penthesilea.°

SIR ANDREW: Before me,° she's a good wench.

SIR TOBY: She's a beagle° true-bred, and one that adores me. What o' that?

SIR ANDREW: I was adored once, too.

SIR TOBY: Let's to bed, knight. Thou hadst need send for more money.

SIR ANDREW: If I cannot recover° your niece, I am a foul way out.°

120. **constantly:** consistently. 121. **time-pleaser:** time-server, sycophant. (Today, someone who says and does what time and circumstance demand.) **affectioned:** affected. **cons . . . book:** learns by heart the phrases and mannerisms of the great. 122. **by great swaths:** in great sweeps, like rows of mown grain. **best persuaded:** having the best opinion. 123. **grounds of faith:** creed, belief. 129. **expressure:** expression. **complexion:** countenance. 130. **personated:** represented. 130–31. **on a forgotten matter:** when we've forgotten which of us wrote something or what it was about. 138. **Ass, I:** (with a pun on "as I"). 140. **physic:** medicine. 142. **construction:** interpretation. 143. **event:** outcome. 144. **Penthesilea:** Queen of the Amazons. (Another ironical allusion to Maria's diminutive stature.) 145. **Before me:** i.e., on my soul. 146. **beagle:** a small, intelligent hunting dog. 149. **recover:** win. **foul way out:** i.e., miserably out of pocket. (Literally, out of my way and in the mire.)

SIR TOBY: Send for money, knight. If thou hast her not i' the end, call me cut.°

SIR ANDREW: If I do not, never trust me, take it how you will.

SIR TOBY: Come, come, I'll go burn some sack.° 'Tis too late to go to bed now. Come, knight; come, knight. *Exeunt.*°

ACT 2, SCENE 4°

Enter Duke [Orsino], Viola, Curio, and others.

ORSINO:
Give me some music. Now, good morrow,° friends.
Now, good Cesario, but° that piece of song,
That old and antique° song we heard last night.
Methought it did relieve my passion much,
More than light airs and recollected terms°
Of these most brisk and giddy-pacèd times.
Come, but one verse.

CURIO: He is not here, so please your lordship, that should sing it.

ORSINO: Who was it?

CURIO: Feste the jester, my lord, a fool that the Lady Olivia's father took much delight in. He is about the house.

ORSINO:
Seek him out, and play the tune the while.
[Exit Curio.] Music plays.
[*To Viola.*] Come hither, boy. If ever thou shalt love,
In the sweet pangs of it remember me;
For such as I am, all true lovers are,
Unstaid and skittish in all motions else°
Save in the constant image of the creature
That is beloved. How dost thou like this tune?

VIOLA:
It gives a very echo to the seat°
Where Love is throned.

ORSINO: Thou dost speak masterly:
My life upon 't, young though thou art, thine eye

151. **cut:** a horse with a docked tail; also, a gelding, or the female genital organ. 153. **burn some sack:** warm some Spanish wine. 154. **s.d.** ***Exeunt:*** (Feste may have left earlier; he says nothing after line 97 and is perhaps referred to without his being present at 141.) **ACT 2, SCENE 4. Location:** Orsino's court. 1. **morrow:** morning. 2. **but:** i.e., I ask only. 3. **antique:** old, quaint, fantastic. 5. **recollected terms:** studied and artificial expressions. 16. **motions else:** other thoughts and emotions. 19. **the seat:** i.e., the heart.

Hath stayed upon some favor° that it loves.
Hath it not, boy?

VIOLA: A little, by your favor.°

ORSINO:
What kind of woman is 't?

VIOLA: Of your complexion.

ORSINO:
She is not worth thee, then. What years, i' faith?

VIOLA: About your years, my lord.

ORSINO:
Too old by heaven. Let still° the woman take
An elder than herself. So wears she° to him,
So sways she level° in her husband's heart.
For, boy, however we do praise ourselves,
Our fancies are more giddy and unfirm,
More longing, wavering, sooner lost and worn,°
Than women's are.

VIOLA: I think it well, my lord.

ORSINO:
Then let thy love be younger than thyself,
Or thy affection cannot hold the bent;°
For women are as roses, whose fair flower
Being once displayed,° doth fall that very hour.

VIOLA:
And so they are. Alas, that they are so,
To die even when° they to perfection grow!

Enter Curio and Clown [*Feste*].

ORSINO:
O, fellow, come, the song we had last night.
Mark it, Cesario, it is old and plain;
The spinsters° and the knitters in the sun,
And the free° maids that weave their thread with bones,°
Do use° to chant it. It is silly sooth,°

22. **stayed . . . favor:** rested upon some face. 23. **by your favor:** if you please (but also hinting at "like you in feature"). 27. **still:** always. 28. **wears she:** she adapts herself. 29. **sways she level:** she keeps a perfect equipoise and steady affection. 32. **worn:** exhausted. (Sometimes emended to *won.*) 35. **hold the bent:** hold steady, stand the strain (like the tension of a bow). 37. **displayed:** full blown. 39. **even when:** just as. 42. **spinsters:** spinners. 43. **free:** carefree, innocent. **bones:** bobbins on which bone-lace was made. 44. **Do use:** are accustomed. **silly sooth:** simple truth.

And dallies with° the innocence of love,
Like the old age.°

FESTE: Are you ready, sir?

ORSINO: Ay, prithee, sing. *Music.*

The Song.

FESTE: [*sings*]

Come away,° come away, death,
And in sad cypress° let me be laid.
Fly away, fly away, breath;
I am slain by a fair cruel maid.
My shroud of white, stuck all with yew,°
O, prepare it!
My part of death, no one so true
Did share it.°

Not a flower, not a flower sweet
On my black coffin let there be strown;°
Not a friend, not a friend greet
My poor corpse, where my bones shall be thrown.
A thousand thousand sighs to save,
Lay me, O, where
Sad true lover never find my grave,
To weep there!

ORSINO: [*offering money*] There's for thy pains.

FESTE: No pains, sir. I take pleasure in singing, sir.

ORSINO: I'll pay thy pleasure then.

FESTE: Truly, sir, and pleasure will be paid, one time or another.°

ORSINO: Give me now leave to leave° thee.

FESTE: Now, the melancholy god° protect thee; and the tailor make thy doublet° of changeable taffeta,° for thy mind is a very opal.° I would have

45. **dallies with:** dwells lovingly on, sports with. 46. **Like . . . age:** as in the good old times. 49. **Come away:** come hither. 50. **cypress:** i.e., a coffin of cypress wood, or bier strewn with sprigs of cypress. 53. **yew:** yew sprigs. (Emblematic of mourning, like cypress.) 55–56. **My . . . it:** no one died for love so true to love as I. 58. **strown:** strewn. 68. **pleasure . . . another:** sooner or later one must pay for indulgence. 69. **leave to leave:** permission to take leave of, dismiss. 70. **the melancholy god:** i.e., Saturn, whose planet was thought to control the melancholy temperament. 71. **doublet:** close-fitting jacket. **changeable taffeta:** a silk so woven of various-colored threads that its color shifts with changing perspective. **opal:** an iridescent precious stone that changes color when seen from various angles or in different lights.

men of such constancy put to sea, that their business might be everything and their intent° everywhere,° for that's it that always makes a good voyage of nothing.° Farewell. *Exit.*

ORSINO:

Let all the rest give place.° [*Curio and attendants withdraw.*]
Once more, Cesario,
Get thee to yond same sovereign cruelty.
Tell her, my love, more noble than the world,
Prizes not quantity of dirty lands;
The parts° that fortune hath bestowed upon her,
Tell her, I hold as giddily as fortune;°
But 'tis that miracle and queen of gems°
That nature pranks° her in attracts° my soul.

VIOLA: But if she cannot love you, sir?

ORSINO:

I cannot be so answered.

VIOLA: Sooth,° but you must.
Say that some lady, as perhaps there is,
Hath for your love as great a pang of heart
As you have for Olivia. You cannot love her;
You tell her so. Must she not then be answered?°

ORSINO:

There is no woman's sides
Can bide° the beating of so strong a passion
As love doth give my heart; no woman's heart
So big, to hold° so much. They lack retention.°
Alas, their love may be called appetite,
No motion° of the liver, but the palate,°
That suffer surfeit,° cloyment,° and revolt;°
But mine is all as hungry as the sea,
And can digest as much. Make no compare°

72–73. **that . . . everywhere:** i.e., so that in the changeableness of the sea their inconstancy could always be exercised. 73. **intent:** destination. 73–74. **for . . . nothing:** because that's the quality that succeeds in making a "good" voyage come to nothing. 75. **give place:** withdraw. 80. **parts:** attributes such as wealth or rank. 81. **I . . . fortune:** I esteem as carelessly as I do fortune, that fickle goddess. 82. **that miracle . . . gems:** i.e., her beauty. 83. **pranks:** adorns. **attracts:** that attracts. 85. **Sooth:** in truth. 89. **be answered:** accept your answer. 91. **bide:** withstand. 93. **to hold:** as to contain. **retention:** constancy, the power of retaining. 95. **motion:** impulse. **liver . . . palate:** (Real love is a passion of the liver, whereas fancy, light love, is born in the eye and nourished in the palate.) 96. **surfeit:** overindulgence. **cloyment:** satiety. **revolt:** sickness, revulsion. 98. **compare:** comparison.

Between that love a woman can bear me
And that I owe° Olivia.

VIOLA: Ay, but I know —

ORSINO: What dost thou know?

VIOLA:
Too well what love women to men may owe.
In faith, they are as true of heart as we.
My father had a daughter loved a man
As it might be, perhaps, were I a woman,
I should your lordship.

ORSINO: And what's her history?

VIOLA:
A blank, my lord. She never told her love,
But let concealment, like a worm i' the bud,
Feed on her damask° cheek. She pined in thought,
And with a green and yellow° melancholy
She sat like Patience on a monument,°
Smiling at grief. Was not this love indeed?
We men may say more, swear more, but indeed
Our shows° are more than will;° for still° we prove
Much in our vows, but little in our love.

ORSINO:
But died thy sister of her love, my boy?

VIOLA:
I am all the daughters of my father's house,
And all the brothers too — and yet I know not.
Sir, shall I to this lady?

ORSINO: Ay, that's the theme.
To her in haste; give her this jewel. [*He gives a jewel.*] Say
My love can give no place, bide no denay.° *Exeunt* [*separately*].

100. **owe:** have for. 109. **damask:** pink and white like the damask rose. 110. **green and yellow:** pale and sallow. 111. **on a monument:** carved in statuary on a tomb. 114. **shows:** displays of passion. **more than will:** greater than our feelings. **still:** always. 121. **can . . . denay:** cannot yield or endure denial.

ACT 2, SCENE 5°

Enter Sir Toby, Sir Andrew, and Fabian.

SIR TOBY: Come thy ways,° Signior Fabian.

FABIAN: Nay, I'll come. If I lose a scruple° of this sport, let me be boiled° to death with melancholy.

SIR TOBY: Wouldst thou not be glad to have the niggardly rascally sheep-biter° come by some notable shame?

FABIAN: I would exult, man. You know he brought me out o' favor with my lady about a bearbaiting° here.

SIR TOBY: To anger him we'll have the bear again, and we will fool him black and blue.° Shall we not, Sir Andrew?

SIR ANDREW: An° we do not, it is pity of our lives.°

Enter Maria [with a letter].

SIR TOBY: Here comes the little villain.° — How now, my metal° of India!

MARIA: Get ye all three into the boxtree.° Malvolio's coming down this walk. He has been yonder i' the sun practicing behavior to his own shadow this half hour. Observe him, for the love of mockery, for I know this letter will make a contemplative° idiot of him. Close,° in the name of jesting! [*The others hide.*] Lie thou there [*throwing down a letter*]; for here comes the trout that must be caught with tickling.° *Exit.*

Enter Malvolio.

MALVOLIO: 'Tis but fortune; all is fortune. Maria once told me she° did affect° me; and I have heard herself come thus near, that, should she fancy,° it should be one of my complexion. Besides, she uses me with a more exalted respect than anyone else that follows° her. What should I think on 't?

SIR TOBY: Here's an overweening rogue!

FABIAN: O, peace! Contemplation makes a rare° turkey-cock of him. How he jets° under his advanced° plumes!

ACT 2, SCENE 5. **Location:** Olivia's garden. 1. **Come thy ways:** come along. 2. **a scruple:** the least bit. **boiled:** (with a pun on "biled"; black bile was the "humor" of melancholy and was thought to be a cold humor). 5. **sheep-biter:** a dog that bites sheep, i.e., a sneak and a censorious fellow. 7. **bearbaiting:** (A special target of Puritan disapproval.) 8–9. **fool . . . blue:** mock him until he is figuratively black and blue. 10. **An:** if. **pity of our lives:** a pity we should live. 11. **villain:** (Here, a term of endearment.) **metal:** gold, i.e., priceless one. 12. **boxtree:** an evergreen shrub. 15. **contemplative:** i.e., from his musings. **Close:** i.e., keep close, stay hidden. 17. **tickling:** (1) stroking gently about the gills — an actual method of fishing (2) flattery. 18. **she:** Olivia. 19. **affect:** have fondness for. 20. **fancy:** fall in love. 21. **follows:** serves. 24. **rare:** excellent. 25. **jets:** struts. **advanced:** raised.

SIR ANDREW: 'Slight,° I could so beat the rogue!

SIR TOBY: Peace, I say.

MALVOLIO: To be Count Malvolio!

SIR TOBY: Ah, rogue!

SIR ANDREW: Pistol him, pistol him.

SIR TOBY: Peace, peace!

MALVOLIO: There is example° for 't. The lady of the Strachy° married the yeoman of the wardrobe.

SIR ANDREW: Fie on him, Jezebel!°

FABIAN: O, peace! Now he's deeply in. Look how imagination blows° him.

MALVOLIO: Having been three months married to her, sitting in my state° —

SIR TOBY: O, for a stone-bow,° to hit him in the eye!

MALVOLIO: Calling my officers about me, in my branched° velvet gown; having come from a daybed,° where I have left Olivia sleeping —

SIR TOBY: Fire and brimstone!

FABIAN: O, peace, peace!

MALVOLIO: And then to have the humour of state;° and after a demure travel of regard,° telling° them I know my place as I would they should do theirs, to ask for my kinsman Toby.°

SIR TOBY: Bolts and shackles!

FABIAN: O peace, peace, peace! Now, now.

MALVOLIO: Seven of my people, with an obedient start, make out for him. I frown the while; and perchance wind up my watch, or play with my° — some rich jewel. Toby approaches; curtsies° there to me —

SIR TOBY: Shall this fellow live?

FABIAN: Though our silence be drawn from us with cars,° yet peace.

MALVOLIO: I extend my hand to him thus, quenching my familiar° smile with an austere regard of control° —

SIR TOBY: And does not Toby take° you a blow o' the lips then?

MALVOLIO: Saying, "Cousin Toby, my fortunes having cast me on your niece give me this prerogative of speech —"

26. **'Slight:** by His (God's) light. 32. **example:** precedent. **lady of the Strachy:** (Apparently a lady who had married below her station; no certain identification.) 34. **Jezebel:** the proud queen of Ahab, King of Israel. 35. **blows:** puffs up. 37. **state:** chair of state. 38. **stone-bow:** crossbow that shoots stones. 39. **branched:** adorned with a figured pattern suggesting branched leaves or flowers. 40. **daybed:** sofa, couch. 43. **have . . . state:** adopt the imperious manner of authority. 43–44. **demure . . . regard:** grave survey of the company. 44. **telling:** indicating to. 45. **Toby:** (Malvolio omits the title *Sir.*) 49. **play with my:** (Malvolio perhaps means his steward's chain but checks himself in time; as "Count Malvolio," he would not be wearing it. A bawdy meaning of playing with himself is also suggested.) 50. **curtsies:** bows. 52. **with cars:** with chariots, i.e., by force. 53. **familiar:** friendly. 54. **regard of control:** look of authority. 55. **take:** deliver.

SIR TOBY: What, what?

MALVOLIO: "You must amend your drunkenness."

SIR TOBY: Out, scab!°

FABIAN: Nay, patience, or we break the sinews of° our plot.

MALVOLIO: "Besides, you waste the treasure of your time with a foolish knight —"

SIR ANDREW: That's me, I warrant you.

MALVOLIO: "One Sir Andrew."

SIR ANDREW: I knew 'twas I, for many do call me fool.

MALVOLIO: What employment° have we here? [*Taking up the letter.*]

FABIAN: Now is the woodcock° near the gin.°

SIR TOBY: O, peace, and the spirit of humors° intimate reading aloud to him!

MALVOLIO: By my life, this is my lady's hand. These be her very c's, her u's, and her t's;° and thus makes she her great° P's. It is in contempt of° question her hand.

SIR ANDREW: Her c's, her u's, and her t's. Why that?

MALVOLIO: [*reads*] "To the unknown beloved, this, and my good wishes." — her very phrases! By your leave, wax.° Soft!° and the impressure° her Lucrece,° with which she uses° to seal. 'Tis my lady. To whom should this be? [*He opens the letter.*]

FABIAN: This wins him, liver° and all.

MALVOLIO: [*reads*]

"Jove knows I love,
But who?
Lips, do not move;
No man must know."

"No man must know." What follows? The numbers altered!° "No man must know." If this should be thee, Malvolio?

SIR TOBY: Marry, hang thee, brock!°

MALVOLIO: [*reads*]

"I may command where I adore;
But silence, like a Lucrece knife,

60. **scab:** scurvy fellow. 61. **break . . . of:** hamstring, disable. 67. **employment:** business. 68. **woodcock:** (A bird proverbial for its stupidity.) **gin:** snare. 69. **humors:** whim, caprice. 71–72. **c's . . . t's:** i.e., *cut,* slang for the female pudenda. 72. **great:** (1) uppercase (2) copious. (*P* suggests "pee.") **in contempt of:** beyond. 76. **By . . . wax:** (Addressed to the seal on the letter.) **Soft:** softly, not so fast. **impressure:** device imprinted on the seal. 77. **Lucrece:** Lucretia, chaste matron who, ravished by Tarquin, committed suicide. **uses:** is accustomed. 79. **liver:** i.e., the seat of passion. 84. **The numbers altered:** more verses, in a different meter. 86. **brock:** badger. (Used contemptuously.)

With bloodless stroke my heart doth gore;
M.O.A.I. doth sway my life."

FABIAN: A fustian° riddle!

SIR TOBY: Excellent wench, say I.

MALVOLIO: "M.O.A.I. doth sway my life." Nay, but first, let me see, let me see, let me see.

FABIAN: What° dish o' poison has she dressed° him!

SIR TOBY: And with what wing° the staniel° checks at it!°

MALVOLIO: "I may command where I adore." Why, she may command me; I serve her, she is my lady. Why, this is evident to any formal capacity.° There is no obstruction in this. And the end — what should that alphabetical position° portend? If I could make that resemble something in me! Softly! M.O.A.I. —

SIR TOBY: O, ay,° make up° that. He is now at a cold scent.

FABIAN: Sowter° will cry upon 't for all this, though it be as rank as a fox.°

MALVOLIO: M — Malvolio. M! Why, that begins my name.

FABIAN: Did not I say he would work it out? The cur is excellent at faults.°

MALVOLIO: M — But then there is no consonancy in the sequel that suffers under probation:° A should follow, but O does.

FABIAN: And O shall end,° I hope.

SIR TOBY: Ay, or I'll cudgel him, and make him cry "O!"

MALVOLIO: And then I comes behind.

FABIAN: Ay, an you had any eye° behind you, you might see more detraction° at your heels° than fortunes before you.

MALVOLIO: M.O.A.I. This simulation° is not as the former. And yet, to crush this a little, it would bow to me, for every one of these letters are in my name. Soft! Here follows prose.

91. **fustian:** bombastic, ridiculously pompous. 95. **What:** what a. **dressed:** prepared for. 96. **wing:** i.e., speed. **staniel:** kestrel, a sparrow hawk. (The word is used contemptuously because of the uselessness of the staniel for falconry.) **checks at it:** turns to fly at it. 98. **formal capacity:** normal understanding. 100. **position:** arrangement. 102. **O, ay:** (playing on *O.I.* of *M.O.A.I.*). **make up:** work out. 103. **Sowter . . . fox:** i.e., the hound, having lost the *cold scent* of the hare, will "give tongue" in picking up the rank new scent of the fox and will dash away on this false trail. **Sowter:** cobbler. (Here, the name for a hound.) 105. **at faults:** i.e., at maneuvering his way past breaks in the line of scent — in this case, on a false trail. 106–07. **consonancy . . . probation:** pattern in the following letters that stands up under examination. (In fact, the letters "M.O.A.I." represent the first, last, second, and next to last letters of Malvolio's name.) 108. **O shall end:** (1) O ends Malvolio's name (2) a noose shall end his life (3) *omega* ends the Greek alphabet (4) his cry of pain will end the joke. 111. **eye:** (punning on the "I" of "O, ay" and "M.O.A.I.") 111–12. **detraction:** defamation. 112. **at your heels:** pursuing you. 113. **simulation:** disguise, puzzle.

[*He reads.*] "If this fall into thy hand, revolve.° In my stars° I am above thee, but be not afraid of greatness. Some are born great, some achieve greatness, and some have greatness thrust upon 'em. Thy Fates open their hands;° let thy blood and spirit embrace them; and, to inure° thyself to what thou art like° to be, cast° thy humble slough° and appear fresh. Be opposite° with a kinsman, surly with servants. Let thy tongue tang° arguments of state;° put thyself into the trick of singularity.° She thus advises thee that sighs for thee. Remember who commended thy yellow stockings, and wished to see thee ever cross-gartered.° I say, remember. Go to,° thou art made, if thou desir'st to be so. If not, let me see thee a steward still, the fellow of servants, and not worthy to touch Fortune's fingers. Farewell. She that would alter services° with thee,

The Fortunate-Unhappy."

Daylight and champaign° discovers° not more! This is open. I will be proud, I will read politic° authors, I will baffle° Sir Toby, I will wash off gross° acquaintance, I will be point-devise° the very man. I do not now fool myself, to let° imagination jade° me; for every reason excites to this,° that my lady loves me. She did commend my yellow stockings of late, she did praise my leg being cross-gartered; and in this° she manifests herself to my love, and with a kind of injunction drives me to these habits° of her liking. I thank my stars, I am happy.° I will be strange,° stout,° in yellow stockings, and cross-gartered, even with the swiftness of putting on. Jove and my stars be praised! Here is yet a postscript. [*He reads.*] "Thou canst not choose but know who I am. If thou entertain'st° my love, let it appear in thy smiling; thy smiles become thee well. Therefore in my presence still° smile, dear my sweet, I prithee."

Jove, I thank thee: I will smile; I will do everything that thou wilt have me. *Exit.*

[*Sir Toby, Sir Andrew, and Fabian come from hiding.*]

116. **revolve:** consider. **stars:** fortune. 118–19. **open their hands:** offer their bounty. 119. **inure:** accustom. 120. **like:** likely. **cast:** cast off. **slough:** skin of a snake; hence, former demeanor of humbleness. 121. **opposite:** contradictory. **tang:** sound loud with. 122. **state:** politics, statecraft. **trick of singularity:** eccentricity of manner. 124. **cross-gartered:** wearing garters above and below the knee so as to cross behind it. **Go to:** (An expression of remonstrance.) 127. **alter services:** i.e., exchange place of mistress and servant. 129. **champaign:** open country. **discovers:** discloses. 130. **politic:** dealing with state affairs. **baffle:** deride, degrade. (A technical chivalric term used to describe the disgrace of a perjured knight.) 131. **gross:** base. **point-devise:** correct to the letter. 132. **to let:** by letting. **jade:** trick (as an unruly horse does). **excites to this:** prompts this conclusion. 134. **this:** this letter. 135. **these habits:** this attire. 136. **happy:** fortunate. **strange:** aloof. **stout:** haughty. 139. **thou entertain'st:** you accept. 141. **still:** continually.

FABIAN: I will not give my part of this sport for a pension of thousands to be paid from the Sophy.°

SIR TOBY: I could marry this wench for this device.

SIR ANDREW: So could I too.

SIR TOBY: And ask no other dowry with her but such another jest.

Enter Maria.

SIR ANDREW: Nor I neither.

FABIAN: Here comes my noble gull-catcher.°

SIR TOBY: Wilt thou set thy foot o' my neck?

SIR ANDREW: Or o' mine either?

SIR TOBY: Shall I play° my freedom at tray-trip,° and become thy bond-slave?

SIR ANDREW: I' faith, or I either?

SIR TOBY: Why, thou hast put him in such a dream that when the image of it leaves him he must run mad.

MARIA: Nay, but say true, does it work upon him?

SIR TOBY: Like aqua vitae° with a midwife.

MARIA: If you will then see the fruits of the sport, mark his first approach before my lady. He will come to her in yellow stockings, and 'tis a color she abhors, and cross-gartered, a fashion she detests; and he will smile upon her, which will now be so unsuitable to her disposition, being addicted to a melancholy as she is, that it cannot but turn him into a notable contempt.° If you will see it, follow me.

SIR TOBY: To the gates of Tartar,° thou most excellent devil of wit!

SIR ANDREW: I'll make one° too.

Exeunt.

ACT 3, SCENE 1°

Enter Viola, and Clown [Feste, playing his pipe and tabor].

VIOLA: Save° thee, friend, and thy music. Dost thou live by° thy tabor?°

FESTE: No, sir, I live by the church.

VIOLA: Art thou a churchman?

145. Sophy: Shah of Persia. **150. gull-catcher:** tricker of *gulls* or dupes. **153. play:** gamble. **tray-trip:** a game of dice, success in which depended on throwing a three (*tray*). **159. aqua vitae:** brandy or other distilled liquors. **165. notable contempt:** notorious object of contempt. **166. Tartar:** Tartarus, the infernal regions. **167. make one:** i.e., tag along. **ACT 3, SCENE 1. Location:** Olivia's garden. **1. Save:** God save. **live by:** earn your living with. (But Feste uses the phrase to mean "dwell near.") **tabor:** small drum.

FESTE: No such matter, sir. I do live by the church, for I do live at my house, and my house doth stand by the church.

VIOLA: So thou mayst say the king lies by° a beggar, if a beggar dwell near him, or the church stands by thy tabor if thy tabor stand by° the church.

FESTE: You have said,° sir. To see this age! A sentence° is but a cheveril° glove to a good wit. How quickly the wrong side may be turned outward!

VIOLA: Nay, that's certain. They that dally nicely° with words may quickly make them wanton.°

FESTE: I would therefore my sister had had no name, sir.

VIOLA: Why, man?

FESTE: Why, sir, her name's a word, and to dally with that word might make my sister wanton. But indeed, words are very rascals since bonds disgraced them.°

VIOLA: Thy reason, man?

FESTE: Troth, sir, I can yield you none without words, and words are grown so false I am loath to prove reason with them.

VIOLA: I warrant thou art a merry fellow and car'st for nothing.°

FESTE: Not so, sir, I do care for something; but in my conscience, sir, I do not care for you. If that be to care for nothing, sir, I would it would make you invisible.°

VIOLA: Art not thou the Lady Olivia's fool?

FESTE: No indeed, sir. The Lady Olivia has no folly. She will keep no fool, sir, till she be married, and fools are as like husbands as pilchars° are to herrings — the husband's the bigger. I am indeed not her fool but her corrupter of words.

VIOLA: I saw thee late° at the Count Orsino's.

FESTE: Foolery, sir, does walk about the orb° like the sun; it shines everywhere. I would be sorry, sir, but° the fool should be as oft with your master as with my mistress.° I think I saw Your Wisdom° there.

VIOLA: Nay, an thou pass upon me,° I'll no more with thee. Hold, there's expenses for thee. [*She gives a coin.*]

6. **lies by:** (1) lies sexually with (2) dwells near. 7: **stands by . . . stand by:** (1) is maintained by (2) is placed near. 8. **You have said:** you've expressed your opinion. **sentence:** maxim, judgment, opinion. **cheveril:** kidskin. 10. **dally nicely:** (1) play subtly (2) toy amorously. 11. **wanton:** (1) equivocal (2) licentious, unchaste. (Feste then "dallies" with the word in its sexual sense; see line 15.) 15–16. **since . . . them:** i.e., since bonds have been needed to make sworn statements good. 20. **car'st for nothing:** are without any worries. (But Feste puns on *care for* in line 21 in the sense of "like.") 23. **invisible:** i.e., nothing; absent. 26. **pilchers:** pilchards, fish resembling herring. 29. **late:** recently. 30. **orb:** earth. 31–32. **I would . . . mistress:** (1) I should be sorry not to visit Orsino's house often (2) it would be a shame if folly were no less common there than in Olivia's household. 31. **but:** unless. 32. **Your Wisdom:** i.e., you. (A title of mock courtesy.) 33. **an . . . me:** if you fence (verbally) with me, pass judgment on me.

FESTE: Now Jove, in his next commodity° of hair, send thee a beard!

VIOLA: By my troth, I'll tell thee, I am almost sick for one° — [*aside*] though I would not have it grow on my chin. — Is thy lady within?

FESTE: Would not a pair of these have bred, sir? [*He holds up the coin.*]

VIOLA: Yes, being kept together and put to use.°

FESTE: I would play Lord Pandarus° of Phrygia, sir, to bring a Cressida to this Troilus.

VIOLA: I understand you, sir. 'Tis well begged. [*She gives another coin.*]

FESTE: The matter, I hope, is not great, sir, begging but a beggar; Cressida was a beggar.° My lady is within, sir. I will conster° to them whence you come. Who you are and what you would are out of my welkin° — I might say "element,"° but the word is overworn. *Exit.*

VIOLA:
This fellow is wise enough to play the fool,
And to do that well craves a kind of wit.
He must observe their mood on whom he jests,
The quality° of persons, and the time,
And, like the haggard,° check at every feather
That comes before his eye.° This is a practice°
As full of labor as a wise man's art;
For folly that he wisely shows is fit,°
But wise men, folly-fall'n,° quite taint their wit.°

Enter Sir Toby and [*Sir*] *Andrew.*

SIR TOBY: Save you, gentleman.

VIOLA: And you, sir.

SIR ANDREW: *Dieu vous garde, monsieur.*°

VIOLA: *Et vous aussi; votre serviteur.*°

SIR ANDREW: I hope, sir, you are, and I am yours.

35. **commodity:** supply. 36. **sick for one.** (1) eager to have a beard (2) in love with a bearded man. 39. **put to use:** put out at interest. 40. **Pandarus:** the go-between in the love story of Troilus and Cressida; uncle to Cressida. 43–44. **begging . . . beggar:** (A reference to Henryson's *Testament of Cresseid* in which Cressida became a leper and a beggar. Feste desires another coin to be the mate of the one he has, as Cressida, the beggar, was mate to Troilus.) 44. **conster:** construe, explain. 45. **welkin:** sky. 46. **"element":** (The word can be synonymous with *welkin,* but the common phrase *out of my element* means "beyond my scope.") 50. **quality:** character, rank. 51. **haggard:** untrained adult hawk, hence unmanageable. 51–52. **check . . . eye:** strike at every bird it sees, i.e., dart adroitly from subject to subject. 52. **practice:** exercise of skill. 54. **folly . . . fit:** the folly he displays is a proper skill. 55. **folly-fall'n:** having fallen into folly. **taint their wit:** infect and impugn their own intelligence. 58. ***Dieu . . . monsieur:*** God keep you, sir. 59. ***Et . . . serviteur:*** and you, too; (I am) your servant. (Sir Andrew is not quite up to a reply in French.)

SIR TOBY: Will you encounter° the house? My niece is desirous you should enter, if your trade° be to her.

VIOLA: I am bound° to your niece, sir; I mean, she is the list° of my voyage.

SIR TOBY: Taste° your legs, sir. Put them to motion.

VIOLA: My legs do better understand° me, sir, than I understand what you mean by bidding me taste my legs.

SIR TOBY: I mean, to go, sir, to enter.

VIOLA: I will answer you with gait and entrance.° — But we are prevented.°

Enter Olivia and gentlewoman [*Maria*].

Most excellent accomplished lady, the heavens rain odors on you!

SIR ANDREW: That youth's a rare courtier. "Rain odors" — well.

VIOLA: My matter hath no voice,° lady, but to your own most pregnant° and vouchsafed° ear.

SIR ANDREW: "Odors," "pregnant," and "vouchsafed." I'll get 'em all three all ready.°

OLIVIA: Let the garden door be shut, and leave me to my hearing. [*Exeunt Sir Toby, Sir Andrew, and Maria.*] Give me your hand, sir.

VIOLA:

My duty, madam, and most humble service.

OLIVIA: What is your name?

VIOLA:

Cesario is your servant's name, fair princess.

OLIVIA:

My servant, sir? 'Twas never merry world
Since lowly feigning was called compliment.°
You're servant to the Count Orsino, youth.

VIOLA:

And he is yours,° and his° must needs be yours,
Your servant's servant is your servant, madam.

61. **encounter:** (High-sounding word to express "approach.") 62. **trade:** business (suggesting also a commercial venture). 63. **I am bound:** (1) I am on a journey. (Continuing Sir Toby's metaphor in *trade.*) (2) I am obliged. **list:** limit, destination. 64. **Taste:** try. 65. **understand:** stand under, support. 68. **gait and entrance:** going and entering (with a pun on *gate:* [1] stride [2] entryway). **prevented:** anticipated. 71. **hath no voice:** cannot be uttered. **pregnant:** receptive. 72. **vouchsafed:** proffered, i.e., attentive. 74. **all ready:** committed to memory for future use. 80–81. **'Twas . . . compliment:** things have never been the same since affected humility (like calling oneself another's servant) began to be mistaken for courtesy. 83. **yours:** your servant. **his:** those belonging to him.

OLIVIA:
For° him, I think not on him. For his thoughts,
Would they were blanks,° rather than filled with me!

VIOLA:
Madam, I come to whet your gentle thoughts
On his behalf.

OLIVIA: O, by your leave,° I pray you.
I bade you never speak again of him.
But, would you undertake another suit,
I had rather hear you to solicit that
Than music from the spheres.°

VIOLA: Dear lady —

OLIVIA:
Give me leave, beseech you. I did send,
After the last enchantment you did here,
A ring in chase of you; so did I abuse°
Myself, my servant, and, I fear me, you.
Under your hard construction° must I sit,
To force° that on you in a shameful cunning
Which you knew none of yours. What might you think?
Have you not set mine honor at the stake°
And baited° it with all th' unmuzzled thoughts
That tyrannous heart can think? To one of your receiving°
Enough is shown; a cypress,° not a bosom,
Hides my heart. So, let me hear you speak.

VIOLA:
I pity you.

OLIVIA: That's a degree to love.

VIOLA:
No, not a grece;° for 'tis a vulgar proof°
That very oft we pity enemies.

85. **For:** as for. 86. **blanks:** blank coins ready to be stamped or empty sheets of paper. 88. **by your leave:** i.e., allow me to interrupt. 92. **music from the spheres:** (The heavenly bodies were thought to be fixed in hollow concentric spheres that revolved one about the other, producing a harmony too exquisite to be heard by human ears.) 95. **abuse:** wrong, mislead. 97. **hard construction:** harsh interpretation. 98. **To force:** for forcing. 100. **at the stake:** (The figure is from bearbaiting.) 101. **baited:** harassed. (Literally, set the dogs on to bite the bear.) 102. **receiving:** capacity, intelligence. 103. **cypress:** a thin, gauzelike, black material. 106. **grece:** step. (Synonymous with *degree* in the preceding line.) **vulgar proof:** common experience.

OLIVIA:
Why then, methinks 'tis time to smile° again.
O world, how apt the poor are to be proud!°
If one should be a prey, how much the better
To fall before the lion than the wolf!° *(Clock strikes.)*
The clock upbraids me with the waste of time.
Be not afraid, good youth, I will not have you;
And yet, when wit and youth is come to harvest
Your wife is like° to reap a proper° man.
There lies your way, due west.

VIOLA: Then westward ho!°
Grace and good disposition attend your ladyship.°
You'll nothing, madam, to my lord by me?

OLIVIA: Stay. I prithee, tell me what thou think'st of me.

VIOLA:
That you do think you are not what you are.°

OLIVIA:
If I think so, I think the same of you.°

VIOLA:
Then think you right. I am not what I am.

OLIVIA:
I would you were as I would have you be!

VIOLA:
Would it be better, madam, than I am?
I wish it might, for now I am your fool.°

OLIVIA: [*aside*]
O, what a deal of scorn looks beautiful
In the contempt and anger of his lip!
A murderous guilt shows not itself more soon
Than love that would seem hid; love's night is noon.° —
Cesario, by the roses of the spring,
By maidhood, honor, truth, and everything,

108. **smile:** i.e., cast off love's melancholy. 109. **how . . . proud:** how ready the unfortunate and rejected (like myself) are to find something to be proud of in their distress. 111. **To fall . . . wolf:** i.e., to fall before a noble adversary. 115. **like:** likely. **proper:** handsome, worthy. 116. **westward ho:** (The cry of Thames watermen to attract westward-bound passengers from London to Westminster.) 117. **Grace . . . ladyship:** may you enjoy God's blessing and a happy frame of mind. 120. **That . . . are:** i.e., that you think you are in love with a man, and you are mistaken. 121. **If . . . you:** (Olivia may interpret Viola's cryptic statement as suggesting that Olivia "does not know herself," i.e., is distracted with passion; she may also hint at her suspicion that "Cesario" is higher born than he admits.) 125. **fool:** butt. 129. **love's . . . noon:** i.e., love, despite its attempt to be secret, reveals itself as plain as day.

I love thee so that, maugre° all thy pride,
Nor° wit nor reason can my passion hide.
Do not extort thy reasons from this clause,
For that I woo, thou therefore hast no cause.°
But rather reason thus with reason fetter:°
Love sought is good, but given unsought is better.

VIOLA:
By innocence I swear, and by my youth,
I have one heart, one bosom, and one truth,
And that no woman has, nor never none
Shall mistress be of it save I alone.
And so adieu, good madam. Nevermore
Will I my master's tears to you deplore.°

OLIVIA:
Yet come again, for thou perhaps mayst move
That heart, which now abhors, to like his love. *Exeunt* [*separately*].

ACT 3, SCENE 2°

Enter Sir Toby, Sir Andrew, and Fabian.

SIR ANDREW: No, faith, I'll not stay a jot longer.

SIR TOBY: Thy reason, dear venom,° give thy reason.

FABIAN: You must needs yield your reason, Sir Andrew.

SIR ANDREW: Marry, I saw your niece do more favors to the Count's servingman than ever she bestowed upon me. I saw 't i' the orchard.°

SIR TOBY: Did she see thee the while, old boy? Tell me that.

SIR ANDREW: As plain as I see you now.

FABIAN: This was a great argument° of love in her toward you.

SIR ANDREW: 'Slight,° will you make an ass o' me?

FABIAN: I will prove it° legitimate, sir, upon the oaths° of judgment and reason.

SIR TOBY: And they have been grand-jurymen since before Noah was a sailor.

132. **maugre:** in spite of. 133. **Nor:** neither. 134–35. **Do . . . cause:** do not rationalize your indifference along these lines, that because I am the wooer you have no cause to reciprocate. 136. **But . . . fetter:** but instead control your reasoning with the following reason. 143. **deplore:** beweep **ACT 3, SCENE 2. Location:** Olivia's house. 2. **venom:** i.e., person filled with venom. (Sir Andrew professes to be angry.) 5. **orchard:** garden. 8. **argument:** proof. 9. **'Slight:** by his (God's) light. 10. **it:** my contention. **oaths:** i.e., testimony under oath.

FABIAN: She did show favour to the youth in your sight only to exasperate you, to awake your dormouse° valour, to put fire in your heart and brimstone in your liver. You should then have accosted her, and with some excellent jests, fire-new from the mint, you should have banged° the youth into dumbness. This was looked for at your hand, and this was balked.° The double gilt° of this opportunity you let time wash off, and you are now sailed into the north° of my lady's opinion, where you will hang like an icicle on a Dutchman's beard° unless you do redeem it by some laudable attempt either of valor or policy.°

SIR ANDREW: An 't be any way, it must be with valor, for policy I hate. I had as lief be a Brownist° as a politician.°

SIR TOBY: Why, then, build me° thy fortunes upon the basis of valor. Challenge me the Count's youth to fight with him; hurt him in eleven places. My niece shall take note of it; and assure thyself, there is no love-broker° in the world can more prevail in man's commendation with woman than report of valor.

FABIAN: There is no way but this, Sir Andrew.

SIR ANDREW: Will either of you bear me a challenge to him?

SIR TOBY: Go, write it in a martial hand. Be curst° and brief; it is no matter how witty, so it be eloquent and full of invention. Taunt him with the license of ink.° If thou "thou"-est° him some thrice, it shall not be amiss; and as many lies° as will lie in thy sheet of paper, although the sheet were big enough for the bed of Ware° in England, set 'em down. Go, about it. Let there be gall° enough in thy ink, though thou write with a goose pen,° no matter. About it.

SIR ANDREW: Where shall I find you?

SIR TOBY: We'll call thee° at the cubiculo.° Go. *Exit Sir Andrew.*

FABIAN: This is a dear manikin° to you, Sir Toby.

SIR TOBY: I have been dear° to him, lad, some two thousand strong or so.

15. **dormouse:** i.e., sleepy and timid. 17. **banged:** struck. 19. **balked:** missed, neglected. **double gilt:** thick layer of gold, i.e., rare worth. 20. **north:** i.e., out of the warmth and sunshine of her favor. 21. **icicle . . . beard:** (Alludes to the arctic voyage of William Barentz in 1596–97.) 22. **policy:** stratagem. 24. **Brownist:** (An early name of the Congregationalists, from the name of the founder, Robert Browne.) **politician:** intriguer. (Sir Andrew misinterprets Sir Toby's more neutral use of *policy,* "clever stratagem.") 25. **build me:** i.e., build. 27. **love-broker:** agent between lovers. 32. **curst:** fierce. 33–34. **with . . . ink:** i.e., with the freedom that may be risked in writing but not in conversation. 34. **"thou"-est:** ("Thou" was used only between friends or to inferiors.) 35. **lies:** charges of lying. 36. **bed of Ware:** A famous bedstead capable of holding twelve persons, about eleven feet square, said to have been at the Stag Inn in Ware, Hertfordshire. 37. **gall:** (1) bitterness, rancor (2) a growth found on certain oaks, used as an ingredient of ink. 37–38. **goose pen:** (1) goose quill (2) foolish style. 40. **call thee:** call for you. **cubiculo:** little chamber. 41. **manikin:** puppet. 42. **dear:** expensive (playing on *dear,* "a source of pleasure," in the previous speech).

FABIAN: We shall have a rare letter from him; but you'll not deliver 't?

SIR TOBY: Never trust me, then; and by all means stir on the youth to an answer. I think oxen and wainropes° cannot hale° them together. For° Andrew, if he were opened and you find so much blood in his liver° as will clog the foot of a flea, I'll eat the rest of th' anatomy.°

FABIAN: And his opposite,° the youth, bears in his visage no great presage of cruelty.

Enter Maria.

SIR TOBY: Look where the youngest wren of nine° comes.

MARIA: If you desire the spleen,° and will laugh yourself into stitches, follow me. Yond gull Malvolio is turned heathen, a very renegado;° for there is no Christian that means to be saved by believing rightly can ever believe such impossible passages of grossness.° He's in yellow stockings.

SIR TOBY: And cross-gartered?

MARIA: Most villanously,° like a pedant° that keeps a school i' the church. I have dogged him like his murderer. He does obey every point of the letter that I dropped to betray him. He does smile his face into more lines than is in the new map° with the augmentation of the Indies. You have not seen such a thing as 'tis. I can hardly forbear hurling things at him. I know my lady will strike him. If she do, he'll smile and take 't for a great favor.

SIR TOBY: Come, bring us, bring us where he is. *Exeunt omnes.*

Act 3, Scene 3°

Enter Sebastian and Antonio.

SEBASTIAN:

I would not by my will have troubled you;
But since you make your pleasure of your pains,
I will no further chide you.

45. **wainropes:** wagon ropes. **hale:** haul. **For:** as for. 46. **liver:** (A pale and bloodless liver was a sign of cowardice.) 47. **anatomy:** cadaver. 48. **opposite:** adversary. 50. **youngest . . . nine:** the last hatched and smallest of a nest of wrens. 51. **the spleen:** a laughing fit. (The spleen was thought to be the seat of immoderate laughter.) 52. **renegado:** renegade, deserter of his religion. 54. **impossible passages of grossness:** gross impossibilities (i.e., in the letter). 56. **villainously:** i.e., abominably. **pedant:** schoolmaster. 59. **new map:** (Probably a reference to a map made by Emmeric Mollineux in 1599 for the purchasers of Hakluyt's *Voyages,* showing more of the East Indies, including Japan, than had ever been mapped before.) **Act 3, Scene 3. Location:** A street.

ANTONIO:
I could not stay behind you. My desire,
More sharp than filèd steel, did spur me forth,
And not all° love to see you — though so much°
As might have drawn one to a longer voyage —
But jealousy° what might befall your travel,
Being skilless in° these parts, which to a stranger,
Unguided and unfriended, often prove
Rough and unhospitable. My willing love,
The rather° by these arguments of fear,
Set forth in your pursuit.

SEBASTIAN: My kind Antonio,
I can no other answer make but thanks,
And thanks; and ever oft good turns°
Are shuffled off° with such uncurrent° pay.
But were my worth° as is my conscience,° firm,
You should find better dealing.° What's to do?
Shall we go see the relics° of this town?

ANTONIO:
Tomorrow, sir. Best first go see your lodging.

SEBASTIAN:
I am not weary, and 'tis long to night.
I pray you, let us satisfy our eyes
With the memorials and the things of fame
That do renown° this city.

ANTONIO: Would you'd pardon me.
I do not without danger walk these streets.
Once in a sea-fight 'gainst the Count his° galleys
I did some service, of such note indeed
That were I ta'en here it would scarce be answered.°

SEBASTIAN:
Belike° you slew great number of his people?

ANTONIO:
Th' offence is not of such a bloody nature,
Albeit the quality of the time and quarrel

6. **all:** only, merely. **so much:** i.e., that was great enough. 8. **jealousy:** anxiety. 9. **skilless in:** unacquainted with. 12. **The rather:** made all the more willing. 15. **And . . . turns:** (This probably corrupt line is usually made to read, "And thanks and ever thanks; and oft good turns.") 16. **shuffled off:** turned aside. **uncurrent:** worthless (such as mere thanks). 17. **worth:** wealth. **conscience:** i.e., moral inclination to assist. 18. **dealing:** treatment, payment. 19. **relics:** antiquities. 24. **renown:** make famous. 26. **Count his:** Count's, i.e., Duke's. 28. **it . . . answered:** I'd be hard put to offer a defense. 29. **Belike:** perhaps.

Might well have given us bloody argument.°
It might have since been answered° in repaying
What we took from them, which for traffic's° sake
Most of our city did. Only myself stood out,
For which, if I be lapsèd° in this place,
I shall pay dear.

SEBASTIAN:
Do not then walk too open.

ANTONIO:
It doth not fit me. Hold, sir, here's my purse. [*He gives his purse.*]
In the south suburbs, at the Elephant,°
Is best to lodge. I will bespeak our diet,°
Whiles you beguile the time and feed your knowledge
With viewing of the town. There shall you have me.

SEBASTIAN: Why I your purse?

ANTONIO:
Haply° your eye shall light upon some toy°
You have desire to purchase; and your store°
I think is not for idle markets,° sir.

SEBASTIAN:
I'll be your purse-bearer and leave you
For an hour.

ANTONIO: To th' Elephant.

SEBASTIAN: I do remember. *Exeunt* [*separately*].

Act 3, Scene 4°

Enter Olivia and Maria.

OLIVIA: [*aside*]
I have sent after him; he says he'll come.°
How shall I feast him? What bestow of° him?
For youth is bought more oft than begged or borrowed.
I speak too loud. —
Where's Malvolio? He is sad and civil,°

32. **bloody argument:** cause for bloodshed. 33. **answered:** compensated. 34. **traffic's:** trade's. 36. **lapsèd:** caught off guard, surprised. 39. **Elephant:** the name of an inn. 40. **bespeak our diet:** order our food. 44. **Haply:** perhaps. **toy:** trifle. 45. **store:** store of money. 46. **idle markets:** unnecessary purchases, luxuries **Act 3, Scene 4. Location:** Olivia's garden. 1. **he . . . come:** i.e., suppose he says he'll come. 2. **of:** on. 5. **sad and civil:** sober and decorous.

And suits well for a servant with my fortunes.
Where is Malvolio?

MARIA: He's coming, madam, but in very strange manner. He is, sure, possessed,° madam.

OLIVIA: Why, what's the matter? Does he rave?

MARIA: No. madam, he does nothing but smile. Your ladyship were best to have some guard about you if he come, for sure the man is tainted in 's° wits.

OLIVIA:
Go call him hither. [*Maria summons Malvolio.*] I am as mad as he,
If sad and merry madness equal be.

Enter Malvolio, [*cross-gartered and in yellow stockings*].

How now, Malvolio!

MALVOLIO: Sweet lady, ho, ho!

OLIVIA: Smil'st thou? I sent for thee upon a sad° occasion.

MALVOLIO: Sad, lady? I could be sad.° This does make some obstruction in the blood, this cross-gartering, but what of that? If it please the eye of one, it is with me as the very true sonnet° is, "Please one, and please all."°

OLIVIA: Why, how dost thou, man? What is the matter with thee?

MALVOLIO: Not black° in my mind, though yellow in my legs. It° did come to his° hands, and commands shall be executed. I think we do know the sweet roman hand.°

OLIVIA: Wilt thou go to bed,° Malvolio?

MALVOLIO: To bed! "Ay, sweetheart, and I'll come to thee."°

OLIVIA: God comfort thee! Why dost thou smile so and kiss thy hand so oft?

MARIA: How do you, Malvolio?

MALVOLIO: At your request? Yes, nightingales answer daws.°

MARIA: Why appear you with this ridiculous boldness before my lady?

MALVOLIO: "Be not afraid of greatness." 'Twas well writ.

OLIVIA: What mean'st thou by that, Malvolio?

MALVOLIO: "Some are born great —"

OLIVIA: Ha?

9. **possessed:** i.e., possessed with an evil spirit. 12–13. **in 's:** in his. 18. **sad:** serious. 19. **sad:** (1) serious (2) melancholy. 21. **sonnet:** song, ballad. **"Please . . . all":** to please one special person is as good as to please everybody. (The refrain of a ballad.) 23. **black:** i.e., melancholic. **It:** i.e., the letter. 24. **his:** Malvolio's. 25. **roman hand:** fashionable italic style of handwriting. 26. **go to bed:** i.e., try to sleep off your mental distress. 27. **"Ay . . . thee":** (Malvolio quotes from a popular song of the day.) 31. **nightingales answer daws:** i.e., (to Maria), do you suppose a fine fellow like me would answer a lowly creature (a *daw,* a "crow") like you.

MALVOLIO: "Some achieve greatness —"
OLIVIA: What sayest thou?
MALVOLIO: "And some have greatness thrust upon them."
OLIVIA: Heaven restore thee!
MALVOLIO: "Remember who commended thy yellow stockings —"
OLIVIA: Thy yellow stockings?
MALVOLIO: "And wished to see thee cross-gartered."
OLIVIA: Cross-gartered?
MALVOLIO: "Go to, thou art made, if thou desir'st to be so —"
OLIVIA: Am I made?
MALVOLIO: "If not, let me see thee a servant still."
OLIVIA: Why, this is very midsummer madness.°

Enter Servant.

SERVANT: Madam, the young gentleman of the Count Orsino's is returned. I could hardly entreat him back. He attends your ladyship's pleasure.

OLIVIA: I'll come to him. [*Exit Servant.*] Good Maria, let this fellow be looked to. Where's my cousin Toby? Let some of my people have a special care of him. I would not have him miscarry° for the half of my dowry.

Exeunt [*Olivia and Maria, different ways*].

MALVOLIO: Oho, do you come near° me now? No worse man than Sir Toby to look to me! This concurs directly with the letter. She sends him on purpose that I may appear stubborn to him, for she incites me to that in the letter. "Cast thy humble slough," says she; "be opposite with a kinsman, surly with servants; let thy tongue tang with arguments of state; put thyself into the trick of singularity." And consequently° sets down the manner how: as, a sad° face, a reverend carriage, a slow tongue, in the habit of some sir of note,° and so forth. I have limed° her, but it is Jove's doing, and Jove make me thankful! And when she went away now, "Let this fellow be looked to." "Fellow!"° Not "Malvolio," nor after my degree,° but "fellow." Why, everything adheres together, that no dram° of a scruple,° no scruple of a scruple, no obstacle, no incredulous° or unsafe° circumstance — what can be said? — nothing that can be can come

48. **midsummer madness:** (A proverbial phrase; the midsummer moon was supposed to cause madness.) 54. **miscarry:** come to harm. 55. **come near:** understand, appreciate. 60. **consequently:** thereafter. 61. **sad:** serious. 62. **habit . . . note:** attire suited to a man of distinction. **limed:** caught like a bird with bird-lime (a sticky substance spread on branches). 64. **"Fellow":** (Malvolio takes the original meaning, "companion.") **after my degree:** according to my position. 65. **dram:** (Literally, one-eighth of a fluid ounce.) 66. **scruple:** (Literally, one-third of a dram.) **incredulous:** incredible. **unsafe:** uncertain, unreliable.

between me and the full prospect of my hopes. Well, Jove, not I, is the doer of this, and he is to be thanked.

Enter [Sir] Toby, Fabian, and Maria.

SIR TOBY: Which way is he, in the name of sanctity? If all the devils of hell be drawn in little,° and Legion° himself possessed him, yet I'll speak to him.

FABIAN: Here he is, here he is. — How is 't with you, sir? How is 't with you, man?

MALVOLIO: Go off. I discard you. Let me enjoy my private.° Go off.

MARIA: Lo, how hollow the fiend speaks within him! Did not I tell you? Sir Toby, my lady prays you to have a care of him.

MALVOLIO: Aha, does she so?

SIR TOBY: Go to, go to! Peace, peace, we must deal gently with him. Let me alone.° — How do you, Malvolio? How is 't with you? What, man, defy° the devil! Consider, he's an enemy to mankind.

MALVOLIO: Do you know what you say?

MARIA: La you,° an you speak ill of the devil, how he takes it at heart! Pray God he be not bewitched!

FABIAN: Carry his water° to the wisewoman.

MARIA: Marry, and it shall be done tomorrow morning, if I live. My lady would not lose him for more than I'll say.

MALVOLIO: How now, mistress?

MARIA: O Lord!

SIR TOBY: Prithee, hold thy peace; this is not the way. Do you not see you move° him? Let me alone with him.

FABIAN: No way but gentleness, gently, gently. The fiend is rough, and will not be roughly used.

SIR TOBY: Why, how now, my bawcock!° How dost thou, chuck?°

MALVOLIO: Sir!

SIR TOBY: Ay, biddy,° come with me. What, man, 'tis not for gravity° to play at cherry-pit° with Satan. Hang him, foul collier!°

MARIA: Get him to say his prayers, good Sir Toby, get him to pray.

71. **drawn in little:** (1) portrayed in miniature (2) gathered into a small space, i.e., in Malvolio's heart. **Legion:** an unclean spirit. ("My name is Legion, for we are many," Mark 5.9.) 75. **private:** privacy. 79–80. **Let me alone:** leave him to me. 81. **defy:** renounce. 83. **La you:** look you. 85. **water:** urine (for medical analysis). 91. **move:** upset, excite. 94. **bawcock:** fine fellow. (From the French *beau-coq.*) **chuck:** (A form of "chick," term of endearment.) 96. **biddy:** chicken. **for gravity:** suitable for a man of your dignity. 97. **cherry-pit:** a children's game consisting of throwing cherry stones into a little hole. **collier:** i.e., Satan. (Literally, a coal vendor.)

MALVOLIO: My prayers, minx?

MARIA: No, I warrant you, he will not hear of godliness.

MALVOLIO: Go hang yourselves all! You are idle,° shallow things; I am not of your element.° You shall know more° hereafter. *Exit.*

SIR TOBY: Is 't possible?

FABIAN: If this were played upon a stage, now, I could condemn it as an improbable fiction.

SIR TOBY: His very genius° hath taken the infection of the device, man.

MARIA: Nay, pursue him now, lest the device take air and taint.°

FABIAN: Why, we shall make him mad indeed.

MARIA: The house will be the quieter.

SIR TOBY: Come, we'll have him in a dark room and bound.° My niece is already in the belief that he's mad. We may carry° it thus for our pleasure and his penance till our very pastime, tired out of breath, prompt us to have mercy on him, at which time we will bring the device to the bar° and crown thee for a finder of madmen.° But see, but see!

Enter Sir Andrew [*with a letter*].

FABIAN: More matter for a May morning.°

SIR ANDREW: Here's the challenge. Read it. I warrant there's vinegar and pepper in 't.

FABIAN: Is 't so saucy?°

SIR ANDREW: Ay, is 't, I warrant him. Do but read.

SIR TOBY: Give me. [*He reads.*] "Youth, whatsoever thou art, thou art but a scurvy fellow."

FABIAN: Good, and valiant.

SIR TOBY: [*reads*] "Wonder not, nor admire° not in thy mind, why I do call thee so, for I will show thee no reason for 't."

FABIAN: A good note,° that keeps you from the blow of the law.

SIR TOBY: [*reads*] "Thou com'st to the Lady Olivia, and in my sight she uses thee kindly. But thou liest in thy throat; that is not the matter I challenge thee for."

FABIAN: Very brief, and to exceeding good sense — less.

SIR TOBY: [*reads*] "I will waylay thee going home, where if it be thy chance to kill me —"

101. **idle:** foolish. 102. **element:** sphere of existence. **know more:** i.e., hear about this. 106. **genius:** i.e., soul, spirit. 107. **take . . . taint:** become exposed to air (i.e., become known) and thus spoil. 110. **in . . . bound:** (The standard treatment for insanity at this time.) 111. **carry:** manage. 113. **bar:** i.e., bar of judgment. 114. **finder of madmen:** member of a jury charged with "finding" if the accused is insane. 115. **matter . . . morning:** sport for May-day plays or games. 118. **saucy:** (1) spicy (2) insolent. 123. **admire:** marvel. 125. **note:** observation, remark.

FABIAN: Good.

SIR TOBY: [*reads*] "Thou kill'st me like a rogue and a villain."

FABIAN: Still you keep o' the windy° side of the law. Good.

SIR TOBY: [*reads*] "Fare thee well, and God have mercy upon one of our souls! He may have mercy upon mine, but my hope is better,° and so look to thyself. Thy friend, as thou usest him, and thy sworn enemy,

Andrew Aguecheek."

If this letter move° him not, his legs cannot. I'll give 't him.

MARIA: You may have very fit occasion for 't. He is now in some commerce° with my lady, and will by and by depart.

SIR TOBY: Go, Sir Andrew. Scout me° for him at the corner of the orchard like a bum-baily.° So soon as ever thou seest him, draw, and as thou draw'st swear horrible;° for it comes to pass oft that a terrible oath, with a swaggering accent sharply twanged off, gives manhood more approbation° than ever proof° itself would have earned him. Away!

SIR ANDREW: Nay, let me alone for swearing.° *Exit.*

SIR TOBY: Now will not I deliver his letter, for the behavior of the young gentleman gives him out to be of good capacity and breeding; his employment between his lord and my niece confirms no less. Therefore this letter, being so excellently ignorant, will breed no terror in the youth. He will find it comes from a clodpoll.° But, sir, I will deliver his challenge by word of mouth, set upon Aguecheek a notable report of valor, and drive the gentleman — as I know his youth will aptly receive it° — into a most hideous opinion of his rage, skill, fury, and impetuosity. This will so fright them both that they will kill one another by the look, like cockatrices.°

Enter Olivia and Viola.

FABIAN: Here he comes with your niece. Give them way° till he take leave, and presently° after him.

SIR TOBY: I will meditate the while upon some horrid° message for a challenge. [*Exeunt Sir Toby, Fabian, and Maria.*]

134. **windy:** windward, i.e., safe, where one is less likely to be driven onto legal rocks and shoals. 136. **my hope is better:** (Sir Andrew's comically inept way of saying he hopes to be the survivor; instead, he seems to say, "May I be damned."). 139. **move:** (1) stir up (2) set in motion. 141. **commerce:** transaction. 142. **Scout me:** keep watch. 143. **bum-baily:** minor sheriff's officer employed in making arrests. 144. **horrible:** horribly. 146. **approbation:** reputation (for courage). **proof:** performance. 147. **let . . . swearing:** don't worry about my ability in swearing. 152. **clodpoll:** blockhead. 154. **his . . . it:** his inexperience will make him all the more ready to believe it. 156. **cockatrices:** basilisks, fabulous serpents reputed to be able to kill by a mere look. 157. **Give them way:** stay out of their way. 158. **presently:** immediately. 159. **horrid:** terrifying. (Literally, "bristling.")

OLIVIA:
I have said too much unto a heart of stone
And laid° mine honour too unchary on 't.°
There's something in me that reproves my fault,
But such a headstrong potent fault it is
That it but mocks reproof.

VIOLA:
With the same havior that your passion bears
Goes on my master's griefs.

OLIVIA: [*giving a locket*]
Here, wear this jewel° for me. 'Tis my picture.
Refuse it not; it hath no tongue to vex you.
And I beseech you come again tomorrow.
What shall you ask of me that I'll deny,
That honor, saved, may upon asking give?°

VIOLA:
Nothing but this: your true love for my master.

OLIVIA:
How with mine honor may I give him that
Which I have given to you?

VIOLA: I will acquit you.°

OLIVIA:
Well, come again tomorrow. Fare thee well.
A fiend like° thee might bear my soul to hell. [*Exit.*]

Enter [*Sir*] *Toby and Fabian.*

SIR TOBY: Gentleman, God save thee.

VIOLA: And you, sir.

SIR TOBY: That defence thou hast, betake thee to 't. Of what nature the wrongs are thou hast done him, I know not, but thy intercepter,° full of despite,° bloody as the hunter,° attends thee at the orchard end. Dismount thy tuck,° be yare° in thy preparation, for thy assailant is quick, skillful, and deadly.

162. laid: hazarded. **unchary on 't:** recklessly on it. **168. jewel:** (Any piece of jewelry; here, seemingly, a locket.) **172. That . . . give:** that can be granted without compromising any honor. **175. acquit you:** release you of your promise. **177. like:** resembling. **181. intercepter:** he who lies in wait. **182. despite:** defiance. **bloody as the hunter:** bloodthirsty as a hunting dog. **182–83. Dismount thy tuck:** draw your rapier. **183. yare:** ready, nimble.

VIOLA: You mistake sir. I am sure no man hath any quarrel to° me. My remembrance is very free and clear from any image of offense done to any man.

SIR TOBY: You'll find it otherwise, I assure you. Therefore, if you hold your life at any price, betake you to your guard, for your opposite° hath in him what° youth, strength, skill, and wrath can furnish man withal.°

VIOLA: I pray you, sir, what is he?

SIR TOBY: He is knight, dubbed with unhatched° rapier and on carpet consideration,° but he is a devil in private brawl. Souls and bodies hath he divorced three, and his incensement at this moment is so implacable that satisfaction can be none but by pangs of death and sepulcher. Hob, nob° is his word;° give 't or take 't.

VIOLA: I will return again into the house and desire some conduct° of the lady. I am no fighter. I have heard of some kind of men that put quarrels purposely on others, to taste° their valour. Belike° this is a man of that quirk.°

SIR TOBY: Sir, no. His indignation derives itself out of a very competent° injury; therefore, get you on and give him his desire. Back you shall not to the house unless you undertake that° with me which with as much safety you might answer him. Therefore, on, or strip your sword stark naked; for meddle° you must, that's certain, or forswear to wear iron° about you.

VIOLA: This is as uncivil as strange. I beseech you, do me this courteous office, as to know of° the knight what my offense to him is. It is something of my negligence, nothing of my purpose.

SIR TOBY: I will do so. — Signior Fabian, stay you by this gentleman till my return. *Exit* [*Sir*] *Toby.*

VIOLA: Pray you, sir, do you know of this matter?

FABIAN: I know the knight is incensed against you, even to a mortal arbitrament,° but nothing of the circumstance more.

VIOLA: I beseech you, what manner of man is he?

FABIAN: Nothing of that wonderful promise, to read him by his form,° as you are like° to find him in the proof of his valor. He is, indeed, sir, the

185. **to:** with. 189. **opposite:** opponent. 190. **what:** whatsoever. **withal:** with. 192. **unhatched:** unhacked, unused in battle. 192–93. **carpet consideration:** (A carpet knight was one whose title was obtained, not in battle, but through connections at court.) 195–96. **Hob, nob:** have or have not, i.e., give it or take it, kill or be killed. 196. **word:** motto. 197. **conduct:** escort. 199. **taste:** test. **Belike:** probably. 200. **quirk:** peculiar humor. 201. **competent:** sufficient. 203. **that:** i.e., to give satisfaction in a duel. 205. **meddle:** engage (in conflict). **forswear . . . iron:** give up your right to wear a sword. 208. **know of:** inquire from. 213–14. **mortal arbitrament:** trial to the death. 216. **read . . . form:** judge him by his appearance. 217. **like:** likely.

most skillful, bloody, and fatal opposite that you could possibly have found in any part of Illyria. Will you° walk towards him, I will make your peace with him if I can.

VIOLA: I shall be much bound to you for 't. I am one that had rather go with° Sir Priest° than Sir Knight. I care not who knows so much of my mettle. *Exeunt.*

Enter [Sir] Toby and [Sir] Andrew.

SIR TOBY: Why, man, he's a very devil; I have not seen such a firago.° I had a pass° with him, rapier, scabbard, and all, and he gives me the stuck in° with such a mortal motion that it is inevitable; and on the answer,° he pays you as surely as your feet hit the ground they step on. They say he has been fencer to° the Sophy.

SIR ANDREW: Pox on 't, I'll not meddle with him.

SIR TOBY: Ay, but he will not now be pacified. Fabian can scarce hold him yonder.

SIR ANDREW: Plague on 't, an I thought he had been valiant and so cunning in fence, I'd have seen him damned ere I'd have challenged him. Let him let the matter slip and I'll give him my horse, grey Capilet.°

SIR TOBY: I'll make the motion.° Stand here, make a good show on 't. This shall end without the perdition of souls.° [*Aside, as he crosses to meet Fabian.*] Marry, I'll ride your horse as well as I ride you.

Enter Fabian and Viola.

[*Aside to Fabian.*] I have his horse to take up° the quarrel. I have persuaded him the youth's a devil.

FABIAN: He is as horribly conceited of him,° and pants and looks pale as if a bear were at his heels.

SIR TOBY: [*To Viola*] There's no remedy, sir, he will fight with you for 's oath's sake. Marry, he hath better bethought him of his quarrel, and he finds that now scarce to be worth talking of. Therefore draw, for the supportance° of his vow; he protests he will not hurt you.

VIOLA: [*aside*] Pray God defend me! A little thing would make me tell them how much I lack of a man.

FABIAN: Give ground, if you see him furious.

219. **Will you:** if you will. 221–22. **go with:** associate with. 222. **Sir Priest:** (*Sir* was a courtesy title for priests.) 224. **firago:** virago. 225. **pass:** bout. **stuck in:** stoccado, a thrust in fencing. 226. **answer:** return hit. 228. **to:** in the service of. 234. **Capilet:** i.e., "little horse." (From "capel," a nag.) 235. **motion:** offer. 236. **perdition of souls:** i.e., loss of lives. 238. **take up:** settle, make up. 240. **He . . . him:** i.e., Cesario has as horrible a conception of Sir Andrew. 245. **supportance:** upholding.

SIR TOBY: [*crossing to Sir Andrew*] Come, Sir Andrew, there's no remedy. The gentleman will, for his honor's sake, have one bout with you. He cannot by the *duello*° avoid it. But he has promised me, as he is a gentleman and a soldier, he will not hurt you. Come on, to 't.

SIR ANDREW: Pray God he keep his oath!

Enter Antonio.

VIOLA: I do assure you, 'tis against my will. [*They draw.*]

ANTONIO: [*drawing, to Sir Andrew*]
Put up your sword. If this young gentleman
Have done offence, I take the fault on me;
If you offend him, I for him defy you.

SIR TOBY: You, sir? Why, what are you?

ANTONIO:
One, sir, that for his love dares yet do more
Than you have heard him brag to you he will.

SIR TOBY: [*drawing*]
Nay, if you be an undertaker,° I am for you.°

Enter Officers.

FABIAN: O good Sir Toby, hold! Here come the officers.

SIR TOBY: [*to Antonio*] I'll be with you anon.

VIOLA: [*to Sir Andrew*] Pray, sir, put your sword up, if you please.

SIR ANDREW: Marry, will I, sir; and for that° I promised you, I'll be as good as my word. He° will bear you easily, and reins well.

FIRST OFFICER: This is the man. Do thy office.

SECOND OFFICER:
Antonio, I arrest thee at the suit
Of Count Orsino.

ANTONIO: You do mistake me, sir.

FIRST OFFICER:
No, sir, no jot. I know your favor° well,
Though now you have no sea-cap on your head. —
Take him away. He knows I know him well.

ANTONIO:
I must obey. [*To Viola.*] This comes with seeking you.
But there's no remedy; I shall answer it.°

251. *duello:* dueling code. 261. **undertaker:** one who takes upon himself a task or business; here, a challenger. **for you:** ready for you. 265. **for that:** as for what. 266. **He:** i.e., the horse. 270. **favor:** face. 274. **answer it:** stand trial and make reparation for it.

What will you do, now my necessity
Makes me to ask you for my purse? It grieves me
Much more for what I cannot do for you
Than what befalls myself. You stand amazed,
But be of comfort.

SECOND OFFICER: Come, sir, away.

ANTONIO: [*to Viola*]
I must entreat of you some of that money.

VIOLA: What money, sir?
For the fair kindness you have showed me here,
And part° being prompted by your present trouble,
Out of my lean and low ability
I'll lend you something. My having° is not much;
I'll make division of my present° with you.
Hold, there's half my coffer.° [*She offers money.*]

ANTONIO:
Will you deny me now?
Is 't possible that my deserts to you
Can lack persuasion?° Do not tempt° my misery,
Lest that it make me so unsound° a man
As to upbraid you with those kindnesses
That I have done for you.

VIOLA: I know of none,
Nor know I you by voice or any feature.
I hate ingratitude more in a man
Than lying, vainness,° babbling, drunkenness,
Or any taint of vice whose strong corruption
Inhabits our frail blood.

ANTONIO: O heavens themselves!

SECOND OFFICER: Come, sir, I pray you, go.

ANTONIO:
Let me speak a little. This youth that you see here
I snatched one half out of the jaws of death,
Relieved him with such° sanctity of love,

283. part: partly. **285. having:** wealth. **286. present:** present store. **287. coffer:** purse. (Literally, strongbox.) **289–90. deserts . . . persuasion:** claims on you can fail to persuade you to help me. **290. tempt:** try too severely. **291. unsound:** morally weak, lacking in self-control. **296. vainness:** vaingloriousness. **302. such:** much.

And to his image,° which methought did promise
Most venerable worth,° did I devotion.

FIRST OFFICER:
What 's that to us? The time goes by. Away!

ANTONIO:
But, O, how vile an idol proves this god!
Thou hast, Sebastian, done good feature shame.°
In nature there's no blemish but the mind;
None can be called deformed but the unkind.°
Virtue is beauty, but the beauteous evil°
Are empty trunks° o'erflourished° by the devil.

FIRST OFFICER:
The man grows mad. Away with him! Come, come, sir.

ANTONIO: Lead me on. *Exit [with Officers].*

VIOLA: [*aside*]
Methinks his words do from such passion fly
That he believes himself. So do not I.°
Prove true, imagination, O, prove true,
That I, dear brother, be now ta'en for you!

SIR TOBY: Come hither, knight. Come hither, Fabian. We'll whisper o'er a couplet or two of most sage saws.° [*They gather apart from Viola.*]

VIOLA:
He named Sebastian. I my brother know
Yet living in my glass;° even such and so
In favor was my brother, and he went
Still° in this fashion, color, ornament,
For him I imitate. O, if it prove,°
Tempests are kind, and salt waves fresh in love! [*Exit.*]

SIR TOBY: A very dishonest° paltry boy, and more a coward than a hare. His dishonesty° appears in leaving his friend here in necessity and denying° him; and for his cowardship, ask Fabian.

FABIAN: A coward, a most devout coward, religious in it.°

303. **image:** what he appeared to be (playing on the idea of a religious icon to be venerated). 304. **venerable worth:** worthiness of being venerated. 307. **Thou . . . shame:** i.e., you have shamed physical beauty by showing that it does not always reflect inner beauty. 309. **unkind:** ungrateful, unnatural. 310. **beauteous evil:** those who are outwardly beautiful but evil within. 311. **trunks:** (1) chests (2) bodies. **o'erflourished:** (1) covered with ornamental carvings (2) made outwardly beautiful. 315. **So . . . I:** i.e., I do not believe myself (in the hope that has arisen in me). 319. **saws:** sayings. 320–21. **I . . . glass:** i.e., I know my brother is virtually alive every time I look in a mirror, because we looked so much alike. 323. **Still:** always. 324. **prove:** prove true. 326. **dishonest:** dishonorable. 327. **dishonesty:** dishonor. 328. **denying:** refusing to acknowledge. 329. **religious in it:** making a religion of cowardice.

SIR ANDREW: 'Slid,° I'll after him again and beat him.
SIR TOBY: Do, cuff him soundly, but never draw thy sword.
SIR ANDREW: An I do not — [*Exit.*]
FABIAN: Come, let's see the event.°
SIR TOBY: I dare lay° any money 'twill be nothing yet.° *Exeunt.*

ACT 4, SCENE 1°

Enter Sebastian and Clown [*Feste*].

FESTE: Will you make me believe that I am not sent for you?

SEBASTIAN: Go to, go to, thou art a foolish fellow. Let me be clear of thee.

FESTE: Well held out,° i' faith! No, I do not know you, nor I am not sent to you by my lady to bid you come speak with her, nor your name is not Master Cesario, nor this is not my nose, neither. Nothing that is so is so.

SEBASTIAN: I prithee, vent° thy folly somewhere else. Thou know'st not me.

FESTE: Vent my folly! He has heard that word of° some great man, and now applies it to a fool. Vent my folly! I am afraid this great lubber,° the world, will prove a cockney.° I prithee now, ungird thy strangeness° and tell me what I shall vent to my lady. Shall I vent to her that thou art coming?

SEBASTIAN: I prithee, foolish Greek,° depart from me. There's money for thee. [*He gives money.*] If you tarry longer, I shall give worse payment.

FESTE: By my troth, thou hast an open° hand. These wise men that give fools money get themselves a good report° — after fourteen years' purchase.°

Enter [*Sir*] *Andrew,* [*Sir*] *Toby, and Fabian.*

SIR ANDREW: Now, sir, have I met you again? There's for you.
[*He strikes Sebastian.*]

SEBASTIAN: Why, there's for thee, and there, and there! [*He beats Sir Andrew with the hilt of his dagger.*] Are all the people mad?

330. **'Slid:** by his (God's) eyelid. 333. **event:** outcome. 334. **lay:** wager. **yet:** nevertheless, after all. ACT 4, SCENE 1. **Location:** Before Olivia's house. 3. **held out:** kept up. 6. **vent:** (1) give vent to (2) void, excrete. 7. **of:** from, suited to the diction of; or, with reference to. 8. **lubber:** lout. 9. **cockney:** effeminate or foppish fellow. (Feste comically despairs of finding common sense anywhere if people start using affected phrases like those Sebastian uses.) **ungird thy strangeness:** put off your affectation of being a stranger. (Feste apes the kind of high-flown speech he has just deplored.) 11. **Greek:** (1) one who speaks gibberish (as in "It's all Greek to me") (2) buffoon (as in "merry Greek"). 13. **open:** generous (with money or with blows). 14. **report:** reputation. 14–15. **after . . . purchase:** i.e., at great cost and after long delays. (Land was ordinarily valued at the price of twelve years' rental; the Fool adds two years to this figure.)

SIR TOBY: Hold, sir, or I'll throw your dagger o'er the house.

FESTE: This will I tell my lady straight.° I would not be in some of your coats for twopence. [*Exit.*]

SIR TOBY: Come on, sir, hold! [*He grips Sebastian.*]

SIR ANDREW: Nay, let him alone. I'll go another way to work with him. I'll have an action of battery° against him, if there be any law in Illyria. Though I struck him first, yet it's no matter for that.

SEBASTIAN: Let go thy hand!

SIR TOBY: Come, sir, I will not let you go. Come, my young soldier, put up your iron. You are well fleshed.° Come on.

SEBASTIAN:
I will be free from thee. [*He breaks free and draws his sword.*] What wouldst thou now?
If thou dar'st tempt° me further, draw thy sword.

SIR TOBY: What, what? Nay, then I must have an ounce or two of this malapert° blood from you. [*He draws.*]

Enter Olivia.

OLIVIA:
Hold, Toby! On thy life I charge thee, hold!

SIR TOBY: Madam —

OLIVIA:
Will it be ever thus? Ungracious wretch,
Fit for the mountains and the barbarous caves,
Where manners ne'er were preached! Out of my sight! —
Be not offended, dear Cesario. —
Rudesby,° begone! [*Exeunt Sir Toby, Sir Andrew, and Fabian.*]
I prithee, gentle friend,
Let thy fair wisdom, not thy passion, sway
In this uncivil and thou unjust extent°
Against thy peace. Go with me to my house,
And hear thou there how many fruitless pranks
This ruffian hath botched up,° that thou thereby
Mayst smile at this. Thou shalt not choose but go.°

20. **straight:** at once. 24. **action of battery:** lawsuit for physical assault. 28. **fleshed:** initiated into battle. 31. **tempt:** make trial of. 33. **malapert:** saucy, impudent. 40. **Rudesby:** ruffian. 42. **extent:** attack. 45. **botched up:** clumsily contrived. 46. **Thou . . . go:** I insist on your going with me.

Do not deny.° Beshrew° his soul for me!°
He started one poor heart of mine, in thee.°

SEBASTIAN: [*aside*]
What relish is in this?° How runs the stream?
Or° I am mad, or else this is a dream.
Let fancy° still° my sense in Lethe° steep;
If it be thus to dream, still let me sleep!

OLIVIA:
Nay, come, I prithee. Would thou'dst be ruled by me!

SEBASTIAN:
Madam, I will.

OLIVIA: O, say so, and so be! *Exeunt.*

ACT 4, SCENE 2°

Enter Maria [*with a gown and a false beard*], *and Clown* [*Feste*].

MARIA: Nay, I prithee, put on this gown and this beard; make him believe thou art Sir° Topas° the curate. Do it quickly. I'll call Sir Toby the whilst.° [*Exit.*]

FESTE: Well, I'll put it on, and I will dissemble° myself in 't, and I would I were the first that ever dissembled in such a gown. [*He disguises himself in gown and beard.*] I am not tall enough to become° the function° well, nor lean° enough to be thought a good student;° but to be said° an honest man and a good housekeeper° goes as fairly as° to say a careful° man and a great scholar. The competitors° enter.

Enter [*Sir*] *Toby* [*and Maria*].

47. **deny:** refuse. **Beshrew:** curse. (A mild oath.) **for me:** on my account. 48. **He . . . thee:** i.e., he alarmed half of my heart, which lies in your bosom. (To *start* is also to drive an animal such as a *hart* [*heart*] from its cover, though the term is more usually applied to rabbits.) 49. **What . . . this?:** i.e., what am I to make of this? (*Relish* means "taste.") 50. **Or:** either. 51. **fancy:** imagination. **still:** ever. **Lethe:** the river of forgetfulness in the underworld; i.e., forgetfulness. **ACT 4, SCENE 2. Location:** Olivia's house. 2. **Sir:** (An honorific title for priests.) **Topas:** (A name perhaps derived from Chaucer's comic knight in the "Rime of Sir Thopas" or from a similar character in Lyly's *Endymion.* Topaz, a semiprecious stone, was believed to be a cure for lunacy.) **the whilst:** in the meantime. 3. **dissemble:** disguise (with a play on "feign"). 5. **become:** grace, adorn. **function:** priestly office. 6. **lean:** (Scholars were proverbially sparing of diet.) **student:** scholar (in divinity). **said:** called, known as. 7. **housekeeper:** household manager, hospitable person. **goes as fairly as:** sounds just as honorable as. **careful:** painstaking in studies. (Feste suggests that honesty and charity are found as often in ordinary men as in clerics.) 8. **competitors:** associates, partners (in this plot).

SIR TOBY: Jove bless thee, Master Parson.

FESTE: *Bonos dies,*° Sir Toby. For, as the old hermit of Prague,° that never saw pen and ink, very wittily said to a niece of King Gorboduc,° "That that is, is"; so I, being Master Parson, am Master Parson; for what is "that" but "that," and "is" but "is"?

SIR TOBY: To him, Sir Topas.

FESTE: What, ho, I say! Peace in this prison!

[*He approaches the door behind which Malvolio is confined.*]

SIR TOBY: The knave counterfeits well; a good knave.

MALVOLIO: (*within*) Who calls there?

FESTE: Sir Topas the curate, who comes to visit Malvolio the lunatic.

MALVOLIO: Sir Topas, Sir Topas, good Sir Topas, go to my lady —

FESTE: Out, hyperbolical° fiend!° How vexest thou this man! Talkest thou nothing but of ladies?

SIR TOBY: Well said, Master Parson.

MALVOLIO: Sir Topas, never was man thus wronged. Good Sir Topas, do not think I am mad. They have laid me here in hideous darkness.

FESTE: Fie, thou dishonest Satan! I call thee by the most modest terms,° for I am one of those gentle ones that will use the devil himself with courtesy. Sayest thou that house° is dark?

MALVOLIO: As hell, Sir Topas.

FESTE: Why, it hath bay windows transparent as barricadoes,° and the clerestories° toward the south north are as lustrous as ebony; and yet complainest thou of obstruction?

MALVOLIO: I am not mad, Sir Topas. I say to you this house is dark.

FESTE: Madman, thou errest. I say there is no darkness but ignorance, in which thou art more puzzled than the Egyptians in their fog.°

MALVOLIO: I say this house is as dark as ignorance, though ignorance were as dark as hell; and I say there was never man thus abused. I am no more mad than you are. Make the trial of it in any constant question.°

FESTE: What is the opinion of Pythagoras concerning wildfowl?°

10. *Bonos dies:* good day. **hermit of Prague:** (Probably another invented authority.) 11. **King Gorboduc:** a legendary king of ancient Britain, protagonist in the English tragedy *Gorbobuc* (1562). 20. **hyperbolical:** vehement, boisterous. **fiend:** i.e., the devil supposedly possessing Malvolio. 25. **modest terms:** mild terms (such as "dishonest" instead of "lying"). 27. **house:** i.e., room. 29. **barricadoes:** barricades (which are opaque. Feste speaks comically in impossible paradoxes, but Malvolio seems not to notice.) 30. **clerestories:** windows in an upper wall. 34. **Egyptians . . . fog:** (Alluding to the darkness brought upon Egypt by Moses; see Exodus 10.21–23.) 37. **constant question:** problem that requires consecutive reasoning. 38. **Pythagoras . . . wildfowl:** (An opening for the discussion of transmigration of souls, a doctrine held by Pythagoras.)

MALVOLIO: That the soul of our grandam might haply° inhabit a bird.

FESTE: What think'st thou of his opinion?

MALVOLIO: I think nobly of the soul, and no way approve his opinion.

FESTE: Fare thee well. Remain thou still in darkness. Thou shalt hold th' opinion of Pythagoras ere I will allow of thy wits,° and fear to kill a woodcock° lest thou dispossess the soul of thy grandam. Fare thee well.

[*He moves away from Malvolio's prison.*]

MALVOLIO: Sir Topas, Sir Topas!

SIR TOBY: My most exquisite Sir Topas!

FESTE: Nay, I am for all waters.°

MARIA: Thou mightst have done this without thy beard and gown. He sees thee not.

SIR TOBY: To him in thine own voice, and bring me word how thou find'st him: I would we were well rid of this knavery. If he may be conveniently delivered,° I would he were, for I am now so far in offense with my niece that I cannot pursue with any safety this sport to the upshot.° Come by and by to my chamber. *Exit* [*with Maria*].

FESTE: [*singing as he approaches Malvolio's prison*]
"Hey, Robin, jolly Robin,
Tell me how thy lady does."°

MALVOLIO: Fool!

FESTE: "My lady is unkind, pardie."°

MALVOLIO: Fool!

FESTE: "Alas, why is she so?"

MALVOLIO: Fool, I say!

FESTE: "She loves another —" Who calls, ha?

MALVOLIO: Good Fool, as ever thou wilt deserve well at my hand, help me to a candle, and pen, ink, and paper. As I am a gentleman, I will live to be thankful to thee for 't.

FESTE: Master Malvolio?

MALVOLIO: Ay, good Fool.

FESTE: Alas, sir, how fell you beside° your five wits?°

MALVOLIO: Fool, there was never a man so notoriously abused.° I am as well in my wits, Fool, as thou art.

39. **haply:** perhaps. 43. **allow of thy wits:** certify your sanity. 44. **woodcock:** (A proverbially stupid bird, easily caught.) 47. **Nay . . . waters:** i.e., indeed, I can turn my hand to anything. 52. **delivered:** i.e., delivered from prison. 53. **upshot:** conclusion. 55–56. **"Hey, Robin . . . does":** (Another fragment of an old song, a version of which is attributed to Sir Thomas Wyatt.) 58. **pardie:** i.e., by God, certainly. 68. **beside:** out of. **five wits:** The intellectual faculties, usually listed as common wit, imagination, fantasy, judgment, and memory. 69. **notoriously abused:** egregiously ill treated.

FESTE: But° as well? Then you are mad indeed, if you be no better in your wits than a fool.

MALVOLIO: They have here propertied me,° keep me in darkness, send ministers to me — asses — and do all they can to face me out of my wits.°

FESTE: Advise you° what you say. The minister is here. [*He speaks as Sir Topas.*] Malvolio, Malvolio, thy wits the heavens restore! Endeavor thyself to sleep, and leave thy vain bibble-babble.

MALVOLIO: Sir Topas!

FESTE: [*in Sir Topas's voice*] Maintain no words with him, good fellow. [*In his own voice.*] Who, I, sir? Not I, sir. God b' wi' you,° good Sir Topas. [*In Sir Topas's voice.*] Marry, amen. [*In his own voice.*] I will, sir, I will.

MALVOLIO: Fool! Fool! Fool, I say!

FESTE: Alas, sir, be patient. What say you, sir? I am shent° for speaking to you.

MALVOLIO: Good fool, help me to some light and some paper. I tell thee I am as well in my wits as any man in Illyria.

FESTE: Welladay° that you were, sir!

MALVOLIO: By this hand, I am. Good Fool, some ink, paper, and light; and convey what I will set down to my lady. It shall advantage thee more than ever the bearing of letter did.

FESTE: I will help you to 't. But tell me true, are you not mad indeed, or do you but counterfeit?

MALVOLIO: Believe me, I am not. I tell thee true.

FESTE: Nay, I'll ne'er believe a madman till I see his brains. I will fetch you light and paper and ink.

MALVOLIO: Fool, I'll requite it in the highest degree. I prithee, begone.

FESTE: [*sings*]

I am gone, sir,
And anon, sir,
I'll be with you again,
In a trice,
Like to the old Vice,°
Your need to sustain;

Who, with dagger of lath,°
In his rage and his wrath,

71. **But:** only. 73. **propertied me:** i.e., treated me as property and thrown me into the lumber-room. 74. **face . . . wits:** brazenly represent me as having lost my wits. 75. **Advise you:** take care. 80. **God b' wi' you:** God be with you. 83. **shent:** scolded, rebuked. 87. **Welladay:** alas, would that. 101. **Vice:** comic tempter of the "old" morality plays. 103. **dagger of lath:** comic weapon of the Vice in at least some morality plays.

Cries, "Aha!" to the devil;
  Like a mad lad,
  "Pare thy nails,° dad?
Adieu, goodman° devil!" *Exit.*

ACT 4, SCENE 3°

Enter Sebastian [with a pearl].

SEBASTIAN:
This is the air; that is the glorious sun;
This pearl she gave me, I do feel 't and see 't;
And though 'tis wonder that enwraps me thus,
Yet 'tis not madness. Where's Antonio, then?
I could not find him at the Elephant;
Yet there he was,° and there I found this credit,°
That he did range the town to seek me out.
His counsel now might do me golden service;
For though my soul disputes well with my sense°
That this may be some error, but no madness,
Yet doth this accident° and flood of fortune
So far exceed all instance,° all discourse,°
That I am ready to distrust mine eyes
And wrangle with my reason that persuades me
To any other trust° but that I am mad,
Or else the lady's mad. Yet, if 'twere so,
She could not sway° her house, command her followers,
Take and give back affairs and their dispatch°
With such a smooth, discreet, and stable bearing
As I perceive she does. There's something in 't
That is deceiveable.° But here the lady comes.

Enter Olivia and Priest.

107. **Pare thy nails:** (Evidently a comic routine in Tudor morality drama, though no samples survive.) 108. **goodman:** title for a person of substance but not of gentle birth. (This line could be Feste's farewell to Malvolio and his "devil.") **ACT 4, SCENE 3. Location:** Olivia's garden. 6. **was:** was previously. **credit:** report. 9. **my soul . . . sense:** i.e., both my rational faculties and my physical senses come to the conclusion. 11. **accident:** unexpected event. 12. **instance:** precedent. **discourse:** reason. 15. **trust:** belief. 17. **sway:** rule. 18. **Take . . . dispatch:** receive reports on matters of household business and see to their execution. 21. **deceivable:** deceptive.

OLIVIA:
Blame not this haste of mine. If you mean well,
Now go with me and with this holy man
Into the chantry by.° There, before him,
And underneath that consecrated roof,
Plight me the full assurance of your faith,
That my most jealous° and too doubtful° soul
May live at peace. He shall conceal it
Whiles° you are willing it shall come to note,°
What time° we will our celebration° keep
According to my birth.° What do you say?

SEBASTIAN:
I'll follow this good man, and go with you,
And, having sworn truth, ever will be true.

OLIVIA:
Then lead the way, good Father, and heavens so shine,
That they may fairly note° this act of mine! *Exeunt.*

ACT 5, SCENE 1°

Enter Clown [Feste] and Fabian.

FABIAN: Now, as thou lov'st me, let me see his letter.
FESTE: Good Master Fabian, grant me another request.
FABIAN: Anything.
FESTE: Do not desire to see this letter.
FABIAN: This is to give a dog and in recompense desire my dog again.°

Enter Duke [Orsino], Viola, Curio, and lords.

ORSINO: Belong you to the Lady Olivia, friends?
FESTE: Ay, sir, we are some of her trappings.°
ORSINO: I know thee well. How dost thou, my good fellow?
FESTE: Truly, sir, the better for° my foes and the worse for my friends.

24. **chantry by:** privately endowed chapel nearby. 27. **jealous:** anxious, mistrustful. **doubtful:** full of doubts. 29. **Whiles:** until. **come to note:** become known. 30. **What time:** at which time. **our celebration:** i.e., the actual marriage. (What they are about to perform is a binding betrothal.) 31. **birth:** social position. 35. **fairly note:** look upon with favor. **ACT 5, SCENE 1. Location:** Before Olivia's house. 5. **This . . . again:** (Apparently a reference to a well-known reply of Dr. Bulleyn when Queen Elizabeth asked for his dog and promised a gift of his choosing in return; he asked to have his dog back.) 7. **trappings:** ornaments, decorations. 9. **for:** because of.

ORSINO: Just the contrary — the better for thy friends.

FESTE: No, sir, the worse.

ORSINO: How can that be?

FESTE: Marry, sir, they praise me and make an ass of me.° Now my foes tell me plainly I am an ass, so that by my foes, sir, I profit in the knowledge of myself, and by my friends I am abused;° so that, conclusions to be as kisses, if your four negatives° make your two affirmatives,° why then the worse for my friends and the better for my foes.

ORSINO: Why, this is excellent.

FESTE: By my troth, sir, no, though° it please you to be one of my friends.°

ORSINO: Thou shalt not be the worse for me. There's gold. [*He gives a coin.*]

FESTE: But° that it would be double-dealing,° sir, I would you could make it another.

ORSINO: O, you give me ill counsel.

FESTE: Put your grace in your pocket,° sir, for this once, and let your flesh and blood obey it.°

ORSINO: Well, I will be so much a sinner to be° a double-dealer. There's another. [*He gives another coin.*]

FESTE: *Primo, secundo, tertio,* is a good play,° and the old saying is, the third pays for all.° The triplex,° sir, is a good tripping measure; or the bells of Saint Bennet,° sir, may put you in mind — one, two, three.

ORSINO: You can fool no more money out of me at this throw.° If you will let your lady know I am here to speak with her, and bring her along with you, it may awake my bounty further.

FESTE: Marry, sir, lullaby to your bounty till I come again. I go, sir, but I would not have you to think that my desire of having is the sin of covetousness. But as you say, sir, let your bounty take a nap. I will awake it anon. *Exit.*

Enter Antonio and Officers.

13. **make an ass of me:** i.e., flatter me into foolishly thinking well of myself. 15. **abused:** flatteringly deceived. 15–16. **conclusions . . . affirmatives:** i.e., as when a young lady, asked for a kiss, says "no, no" really meaning "yes"; or, as in grammar, two negatives make an affirmative. 16. **your four negatives:** the four negatives that people talk about. 19. **though:** even though. **friends:** i.e., those who, according to Feste's syllogism, flatter him. 21. **But:** except for the fact. **double-dealing:** (1) giving twice (2) deceit, duplicity. 24. **Put . . . pocket:** (1) pocket up your virtue, your grace before God (2) reach in your pocket or purse and show your customary grace or munificence. (*Your Grace* is also the formal way of addressing a duke.) 25. **it:** i.e., my "ill counsel." 26. **to be:** as to be. 28. **play:** (Perhaps a methematical game or game of dice.) 28–29. **the third . . . all:** the third time is lucky. (Proverbial.) 29. **triplex:** triple time in music. 30. **Saint Bennet:** church of St. Benedict. 31. **throw:** (1) time (2) throw of the dice.

VIOLA:
Here comes the man, sir, that did rescue me.

ORSINO:
That face of his I do remember well,
Yet when I saw it last it was besmeared
As black as Vulcan° in the smoke of war.
A baubling° vessel was he captain of,
For° shallow draft° and bulk unprizable,°
With which such scatheful° grapple did he make
With the most noble bottom° of our fleet
That very envy° and the tongue of loss°
Cried fame and honour on him. What's the matter?

FIRST OFFICER:
Orsino, this is that Antonio
That took the *Phoenix* and her freight from Candy,°
And this is he that did the *Tiger* board
When your young nephew Titus lost his leg.
Here in the streets, desperate of shame and state,°
In private brabble° did we apprehend him.

VIOLA:
He did me kindness, sir, drew on my side,
But in conclusion put strange speech upon me.°
I know not what 'twas but distraction.°

ORSINO:
Notable° pirate, thou saltwater thief,
What foolish boldness brought thee to their mercies
Whom thou in terms so bloody° and so dear°
Hast made thine enemies?

ANTONIO: Orsino, noble sir,
Be pleased that I° shake off these names you give me.
Antonio never yet was thief or pirate,
Though, I confess, on base and ground° enough

41. **Vulcan:** Roman god of fire and smith to the other gods; his face was blackened by the fire. 42. **baubling:** insignificant, trifling. 43. **For:** because of. **draft:** depth of water a ship draws. **unprizable:** of value too slight to be estimated, not worth taking as a "prize." 44. **scatheful:** destructive. 45. **bottom:** ship. 46. **very envy:** i.e., even those who had most reason to hate him, his enemies. **loss:** i.e., the losers. 49. **from Candy:** on her return from Candia, or Crete. 52. **desperate . . . state:** recklessly disregarding the disgrace that public quarreling would bring on him and his dangerous status as a wanted man. 53. **brabble:** brawl. 55. **put . . . me:** spoke to me strangely. 56. **but distraction:** unless (it was) madness. 57. **Notable:** notorious. 59. **in terms so bloody:** in so bloodthirsty a manner. **dear:** costly, grievous. 61. **Be pleased that I:** allow me to. 63. **base and ground:** solid grounds.

Orsino's enemy. A witchcraft drew me hither.
That most ingrateful boy there by your side
From the rude sea's enraged and foamy mouth
Did I redeem; a wreck° past hope he was.
His life I gave him, and did thereto add
My love, without retention° or restraint,
All his in dedication.° For his sake
Did I expose myself — pure° for his love —
Into° the danger of this adverse° town,
Drew to defend him when he was beset;
Where being apprehended, his false cunning,
Not meaning to partake with me in danger,
Taught him to face me out of his acquaintance°
And grew a twenty years' removèd thing
While one would wink;° denied me mine own purse,
Which I had recommended° to his use
Not half an hour before.

VIOLA: How can this be?

ORSINO: When came he to this town?

ANTONIO:
Today, my lord; and for three months before,
No interim, not a minute's vacancy,
Both day and night did we keep company.

Enter Olivia and attendants.

ORSINO:
Here comes the Countess. Now heaven walks on earth.
But for° thee, fellow — fellow, thy words are madness.
Three months this youth hath tended upon me;
But more of that anon. Take him aside.

OLIVIA: [*to Orsino*]
What would my lord — but that he may not have° —
Wherein Olivia may seem serviceable? —
Cesario, you do not keep promise with me.

VIOLA: Madam?

67. **wreck:** person cast ashore from a wrecked vessel. 69. **retention:** reservation. 70. **All . . . dedication:** devoted wholly to him. 71. **pure:** entirely, purely. 72. **Into:** unto. **adverse:** hostile. 76. **face . . . acquaintance:** brazenly deny he knew me. 77–78. **grew . . . wink:** in the twinkling of an eye acted as though we had been estranged for twenty years. 79. **recommended:** consigned. 87. **for:** as for. 90. **but . . . have:** except that which he may not have — i.e., my love.

ORSINO: Gracious Olivia —
OLIVIA:
What do you say, Cesario? — Good my lord° —
VIOLA:
My lord would speak. My duty hushes me.
OLIVIA:
If it be aught to the old tune, my lord,
It is as fat and fulsome° to mine ear
As howling after music.
ORSINO: Still so cruel?
OLIVIA: Still so constant, lord.
ORSINO:
What, to perverseness? You uncivil lady,
To whose ingrate° and unauspicious° altars
My soul the faithfull'st offerings hath breathed out
That e'er devotion tendered! What shall I do?
OLIVIA:
Even what it please my lord that shall become° him.
ORSINO:
Why should I not, had I the heart to do it,
Like to th' Egyptian thief° at point of death
Kill what I love? — a savage jealousy
That sometimes savors nobly.° But hear me this:
Since you to nonregardance° cast my faith,
And that° I partly know the instrument
That screws° me from my true place in your favor,
Live you the marble-breasted tyrant still.
But this your minion,° whom I know you love,
And whom, by heaven I swear, I tender° dearly,
Him will I tear out of that cruel eye
Where he sits crownèd in his master's spite.° —
Come, boy, with me. My thoughts are ripe in mischief.

95. **Good my lord:** (Olivia urges Orsino to listen to Cesario.) 98. **fat and fulsome:** gross and offensive. 103. **ingrate:** ungrateful. **unauspicious:** unpropitious, not disposed to be favorable. 106. **become:** suit. 108. **Egyptian thief:** (An allusion to the story of Theagenes and Chariclea in the *Ethiopica,* a Greek romance by Heliodorus. The robber chief, Thyamis of Memphis, having captured Chariclea and fallen in love with her, is attacked by a larger band of robbers; threatened with death, he attempts to slay her first.) 110. **savors nobly:** is not without nobility. 111. **nonregardance:** neglect. 112. **that:** since. 113. **screws:** pries, forces. 115. **minion:** darling, favorite. 116. **tender:** regard. 118. **in . . . spite:** to the vexation of his master.

I'll sacrifice the lamb that I do love,
To spite a raven's heart within a dove.° [*Going.*]

VIOLA:
And I, most jocund, apt,° and willingly,
To do you rest,° a thousand deaths would die.° [*Going.*]

OLIVIA:
Where goes Cesario?

VIOLA: After him I love
More than I love these eyes, more than my life,
More by all mores° than e'er I shall love wife.
If I do feign, you witnesses above
Punish my life for tainting of my love!°

OLIVIA:
Ay me, detested!° How am I beguiled!

VIOLA:
Who does beguile you? Who does do you wrong?

OLIVIA:
Hast thou forgot thyself? Is it so long?
Call forth the holy father. [*Exit an attendant.*]

ORSINO: [*to Viola*] Come, away!

OLIVIA:
Whither, my lord? Cesario, husband, stay.

ORSINO:
Husband?

OLIVIA: Ay, husband. Can he that deny?

ORSINO: [*to Viola*]
Her husband, sirrah?°

VIOLA: No, my lord, not I.

OLIVIA:
Alas, it is the baseness of thy fear
That makes thee strangle thy propriety.°
Fear not, Cesario; take thy fortunes up;
Be that° thou know'st thou art, and then thou art
As great as that thou fear'st.°

120–21. **I'll . . . dove:** i.e., I'll kill Cesario, whom I love, to revenge myself on this beautiful but black-hearted lady. 122. **apt:** readily. 123. **do you rest:** give you ease. **die:** (with possible suggestion of "have an orgasm".) 126. **by all mores:** by all such comparisons. 128. **Punish . . . love:** punish me with death for being disloyal to the love I feel. 129. **detested:** hated and denounced by another. 135. **sirrah:** (The normal way of addressing an inferior.) 137. **strangle thy propriety:** i.e., deny what you are. 139. **that:** that which. 140. **that thou fear'st:** him you fear, i.e., Orsino.

Enter Priest.

O, welcome, Father!
Father, I charge thee by thy reverence
Here to unfold — though lately we intended
To keep in darkness what occasion now
Reveals before 'tis ripe — what thou dost know
Hath newly passed between this youth and me.

PRIEST:
A contract of eternal bond of love,
Confirmed by mutual joinder° of your hands,
Attested by the holy close° of lips,
Strengthened by interchangement of your rings,
And all the ceremony of this compact
Sealed in my function,° by my testimony;
Since when, my watch hath told me, toward my grave
I have traveled but two hours.

ORSINO: [*to Viola*]
O thou dissembling cub! What wilt thou be
When time hath sowed a grizzle° on thy case?°
Or will not else thy craft so quickly grow
That thine own trip° shall be thine overthrow?
Farewell, and take her, but direct thy feet
Where thou and I henceforth may never meet.

VIOLA:
My lord, I do protest —

OLIVIA: O, do not swear!
Hold little faith,° though thou hast too much fear.

Enter Sir Andrew.

SIR ANDREW: For the love of God, a surgeon! Send one presently° to Sir Toby.

OLIVIA: What's the matter?

SIR ANDREW: He's broke° my head across, and has given Sir Toby a bloody coxcomb° too. For the love of God, your help! I had rather than forty pound I were at home.

147. **joinder:** joining. 148. **close:** meeting. 151. **Sealed in my function:** ratified through my carrying out of my priestly office. 155. **a grizzle:** scattering of gray hair. **case:** skin. 157. **trip:** wrestling trick used to throw an opponent. (You'll get overclever and trip yourself up.) 161. **Hold little faith:** keep at least a little part of what you promised. 162. **presently:** immediately. 165. **broke:** broken the skin, cut. 166. **coxcomb:** fool's cap resembling the crest of a cock; here, head.

OLIVIA: Who has done this, Sir Andrew?

SIR ANDREW: The Count's gentleman, one Cesario. We took him for a coward, but he's the very devil incardinate.°

ORSINO: My gentleman, Cesario?

SIR ANDREW: 'Od's lifelings,° here he is! — You broke my head for nothing, and that that I did I was set on to do 't by Sir Toby.

VIOLA:
Why do you speak to me? I never hurt you.
You drew your sword upon me without cause,
But I bespake you fair,° and hurt you not.

SIR ANDREW: If a bloody coxcomb be a hurt, you have hurt me. I think you set nothing by° a bloody coxcomb.

Enter [*Sir*] *Toby and Clown* [*Feste*].

Here comes Sir Toby, halting.° You shall hear more. But if he had not been in drink, he would have tickled you othergates° than he did.

ORSINO: How now, gentleman? How is 't with you?

SIR TOBY: That's all one.° He's hurt me, and there's th' end on 't.° — Sot,° didst see Dick surgeon, sot?

FESTE: O, he's drunk, Sir Toby, an hour agone;° his eyes were set° at eight i' the morning.

SIR TOBY: Then he's a rogue, and a passy measures pavane.° I hate a drunken rogue.

OLIVIA: Away with him! Who hath made this havoc with them?

SIR ANDREW: I'll help you, Sir Toby, because we'll be dressed° together.

SIR TOBY: Will you help? An ass-head and a coxcomb and a knave, a thin-faced knave, a gull!

OLIVIA:
Get him to bed, and let his hurt be looked to.
[*Exeunt Feste, Fabian, Sir Toby, and Sir Andrew.*]

Enter Sebastian.

170. **incardinate:** (For "incarnate.") 172. **'Od's lifelings:** by God's little lives. 176. **bespake you fair:** addressed you courteously. 178. **set nothing by:** regard as insignificant. 179. **halting:** limping. 180. **othergates:** otherwise. 182. **That's all one:** it doesn't matter; never mind. **there's . . . on 't:** that's all there is to it. **Sot:** (1) fool (2) drunkard. 184. **agone:** ago. **set:** fixed or closed. 186. **passy measures pavane:** passe-measure pavane, a slow-moving stately dance (suggesting Sir Toby's impatience to have his wounds dressed). 189. **be dressed:** have our wounds surgically dressed.

SEBASTIAN:

I am sorry, madam, I have hurt your kinsman;
But, had it been the brother of my blood,°
I must have done no less with wit and safety.° —
You throw a strange regard° upon me, and by that
I do perceive it hath offended you.
Pardon me, sweet one, even for the vows
We made each other but so late ago.

ORSINO:

One face, one voice, one habit,° and two persons,
A natural perspective,° that is and is not!

SEBASTIAN:

Antonio, O my dear Antonio!
How have the hours racked° and tortured me,
Since I have lost thee!

ANTONIO: Sebastian are you?

SEBASTIAN: Fear'st thou that,° Antonio?

ANTONIO:

How have you made division of yourself?
An apple cleft in two is not more twin
Than these two creatures. Which is Sebastian?

OLIVIA: Most wonderful!

SEBASTIAN: [*seeing Viola*]

Do I stand there? I never had a brother;
Nor can there be that deity in my nature
Of here and everywhere.° I had a sister,
Whom the blind° waves and surges have devoured.
Of charity,° what kin are you to me?
What countryman? What name? What parentage?

VIOLA:

Of Messaline. Sebastian was my father.
Such a Sebastian was my brother, too.
So went he suited° to his watery tomb.

194. **the brother of my blood:** my own brother. 195. **with wit and safety:** with intelligent concern for my own safety. 196. **strange regard:** look such as one directs at a stranger. 200. **habit:** dress. 201. **A natural perspective:** an optical device or illusion created in this instance by nature. 203. **racked:** tortured. 206. **Fear'st thou that:** do you doubt that. 213. **here and everywhere:** omnipresence. 214. **blind:** heedless, indiscriminating. 215. **Of charity:** (tell me) in kindness. 219. **suited:** dressed; clad in human form.

If spirits can assume both form and suit,°
You come to fright us.

SEBASTIAN: A spirit I am indeed,
But am in that dimension grossly clad°
Which from the womb I did participate.°
Were you a woman, as the rest goes even,°
I should my tears let fall upon your cheek
And say, "Thrice-welcome, drownèd Viola!"

VIOLA:
My father had a mole upon his brow.

SEBASTIAN: And so had mine.

VIOLA:
And died that day when Viola from her birth
Had numbered thirteen years.

SEBASTIAN:
O, that record° is lively in my soul!
He finishèd indeed his mortal act
That day that made my sister thirteen years.

VIOLA:
If nothing lets° to make us happy both
But this my masculine usurped attire,
Do not embrace me till each circumstance
Of place, time, fortune, do cohere and jump°
That I am Viola — which to confirm
I'll bring you to a captain in this town
Where lie my maiden weeds,° by whose gentle help
I was preserved to serve this noble count.
All the occurrence of my fortune since
Hath been between this lady and this lord.

SEBASTIAN: [*to Olivia*]
So comes it, lady, you have been mistook.
But nature to her bias drew in that.°
You would have been contracted to a maid,
Nor are you therein, by my life, deceived.
You are betrothed both to a maid° and man.

220. **form and suit:** physical appearance and dress. 222. **in . . . clad:** clothed in that fleshly shape. 223. **participate:** possess in common with all humanity. 224. **as . . . even:** since everything else agrees. 231. **record:** recollection. 234. **lets:** hinders. 237. **jump:** coincide, fit exactly. 240. **weeds:** clothes. 245. **nature . . . that:** nature followed her bent in that. (The metaphor is from the game of bowls.) 248. **a maid:** i.e., a virgin man.

ORSINO: [*to Olivia*]
Be not amazed; right noble is his blood.
If this be so, as yet the glass° seems true,
I shall have share in this most happy wreck.°
[*To Viola.*] Boy, thou hast said to me a thousand times
Thou never shouldst love woman like to me.°

VIOLA:
And all those sayings will I over swear,°
And those swearings keep as true in soul
As doth that orbèd continent the fire°
That severs day from night.

ORSINO: Give me thy hand,
And let me see thee in thy woman's weeds.

VIOLA:
The captain that did bring me first on shore
Hath my maid's garments. He upon some action°
Is now in durance,° at Malvolio's suit,
A gentleman and follower of my lady's.

OLIVIA:
He shall enlarge° him. Fetch Malvolio hither.
And yet, alas, now I remember me,
They say, poor gentleman, he's much distract.

Enter Clown [Feste] with a letter, and Fabian.

A most extracting° frenzy of mine own
From my remembrance clearly banished his.°
How does he, sirrah?

FESTE: Truly, madam, he holds Beelzebub at the staves's end° as well as a man in his case may do. He's here writ a letter to you; I should have given 't you today morning. But as a madman's epistles are no gospels,° so it skills° not much when they are delivered.°

OLIVIA: Open 't and read it.

250. **the glass:** i.e., the *natural perspective* of line 201. 251. **wreck:** shipwreck, accident. 253. **like to me:** as well as you love me. 254. **over swear:** swear again. 256. **As . . . fire:** i.e., as the sphere of the sun keeps the fire. 260. **action:** legal charge. 261. **durance:** imprisonment. 263. **enlarge:** release. 266. **extracting:** i.e., that obsessed me and drew all thoughts except of Cesario from my mind. 267. **his:** i.e., his madness. 269. **holds . . . end:** i.e., keeps the devil at a safe distance. (The metaphor is of fighting with quarterstaffs or long poles.) 271. **a madman's . . . gospels:** i.e., there is no truth in a madman's letters. (An allusion to readings in the church service of selected passages from the epistles and the gospels.) 272. **skills:** matters. **delivered:** (1) delivered to their recipient (2) read aloud.

FESTE: Look then to be well edified when the fool delivers° the madman. [*He reads loudly.*] "By the Lord, madam —"

OLIVIA: How now, art thou mad?

FESTE: No, madam, I do but read madness. An your ladyship will have it as it ought to be, you must allow *vox.*°

OLIVIA: Prithee, read i' thy right wits.

FESTE: So I do, madonna; but to read his right wits° is to read thus. Therefore perpend,° my princess, and give ear.

OLIVIA: [*to Fabian*] Read it you, sirrah.

FABIAN: [*reads*] "By the Lord, madam, you wrong me, and the world shall know it. Though you have put me into darkness and given your drunken cousin rule over me, yet have I the benefit of my senses as well as your ladyship. I have your own letter that induced me to the semblance I put on, with the which° I doubt not but to do myself much right or you much shame. Think of me as you please. I leave my duty a little unthought of, and speak out of my injury.°

The madly used Malvolio."

OLIVIA: Did he write this?

FESTE: Ay, madam.

ORSINO: This savours not much of distraction.

OLIVIA:

See him delivered,° Fabian. Bring him hither. [*Exit Fabian.*]
My lord, so please you, these things further thought on,°
To think me as well a sister as a wife,°
One day shall crown th' alliance on 't,° so please you,
Here at my house and at my proper° cost.

ORSINO:

Madam, I am most apt° t' embrace your offer.
[*To Viola.*] Your master quits° you; and for your service done him,
So much against the mettle° of your sex,
So far beneath your soft and tender breeding,
And since you called me master for so long,

274. **delivers:** speaks the words of. 278. ***vox:*** voice, i.e., an appropriately loud voice. 280. **to read . . . wits:** to express his true state of mind. 281. **perpend:** consider, attend. (A deliberately lofty word.) 287. **the which:** i.e., the letter. 288–89. **I leave . . . injury:** i.e., in saying this, I speak for the moment not as your steward should, but as an injured party. 294. **delivered:** released. 295. **so . . . on:** if you are pleased on further consideration of all that has happened. 296. **To . . . wife:** to regard me as favorably as a sister-in-law as you had hoped to regard me as a wife. 297. **crown . . . on 't:** i.e., serve as occasion for two marriages confirming our new relationship. 298. **proper:** own. 299. **apt:** ready. 300. **quits:** releases. 301. **mettle:** natural disposition.

Here is my hand. You shall from this time be
Your master's mistress.

OLIVIA: A sister! You are she.

Enter [Fabian, with] Malvolio.

ORSINO:
Is this the madman?

OLIVIA: Ay, my lord, this same.
How now, Malvolio!

MALVOLIO: Madam, you have done me wrong,
Notorious wrong.

OLIVIA: Have I, Malvolio? No.

MALVOLIO: [*showing a letter*]
Lady, you have. Pray you, peruse that letter.
You must not now deny it is your hand.
Write from it,° if you can, in hand or phrase,
Or say 'tis not your seal, not your invention.°
You can say none of this. Well, grant it then,
And tell me, in the modesty of honor,°
Why you have given me such clear lights° of favor,
Bade me come smiling and cross-gartered to you,
To put on yellow stockings, and to frown
Upon Sir Toby and the lighter° people?
And, acting this in an obedient hope,°
Why have you suffered me to be imprisoned,
Kept in a dark house, visited by the priest,°
And made the most notorious geck° and gull
That e'er invention played on?° Tell me why?

OLIVIA:
Alas, Malvolio, this is not my writing,
Though, I confess, much like the character;°
But out of° question 'tis Maria's hand.
And now I do bethink me, it was she
First told me thou wast mad; then cam'st° in smiling,
And in such forms which here were presupposed°

311. **from it:** differently. 312. **invention:** composition. 314. **in . . . honor:** in the name of all that is decent and honorable. 315. **clear lights:** evident signs. 318. **lighter:** lesser. 319. **acting . . . hope:** when I acted thus out of obedience to you and in hope of your favor. 321. **priest:** i.e., Feste. 322. **geck:** dupe. 323. **invention played on:** contrivance sported with. 325. **the character:** my handwriting. 326. **out of:** beyond. 328. **cam'st:** you came. 329. **presupposed:** specified beforehand.

Upon thee in the letter. Prithee, be content.
This practice° hath most shrewdly° passed° upon thee;
But when we know the grounds and authors of it,
Thou shalt be both the plaintiff and the judge
Of thine own cause.

FABIAN: Good madam, hear me speak,
And let no quarrel nor no brawl to come°
Taint the condition° of this present hour,
Which I have wondered at. In hope it shall not,
Most freely I confess, myself and Toby
Set this device against Malvolio here,
Upon° some stubborn and uncourteous parts°
We had conceived against him.° Maria writ
The letter at Sir Toby's great importance,°
In recompense whereof he hath married her.
How with a sportful malice it was followed°
May rather pluck on° laughter than revenge,
If that° the injuries be justly weighed
That have on both sides passed.

OLIVIA: [*to Malvolio*]
Alas, poor fool, how have they baffled° thee!

FESTE: Why, "Some are born great, some achieve greatness, and some have greatness thrown upon them." I was one, sir, in this interlude,° one Sir Topas, sir, but that's all one.° "By the Lord, fool, I am not mad." But do you remember? "Madam, why laugh you at such a barren rascal? An you smile not, he's gagged." And thus the whirligig° of time brings in his revenges.

MALVOLIO: I'll be revenged on the whole pack of you. [*Exit.*]

OLIVIA:
He hath been most notoriously abused.

ORSINO:
Pursue him, and entreat him to a peace.
He hath not told us of the captain yet.
When that is known, and golden time convents,°

331. **practice:** plot. **shrewdly:** mischievously. **passed:** been perpetrated. 335. **to come:** in the future. 336. **condition:** (happy) nature. 340. **Upon:** on account of. **parts:** qualities, deeds. 341. **conceived against him:** seen and resented in him. 342. **importance:** importunity. 344. **followed:** carried out. 345. **pluck on:** induce. 346. **If that:** if. 348. **baffled:** disgraced, quelled. 350. **interlude:** little play. 351. **that's all one:** no matter for that. 353. **whirligig:** spinning top. 359. **convents:** (1) summons, calls together (2) suits.

A solemn combination shall be made
Of our dear souls. Meantime, sweet sister,
We will not part from hence. Cesario, come —
For so you shall be, while you are a man;
But when in other habits° you are seen,
Orsino's mistress and his fancy's° queen. *Exeunt* [*all, except Feste*].

FESTE: (*sings*)

When that I was and a little° tiny boy,
With hey, ho, the wind and the rain,
A foolish thing was but a toy,°
For the rain it raineth every day.

But when I came to man's estate,
With hey, ho, the wind and the rain,
'Gainst knaves and thieves men shut their gate,
For the rain it raineth every day.

But when I came, alas, to wive,
With hey, ho, the wind and the rain,
By swaggering could I never thrive,
For the rain it raineth every day.

But when I came unto my beds,°
With hey, ho, the wind and the rain,
With tosspots° still had drunken heads,
For the rain it raineth every day.

A great while ago the world begun,
With hey, ho, the wind and the rain,
But that's all one, our play is done,
And we'll strive to please you every day.

[*Exit.*]

FINIS

364. **habits:** attire. 365. **fancy's:** love's. 366. **and a little:** a little. 368. **toy:** trifle. 378. **unto my beds:** i.e., (1) drunk to bed, or, perhaps, (2) in the evening of life. 380. **tosspots:** drunkards.

Textual Notes for Twelfth Night

Copy text: the First Folio. Act and scene divisions follow the Folio text throughout.

Act 1, Scene 1. 1. s.p. [and throughout] **Orsino:** *Duke.* 10–11. **capacity / Receiveth:** capacitie, / Receiueth. 11. **sea, naught:** sea. Nought.

Act 1, Scene 2. 15. **Arion:** *Orion.*

Act 1, Scene 3. 43. s.p. **Sir Andrew:** *Ma.* 45. **Mary Accost:** *Mary,* accost. 82. **curl by:** coole my. 83. **me:** we. 109. **dun:** dam'd. 110. **set:** sit. 112. **That's:** That.

Act 1, Scene 5. 4. s.p. [and throughout] **Feste:** *Clo.* 68. **gagged:** gag'd [also at 5.1. 353]. 115. **He's:** Ha's. 131. s.d. **Viola:** *Uiolenta.* 246. **County's:** Countes. 256. s.d. [F adds *"Finis, Actus primus"*].

Act 2, Scene 2. 15. **That sure:** That. 26. **our:** O. 27. **made of, such:** made, if such.

Act 2, Scene 3. 20. **leman:** Lemon.

Act 2, Scene 4. 49. s.p. **Feste:** [not in F]. 51. **Fly . . . fly:** Fye . . . fie. 53. **yew:** Ew. 85. **I:** It.

Act 2, Scene 5. 96. **staniel:** stallion. 100. **portend?:** portend. 117. **born:** become. **achieve:** atcheeues. 128–29. **Unhappy." Daylight:** vnhappy daylight. 141. **dear:** deero. 167. s.d. [F adds *"Finis Actus secundus"*].

Act 3, Scene 1. 6. **king:** Kings. 55. **wise men:** wisemens. 74. **all ready:** already. 106. **grece:** grize.

Act 3, Scene 2. 6. **thee the:** the. 50. **nine:** mine.

Act 3, Scene 4. 15. s.d.: [at line 14 in F, after "hither"]. 23. s.p.: **Olivia:** *Mal.* 54. s.d.: **Exeunt:** *exit.* 59. **tang:** langer. 140. **You:** Yon. 180. **thee:** the. 185. **sir. I am sure no:** sir I am sure, no. 201. **competent:** computent. 334. s.d.: **Exeunt:** *Exit.*

Act 4, Scene 2. 4. **in:** in in. 30. **clerestories:** cleere stores. 53. **sport to:** sport.

Act 4, Scene 3. 1. s.p.: **Sebastian:** [not in F] 35. s.d. [F adds *"Finis Actus Quartus"*].

Act 5, Scene 1. 165. **He's:** H'as. 179. s.d. [after line 176 in F]. 182. **He's:** has. 186. **pavane:** panyn. 190. **help? An:** helpe an. 269. **He's:** has. 366. **tiny:** tine. 383. **With hey:** *hey.*

PART TWO

Cultural Contexts

CHAPTER 1

Romance

Illyria is no one's intended destination. All of us — Viola and Sebastian, John Manningham and other members of the original audience, you and I as readers today — arrive there quite by accident, as the result of a shipwreck. Wherever we happen to be situated — on the coast of Illyria, on the benches in Middle Temple Hall, in a theater seat, in a chair by a reading lamp — act one, scene one, of *Twelfth Night* forces us to get our bearings in this strange new location. What we hear first is music. What we see first is a lover. "If music be the food of love, play on" (1.1.1): the lover's speeches turn sounds into tastes, tastes into touches, touches into sights, sights into smells. We are not on *terra firma.* An image of the sea defines our new surroundings as a place of flux and flow:

> O spirit of love, how quick and fresh art thou,
> That, notwithstanding thy capacity
> Receiveth as the sea, naught enters there,
> Of what validity and pitch soe'er,
> But falls into abatement and low price
> Even in a minute! So full of shapes is fancy
> That it alone is high fantastical. (1.1.9–15)

Here even words lose their solidity. "Pitch" is a property of waves, of value, of melody, all at once. The presiding genius of the place in which we find ourselves seems to be the Ovid of *Metamorphoses,* the poet of love and of the transformations that love works on individuals. Orsino acknowledges as much when he casts himself in the guise of one of Ovid's myths, as Actaeon to Olivia's Diana. The sight of her beauty has turned him into a hart (hear also *heart*), leaving him to be devoured by his desires "like fell and cruel hounds" (1.1.21). Ovid's version of the story occurs in *Metamorphoses* 3.155–252.

In such a place, time too is altered. Time in *Twelfth Night* is not the regular sequence of minutes, hours, days, and years that we ordinarily experience. As an artful ordering of sounds in time, music speeds things up and slows things down. So, too, does the artful ordering of phonemes in the pentameter verse that Orsino speaks: "If music be the food of love, play on. . . ." Heard in this context, "be the food" is quick, "play on" is slow. Orsino's expressed experience of time is anything but regular. First he apprehends time in seconds, as the spirit of love changes its affections "even in a minute." Next it is the life-altering before and after of his first sight of Olivia: "O, when mine eyes did see Olivia first, / Methought she purged the air of pestilence" (1.1.18–19). Then it is the long "seven years' heat" of Olivia's mourning for her brother (1.1.25). For the play's original audience time was, above all, the ritual time of Twelfth Night, the climax of twelve days of feasting, revelry, and religious observation that by its very nature was time out from the concerns of everyday life.

When in scene two Viola asks her shipwrecked fellows, "What country, friends, is this?" a name is given to a configuration of place and time that the audience has already started to experience: "Illyria" (1.2.1–2). The readiest term to describe these circumstances of time and place is *romance.* Both the root meaning of the word *romance* as something "having to do with Rome" (*Romanicus*) and its meanings today — a love affair, an emotional appeal, an improbable story of erotic desire — figure in early modern understandings of what goes on in *Twelfth Night.* Originally a romance denoted anything translated out of Latin into a vernacular language like French. The story at hand might be "the matter of Troy" or "the matter of Thebes" or "the matter of Rome." To a listener or a reader in northern Europe, all three were both exotic in location and familiar in language (Gibbs 1–27). That poise of distance and immediacy is established also in *Twelfth Night,* which is set in a distant place on the eastern shores of the Adriatic, in a land ruled by a duke with a well-known contemporary Italian name and peopled in part by folk with such thoroughly English names as Toby Belch and Andrew Aguecheek. The English that the Illyrians speak comes in two registers: the earthy immediacy of the revelers' prose and the etherial musicality of the lovers' verse. Romance has to do with dislocations in both time and place.

Like pastoral poetry, the aspect of romance most apt to strike audiences and readers today is, in Orsino's words, "high fantastical." Such a view neglects, however, the tensions between escapist fantasies and here-and-now anxieties that made romance so compelling to John Manningham and other members of the original audience. The texts in this chapter have been chosen to illustrate some of the ways in which *Twelfth Night* engages very present concerns about viewers' social status, national identity, and gender, even as it offers them an escape from the constraints of ordinary life. Let us begin with a specific example, the Middle Temple's Christmas revels of 1597–98, and then proceed to consider texts that address the two dimensions — space and time — in which *Twelfth Night* reorients watchers, listeners, and readers.

SIR BENJAMIN RUDYERD

From Le Prince d'Amour, or The Prince of Love *1660*

Sir Benjamin Rudyerd (1572–1658), a friend of John Manningham and likely a member of the audience for *Twelfth Night* at the Middle Temple in 1602, was admitted to the Temple as a law student in 1590 and called to the bar in 1600. His skills as a poet were widely appreciated — by Ben Jonson and other poetical wits who gathered in the Mermaid Tavern — but his primary reputation as a member of Parliament after 1620 was his role as a mediator between the king and the increasingly critical parliamentary majority. *Le Prince d'Amour,* Rudyerd's account of the Middle Temple Christmas revels of 1597–98, was probably written soon after the event (indeed, Rudyerd was probably the author of many of the speeches and devices it contains) but it was not printed until 1660, when it took its place in a series of books published during the Interregnum that celebrate a golden age of poetry that ended in 1642 with civil war and the execution of Charles I seven years later.[1] In those republican years between the reigns of Charles I and Charles II, the cult of chivalry was associated with the royalist cause. Earlier books of this type, such as *Musarum Deliciae* (1655), *Sportive Wit* (1656), *Parnassus Biceps* (1656), *Wit and Drollery* (1656), and *Wit Restored* (1658), print poems that had originally been passed around in manuscript by students in Oxford colleges in the 1620s and 1630s. Some of these miscellanies also include pseudo-rustic poems depicting morris dancing, church ales, and traditional holiday pastimes that had been

[1] On the 1597–98 Middle Temple revels see Arlidge and Gras.

banned by Puritan authorities after 1642.[2] Both concerns are represented in *Le Prince d'Amour, or The Prince of Love, with a Collection of Several Ingenious Poems and Songs by the Wits of the Age.* The volume collects some of the verse written by Rudyerd's contemporaries at the Temple seventy years before, even as Rudyerd's chronicle of the Christmas festivities of 1597–98 is presented as a nostalgic account of revelry that could no longer be countenanced in the 1650s. *Le Prince d'Amour* in its 1660 printing is thus itself an exercise in romance. It evokes a distant time and place where love and daring were the order of the day.

For the 1597–98 revels, law students at the Middle Temple elected one of their fun-loving contemporaries, Richard Martin (1570–1616), to preside over the forty days of festivities that stretched from Christmas to Candlemas. The Middle Temple's old tradition of electing a Lord of Misrule had been banned in 1584, along with dicing, card playing, and "outcries in the night" (Manningham 261–62), but Martin and his friends found plenty of opportunities for high spirits, as Rudyerd's account makes clear. The mock-heroic air about the whole affair is indicated by Martin's official title: "Lucius, Elius, Pulcher, Eratosthenes, Aphroditomanes, Potharcus, Erotopegniopolimarchus, Lypothumyacranter, Pomphilopolinices, Prince d'Amours, Palsgrave of Heartbroken, Duke of Suspircia, Marquess of Brainswound, Governor of Florida and Excultantia, Great Commander of all the Seas from the Streits of Genua to the Bay of Porto Desiderato, and Chief General of all Venus's Forces from Japan to Quevera by the West and from Rio des Amazones to Lapland by the North, in all people and nations that understand the language of seeing and feeling." As sportive as that may seem, Martin and his comrades were training in earnest for the very roles in diplomacy and public speaking that would occupy them as future attorneys and members of Parliament. The court of the Prince of Love was set up as a microcosm of the court of the realm, complete with a retinue of royal officials, protracted dealings with the neighboring prince of Lincoln's Inn (another of the centers for legal study), a mock tournament, a procession about the streets of London, and a series of entertainments on a royal scale — including the performance of several comedies. As Rudyerd's account indicates, evening festivities usually comprised a banquet, followed by a play, concluded with dancing or "solemn revels" involving ladies whose presence in the normally all-male household added an element of flirtation to the whole affair. Training in courtship was no less a serious business than training in public speaking and diplomacy. After being called to the bar in 1602, Martin himself went on to become a member of Parliament and the official recorder of the City of London, an office he achieved just a few months before his death, which was said to have been brought on by excessive drinking. His tomb, with a brightly painted portrait statue, still stands in Temple Church. Details about the Middle Temple's Christmas revels of 1602 do not survive, but Rudyerd's chronicle of the 1597–98 proceedings gives some idea of the romantic trappings in which plays like *Twelfth Night* were watched, relished, and remembered.

[2] On the cultural circumstances that produced these volumes see Rayler.

From *Le Prince d'Amour, or The Prince of Love*

A Brief Chronicle of the Dark Reign of the Bright Prince of Burning Love

Anno ab Aula condita the 27[3] the Lincolnians[4] (the most noble confederates with the *Medio Templarians*[5]), to bring that ancient and general league to particular feeling and affection of the gentlemen on both sides, invited the Templarians to their solemnities, entertained them with variety of music, and ended their friendly revels and discourses with a sumptuous banquet that exceeded the plentifullest vein of description. The great number of their able company occasioned in us (that took ourselves but beholders) an offer to create some one man, amongst so many worthy, to be the prince and head of all the rest. But our offer rebounded back upon us with more vehemency than it was made. Whereupon we were withdrawn into the senate house to consult further, where matters were handled by way of comparison, and it was thus and thus found that they were fitter for the multitude, we for a man and hall of capacity.

One Stradilax, a Templarian (who was in great danger to have been prince himself, if any man had thought him fit) ran down amongst them, like Laocoonardens,[6] and with a most furious and turbulent action uttered these two proverbs, the one borrowed from a smith, the other from a clown: "My masters, strike while the iron is hot," "Make hay while the sun shineth." They presently with acclamation and sound of trumpets named Signior Martino prince, promised him all their aid and furtherance, waited on him home to the Temple, and in making themselves believe he was a prince thought to have made him believe so, too. He, esteeming it rather a solemn leading to some fatal execution, fled from them. Then Stradilax stepped up upon the stone stairs in the porch of the Temple hall, from whence nothing but oysters ever opened their mouths with eloquence, and spake as followeth:

> Forasmuch as, most dear league fellows, ye are not only come down from your own house but have also taken the pains to bring us home, like the tile that doth not only fall from the roof but doth also fall to the ground, I am to tell you etc.

[3] ***Anno ab Aula condita* the 27:** in the twenty-seventh year of the hall's founding. [4] **Lincolnians:** residents of Lincoln's Inn, another of the Inns of Court. [5] ***Medio Templarians:*** residents of the Middle Temple. [6] **Laocoonardens:** Laocoön and his two sons struggling with two sea serpents, the subject of a famous Roman statuary group.

Benjamin Rudyerd, *Le Prince d'Amour, or The Prince of Love* (London: William Leake, 1660), 78–90.

But they went to bed, and so he did not tell them.

All that week was Signior Martino coninually importuned by his own friends, pressed by mighty expectation, and overborn with the stream of rumor, all which he answered more than for fashion's sake with these reasons: that other men heretofore, if they denied it, might hide their willingness under form of denial, for they for their years were unsettled, for their life not so well known as they would be, for their experience untravelled, and for their course unresolved. For his part, he rather now desired to settle his name than to spread it and thought it would be but a subject to spend his former credit upon. Only he could object to himself against all these reasons, but a gain of a more inward love of that company, which before time he had lived in, and now chosen for continuance. And that made him yield. Then were privy seals directed to all within these dominions towards the charge of this undertaking, but slowly returned. Yet notwithstanding did Stradilax make a great feast, and instead of grace after it there was a libel set up against him in all famous places of the City, as Queenhithe, Newgate, the stocks, pillory, Pissing Conduit, and (but that the Provost Marshall was his inward friend) it should not have missed Bridewell.[7]

Now did many of Signior Martino's own company forsake him, but some of them not without excuse. For one said he would willingly stay, but he must always have a care to the main chance. Another protested he would do him any service at any other time, but now he must needs go home to register his father's new year's gifts into the capon book, because the clerk was newly put away for a pre-contract with his mother's chambermaid. A third swore he would attend upon him, but his promise bound him to play the prologue at Christmas before a chine of brawn[8] at a great man's table. A fourth would needs be gone because he had no money, and his wit was not yet come to his head, nor his land to his hands. There were many more left their departure to construction.[9]

This revolt and defection notwithstanding, the hope of the Lincolnian aid kept life in our resolution, until Palmorin de Olivia, the prince's perfumer, carried a false scent in his clothes, which had like utterly to have choked the league and amity between us, but did altogether lay flat our purposes. For Signior Martino himself openly gave it over, tailors were forbidden to proceed in their work, and Stradilax had like to have lost the two shillings he delivered in earnest for a pair of pantofles.[10] Yet at the last did Signior Martino, at the earnestness of some honorable personages urging reasons of necessity, raise from the ground his own burden upon his own

[7] **Bridewell:** a prison. [8] **chine of brawn:** joint of beef. [9] **to construction:** to be inferred, to be guessed. [10] **pantofles:** slippers.

shoulders against all these difficulties, and was upheld by some of his own house that were strangers to his love, rather for the true judgement of his parts than for hope or desire of his acquaintance. Then went the tailors forward, and everyone else had more work than a tailor against Christmas, for these uncertainties made both inventions and other provisions like the tillage of Ireland, half mowed, half fallowed, half ploughed, half harrowed, half sowed, all rude.

The price of feathers during this staggering did rise and fall ten groats a day.

1. Upon Saturday at night, being Christmas Eve, Signior Martino was publicly elected Prince by the common consent of all his nobles and subjects. The Lord Chancellor made a gratulatory oration to the company. The elected Prince answered it with sweet and clear eloquence. That night the Orator presented himself in a clean ruff, and Stradilax appeared in a marmelade-color taffeta gown that was never seen after.

2. Christmas day was disposed to private meditations, the Prince resolving that all his devotions should be done rather with secret zeal than public ostentation.

3. Upon Monday night was the ceremonious inauguration and pompous coronation of the most flourishing Prince Luc. El. Pulcher Prince d'Amours with trumpets, divers sorts of rare music, and a peal of ordnance to the number of six score chambers and one gentleman's chamber broken up, which made six score and one. The Prince's title was proclaimed by the herald, justified by a champion, and excepted against[11] by a stranger knight. The fame of the Prince's entertainment drew many strangers unto his allegiance, who were received into service, rewarded with dignities, and his favor mediated peace between them and some foreign princes.

4. Tuesday night the battle between the two knights was deraigned[12] upon advice whether it were convenient the Prince should hazard all his kingdom upon the fortune of one man, which was handled by three of the council. This night Stradilax in great pomp with a left-handed truncheon[13] marshalled himself a lord, no man gainsaying it or crying "God save thy lordship" but poet Matagonius, who presented him a shield wherein was drawn the monster Sphinx — the word was *"Davus sum, non Oedipus"* ["I am David, not Oedipus"][14] — and saluted him by the name of Stradilax, to the tune of "The Tanner and the King."

[11] **excepted against:** challenged. [12] **deraigned:** set aside, cancelled. [13] **truncheon:** club. [14] ***Davus . . . Oedipus:*** motto alluding to Oedipus's solving the riddle of the Sphinx, and likely identifying Stradilax as John Davies.

5. Wednesday night there was a comedy. The Prince's officers had their charge read unto them, which the people were glad to hear.

6. Upon Thursday night there was set forth a prognostication,[15] which with great skill foretold many things that were past. The Orator made a neat tuftaffeta[16] oration, which was answered in a handsome fustian[17] speech by the Clerk of the Council, in the middle of which tuftaffeta oration the Orator took tobacco, and being charged with it in the fustian answer, at first denied it.

7. Upon Friday night there was a general fast proclaimed, suppers forbidden in the Prince's hall, except eggs in moonshine[18] and pippin pies,[19] that everyone might better prepare himself for the sacrifice of love,[20] which is usually celebrated upon the last day of every year.

8. Upon Saturday the sacrifice of love was performed, in which many misliked the confessions but few the sin. The best part of this night's show was eaten up at supper, and yet the people said there was a good masque done by eight gentlemen. Milorsius Stradilax made three confessions, for a soldier, a traveler, and a country gentleman, but two so bad that the meanest wit would not undertake to bring them in, and soldier's speech in the style of a tailor's bill or a memorandum, with *imprimis* and *items,* yet did disclaim in the night's device, because it wanted applause. Milorsius Stradilax usurped upon the commendation of all tolerable speeches, insomuch that one praising the Herald's coat, he reported that he penned it, and so far refused all matters of ill success that this night when one of the Prince's ordnance broke, he protested it was none of his project. Many found great faults with our sports because they could not come in to see the faults. This night there were six knights created of the most ancient and honorable Order of the Quiver.[21]

9. Sunday, being the first day of the new year, and the second year of the Prince's most happy reign, the hard-hearted Thames had thought to have frozen quite over, but upon better advisement it forebare, yet was it so hard that a sculler[22] in the middest of the ice was like a rat in a glazier's shop.[23] A farmer of Kingston sent down five hundred quarters of malt upon a piece of ice, which suffered shipwreck against the middle arch of the bridge and made honest small beer as far as Ratcliff.[24]

[15] **prognostication:** prophecy. [16] **tuftaffeta:** puffy (from taffeta, a fabric, that has been tufted or quilted). [17] **fustian:** inflated, bombastic. [18] **eggs in moonshine:** blancmange or custard decorated with a half-moon and stars in jelly. [19] **pippin pies:** apple pies. [20] **sacrifice of love:** an entertainment in which various characters prepare for the new year by confessing the sins they have committed in the name of love. [21] **Quiver:** arrow, with a traditional pun on arrow as penis. [22] **sculler:** boatman. [23] **glazier's shop:** shop of an installer of windowpanes. [24] **Kingston . . . the bridge . . . Ratcliff:** Kingston-upon-Thames is upriver from London, Ratcliff is downriver, and London Bridge until the eighteenth century was built on closely spaced arches.

10. Upon Monday at night there happened a comedy, and dancing, which was no wonder, and a banquet which was not looked for. There was this night a discovery of pickpurses, more fit to be put into the stocks than a chronicle, for the strangeness of their inventions. For one cut off a piece of a gentleman's left ear, and a jewel in it, with such dexterity that he never heard it. Another gentleman had his nose cut off with a ruby upon it so cunningly that until he missed his handkerchief he knew not that he had lost his nose.

11. Upon Tuesday night there came not so much as a whale up the Thames, nor a wild boar down the street. No man's purse was picked but by himself. Fabricius Spurcus shifted not his shirt because of the good service it had done him the week before. This night one had like to have commended women for their inconstancy, but he was disappointed. Therefore now let them never look to be praised for that quality.

12. Wednesday the Prince's Excellency was invited to the Lord Mayor's and expected, but he deferred his coming because of preparation for barriers and a masque to the court.

13. Thursday was also spent in the business.

14. Upon Friday, being Twelfth Day, at night there went to the court 11 knights and 11 esquires, 9 maskers, and 9 torchbearers. Their setting forth was with a peal of ordnance,[25] a noise of trumpets always sounding before them, the Herald next, and after two esquires and two knights. The knights for their upper parts in bright armor, their hose of cloth of gold and silver; the esquires in jerkins laced with gold and silver, and their hose as fair; all upon great horses, all richly furnished. Then came the maskers by couples upon velvet footcloths, their short cloaks, doublets, and hose of cloth of gold and silver of nine several colors, representing nine several passions; to every masker a torchbearer upon a footcloth carrying his device, besides a hundred torches born by servants. Never any prince in this kingdom or the like made so glorious and so rich a show. When they came to the court, the knights broke every man a lance and two swords.[26] The nine maskers like passions issued out of a heart. All was fortunately performed and received gracious commendation.

15. Upon Saturday at night there was a solemn barriers[27] by two knights challengers against all commoners in honor of the Prince's fair mistress. Cavaliero Saint George and Cavaliero de Bombardo began a quarrel in their combat, which had not so ended but that the Prince's wise care moderated their choler[28] and prevented further danger. There was a masque that night, and therefore why should it not be set down?

[25] **ordnance:** large hand-held gun. [26] **broke . . . swords:** competed three times, once with a lance and twice with a sword. [27] **barriers:** tilting, running lances across a low railing. [28] **choler:** anger.

16. Upon Sunday the Prince was invited to supper to a royal gentleman, where he was royally welcomed with great plenty of all things, but the provision of ladies fell short. Here Milorsius Stradilax, scorning the soberness of the company, fell drunk without a rival, he made a festival oration, and in his new drunkenness repeated his old comparison of pork, to the dispraise of noble women there present. Coming home he went to sleep upon a stall, where the bellman found him and delivered him to the Prince's Porter to be sent according to the superscription.[29]

17. Upon Monday was the Prince invited the second time to the Lord Mayor's, whither he went in great state, all his pensioners mounted upon great horses, his revellers upon velvet footclothes, his council next him, His Excellency last, saving the Master of the Horse, which led a spare horse behind him. His entertainment, for magnificence, bounty, and daintiness, was enough to fill a whole chronicle, but with due commendations. The streets were so slippery with the frost that many durst not ride with the Prince but stayed at home for lack of good clothes.

18. Upon Tuesday at night the Prince supped privately abroad.

19. Upon Wednesday the Prince undertook a progress[30] and visited all the corners of his court to see how his subjects were furnished with household stuff, where he found some to be well and fairly provided, many that had need of the tinker,[31] but most were not worth the mending.

20. Upon Thursday at night the Lincolnians intended to see the Prince's court, and so did all the town, which bred such disorder that the Prince could not receive them according to their worthiness nor his own desire. Upon this Milorsius Stradilax practiced factiously against the Prince and earnestly stirred enmity betwixt him and the Lincolnians.

21. Upon Friday the Lincolnians came with an ambassador, who proffered their Prince's love unto ours. There was a masque of eight gallant gentlemen gallantly apparelled, exactly performed, exceedingly commended, but not sufficiently. There was that night also an arraignment of a discontented lover. Milorsius Stradilax, made commissioner in the arraignment, puffed up with a poor-witted ambition, would needs be called Erophilus, in saucy imitation of the great Earl of the time.

22. Upon Saturday the Lincolnians were entertained with a banquet by our Prince, where our league was renewed. Thus ended our sports, and it was a wonder that they so long lasted, considering the tottering beginnings, the small comfort of a smaller number, the narrowness of time, that it passed all

[29] **superscription:** written-out address, as on a parcel. [30] **progress:** extended journey around a ruler's realm. [31] **tinker:** mender of metal.

hope to see such success raised out of such unlikelihoods, minds so straggling, as it might be praise enough for a Prince to do nothing but hold them together and to take away discontentments in unequality of employments. The Prince himself descended into all particular charges and regards and departed with much of majesty to gain somewhat of every man's love and to assure his court of a good report of strangers' entertainment.

23. Upon Candlemas night the Prince, wearied with the weight of government, made a voluntary resignation into the hands of the optimates, intending a private life, where he required the advice of his council. One advised him to follow the sea, another to land travel, a third to marry a rich widow, and a fourth to study the common law. He chose the last, and refused not the third if she stood in his way. The Prince was of face thin and lean, but of a cheerful and gracious countenance; black-haired, tall bodied, and well proportioned; of a sweet and fair conversation to every man that kept his distance. Fortune never taught him to temper his own wit or manhood. His company, commonly weaker than himself, put him into a just opinion of his own strength; of a noble and high spirit; as far from base and infamous stains as he was from want; so wise, that he knew how to make use of all his subjects, and that to their own contentment; so eloquent in ordinary speech, by extraordinary practice, and loss of too much time, that his judgement (which was good) and study could not mend it. He was very fortunate and discreet in the love of women; a great lover and complainer of good company, having more judgement to mislike than power to forebear. This Prince reigned not full forty years. He died of a common infectious disease, called opinion, upon the sixth month of Candlemas Day, and may be buried in Oblivion with his ancestors, if tongues dig him not up.

Place

Getting one's bearings in Illyria is quite literally a matter of *orientation,* of positioning oneself with respect to the East. It was the eastern and southern Mediterranean that provided the setting for most of the founding texts in the tradition of romance writing, texts like Achilles Tatius's *Clitophon and Leucippe,* Heliodorus's *Aethiopica,* and the anonymous *Apollonius of Tyre,* all from the third century C.E. Readers since the eighteenth century may have spurned these tales of love and adventure for lacking the epic pitch of Homer and Virgil, but Shakespeare and his contemporaries loved them, as witness the fact that most of them were translated into English and enjoyed frequent reprintings (see Gesnor; Wolff). Furthermore, they inspired many

Renaissance imitations, including the sources from which Shakespeare drew the plot of *Twelfth Night.* Guides to these exotic destinations — and to Italy as the point of embarkation — can be found in a number of sixteenth- and seventeenth-century English writers.

GEORGE SANDYS

From A Relation of a Journey Begun Anno Domini 1610

1615

Travel and writing distinguish the career of George Sandys (1578–1644). His journey to the Near East in 1610 was followed a decade later by a sojourn in Virginia that may have lasted ten years. While in Virginia he completed his verse translation of Ovid's *Metamorphoses,* published in three successive editions (1621, 1626, 1632). He also wrote a verse *Paraphrase upon the Psalms* (1636) and translated Hugo Grotius's Latin dramatization of *Christ's Passion* (1640). *A Relation of a Journey Begun Anno Domini 1610* chronicles Sandys' trip around the Near East. In the course of the outward voyage he stopped along the coast of Dalmatia, in modern Croatia. (See Figure 6.) His brief remarks on the region note that it was anciently called Illyria. In Sandys's own day, the region stood just at the contested border between Christendom and Islam, between Austria and the Ottoman empire. As such it occupied liminal space between "us" and "them" that can also be apprehended in Shakespeare's play with respect to sexual mores if not religion. Sandys is careful to note that the Christian inhabitants of the region were able to secure their peace only by paying tribute to the Turks.

We sailed all along in the sight of Dalmatia, which lieth between Istria and Epirus, a province of Macedon, called anciently Illyria of Illyrius the son of Cadmus,[1] afterwards Dalmatia, of the city Dalminium, and at this day Sclavonia, of the Sclavi, a people of Sarmatia, who leaving their own homes in the reign of Justinian, were planted by him in Thracia,[2] and after in the days of Mauritius and Phocas became possessors of this country. Patient they are of labor, and able of body. The meaner sort will tug lustily at an oar and are, by their sovereigns of Venice, such as remain under that state, employed to that purpose. The women marry not till the age of twenty-four, nor the men until thirty: perhaps the cause of their strength,

[1] **Cadmus:** founder of Thebes. [2] **Thracia:** Thrace, region of northern Greece.

George Sandys, *A Relation of a Journey Begun Anno Domini 1610* (London: W. Barrett, 1615), 2–3.

FIGURE 6 *Locating Illyria, from George Sandys,* A Relation of a Journey Begun Anno Domini 1610 *(1615).*

and so big proportions, or for that bred in a mountainous country, who are generally observed to oversize those that dwell on low levels. Three thousand horsemen of this country and the islands hereabout are enrolled in the Venetian militia. They dissent not from the Greek church in their religion. Throughout the north part of the world their language is understood and spoken, even from thence almost to the confines of Tartary. The men wear half-sleeved gowns of violet cloth with bonnets of the same. They nourish only a lock of hair on the crown of their heads, the rest all shaven. The women wear theirs not long and dye them black for the most part. Their chief city is Ragusa, heretofore Epidaurus, a commonwealth of itself, famous for merchandise and plenty of shipping. Many small islands belong thereunto, but little of the continent. They pay tribute to the Turk 14,000 Zecchins yearly and spend as much more upon them in gifts and entertainment, sending the Grandsignior[3] every year a ship laden with pitch for the use of his galleys. Whereby they purchase their peace and a discharge of duties throughout the Ottoman Empire.

3. **Grandsignior:** the ruler of the Turkish empire.

ROGER ASCHAM

From The Schoolmaster

1570

Tutor to Elizabeth when she was a princess and Latin secretary to her when she became queen (as he had been to her sister Queen Mary), Roger Ascham (1516–1568) is most famous today as the author of *The Schoolmaster.* This how-to manual for teachers, published two years after the author's death, advocates acquaintance with Roman civilization and literature even as it warns against travel to modern-day Italy. Ascham had himself traveled on the Continent as secretary to Sir Richard Morison, English ambassador to the emperor Charles V, but Ascham reports that he spent only nine days in Italy — and was glad of it. Shakespeare's feelings about Italy and things Italian was clearly different. As do most of his comedies, *Twelfth Night* incorporates Italian names, even if the setting itself is not Italy. Viola and Sebastian hail from "Messaline," an anglicized version of the Latin name for Marseilles, but their names ally them with Italy as surely as do the names of Orsino and Olivia. Many of the plots for Shakespeare's comedies (including *Twelfth Night*) come from Italian sources. John Manningham recognized as much when he noted that the plot of *Twelfth Night* is "most like and near to that in Italian called 'Inganni'" [the Deceived]. (See the Introduction.) There are three plays to which Manningham may be referring: one by a group of Sienese writers who called themselves the Academy of the Thunderstruck, published in 1537; one by Nicolò Secchi, first acted in 1547 and printed at Florence in 1562; and one by Curzio Gonzaga, printed in Venice in 1592. All three involve a brother and a sister who look alike, caught up in circumstances that require the sister to dress like her brother. In geographical terms, Italy, particularly Venice, was a staging ground for voyages further east, as Sandys's itinerary illustrates. (See Figure 6.)

A look at one of the images of Venice in Georg Braun and Franz Hogenberg's *Civitates Orbis Terrarum* ("Cities of the Lands of the Globe," 1606–18) shows that Venice itself is colored by this eastern aura. (See Figures 7 and 8.) Braun and Hogenberg's view of the Piazza San Marco in Venice is, literally, "oriented," as the label "Oriens" (East) proclaims at the center top. The arched openings in the basilica's façade and the placement of gesticulating people in the piazza's rectilinear space invite a comparison of the piazza with an urban stage set of the sort Sebastiano Serlio describes in his *Architettura* (1545) and that Palladio had built in the Teatro Olimpico at Vicenza (1585).[1] Indeed, some sort of theatrical performance seems to be going on in front of the mechanical clock in the upper left of the piazza. Most prominent among the piazza's personages are three ladies in the foreground. Their accoutrements of fans and feathers, their half-bared bosoms and unmasked faces, and their lack of male escorts suggest that the figures are in fact three of the courtesans for which Venice was famous — visible testimony to Ascham's claim that Italy seduced unwary Englishmen with "all the enchantments of Circe" (see p. 132). In addition to the domes of the basilica, the eastern atmosphere of the whole scene is embodied in three pairs of strolling male figures, one of whom is dressed in familiar European clothes, the other in robes with a turban. (See the detail in Figure 8.) The Italy of Shakespeare's comedies was, in Ascham's sober judgment, a place of danger on religious, social, political, and sexual fronts. As such, it was a place of special danger to young men the age of John Manningham and others in the original audience of *Twelfth Night.* (See Introduction.) For young Englishmen unable to go to Italy in person, the booksellers' stalls of London offered collections of tales translated from Italian. Ascham recognizes the similar appeal between these books and medieval romances like *Morte D'Arthur.* For him there is just one difference: the Italian tales are ten times more dangerous.

[1]On these designs see Smith, *Ancient Scripts,* 84–89.

From *The Schoolmaster*

The Bringing-up of Youth

. . . Time was when Italy and Rome have been, to the great good of us that now live, the best breeders and bringers-up of the worthiest men, not only for wise speaking, but also for well-doing, in all civil affairs, that ever was in the world. But now that time is gone and, though the place remain, yet the

Roger Ascham, *The Schoolmaster* (1570), ed. Lawrence V. Ryan (Ithaca: Cornell University Press for the Folger Shakespeare Library, 1967), 59–72.

FIGURE 7 *Looking East in the Piazza San Marco, Venice, from Georg Braun and Franz Hogenberg,* Civitates Orbis Terrarum *(1606–08).*

FIGURE 8 *Looking East in the Piazza San Marco, Venice (Detail) from Georg Braun and Franz Hogenberg,* Civitates Orbis Terrarum *(1606–08).*

old and present manners do differ as far as black and white, as virtue and vice. Virtue once made that country mistress over all the world. Vice now maketh that country slave to them that before were glad to serve it. All men seeth it; they themselves confess it, namely, such as be best and wisest amongst them. For sin, by lust and vanity, hath and doth breed up everywhere common contempt of God's word, private contention in many families, open factions in every city, and so, making themselves bond to vanity and vice at home, they are content to bear the yoke of serving strangers abroad. Italy now is not that Italy that it was wont to be and therefore now not so fit a place as some do count it for young men to fetch either wisdom or honesty from thence. For surely they will make other but bad scholars that be so ill masters to themselves. Yet if a gentleman will needs travel into Italy, he shall do well to look on the life of the wisest traveler that ever traveled thither, set out by the wisest writer that ever spake with tongue (God's doctrine only excepted), and that is Ulysses in Homer. Ulysses and his travel, I wish our travelers to look upon, not so much to fear them with the great dangers that he many times suffered as to instruct them with his excellent wisdom, which he always and everywhere used. Yea, even those that be learned and witty travelers, when they be disposed to praise traveling, as a great commendation and the best scripture they have for it, they gladly recite the third verse of Homer in his first book of *Odyssea,* containing a great praise of Ulysses for the wit he gathered and wisdom he used in his traveling. . . .

And yet is not Ulysses commended so much nor so oft in Homer because he was πολὺτροπος, that is, skillful in many men's manners and fashions, as because he was πολὺμητις, that is, wise in all purposes and ware in all places; which wisdom and wariness will not serve neither a traveler except Pallas[2] be always at his elbow, that is, God's special grace from heaven, to keep him in God's fear in all his doings, in all his journey. For he shall not always, in his absence out of England, light upon a gentle Alcinous[3] and walk in his fair gardens full of all harmless pleasures, but he shall sometimes fall either into the hands of some cruel Cyclops[4], or into the lap of some wanton and dallying Dame Calypso,[5] and so suffer the danger of many a deadly den, not so full of perils to destroy the body as full of vain pleasures to poison the mind. Some Siren shall sing him a song, sweet in tune, but sounding in the end to his utter destruction. If Scylla drown him not, Charybdis[6] may fortune[7] swallow him. Some Circe[8] shall make him, of a plain Englishman, a right Italian. . . .

If some yet do not well understand what is an Englishman Italianated, I will plainly tell him: he that by living and traveling in Italy bringeth home into England out of Italy the religion, the learning, the policy, the experience, the manners of Italy. That is to say, for religion, papistry or worse; for learning, less, commonly, than they carried out with them; for policy, a factious heart, a discoursing head, a mind to meddle in all men's matters; for experience, plenty of new mischiefs never known in England before; for manners, variety of vanities and change of filthy living. These be the enchantments of Circe brought out of Italy to mar men's manners in England: much by example of ill life but more by precepts of fond books, of late translated out of Italian into English, sold in every shop in London, commended by honest titles the sooner to corrupt honest manners, dedicated overboldly to virtuous and honorable personages, the easilier to beguile simple and innocent wits. It is pity that those which have authority and charge to allow and disallow books to be printed be no more circumspect herein than they are. Ten sermons at Paul's Cross[9] do not so much good for moving men to true doctrine as one of those books do harm with enticing men to ill-living. . . . Yea, I say farther, those books tend not so much to corrupt honest living as they do to subvert true religion. More papists be made by your merry books of Italy than by your earnest books of Louvain. . . .

In our forefathers' time, when papistry as a standing pool covered and overflowed all England, few books were read in our tongue, saving certain

[2] **Pallas:** Athena. [3] **Alcinous:** king who sheltered the shipwrecked Ulysses. [4] **Cyclops:** giant one-eyed cannibal who imprisoned Ulysses. [5] **Calypso:** nymph with whom Ulysses fell in love. [6] **Scylla . . . Charybdis:** whirlpools in the straits between Italy and Sicily. [7] **fortune:** happen to. [8] **Circe:** enchantress who turned men into swine. [9] **Paul's Cross:** outdoor pulpit outside St. Paul's Cathedral.

books of chivalry, as they said, for pastime and pleasure, which, as some say, were made in monasteries by idle monks or wanton canons; as one for example, *Morte D'Arthur,* the whole pleasure of which book standeth in two special points — in open manslaughter and bold bawdry; in which book those be counted the noblest knights that do kill most men without any quarrel and commit foulest adulteries by subtlest shifts: as Sir Lancelot with the wife of King Arthur his master, Sir Tristram with the wife of King Mark his uncle, Sir Lamorak with the wife of King Lot that was his own aunt. This is good stuff for wise men to laugh at or honest men to take pleasure at. Yet I know when God's Bible was banished the court and *Morte D'Arthur* received into the prince's chamber. What toys[10] the daily reading of such a book may work in the will of a young gentleman or a young maid that liveth wealthily and idly, wise men can judge and honest men do pity. And yet ten *Morte D'Arthurs* do not the tenth part so much harm as one of these books made in Italy and translated in England. . . .

I was once in Italy myself, but, I thank God, my abode there was but nine days. And yet I saw in that little time, in one city, more liberty to sin than ever I heard tell of in our noble city of London in nine year.

[10] **toys:** fantastic or wanton notions.

BARNABY RICH

From Barnaby Rich His Farewell to the Military Profession

1581

Although the Italian plays called *Gli Ingannati* provided the ultimate inspiration for the plot of *Twelfth Night,* Shakespeare's more immediate source was a collection of stories written by Barnaby Rich (1542–1617), an army captain whose fighting career took him to Ireland, Le Havre, and the Netherlands. At age thirty-six Rich took up the pen at the suggestion of his friends Thomas Churchyard, George Gascoigne, and Thomas Lodge — professional writers all three — and produced, among other things, the collection of stories he styled his "farewell to the military profession." An entry in the register of the Stationers' Company suggests that the first edition of 1581 may have been followed by a second in 1591, ten years before Shakespeare took up one of the stories for *Twelfth Night.*[1] It is always interesting to read Shakespeare's sources, to see what he chose to emphasize, what to leave out, what to add, but Rich's book is even

[1]Full discussions of the sources of *Twelfth Night* are offered by Muir, 132–40, and Bullough, 2: 269–85.

more interesting, since it sets in place some major ideas about romance in Renaissance culture. *His Farewell to the Military Profession* presents itself as one of the pernicious books that Ascham so abhorred.

All the key elements of romance are present in Rich's second tale, "Of Apolonius and Silla": a voyage to exotic distant places, the framing of events in time, the exclusion of all motives but love, the flirtation with sexual mores other than those of one's own country, the happenstances that bring about a happy ending against expectations. The place of romance in this case is even further east than Illyria. After serving in wars against the Turks, the Orsino figure is driven by a storm to Cyprus, where the Viola figure falls in love with him. Donning the clothing of her brother and taking on his identity, she follows the Orsino figure to Constantinople, where the Olivia figure duly falls in love with her in her male disguise. Cyprus, Constantinople, Illyria: the fascinating otherness of these places can be witnessed in Figure 9, which shows clothing worn by men and women in the lands east of Venice during the years of Shakespeare's youth. The arrival of the Viola figure's brother in Constantinople leads to the revelation of true identities and to two marriages — but not before the Sebastian figure has been seduced by the Olivia figure and impregnated her. The interplay between West and East in this story is heightened by Rich's note that the events took place in time past, when "the famous city of Constantinople remained in the hands of the Christians," before the city fell to the Turks in 1453 (see p. 137). Time past is also time fast. Apologizing for the philosophical reflections about love and deserving that open his story, Rich promises to write thereafter "with such celerity as the matter that I pretend to pen may in any wise permit me" (see p. 137) and indeed several times appeals to his readers' own sense of urgency.

The readers whom Rich addresses in these frequent asides are specifically women: "Gentlewomen, according to my promise, I will here for brevity's sake omit to make repetition of the long and dolorous discourse" that Silla, the Viola

FIGURE 9 *Eastern Apparel, from Abraham de Bruyn,* Omnium Gentium Habitus *(1581).*

figure, made when the Orsino figure had left Cyprus, "knowing you to be as tenderly hearted as Silla herself, whereby you may the better conjecture the fury of her fever" (see p. 138). Rich's *Farewell to the Military Profession* begins, in fact, with three epistles to three kinds of readers. Women come first: "To the right courteous gentlewomen, both of England and Ireland, Barnaby Rich wisheth all things they should have appertaining to their honor, estimation, and all other honest delights" (Rich 124). Mars has been left behind, Rich tells the "gentlewomen" who take his book in hand; now, in his "riper years," all he desires is "to live in peace amongst women and to consecrate myself wholly unto Venus" (123). His second epistle, "To the Noble Soldiers both of England and Ireland," shows Rich to be very skittish indeed about taking up love as a subject, as if doing so will call his masculinity into question:

> Herein I do but follow the course of the world, for many nowadays go about by a great device as may be how they might become women themselves. How many gentlemen shall you see at this present date that, I dare undertake, in the wearing of their apparel, in the setting of their ruffs and the frizzling of their hair, are more newfangled and foolish than any courtesan of Venice. (128)

The gender anxieties of the second epistle become social anxieties in the third epistle, "To the Readers in General," as Rich begs pardon in advance for any "indecent" words and terms that his subject might lead him to use (135).

All of Rich's anxieties about romance are carried over into *Twelfth Night*. Rich's catalogue, in his epistle to "courteous gentlewomen," of all the dances he *cannot* do perhaps inspires Sir Andrew's boast about all the dances he *can* do, including the "back-trick" in a galliard (1.3.97–101). Above all, Rich's anxieties about effeminization seem to be registered in Orsino, a man who languishes *like* a woman in his love *for* a woman. "High fantastical" it may be, but the romance of *Twelfth Night* addresses anxieties about self-identity that were of immediate concern to young men like John Manningham and the other young men who saw the play at Middle Temple Hall in February 1602: they were all still unmarried,

still unsure of their future prospects as adult men. In an exotic world where the rules are different — or where there seem to be no rules at all — one can become, for the space and time of the play, someone else. One question remains: How does one get home?

From *Barnaby Rich His Farewell to the Military Profession*

Of Apolonius and Silla

The Argument of the Second History

Apolonius, duke, having spent a year's service in the wars against the Turk, returning homeward with his company by sea, was driven by force of weather to the isle of Cyprus, where he was well-received by Pontus governor of the same isle, with whom Silla, daughter to Pontus, fell so strangely in love that after Apolonius was departed to Constantinople, Silla with one man followed, and coming to Constantinople she served Apolonius in the habit of a man, and after many pretty accidents falling out, she was known to Apolonius, who, in requital of her love, married her.

There is no child that is born into this wretched world but before it doth suck the mother's milk it taketh first a sup[2] of the cup of error, which maketh us when we come to riper years not only to enter into actions of injury, but many times to stray from that is right and reason. But in all other things wherein we shew ourselves to be most drunken with this poisoned cup, it is in our actions of love, for the lover is so estranged from what is right and wandereth so wide from the bounds of reason that he is not able to deem white from black, good from bad, virtue from vice, but only led by the appetite of his own affections, and grounding them on the foolishness of his own fancies, will so settle his liking on such a one as either by desert or unworthiness will merit rather to be loathed than loved.

If a question might be asked, "what is the ground indeed of reasonable love whereby the knot is knit of true and perfect friendship?" I think those that be wise would answer, "desert," that is, where the party beloved doth requite us with the like. For otherwise, if the bare show of beauty or the comeliness of personage might be sufficient to confirm us in our love, those

[2] **sup:** sip.

Barnaby Rich, *Barnaby Rich His Farewell to the Military Profession* (1581), ed. Donald Beecher (Ottawa: Doverhouse Editions, 1992), 180–201.

that be accustomed to go to fairs and markets might sometimes fall in love with twenty in a day; desert must then be, of force, the ground of reasonable love, for to love them that hate us, to follow them that fly from us, to fawn on them that frown on us, to curry favor with them that disdain us, to be glad to please them that care not how they offend us — who will not confess this to be an erroneous love, neither grounded upon wit nor reason? Wherefore, right courteous gentlewomen, if it please you with patience to peruse this history following, you shall see Dame Error so play her part with a leash[3] of lovers, a male and two females, as shall work a wonder to your wise judgment in noting the effect of their amorous devices and conclusions of their actions: the first, neglecting the love of a noble dame, young, beautiful and fair, who only for his good will[4] played the part of a serving man, contented to abide any manner of pain only to behold him; he again setting his love of a dame that, despising him — being a noble duke — gave herself to a serving man, as she had thought, but it otherwise fell out, as the substance of this tale shall better describe. And because I have been something tedious in my first discourse, offending your patient ears with the hearing of a circumstance overlong, from henceforth that which I mind to write shall be done with such celerity as the matter that I pretend to pen may in any wise permit me, and thus followeth the history.

During the time that the famous city of Constantinople remained in the hands of the Christians, amongst many other noblemen that kept their abiding in that flourishing city there was one whose name was Apolonius, a worthy duke, who, being but a very young man and even then new come to his possessions, which were very great, levied a mighty band of men at his own proper charges with whom he served against the Turk during the space of one whole year, in which time, although it were very short, this young duke so behaved himself — as well by prowess and valiance showed with his own hands as otherwise by his wisdom and liberality used towards his soldiers — that all the world was filled with the fame of this noble duke. When he had thus spent one year's service, he caused his trumpet to sound a retreat, and gathering his company together and embarking themselves he set sail, holding his course towards Constantinople. But being upon the sea, by the extremity of a tempest which suddenly fell, his fleet was dissevered, some one way and some another; but he himself recovered the isle of Cyprus where he was worthily received by Pontus, duke and governor of the same isle, with whom he lodged while his ships were new repairing.

This Pontus that was lord and governor of this famous isle was an ancient duke and had two children, a son and a daughter. His son was

[3] **leash:** a brace and a half of hunting dogs, i.e., three. [4] **good will:** i.e., to gain his favor.

named Silvio, of whom hereafter we shall have further occasion to speak, but at this instant he was in the parts of Africa serving in the wars.

The daughter her name was Silla, whose beauty was so peerless that she had the sovereignty amongst all other dames, as well for her beauty as for the nobleness of her birth. This Silla, having heard of the worthiness of Apolonius, this young duke, who besides his beauty and good graces had a certain natural allurement, that being now in his company in her father's court, she was so strangely attached[5] with the love of Apolonius that there was nothing might content her but his presence and sweet sight. And although she saw no manner of hope to attain to that she most desired, knowing Apolonius to be but a guest and ready to take the benefit of the next wind and to depart into a strange country, whereby she was bereaved of all possibility ever to see him again, and therefore strived with herself to leave her fondness, but all in vain — it would not be, but like the fowl which is once limed,[6] the more she striveth, the faster she tieth herself.

So Silla was now constrained, perforce[7] her will, to yield to love; wherefore from time to time she used so great familiarity with him as her honor might well permit, and fed him with such amorous baits as the modesty of a maid could reasonably afford, which when she perceived did take but small effect, feeling herself so much outraged with the extremity of her passion, by the only countenance that she bestowed upon Apolonius it might have been well perceived that the very eyes pleaded unto him for pity and remorse. But Apolonius, coming but lately from out the field from the chasing of his enemies, and his fury not yet thoroughly dissolved nor purged from his stomach, gave no regard to those amorous enticements which, by reason of his youth, he had not been acquainted withal. But his mind ran more to hear his pilots bring news of a merry wind to serve his turn to Constantinople, which in the end came very prosperously; and giving Duke Pontus hearty thanks for his great entertainment, taking his leave of himself and the lady Silla his daughter, departed with his company and with a happy gale arrived at his desired port.

Gentlewomen, according to my promise, I will here for brevity's sake omit to make repetition of the long and dolorous discourse recorded by Silla for this sudden departure of her Apolonius, knowing you to be as tenderly hearted as Silla herself, whereby you may the better conjecture the fury of her fever.

But Silla, the further that she saw herself bereaved of all hope ever any more to see her beloved Apolonius, so much the more contagious were her

[5] **attached:** seized, taken. [6] **limed:** trapped on a stick smeared with lime. [7] **perforce:** in spite of.

passions, and made the greater speed to execute that she had premeditated in her mind, which was this: amongst many servants that did attend upon her there was one whose name was Pedro, who had a long time waited upon her in her chamber, whereby she was well-assured of his fidelity and trust; to that Pedro, therefore, she bewrayed[8] first the fervency of her love borne to Apolonius, conjuring him in the name of the goddess of love herself and binding him by the duty that a servant ought to have that tendereth his mistress' safety and good liking, and desiring him with tears trickling down her cheeks that he would give his consent to aid and assist her in that she had determined, which was — for that she was fully resolved to go to Constantinople where she might again take the view of her beloved Apolonius — that he, according to the trust she had reposed in him, would not refuse to give his consent secretly to convey her from out her father's court according as she would give him direction, and also to make himself partaker of her journey and to wait upon her till she had seen the end of her determination.

Pedro, perceiving with what vehemency his lady and mistress had made request unto him, albeit he saw many perils and doubts depending in her pretence,[9] notwithstanding, gave his consent to be at her disposition, promising her to further her with his best advice and to be ready to obey whatsoever she would please to command him. The match[10] being thus agreed upon and all things prepared in a readiness for their departure, it happened there was a galley of Constantinople ready to depart, which Pedro understanding, came to the captain desiring him to have passage for himself and for a poor maid that was his sister which were bound to Constantinople upon certain urgent affairs — to which request the captain granted, willing him to prepare[11] aboard with all speed because the wind served him presently to depart.

Pedro now coming to his mistress and telling her how he had handled the matter with the captain, she liking very well of the device, disguising herself into very simple attire, stole away from out her father's court and came with Pedro, whom now she calleth brother, aboard the galley, where all things being in readiness and the wind serving very well, they launched forth with their oars and set sail. . . .

[The captain of the vessel attempts to seduce Silla, who sees suicide as her only escape. Just as she is about to kill herself, a storm arises.]

This storm continued all that day and the next night, and they, being driven to put romer[12] before the wind to keep the galley ahead the billow,

[8] **bewrayed:** revealed. [9] **depending in her pretence:** relating to her plan. [10] **match:** appointment; bargain. [11] **prepare:** repair, go. [12] **romer:** either to trim the sails, or allow to be driven by the wind, or to use a sea anchor to keep the ship properly oriented to the wind.

were driven upon the main shore where the galley brake all to pieces; there was every man providing to save his own life: some got upon hatches, boards, and casks, and were driven with the waves to and fro; but the greatest number were drowned, amongst the which Pedro was one. But Silla herself being in the cabin, as you have heard, took hold of a chest that was the captain's, the which by the only providence of God brought her safe to the shore; the which when she had recovered, not knowing what was become of Pedro her man, she deemed that both he and all the rest had been drowned for that she saw nobody upon the shore but herself.

Wherefore, when she had awhile made great lamentations, complaining her mishaps, she began in the end to comfort herself with the hope that she had to see her Apolonius, and found such means that she brake open the chest that brought her to land, wherein she found good store of coin, and sundry suits of apparel that were the captain's. And now, to prevent a number of injuries that might be proffered to a woman that was left in her case, she determined to leave her own apparel and to sort herself into some of those suits, that, being taken for a man, she might pass through the country in the better safety. And as she changed her apparel, she thought it likewise convenient to change her name, wherefore, not readily happening of any other, she called herself Silvio, by the name of her own brother whom you have heard spoken of before.

In this manner she travelled to Constantinople where she inquired out the palace of the Duke Apolonius, and thinking herself now to be both fit and able to play the servingman, she presented herself to the duke, craving his service. The duke, very willing to give succor unto strangers, perceiving him to be a proper smug[13] young man, gave him entertainment. Silla thought herself now more than satisfied for all the casualties that had happened unto her in her journey, that she might at her pleasure take but the view of the Duke Apolonius, and above the rest of his servants was very diligent and attendant upon him, the which the duke perceiving, began likewise to grow into good liking with the diligence of his man, and therefore made him one of his chamber. Who but Silvio then was most neat[14] about him, in helping of him to make him ready in a morning, in the setting of his ruffs, in the keeping of his chamber? Silvio pleased his master so well that above all the rest of his servants about him, he had the greatest credit, and the duke put him most in trust.

At this very instant there was remaining in the city a noble dame, a widow, whose husband was but lately deceased, one of the noblest men that were in the parts of Greece, who left his lady and wife large possessions and

[13] **smug:** neat and trim. [14] **neat:** skillful and precise.

great livings. This lady's name was called Julina, who, besides the abundance of her wealth and the greatness of her revenues, had likewise the sovereignty of all the dames of Constantinople for her beauty. To this lady Julina Apolonius became an earnest suitor, and according to the manner of wooers, besides fair words, sorrowful sighs, and piteous countenances, there must be sending of loving letters, chains, bracelets, brooches, rings, tablets, gems, jewels, and presents — I know not what. So my duke, who in the time that he remained in the isle of Cyprus had no skill at all in the art of love, although it were more than half proffered unto him, was now become a scholar in love's school and had already learned his first lesson, that is, to speak pitifully, to look ruthfully, to promise largely, to serve diligently, and to please carefully. Now he was learning his second lesson, that is, to reward liberally, to give bountifully, to present willingly, and to write lovingly. Thus Apolonius was so busied in his new study that I warrant you there was no man that could challenge him for playing the truant, he followed his profession with so good a will. And who must be the messenger to carry the tokens and love letters to the lady Julina but Silvio his man; in him the duke reposed his only confidence to go between him and his lady.

Now gentlewomen, do you think there could have been a greater torment devised wherewith to afflict the heart of Silla than herself to be made the instrument to work her own mishap and to play the attorney in a cause that made so much against herself? But Silla, altogether desirous to please her master, cared nothing at all to offend herself, followed his business with so good a will as if it had been in her own preferment.

Julina, now having many times taken the gaze of this young youth Silvio, perceiving him to be of such excellent perfect grace, was so entangled with the often sight of this sweet temptation that she fell into as great a liking with the man as the master was with herself. And on a time Silvio, being sent from his master with a message to the lady Julina, as he began very earnestly to solicit in his master's behalf, Julina interrupting him in his tale, said:

"Silvio, it is enough that you have said for your master; from henceforth either speak for yourself or say nothing at all."

Silla, abashed to hear these words, began in her mind to accuse the blindness of love, that Julina, neglecting the good will of so noble a duke, would prefer her love unto such a one as nature itself had denied to recompense her liking.

And now for a time leaving matters depending,[15] as you have heard, it fell out that the right Silvio indeed — whom you have heard spoken of before, the brother of Silla — was come to his father's court into the isle of

[15] **depending:** suspended.

Cyprus, where, understanding that his sister was departed in manner as you have heard, conjectured that the very occasion did proceed of some liking had between Pedro her man — that was missing with her — and herself. But Silvio, who loved his sister as dearly as his own life, and the rather for that as she was his natural sister both by father and mother — so the one of them was so like the other in countenance and favor that there was no man able to discern one from the other by their faces, saving by their apparel, the one being a man, the other a woman — Silvio therefore vowed to his father not only to seek out his sister Silla, but also to revenge the villainy which he conceived in Pedro for the carrying away of his sister. And thus departing, having travelled though many cities and towns without hearing any manner of news of those he went to seek for, at the last he arrived at Constantinople, where, as he was walking in an evening for his own recreation on a pleasant green yard without the walls of the city, he fortuned to meet with the lady Julina, who likewise had been abroad to take the air. And as she suddenly cast her eyes upon Silvio, thinking him to be her old acquaintance by reason they were so like one another as you have heard before, said unto him:

"Sir Silvio, if your haste be not the greater, I pray you let me have a little talk with you, seeing I have so luckily met you in this place."

Silvio, wondering to hear himself so rightly named, being but a stranger not of above two days' continuance in the city, very courteously came towards her, desirous to hear what she would say.

Julina, commanding her train something to stand back, said as followeth: "Seeing my good will and friendly love hath been the only cause to make me so prodigal to offer that I see is so lightly rejected, it maketh me to think that men be of this condition, rather to desire those things which they cannot come by than to esteem or value of that which both largely and liberally is offered unto them; but if the liberality of my proffer[16] hath made to seem less the value of the thing that I meant to present, it is but in your own conceit,[17] considering how many noble men there hath been here before, and be yet at this present, which hath both served, sued, and most humbly entreated to attain that which to you of myself I have freely offered, and I perceive is despised or at the least very lightly regarded."

Silvio, wondering at these words, but more amazed that she could so rightly call him by his name, could not tell what to make of her speeches, assuring himself that she was deceived and did mistake him, did think, notwithstanding, it had been a point of great simplicity[18] if he should forsake that which fortune had so favorably proffered unto him, perceiving by

[16] **liberality of my proffer:** generosity of my offer. [17] **conceit:** opinion, fancy. [18] **great simplicity:** lack of intelligence or judgment.

her train that she was some lady of great honor, and viewing the perfection of her beauty and the excellency of her grace and countenance did think it impossible that she should be despised, and therefore answered thus:

"Madam, if before this time I have seemed to forget myself in neglecting your courtesy which so liberally you have meant unto me, please it you to pardon what is past, and from this day forwards Silvio remaineth ready prest[19] to make such reasonable amends as his ability may any ways permit, or as it shall please you to command."

Julina, the gladdest woman that might be to hear these joyful news, said: "Then, my Silvio, see you fail not tomorrow at night to sup with me at my own house where I will discourse further with you what amends you shall make me."

To which request Silvio gave his glad consent, and thus they departed very well pleased. And as Julina did think the time very long till she had reaped the fruit of her desire, so Silvio, he wished for harvest before corn could grow, thinking the time as long till he saw how matters would fall out. But not knowing what lady she might be, he presently — before Julina was out of sight — demanded of one that was walking by what she was and how she was called, who satisfied Silvio in every point, and also in what part of the town her house did stand whereby he might inquire it out.

Silvio, thus departing to this lodging, passed the night with very unquiet sleep, and the next morning his mind ran so much of his supper that he never cared neither for his breakfast nor dinner; and the day, to his seeming, passed away so slowly that he had thought the stately steeds had been tired that draw the chariot of the sun, or else some other Joshua had commanded them again to stand, and wished that Phaethon had been there with a whip.

Julina, on the other side, she had thought the clock-setter had played the knave, the day came no faster forwards; but six o'clock being once struck, recovered comfort to both parties, and Silvio hastening himself to the palace of Julina, where by her he was friendly welcomed, and a sumptuous supper being made ready, furnished with sundry sorts of delicate dishes, they sat them down, passing the supper time with amorous looks, loving countenances, and secret glances conveyed from the one to the other, which did better satisfy them than the feeding of their dainty dishes.

Supper time being thus spent, Julina did think it very unfitly[20] if she should turn Silvio to go seek his lodging in an evening, desired him therefore that he would take a bed in her house for that night; and bringing him up into a fair chamber that was very richly furnished, she found such means that when all the rest of her household servants were abed and quiet, she

[19] **ready prest:** prepared, at hand. [20] **unfitly:** inappropriate.

came herself to bear Silvio company, where concluding upon conditions that were in question between them, they passed the night with such joy and contentation as might in that convenient time be wished for, but only that Julina, feeding too much of some one dish above the rest, received a surfeit whereof she could not be cured in forty weeks after, a natural inclination in all women which are subject to longing and want the reason to use a moderation in their diet. But the morning approaching, Julina took her leave and conveyed herself into her own chamber; and when it was fair daylight, Silvio making himself ready departed likewise about his affairs in the town, debating with himself how things had happened, being well assured that Julina had mistaken him, and therefore, for fear of further evils, determined to come no more there, but took his journey towards other places in the parts of Greece to see if he could learn any tidings of his sister Silla.

The Duke Apolonius, having made a long suit and never a whit the nearer of his purpose, came to Julina to crave her direct answer, either to accept of him and of such conditions as he proffered unto her, or else to give him his last farewell.

Julina, as you have heard, had taken an earnest penny[21] of another, whom she had thought had been Silvio the duke's man, was at a controversy in herself what she might do. One while she thought, seeing her occasion served so fit, to crave the duke's good will for the marrying of his man. Then again she could not tell what displeasure the duke would conceive in that she should seem to prefer his man before himself, did think it therefore best to conceal the matter till she might speak with Silvio to use his opinion how these matters should be handled. . . .

[When the duke comes to Julina's house to press his suit, she confides that she is promised to another suitor, and asks the duke permission to marry that suitor. The duke refuses. While the duke is in Julina's house, Julina's servants tell the duke's servants how much more familiar and courteous Julina has been to Silvio than she is to the duke. The duke hears about the gossip and concludes the other suitor could only be Silvio.]

Poor Silvio, having got intelligence by some of his fellows what was the cause that the duke his master did bear such displeasure unto him, devised all the means he could, as well by mediation by his fellows as otherwise by petitions and supplication to the duke that he would suspend his judgment till perfect proof were had in the matter, and then if any manner of thing did fall out against him whereby the duke had cause to take any grief, he would confess himself worthy not only of imprisonment, but also of most vile and

[21] **earnest penny:** money paid to seal a bargain, a down payment.

shameful death; with these petitions he daily plied the duke, but all in vain, for the duke thought he had made so good proof that he was thoroughly confirmed in his opinion against his man.

But the lady Julina, wondering what made Silvio that he was so slack in his visitation and why he absented himself so long from her presence, began to think that all was not well. But in the end, perceiving no decoction[22] her former surfeit received as you have heard, and finding in herself an unwonted swelling in her belly, assuring herself to be with child, fearing to become quite bankrupt of her honor, did think it more than time to seek out a father, and made such secret search and diligent inquiry that she learned the truth how Silvio was kept in prison by the duke his master. And minding to find a present remedy, as well as for the love she bare to Silvio as for the maintenance of her credit, and estimation, she speedily hasted to the palace of the duke. . . .

[Julina pleads with the duke to release Silvio from prison, since it was she who chose Silvio and not the other way around. Silvio is sent for. He protests, "I have not otherwise used myself than according to the bond and duty of a servant, that is both willing and desirous to further his master's suits." In response, Julina claims Silvio as "my husband by plighted faith." Silvio denies everything. Julina then reveals that she is pregnant with Silvio's child.]

I pray you gentlewomen, was not this a foul oversight of Julina, that would so precisely swear so great an oath that she was gotten with child by one that was altogether unfurnished with implements for such a turn? For God's love take heed, and let this be an example to you, when you be with child, how you swear who is the father before you have had good proof and knowledge of the party, for men be so subtle and full of sleight that, God knoweth, a woman may quickly be deceived.

But now to return to our Silvio, who, hearing an oath sworn so divinely that he had gotten a woman with child, was like to believe that it had been true in very deed; but remembering his own impediment thought it impossible that he should commit such an act, and therefore half in a chafe, he said:

"What law is able to restrain the foolish indiscretion of a woman that yieldeth herself to her own desires? What shame is able to bridle or withdraw her from her mind and madness, or with what snaffle[23] is it possible to hold her back from the execution of her filthiness? But what abomination is this, that a lady of such a house should so forget the greatness of her estate,

[22] **decoction:** reduction. [23] **snaffle:** a simple bridle.

the alliance whereof she is descended, the nobility of her deceased husband, and maketh no conscience to shame and slander herself with such a one as I am, being so far unfit and unseemly for her degree. But how horrible is it to hear the name of God so defaced, that we make no more account but for the maintenance of our mischiefs, we fear no whit at all to forswear His holy name, as though He were not in all His dealings most righteous, true, and just, and will not only lay open our leasings[24] to the world, but will likewise punish the same with most sharp and bitter scourges."

Julina, not able to endure him to proceed any farther in his sermon, was already surprised with a vehement grief, began bitterly to cry out uttering these speeches following:

"Alas, is it possible that the sovereign justice of God can abide a mischief so great and cursed? Why may I not now suffer death rather than the infamy which I see to wander before mine eyes? Oh happy and more than right happy had I been if inconstant fortune had not devised this treason wherein I am surprised and caught. Am I thus become to be entangled with snares, and in the hands of him who, enjoying the spoils of my honor, will openly deprive me of my fame by making me a common fable to all posterity in time to come? Ah, traitor and discourteous wretch, is this the recompense of the honest and firm amity which I have borne thee? Wherein have I deserved this discourtesy? By loving thee more than thou art able to deserve? Is it I, arrant thief, is it I upon whom thou thinkest to work thy mischiefs? Doest thou think me no better worth but that thou mayest prodigally waste my honor at thy pleasure? Didst thou dare to adventure upon me, having thy conscience wounded with so deadly a treason? Ah, unhappy and above all other most unhappy, that have so charily[25] preserved mine honor, and now am made a prey to satisfy a young man's lust that hath coveted nothing but the spoil of my chastity and good name."

Herewithal the tears so gushed down her cheeks that she was not able to open her mouth to use any further speech.

The duke, who stood all this while and heard this whole discourse, was wonderfully moved with compassion towards Julina, knowing that from her infancy she had ever honorably used herself that there was no man able to detect[26] her of any misdemeanor otherwise than beseemed a lady of her estate. Wherefore being fully resolved that Silvio his man had committed this villainy against her, in a great fury drawing his rapier, he said unto Silvio:

"How canst thou, arrant thief, show thyself so cruel and careless to such as do thee honor? Hast thou so little regard of such a noble lady as humbleth

[24] **leasings:** lies, falsehoods. [25] **charily:** carefully, cautiously. [26] **detect:** accuse.

herself to such a villain as thou art, who, without any respect either of her renown or noble estate, canst be content to seek the wrack and utter ruin of her honor? But frame thyself to make such satisfaction as she requireth — although I know, unworthy wretch, that thou art not able to make her the least part of amends — or I swear by God that thou shall not escape the death which I will minister to thee with my own hands, and therefore advise thee well what thou doest."

Silvio, having heard this sharp sentence, fell down on his knees before the duke, craving for mercy, desiring that he might be suffered to speak with the lady Julina apart, promising to satisfy her according to her own contentation.

"Well," quoth the duke, "I take thy word, and therewithal I advise thee that thou perform thy promise, or otherwise I protest before God I will make thee such an example to the world that all traitors shall tremble for fear how they do seek the dishonoring of ladies."

But now Julina had conceived so great grief against Silvio that there was much ado to persuade her to talk with him. But remembering her own case, desirous to hear what excuse he could make, in the end she agreed, and being brought into a place severally[27] by themselves, Silvio began with a piteous voice to say as followeth:

"I know not, madam, of whom I might make complaint, whether of you or of myself, or rather of fortune, which hath conducted and brought us both into so great adversity. I see that you receive great wrong, and I am condemned against all right: you in peril to abide the bruit[28] of spiteful tongues, and I in danger to lose the thing that I most desire. And although I could allege many reasons to prove my sayings true, yet I refer myself to the experience and bounty of your mind."

And herewithal, loosing his garments down to his stomach, and showed Julina his breasts and pretty teats surmounting far the whiteness of snow itself, saying: "Lo, madam, behold here the party whom you have challenged[29] to be the father of your child; see, I am a woman, the daughter of a noble duke, who only for the love of him whom you so lightly have shaken off, have forsaken my father, abandoned my country, and in manner as you see, am become a servingman, satisfying myself but with the only sight of my Apolonius. And now madam, if my passion were not vehement and my torments without comparison, I would wish that my feigned griefs might be laughed to scorn and my dissembled pains to be rewarded with flouts. But my love being pure, my travail continual, and my griefs endless, I trust

[27] **severally:** apart from the others. [28] **bruit:** gossip, news. [29] **challenged:** declared.

madam, you will not only excuse me of crime but also pity my distress, the which I protest I would still have kept secret if my fortune would so have permitted."

Julina did now think herself to be in a worse case than ever she was before, for now she knew not whom to challenge to be the father of her child. Wherefore, when she had told the duke the very certainty of the discourse which Silvio had made unto her, she departed to her own house with such grief and sorrow that she purposed never to come out of her own doors again alive to be a wonder and mocking stock to the world.

But the duke, more amazed to hear this strange discourse of Silvio, came unto him whom, when he had viewed with better consideration, perceived indeed that it was Silla the daughter of Duke Pontus, and embracing her in his arms, he said:

"O the branch of all virtue and the flower of courtesy itself, pardon me I beseech you of all such discourtesies as I have ignorantly committed towards you, desiring you that without further memory of ancient griefs, you will accept of me who is more joyful and better contented with your presence than if the whole world were at my commandment. Where hath there ever been found such liberality in a lover, which having been trained up and nourished amidst the delicacies and banquets of the court, accompanied with trains of many fair and noble ladies, living in pleasure and in the midst of delights, would so prodigally[30] adventure yourself, neither fearing mishaps nor misliking to take such pains as I know you have not been accustomed unto? O liberality never heard of before! O fact that can never be sufficiently rewarded! O true love most pure and unfeigned!"

Herewithal, sending for the most artificial[31] workmen, he provided for her sundry suits of sumptuous apparel, and the marriage day appointed, which was celebrated with great triumph through the whole city of Constantinople, everyone praising the nobleness of the duke; but so many as did behold the excellent beauty of Silla gave her the praise above all the rest of the ladies in the troupe.

The matter seemed so wonderful and strange that the bruit was spread throughout all the parts of Greece insomuch that it came to the hearing of Silvio, who as you have heard, remained in those parts to inquire of his sister. He, being the gladdest man in the world, hastened to Constantinople, where coming to his sister he was joyfully received and most lovingly welcomed and entertained of the duke his brother-in-law. After he had remained there two or three days, the duke revealed unto Silvio the whole discourse how it happened between his sister and the lady Julina, and how

[30] **prodigally:** recklessly. [31] **artificial:** clever at artifice.

his sister was challenged for getting a woman with child. Silvio, blushing with these words, was stricken with great remorse to make Julina amends, understanding her to be a noble lady, and was left defamed to the world through his default. He therefore bewrayed the whole circumstance to the duke, whereof the duke being very joyful, immediately repaired with Silvio to the house of Julina, whom they found in her chamber in great lamentation and mourning, to whom the duke said:

"Take courage madam, for behold here a gentleman that will not stick[32] both to father your child and to take you for his wife — no inferior person but the son and heir of a noble duke, worthy of your estate and dignity."

Julina, seeing Silvio in place, did know very well that he was the father of her child, and was so ravished with joy that she knew not whether she were awake or in some dream. Silvio, embracing her in his arms, craving forgiveness of all that passed, concluded with her the marriage day, which was presently accomplished with great joy and contentation to all parties. And thus Silvio, having attained a noble wife, and Silla his sister her desired husband, they passed the residue of their days with such delight as those that have accomplished the perfection of their felicities.

[32] **stick:** persevere, continue steadfast.

Time

For readers and viewers today, time in *Twelfth Night* is likely to be even more elusive than place. For us, a visit to the theater can occur almost anytime: on a weekday night as well as on the weekend, on an ordinary Monday as well as on a special occasion. With the exception of the six weeks of Lent and outbreaks of the plague, the public playhouses in London offered similar opportunities. The performance of *Twelfth Night* at the Middle Temple at Candlemas 1602 belongs, however, to a different set of circumstances. The play was part of a ritual celebration and took its place amid processions, feasting, and dancing. As such, *Twelfth Night* at the Middle Temple was more typical of how drama has been experienced in traditional cultures all over the world, throughout history. In early modern Europe, only England and Spain offered commercial theater as an entertainment available anytime a spectator took a fancy to it. Although *Twelfth Night* was almost certainly performed in the Lord Chamberlain's Men's public playhouse as well as at the Middle Temple, the play nonetheless seems unusually attuned to playacting as something that happens in ritual time. Two texts can help us appreciate those connections.

➔ *From* The Book of Common Prayer *1559*

To the fascinations of geography Twelfth Night as a religious event added a dimension of mystery and revelation. The twelfth day after Christmas marked the visit of "wise men from the east" to the newly born Christ in Bethlehem. In the liturgy of the Church of England the occasion was commemorated by a special prayer and two special readings from the Bible that were added to the form of Holy Communion prescribed for use on all occasions. That prayer or collection and the two scripture readings, from Paul's epistle to the Romans and from the gospel according to Luke, are transcribed here from *The Book of Common Prayer and Administration of the Sacraments and Other Rites and Ceremonies in the Church of England,* as adopted in the first year of Queen Elizabeth's reign, 1559.

Time is precisely what *The Book of Common Prayer* is designed to manage. In its pages are to be found forms of observance for regular week-by-week services, for special occasions like the twelfth day after Christmas, and for great events in the life cycle like birth, baptism, confirmation, marriage, sickness, and death. The book thus embraces five ways of reckoning time: the diurnal time of morning prayer and evening prayer, the weekly time of Sunday services, the annual time of recurring holidays, the generational time of a parishioner's life, and the apocalyptic time of Christ's birth, death, resurrection, and promise of return. Graphic evidence of the place of Twelfth Night in these schemes of time can be witnessed in the calendar for January included in the Bishops' Bible, printed in 1575. (See Figure 10.) A woodcut in the upper right shows adults feasting by a fire while children throw snowballs at each other outside. The table of religious holidays places Twelfth Night vis-à-vis the other religious events of the month. Of the five measures of time in *The Book of Common Prayer,* Shakespeare's *Twelfth Night* seems to recognize at least four in its focus on night, on holiday time, on youths preparing to marry, on mystery. Epiphany, as the twelfth day after Christmas is called in *The Book of Common Prayer,* celebrates the revelation of Christ's birth to the wise men through the appearance of a star in the east. *Epiphaneia* in Greek derives from a verb that means "to show." The revelations that conclude *Twelfth Night* in act 5 come indeed as an epiphany, a revelation of identities that conspires to make possible the play's happy ending. Olivia's response there gives the audience their cue: "Most wonderful" (5.1.210). When Viola exclaims earlier in the play, "O Time, thou must untangle this, not I" (2.2.35), she may have in mind quite specifically the special time announced in the play's title.

Ianuarie hath xxxi. dayes.

The Moone.xxx.

Sunne riseth / falleth — Houres vi. min. xviii. / v. min. xlii.

					Morning prayer.		Euening prayer.	
					i. Lesson	ii. Lesson.	i. Lesson	ii. Lesson
iii	A	Kalend.	Circumcision.	i	Gen.xvii.	Rom.ii	Deut.x.	Colos.ii.
	b	iiii. No.		ii	Gene.i.	Math.i.	Gene.ii.	Rom.i.
xi	c	iii No.		iii	iii	ii	iiii	ii
	d	prid. No.		iiii	v	iii	vi	iii
xix	e	Nonas.		v	vii	iiii	viii	iiii
viii	f	viii. Id.	Epiphanie.	vi	Esai.lx.	Luke.iii.	Esai.xlix	John.ii.
	g	vii Id.	Perpetue.	vii	Gene.ix.	Math.v.	Gen.xii.	Rom.v.
xvi	A	vi Id.	Lucian.	viii	xiii	vi	xiiii	vi
v	b	v Id.		ix	xv	vii	xvi	vii
	c	iiii Id.		x	xvii	viii	xviii	viii
xiii	d	iii Id.		xi	xix	ix	xx	ix
ii	e	prid. Id.	Sol in Aquario.	xii	xxi	x	xxii	x
	f	Idus.	Hyllarie.	xiii	xxiii	xi	xxiiii	xi
x	g	xix Kl.	Februarij.	xiiii	xxv	xii	xxvi	xii
	A	xviii Kl.		xv	xxvii	xiii	xxviii	xiii
xviii.	b	xvii Kl.		xvi	xxix	xiiii	xxx	xiiii
vii	c	xvi Kl.		xvii	xxxi	xv	xxxii	xv
	d	xv Kl.	Prisca.	xviii	xxxiii	xvi	xxxiiii	xvi
xv	e	xiiii Kl.		xix	xxxv	xvi	xxxvii	i.Cor.i.
iiii	f	xiii Kl.	Fabian.	xx	xxxviii	xviii	xxxix	ii
	g	xii Kl.	Agnes.	xxi	xl	xix	xli	iii
xii	A	xi Kl.	Vincent.	xxii	xlii	xx	xliii	iiii
i	b	x Kl.		xxiii	xliiii	xxi	xlv	v
	c	ix Kl.		xxiiii	xlvi	xxii	xlvii	vi
ix	d	viii Kl.	Conuer.Paul.	xxv	Wisd.v.	Actes.xxii.	Wisd.vi	Act.xxvi
	e	vii Kl.		xxvi	Gene.48.	Mat.xxiii	Gene.49.	i.Cor.vii
xvii	f	vi Kl.		xxvii	l	xxiiii	Exod.i.	viii
vi	g	v Kl.		xxviii	Exod.ii.	xxv	iii	ix
	A	iiii Kl.		xxix	iiii	xxvi	v	x
xiiii	b	iii Kl.		xxx	vii	xxvii	viii	xi
iii	c	prid. Kl.		xxx	ix	xxviii	x	xii
							***.iii.	

FIGURE 10 *Calendar for January, from* The Bishops' Bible *(1575).*

From *The Book of Common Prayer*

The Epiphany

The Collect

O God, which by the leading of a star didst manifest thy only begotten Son to the Gentiles: Mercifully grant, that we which know thee now by faith, may after this life have the fruition of thy glorious Godhead; through Christ our Lord.

The Epistle {Ephesians 3}

For this cause I, Paul, am a prisoner of Jesus Christ for you heathen, if ye have heard of the ministration of the grace of God, which is given me to youward[1] For by revelation showed he the mystery unto me (as I wrote afore in few words, whereby when ye read, ye may understand my knowledge in the mystery of Christ) which mystery in times past was not opened unto the sons of men, as it is now declared unto his holy Apostles and prophets by the Spirit, that the Gentiles should be inheritors also, and of the same body, and partakers of his promise of Christ, by the means of the gospel, whereof I am made a minister according to the gift of the grace of God, which is given unto me after the working of his power. Unto me the least of all saints is this grace given, that I should preach among the Gentiles the unsearchable riches of Christ; and to make all men see what the fellowship of the mystery is, which from the beginning of the world hath been hid in God, which made all things through Jesus Christ; to the intent, that now unto the rulers and powers in heavenly things, might be known by the congregation, the manifold wisdom of God, according to the eternal purpose which he wrought in Christ Jesu our Lord, by whom we have boldness and entrance with the confidence which is by the faith of him.

The Gospel {Matthew 2}

When Jesus was born in Bethlehem, a city of Jewry, in the time of Herod the king, behold, there came Wise men from the east to Jerusalem, saying, Where is he that is born King of the Jews? For we have seen his star in the east, and are come to worship him. When Herod the king had heard these things, he was troubled and all the city of Jerusalem with him. And when he

[1] **to youward:** for you.

The 1559 Book of Common Prayer, ed. John E. Booty (Charlottesville: University of Virginia Press for the Folger Shakespeare Library, 1976), 92–94.

had gathered all the chief priests and scribes of the people together, he demanded of them where Christ should be born. And they said unto him, At Bethlehem in Jewry. For thus it is written by the prophet, And thou Bethlehem in the land of Jewry art not the least among the princes of Judah, for out of thee there shall come unto me the captain that shall govern my people Israel. Then Herod, when he had privily[2] called the Wise men, he enquired of them diligently what time the star appeared, and he bade them go to Bethlehem, and said, Go your way thither, and search diligently for the child. And when ye have found him, bring me word again, that I may come and worship him also. When they had heard the king, they departed; and lo, the star, which they saw in the east, went before them till it came and stood over the place wherein the child was. When they saw the star, they were exceeding glad, and went into the house, and found the child with Mary his mother, and fell down flat, and worshiped him, and opened their treasures, and offered unto him gifts: gold, frankincense, and myrrh. And after they were warned of God in sleep that they should not go again to Herod, they returned into their own country another way.

[2] **privily:** secretly.

→ **HENRY BOURNE**

From Antiquitates Vulgares, or the Antiquities of the Common People

1725

Traditionally, in country villages and in cities, in academic households and in the court of the realm, Twelfth Night saw the most extravagent festivities of the year. Religious services involving a gilded star would be followed by feasting, by plays, by dancing, by gift-giving inspired by the wise men's gifts of gold, frankincense, and myrrh. In academic households like the Middle Temple it was customary to elect a Lord of Misrule to preside over the proceedings — until Protestant sentiment and new ideas of propriety ended the tradition in 1584. By that date the whole paraphernalia of traditional festivities had been abolished by Protestant extremists under Edward VI (reigned 1547–1553), reinstated under the Catholic Mary (reigned 1553–1558), and tolerated to a degree under Elizabeth (reigned 1558–1603). The Middle Temple's Prince of Love strode into a contested arena in 1597–98 (Hutton 13–18). Popular ways of celebrating Epiphany persisted, despite the hostility of real-life counterparts to Malvolio.

The first systematic, book-length account of popular customs in Britain was produced by Henry Bourne (1696–1733), a clergyman who was curate of the Chapel of All Saints at Newcastle-upon-Tyne. Dedicated to the mayor and aldermen of Newcastle, the volume was printed at Bourne's own expense. The book's full subtitle — *The Antiquities of the Common People, Giving An Account of Several of their Opinions and Ceremonies, With Proper Reflections upon Each of Them, Showing Which May be Retained and Which Ought to be Laid Aside* — makes clear that Bourne's purpose was not just to describe popular customs but to pass judgment on them. His criteria for doing so are two: Christian dogma and middle-class propriety. The authorities he cites are mainly chroniclers of the Christian church like Bede (673–735), scholars of Greek and Roman customs like Polydore Virgil (c. 1470–c. 1555), and historians of Saxon antiquities like Edward Stillingfleet (1635–1699). Though written more than a century after *Twelfth Night* was first performed, Bourne's account "Of the Twelfth Day" records customs that date back to Shakespeare's time and before.

From *Antiquitates Vulgares, or the Antiquities of the Common People*

Of the Twelfth Day

The Twelfth Day itself is one of the greatest of the twelve, and of more jovial observation than the others, for the visiting of friends and Christmas gambols.[1] The rites of this day are different in divers places, though the end of them is much the same in all; namely, to do honor to the memory of the Eastern Magi, whom they suppose to have been kings. In France, one of the courtiers is chosen king, whom the king himself, and the other nobles attend to an entertainment. In Germany, they observe the same thing on this day in academies and cities, where the students and citizens create one of themselves king, or a stranger guest. Now this is answerable to that custom of the Saturnalia, of masters making banquets for their servants, and waiting on them; and no doubt this custom was in past sprung from that.

Not many years ago, this was a common Christmas gambol in both our universities; and it is still usual in other places of our land, to give the name of King or Queen to that person, whose extraordinary luck hits upon that part of the divided cake, which is honored above the others, with a bean in it.

But though this be generally the greatest of the twelve, yet the others preceding are observed with mirth and jollity, generally to excess. Was this feasting confined within the bounds of decency and moderation, and gave

[1] **gambol:** game, entertainment.

Henry Bourne, *Antiquitates Vulgares, or The Antiquities of the Common People . . .* (Newcastle: J. White for the Author, 1725), 151–54.

more way than it does to the exercises and the religious duties of the season, it would have nothing in it immoral or sinful. The keeping up of friendship, and love, and old acquaintance, has nothing in it harmful; but the misfortune is, men upon that bottom, act rather like brutes than men, and like heathens than Christians; and the preservation of friendship and love, is nothing else but a pretense for drunkenness, and rioting, and wantonness. And such I am afraid hath been the observation of the Christmas holiday, since the holiest times of the Christian Church; and the generality of men have looked upon them, as a time of eating and drinking, and playing, than of returning praises and thanksgivings to God, for the greatest benefit He ever bestowed upon the sons of men.

CHAPTER 2

Music

With the possible exception of *The Tempest,* written late in Shakespeare's career, *Twelfth Night* is Shakespeare's most musical play. From the "dying" strains of melody that inspire Orsino's opening speech to the wistful, folk-like song by Feste that serves as an epilogue, the atmosphere of Illyria is suffused with music. Feste is responsible for much it. When Feste joins Sir Toby and Sir Andrew in their midnight revels in act 2, scene 3, Sir Toby proposes the three of them sing a round or "catch." "By my troth," Sir Andrew enthuses, "the Fool has an excellent breast. I had rather than forty shillings I had such a leg, and so sweet a breath to sing, as the Fool has" (2.3.16–18). In the original performances Feste was played by Robert Armin, who brought to Shakespeare's troupe not only his sardonic improvisatory wit but an ability to sing. With Armin in one of the primary roles, the songs in *Twelfth Night* were very much part of the show, part of what audiences paid to hear.[1] Let's have a song, then, Sir Andrew suggests. A love song, Feste asks, or "a song of good life"? Accepting Feste's dubious implication that you can't have both, Sir Andrew opts for love. Feste obliges with "O mistress mine," a popular tune that survives in artful settings by the composers William Byrd and Thomas Morley, among others. Later in the scene come the boisterous

[1]Armin's career is reconstructed in Wiles, *Shakespeare's Clown,* 144–87.

catches — "Hold thy peace," "Three merry men are we," and "O' the twelfth day of December" — that rouse Malvolio from his sleep and inspire the boon companions to a riotous rendition of Robert Jones's lute song, "Farewell, dear heart, since I must needs be gone." In the next scene, to Orsino's request for more sad music Feste responds with "Come away, come away, Death" (2.4.49 ff). Orsino describes it to Viola/"Cesario" as "old and plain" (2.4.41), a song that belongs to women and times gone by:

> The spinsters and the knitters in the sun,
> And the free maids that weave their thread with bones,
> Do use to chant it. It is silly sooth,
> And dallies with the innocence of love,
> Like the old age. (2.4.42–46)

Music in *Twelfth Night* thus runs the social gamut, from the fashionably melancholy instrumental music that opens the play to the popular catches bellowed out by Sir Toby and Sir Andrew to the artful "O mistress mine" performed by Feste to the purportedly traditional ballad "Come away, come away, Death" to the folk-like "When that I was and a little tiny boy." As different as these musical numbers may be in origin, all of them except for the catches share the same feeling: an amorous melancholy of just the sort Orsino describes in his opening speech. The central element in the name Il-*lyre*-ia is a stringed musical instrument; the place itself is conjured into presence with song.

Music in *Twelfth Night* is not limited, however, to the play's atmosphere; it also defines the philosophical universe in which the events of the play take place and the psychology of the characters who inhabit that universe. From Greek and Roman culture Shakespeare and his contemporaries inherited two quite opposite ideas about music. On the one hand, the intervals of the musical scale were thought to be coincident with the distances between the planets, producing cosmic harmonies that could have visceral effects on human beings. On the other hand, music that lacked those proportions, especially music that was devoid of words, could seduce the senses and produce madness. Malvolio knows which of the two kinds he is hearing when he interrupts Sir Toby's and Sir Andrew's drunken catches: "My masters, are you mad?" (2.3.73). Through music man might come closer to divine order; through music he might descend into the brute sensuality of beasts. Malvolio, for one, identifies Sir Toby's and Sir Andrew's music with the lower social orders:

> what are you? Have you no wit, manners, nor honesty but to gabble like tinkers at this time of night? Do ye make an alehouse of my lady's house, that ye squeak out your coziers' catches without any mitigation or remorse of voice? Is there no respect of place, persons, nor time in you? (2.3.73–77)

Equally dangerous is the power of sensual music to effeminate a man, to turn him into the love-longing creature that Orsino shows himself to be in act 1, scene 1. A visual representation of music's effeminating power is provided by an emblem of Ulysses and the Sirens in Geoffrey Whitney's *A Choice of Emblems.* (See Figure 11.) To hear the Sirens' music, but not succumb to the singers' temptations, is one of the trials Ulysses has to undergo in book 12 of Homer's *Odyssey.* In Whitney's version the Sirens' singing becomes specifically a test of Ulysses' masculinity: "But nothing could his manly heart procure." Malvolio thus loses his social status and his manhood when he falls for the revelers' trick and tries to woo Olivia with a ballad refrain (3.4.20–21). With its potential to ennoble or to bestialize, music provides another key to the concern with self-identity that occupied the original audiences of *Twelfth Night.* Let us take stock of the musical instruments available to Shakespeare's troupe — including human voices — before investigating the philosophical issues that music engages.

Musical Resources

In the absence of any surviving papers from Shakespeare's acting company, we are lucky to have some of the inventories and financial records kept by Philip Henslowe (d. 1616), the impresario of a rival company, the Lord Admiral's Men, at the Rose Theater in the 1590s. His careful accounts of expenditures for scripts, costumes, and properties are matched by records of what the take was for a given play on a given date. An inventory of costumes from Henslowe's papers is included in Chapter 4. Among the company's properties that Henslowe inventoried at about the same time are four groupings of musical instruments: (1) four stringed instruments in the form of a treble viol, a bass viol, a guitar-like bandore, and a cittern, (2) one trombone-like sackbut, (3) three tambourine-like timbrels, and (4) three trumpets and a drum. Scripts written for the Lord Admiral's Men in these years indicate that one or more recorders or flutes were also available. The instruments could be deployed individually for special effects or, in the case of bass and treble viols, bandore or cittern, and recorder, played together in what contemporary musicians knew as a "broken consort" — "broken" because the instruments came from different "families" (Smith, *Acoustic World* 218–19). Possibly it was the music of a broken consort that Orsino, and Manningham and his friends in the audience (see Introduction), heard at the opening of *Twelfth Night* in 1602. Feste's solo songs were likely accompanied by a bandore, cittern, or lute. For their catches Sir Toby and Sir Andrew needed no support.

10

Sirenes.

Virg. Aeneid. lib. 5. & Ouidius lib. 5. Metamorph.

WITHE pleaſaunte tunes, the SYRENES did allure
Vliſſes wiſe, to liſten theire ſonge:
But nothinge could his manlie harte procure,
Hee ſailde awaie, and ſcap'd their charming ſtronge,
The face, he lik'de: the nether parte, did loathe:
For womans ſhape, and fiſhes had they bothe.

Nic. Reuſnerus. *Illectos nautas dulci modulamine vocis, Mergebant auida fluctibus Ioniis.*

Which ſhewes to vs, when Bewtie ſeekes to ſnare
The careleſſe man, whoe dothe no daunger dreede,
That he ſhoulde flie, and ſhoulde in time beware,
And not on lookes, his fickle fancie feede:
Suche Mairemaides liue, that promiſe onelie ioyes:
But hee that yeldes, at lengthe him ſelffe diſtroies.

Laërtij tetraſticon ſic per Claud. Minoëm conuerſum.

Hæc Venus ad muſas: Venerem exhorreſcite Nimphæ,
In vos armatus aut amor inſiliet.
Cui contrà muſæ, verba hæc age dicito marti:
Aliger huc ad nos non volat ille puer.

FIGURE 11 *Sirens, from Geoffrey Whitney,* A Choice of Emblems *(1586).*

What the audience heard most of the time in Middle Temple Hall on February 2, 1602, was not, of course, musical instruments but human voices. Music, however, provides a key to appreciating how those voices were deployed. The disquisition on rhetoric written by Aristotle (384–322 B.C.E.) is the earliest in a series of rhetorical treatises that taught Renaissance schoolmasters, their students, and professional actors to think about the human voice as an instrument that, like a lute or a trumpet, possessed certain qualities and demanded certain kinds of discipline. Other influential rhetorical manuals were written by Cicero (106–43 B.C.E.) and Quintilian (d. 95 C.E.). Aristotle distinguishes three factors in the artful deployment of the speaking voice: volume (*megethos*), rhythm (*rhythmos*), and pitch (*harmonia*) (*Rhetoric* 3.1.4). With respect to pitch and volume, if not rhythm, Shakespeare's company was composed of two kinds of voices: men's and boys'. They could be orchestrated in different ways, depending on the kind of play at hand — history, comedy, or tragedy — as well as the venue in which it was to be played. Indoor spaces like the Middle Temple Hall fostered a quieter, more "rounded" sound than the outdoor amphitheaters, inviting the prominence of treble sounds that we find in *Twelfth Night.*[1]

In terms of sound, *Twelfth Night* (likely written 1601) contrasts with the plays Shakespeare wrote just before (*Hamlet,* 1600) and just after (*Troilus and Cressida,* 1602). The plays are *scored* differently: they call for different combinations of musical instruments, different ranges of human voices. *Hamlet* and *Troilus and Cressida* are both dominated by men's voices. In the earlier play the treble of boy actors is heard only in Ophelia's part and Gertrude's; in the later play, only in Cressida's, Helen's, and Cassandra's. In *Twelfth Night,* by contrast, Viola's voice sounds the keynote. "I'll serve this duke [. . .]," she declares moments after her first appearance in the play, "for I can sing / And speak to him in many sorts of music" (1.2.55, 57–58). As well she might, being a boy actor playing a girl playing a boy. *Viola,* let it be noted, is not only a type of violet but a stringed musical instrument. As Viola predicts, the duke turns out to be appreciative of his new servant's vocal skills. "Thy small pipe," he tells "Cesario," "Is as the maiden's organ, shrill and sound" (1.4.30–31). The boy actor playing Viola is scripted to speak about 300 of the play's approximately 2,400 lines, second only (and not by much) to Sir Toby. The unusually equitable distribution of lines in *Twelfth Night* means that what the audience heard in the original performances was a *consort* of vocal sounds, the equivalent of the "true love" in "O mistress mine" who "can sing both high and low" (2.3.32–35). The instrumental sounds in *Twelfth Night* are equally distinctive. Where *Hamlet* calls

[1]On these differing spaces and differing sorts of effects see Smith, *Acoustic World,* 206–45.

at the end for trumpets ("the soldiers' music") and *"a peal of ordnance"* ("the rites of war") (5.2.353, stage direction after 357) and *Troilus and Cressida* for battle noises, *Twelfth Night* features temperate accompaniment to Feste's singing, probably on a lute, possibly with recorders.[2] The effect, as with the pitch range of speaking voices, would have been that of a musical consort.

→ ARISTOTLE (ATTRIBUTED)

From The Problems of Aristotle, with Other Philosophers and Physicians

1597

A physiological explanation of the special qualities of Viola's voice is to be found in one of the works no longer assigned to Aristotle but thought to be his in Shakespeare's time. *The Problems of Aristotle, with Other Philosophers and Physicians,* as collected, translated, and printed in 1597, follows a question-and-answer format that was a recognized way of writing philosophy in the Renaissance. Among the questions "Aristotle" takes up in this edition is why the voices of boys and women are "smaller" than men's voices. The English translator alters the Latin original by specifying that it was at age fourteen — the legal age of marriage for males — when a boy's voice began to change. Aristotle's *Problems* helps to situate Viola/"Cesario" vocally, just as Malvolio's description situates her/"him" visually: "not yet old enough for a man, nor young enough for a boy." In sum, "He is very well-favored, and he speaks very shrewishly" (1.5.122–25). "Shrewish" is Malvolio's impolite way of saying "acutely," "with a high pitch," "in the manner of a woman."

Question. *Why have all the females of all living creatures the shrillest voices, a cow only excepted, and a woman shriller than a man and smaller?*

Answer. According unto Aristotle, by reason of the composition of the veins, and vocal arteries, that is, where the air doth enter in, by which veins and arteries the voice is formed: as it appeareth by a similitude, because a small pipe doth sound shriller than a great. And so also in women, because the passage where the voice is formed, is made narrow and strait, by reason of cold, because it is the nature of cold to bind: but in men that passage is open and wider through heat, because it is the property of heat to open and

[2]The musical instruments typically used in the outdoor theaters of the 1590s are described in Long, 1: 28–29.

Aristotle [attributed], *The Problems of Aristotle, with other Philosophers and Physicians* (London: Arnold Hatfield, 1597), C1–C1v, I8v, L8v, M1.

dissolve. Also it proceedeth in women through the moistness of the lungs and weakness of heat. Young men and diseased men have sharp and shrill voices for the same cause. And that is the natural cause why a man-child at his birth time doth cry *"a, i,"* which is a bigger sound, and the female *"e,"* which is a slenderer sound, as it pleaseth Laberintus,[3] when he sayeth, *"Masculus a profert."*[4]

Question. *Why doth the voice change in men and women, in men at 14, in women at 12,*[5] *in men when they begin to yield seed, in women, when their breasts begin to grow, as Aristotle doth say,* Lib[er] de Animal[ibus] [Treatise on Animals].

Answer. Because that then, sayeth Aristotle, the beginning of the voice is slackened and loosed: and he proveth this by a similitude of a string of an instrument let down or loosed, which giveth a greater sound. And he proveth it another way, because that beasts which are gelded,[6] as capons, eunuchs, and gelded men, have softer and slenderer voices than others, by reason they want stones.

Question. *Why have women such weak small voices?*

Answer. Because their instruments and organs of speaking, by reason they are cold, are small and narrow: and therefore receiving but little air, causeth the voice to be small and effeminate. . . .

Question: *Why are boys apt to change their voice about fourteen years of age?*

Answer: Because that then nature doth cause a great and sudden change of age. Experience proveth this to be true: for at that time we may see that women's paps[7] do grow great, to hold and gather milk, and also those places which are about the hips, in which the young fruit should remain. Likewise men's breasts and shoulders which then bear great and heavy burdens. Also their stones in which the seed may increase and abide: and his privy member, to let out the seed with ease. Further all the whole body is made bigger and dilated, as the alteration and change of every part doth testify. And the harshness of the voice and hoarseness: for the rough artery or windpipe being made wide in the beginning, and the exterior or outward part within unequal even to the throat, the air going out at that rough unequal and uneven pipe, doth become unequal and sharp, and after a sort hoarse. Like unto the voice of a goat, whereof it hath his name *Branchus.* The same doth happen unto them into whose rough artery any distillation doth flow. It happeneth by reason of the dropping humidity, that a light small skin filled unequally, causeth an uneven going forth of the spirit and air. Understand

[3] **Laberintus:** an ancient medical authority. [4] ***"Masculus a profert"*:** the male puts forth an "a." [5] ***at 14 . . . at 12:*** Aristotle does not specify these ages in the passage cited below from *De Animalibus* (On Animals). [6] **gelded:** castrated. [7] **paps:** breasts.

that the windpipe of goats is such, by reason of the abundance of humidity. The like doth happen unto all such, as nature hath given a rough artery, as unto cranes. After the years of fourteen they leave off that voice, because the artery is made wider, and receiveth his natural evenness and equality.

ANTHONY GIBSON

From A Woman's Worth Defended Against All the Men in the World

1599

A remarkable feature of the acoustic design of *Twelfth Night* is the prominence given to boys' voices, with their distinctive pitch in the treble range and their clear, ringing tone. In keeping with casting traditions in schools and in Oxford and Cambridge colleges, the low-comic role of Maria might have been played by a man whose deeper voice was part of the satire, but the voices of Viola and Olivia enjoy a special prominence. As the focus of the plot, Viola in her speaking establishes a keynote in accord with which all the other sounds in the play are tuned. The musical quality of women's voices is one of the arguments advanced by the obscure author Anthony Gibson in *A Woman's Worth Defended Against All the Men in the World,* printed in 1599. Voice quality, he implies, is partly the result of balances among the body's four basic fluids, or "humors" as they were called. Men's voices, Gibson alleges, are choked with choler, the hottest of the four humors, while melancholy men like Orsino, enervated by an excess of black bile, are at the opposite extreme, possessing voices that are too soft. Women's voices, by contrast, offer a natural harmony. Examples from ancient times demonstrate the special affinity that women have for music. All of the author's arguments invite us to hear Viola's speeches, as Orsino does, with culturally attuned ears. A page from Richard Day's *A Book of Christian Prayers* (1578), sometimes called "Queen Elizabeth's Prayerbook," gives us an image for what the author of *A Woman's Worth* says about women and music. (See Figure 12.) Like the illuminated books of hours that wealthy people once possessed in manuscript, Day's printed book surrounds prayers for particular occasions with illustrations suggestive of those occasions. "A Prayer Against Despair" seems especially appropriate for the shipwrecked Viola: "Depart not from me in the time of my need, but defend thou me till this storm be overpast." The woodcuts surrounding this prayer illustrate hearing. On the right a woman is shown playing a lute; below, a recumbent deer is shown surrounded by musical instruments, charmed into tameness by the concord of music.

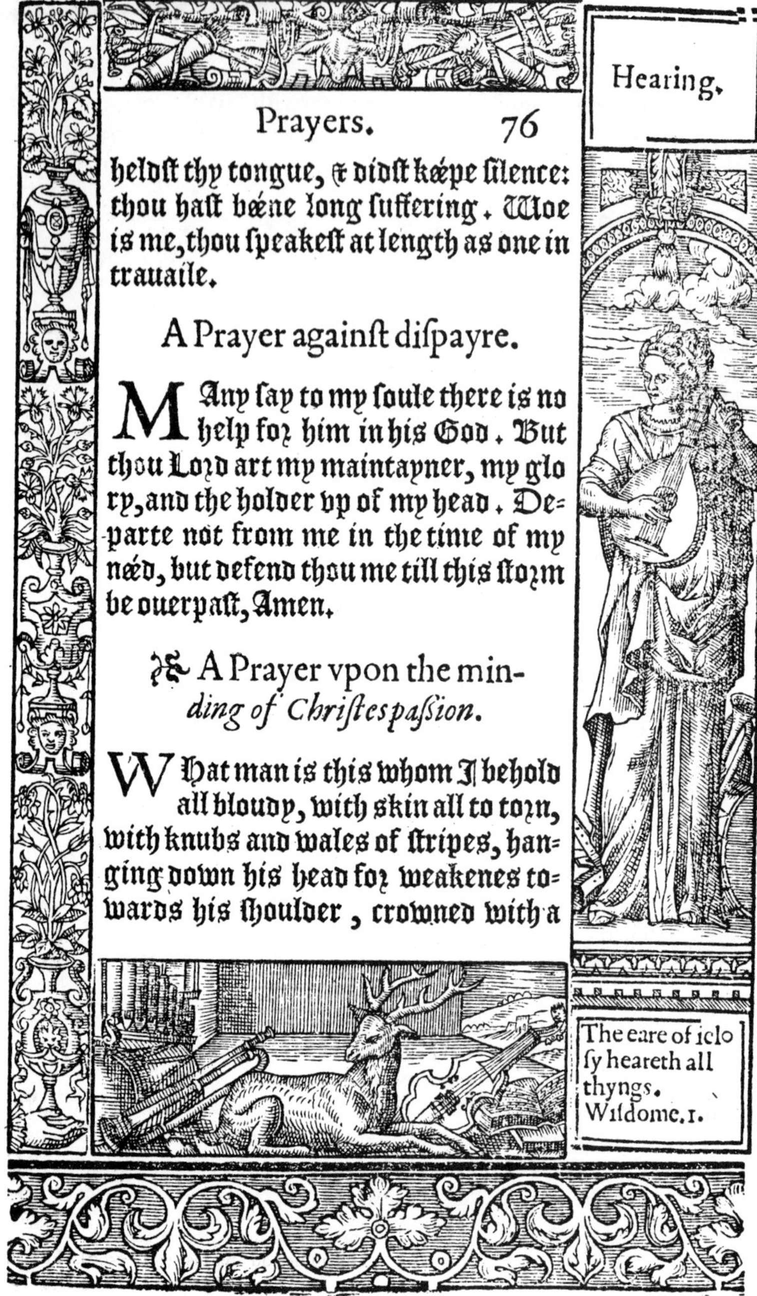

Hearing.

Prayers. 76

heldst thy tongue, & didst kéepe silence: thou hast béene long suffering. Woe is me, thou speakest at length as one in trauaile.

A Prayer against dispayre.

MAny say to my soule there is no help for him in his God. But thou Lord art my maintayner, my glory, and the holder vp of my head. Departe not from me in the time of my néed, but defend thou me till this storm be ouerpast, Amen.

A Prayer vpon the minding of Christes passion.

WHat man is this whom I behold all bloudy, with skin all to torn, with knubs and wales of stripes, hanging down his head for weakenes towards his shoulder, crowned with a

The eare of ielosy heareth all thyngs. Wisdome. I.

FIGURE 12 *Hearing, Women, the Power of Music, and a Prayer against Despair, from Richard Day,* A Book of Christian Prayers *(1578).*

From *A Woman's Worth Defended Against All the Men in the World*

Nature teacheth us that women are or may be most eloquent, considering the organs and instruments of their voice is more mild and gentle, than those in men, whose pronunciation is very rough, sharp and coarsely shaped, by reason of the abundance of choler,[1] which (with their words) drives forth so much vehemence of spirit, as they are well near choked therewith, or break their wind in uttering of their speech. Yet, we must confess that melancholy[2] men are softer in words, than the swarthy and sanguine,[3] such several qualities remain in men [. . .].

As for music, among women it is so familiar, as their very voice is naturally a harmony. Aelianus recounteth, that there was a woman musician in Rome so excellent as everyone imagined she helped herself by magic. So rarely could she ravish by the ear of minds of them that heard her. Yea, it grew to such effect, as many frantic people were thereby recovered from their fury. Most certain is it that Philliada the Tiriane invented the lute, whence rose the proverb "the harp of Idumea and the lute of Phoenicia," and the testimony hereof is drawn from others, by the Lord of Bartas:[4]

> The cunning Tirianes, who on bark of trees
> Did first set down the voice's harmonies.

And a Grecian, thus:

> Inventress was Philliada,
> Of lutes in fair Phoenicia.
> She first gave spirit and quick life
> To dull dead wood, and made so rife
> The several sweets of harmony,
> By her rare wit and industry.

When Alexander the Great had conquered the kingdom of Darius, he found so skillful a woman musician in the city of Sufa, as could accommodate the varieties of her voice, to the several notes of all kind of birds, and that with such exceeding dexterity, as they which saw her not, could make no difference from the very thing itself. Great Caesar likewise was wont to

[1] **choler:** yellow bile, producing anger. [2] **melancholy:** dominated by black bile. [3] **sanguine:** dominated by blood. [4] **the lord of Bartas:** Guillaume du Bartas (1544–1590), French Huguenot poet.

Anthony Gibson, *A Woman's Worth Defended Against All the Men in the World* (London: John Wolfe, 1599), 20–27.

say, that men's tunes were learned from the birds chattering on trees, but the voice of women came from the gods themselves. The Sirens, so much described the Grecians, had songs so wonderful sweet and melodious, as they could out-ear[5] the winds, and rob all mouths of their natural offices. The Greeks returning from the wars of Troy rested themselves a long while in the isles where they inhabited, little caring for return home into their own country, by being rapt, or rather charmed with such a harmonious delight.

Perhaps someone will say unto me, that the Tritons are very excellent musicians, but he must withal confess, that they never had like power and virtue as the Sirens have, of whom they learned their very deepest knowledge, albeit their music stretch no further than the sound of a trumpet, which Misenus the trumpeter to Aeneas well perceiving, provoked them to sound, to try whether he could go beyond them or no. Marry, he lost his life therefore, if this narration be of any certainty:

But whilst his trumpet he did sound,
  with glory indiscrete
Upon the marble of the waves,
  the Tritons' notes to meet.
They jealous to be so defied,
  in their own pleasing art,
In anger threw him in the waves,
  and so his life did part.

Istrina, the mother to Ariphita, king of Scythia, was of such estimation in music, as the poets have feigned, that the seas would never be calm but when this lady stood exchanging her sweet zephyrs with the northern gusts, which blew very bitterly upon them continually. The astronomers do hold that Venus is the patroness of music, and that the influence of her planet brings most special felicity to such as deal in that faculty.

Let us admit that Thespian the priest of the Gymnosophists, Zoroastes of the Persians, Hermes of the Egyptians, Buddha of the Chaldeans, Abbares of the Scythians, and Zalmosis of the Thracians excelled no less in music than in piety and knowledge of sacred matters. Yet, notwithstanding, they were but simple admirers of fair Clora, daughter to God Anubis, who could charm crocodiles of Nylus, as also them of hot Cyrena, by the benefit of her voice, reputed incomparable, which Lycosthenes[6] reports such wonders of, as they seem to move more astonishment than belief.

[5] **out-ear:** drown out. [6] **Lycosthenes:** Konrad Lykosthenes (1518–1561), humanist scholar.

Minds and Bodies

To Renaissance thinkers, if not Renaissance listeners, music presented a philosophical paradox. In its numerosity, it embodied the very order of the universe and thus appealed to reason; in its physicality, it struck the ear in airwaves, appealing to the senses and capable of distracting the listener's reason. In effect, music forced the issue of how souls are related to bodies. For Plato, soul and body are two separate entities. Indeed, the soul pre-exists the body and will survive after the body's demise. In this understanding of the soul-body nexus, the essence of music is something that the soul alone apprehends. Ears are incidental. Socrates deftly leads Theaetetus to a general truth about being, order and number: "these, unlike objects of sense, have no separate organ, but . . . the mind, by a power of its own, contemplates the universals in all things" (*Dialogues* 3:286). For Aristotle, on the other hand, the soul is always an *embodied* soul: "all the affections of soul involve a body — passion, gentleness, fear, pity, courage, joy, loving, and hating; in all these there is a concurrent affection of the body" (*Complete Works* 1: 642). Renaissance writing about music in general — and the functions of music in *Twelfth Night* in particular — negotiate these alternative ways of relating soul to body.

→ **OVID**

From Ovid's Metamorphosis Englished, Mythologized, and Represented in Figures *1632*

Translated by George Sandys

The divided sensibility that Renaissance listeners had about music finds graphic embodiment in the ancient myth of the contest between Marsyas and Apollo over who was the greater musician. Marsyas's instrument was the double flute; Apollo's, the lyre. Celebrated by some as the inventor of the flute, Marsyas in other versions of the story found the instrument after it had been cast aside by Athena (called Minerva in Latin tradition), the presiding deity of wisdom. Varying versions of the story tell how Athena, playing on the instrument, happened to see her reflection in water. She looked so ridiculous that she threw the instrument away in disgust. After he took it up, Marsyas was so impressed with his own playing that he challenged Apollo to a contest. Apollo accepted, on condition that the winner could punish the loser in whatever way he chose. By some accounts, the first trial was a draw, but when Apollo challenged Marsyas to play his instrument upside down, Apollo with his lyre was victorious. The Roman poet Ovidius Naso (43 B.C.E.–17 C.E.) offers two accounts of the myth.

In *Fasti,* his long poem on Roman holidays, Ovid reads the contest of Apollo and Marsyas as the presiding myth for *turba* (literally "hubbub," "uproar," "racket"), the professional band of flute-players. *Turba* becomes "waits," musicians waiting for hire in taverns or other locations about town, in John Gower's English translation, *Ovid's Festivals, or Roman Calendar,* printed in 1640. Minerva is the speaker in Ovid's account of Apollo's contest with Marsyas. She claims to be the inventor of Marsyas's favored instrument, the flute, but says she cast it aside once she saw how playing it distorted her cheeks:

'Twas my invention raised this company.
I first the pipe of bored box did frame
With certain holes, and played upon the same.
Sweet were the notes; but when as I beheld
My face in the spring, I spied my cheeks all swelled.
"I prize thee not so high, my pipe," said I:
"Farewell." And cast it on a bank thereby.[1]

In keeping with the violent transformations that constitute his theme, Ovid's other account of the contest of Apollo and Marsyas in *Metamorphoses* stresses Marsyas's fleshly physicality, his half-completed metamorphosis as a satyr — goat from the waist down, man from the waist up. His punishment at the hands of Apollo is particularly gory. The translation by George Sandys (1578–1644) was completed in Virginia in the 1620s and published in England in three successive editions of 1621, 1626, and 1632. The last of these editions features elegant engravings of the events described in each book (see Figure 13), as well as a learned commentary that gathers interpretations of each myth from ancient and modern sources. In Sandys's digest, Marsyas figures as an embodiment of mindless, wordless music, Apollo as the translator of the mathematical music of the spheres into audible form. Apollo could manage that translation because the varying lengths of the strings of his lyre were thought to be proprotionate to the distances between the planets. It was with weighted strings, as we noted in the Introduction, that Pythagoras was supposed to have invented the musical scale. An illustration in Robert Fludd's book on cosmic order, *Utriusque Cosmi Maioris Scilicet et Minoris Metaphysica, Physica, atque Technica Historia* (*The Metaphysical, Physical, and Technical Story of both the Greater and the Lesser Cosmos*) (1617) figures the universe as giant viol that is tuned according to precise mathematical ratios. (See Figure 14.) The addition of words to stringed music completed its claims to superiority. Apollo was, after all, the god of poetry. Some Greek commentators regarded pipe music is Asiatic in origin, the cultural antithesis to the *logos*-inspired music that could be sung to Apollo's lyre.

[1]Ovid, *Fasti,* trans. John Gower as *Ovid's Festivals, or Roman Calendar* (Cambridge: Roger Daniel, 1640), 143.

FIGURE 13 *Apollo Flaying Marsyas, from George Sandys,* Ovid's Metamorphosis Englished, Mythologized, and Represented in Figures *(1632).*

From *Metamorphosis*

Thus much, I know not by what Theban, said:
Another mention of a satyr made,
By Phoebus, with Tritonia's reed[2] o'ercome
Who for presuming felt a heavy doom.
Me from my self, ah, why do you distract?
(Oh!) I repent, he cried: Alas! this fact
Deserves not such a vengeance![3] Whilst he cried,
Apollo from his body stript his hide.
His body was one wound, blood every way

[2] **reed:** Minerva's pipe, whereon Marsyas the satyr played [Sandys's note]. [3] **Alas . . . vengeance:** Marsyas's words [Sandys's note].

Ovid, *Ovid's Metamorphosis Englished, Mythologized, and Represented in Figures,* trans. George Sandys (Oxford: J. Lichfield, 1632), 209–10, 224–25.

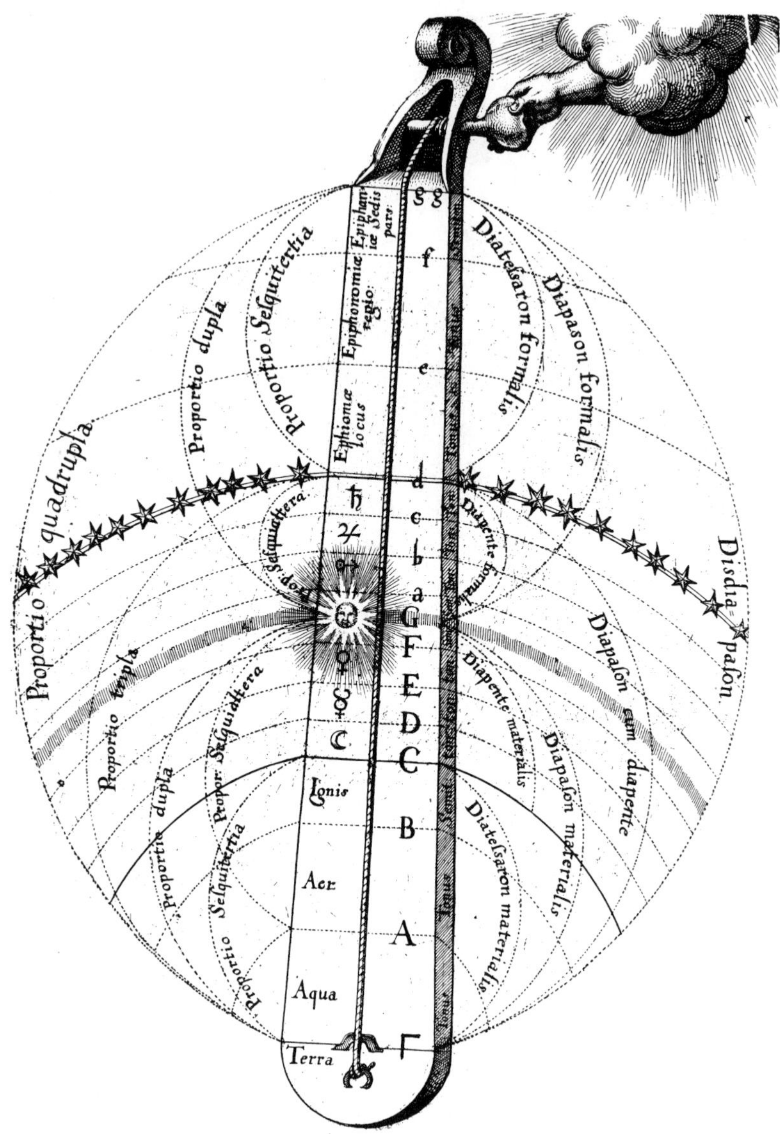

FIGURE 14 *The Tuning of the Spheres, from Robert Fludd,* Utriusque Cosmi Maioris Scilicet et Minoris Metaphysica, Physica, atque Technica Historia *(1617).*

Streams from all parts: his sinews naked lay.
His bare veins pant: his heart you might behold;
And all the fibers in his breast have told.
For him the fauns, that in the forests keep:
For him the nymphs, and brother satyrs weep:
His end, Olympus[4] (famous then) bewails:
With all the shepherds of those hills and dales.
The pregnant Earth conceiveth with their tears;
Which in her penetrated womb she bears,
Till big with waters: then discharg'd her fraught.
This purest Phrygian stream a way out sought
By down-falls, till to toiling seas he came:
Now called Marsyas of the satyr's name. . . .

This story is seconded by another of the excoriating of Marsyas: a musician excelling in wind instruments; and called a satyr, for his rude and lascivious composures: who finding the flute, which Minerva cast away, when she beheld in the river how the blowing thereof distorted her visage, was the first of mortals that played thereon: and so cunningly, that he presumed to challenge Apollo with his harp: by whom overcome, he had his skin stripped over his ears by the victor. It is said that Minerva threw the flute away, not only for deforming her face, but that such music conferreth nothing to the knowledge of the mind; presented[5] by that goddess, the patroness of wit and learning. The fiction of the satyr's punishment was invented not only to deter from such self-exaltation: but to dehort the Athenians from the practice of an art so illiberal,[6] whereunto the Thebans were generally addicted. To which purpose thus spake Alcibiades. "Let the Thebans play on the flute, who know not how to speak: but for us Athenians, we have Pallas and Apollo for the patrons of our country; of whom, in times past, the one threw away the pipe, and the other uncased the piper." Marsyas is fained to have the tail of a swine; in that audacious attempts have but shameful ends. But the rurals deplore the death of their piper, and raise a river with their tears which carries his name: the Phrygians themselves believing that it sprung from the blood of the satyr. A violent stream, which meeting with Maeander, hath his speed abated by the slowness of the other.

By Mycale into th' Icarian deep
United Marsyas and Maeander creep.
Straight Marsyas wondrous swift while yet his own;

[4] **Olympus:** an excellent piper remembered by Plato and beloved of Marsyas, of whom that mountain in Mysia was so called [Sandys' note, citing *Symposium* 215c and *Laws* 3.677d].
[5] **presented:** represented. [6] **illiberal:** unbefitting a free (*liber*) man.

Now, dull'd by crook'd Maeander, tardy grown.
Far otherwise, smooth Araris' slow pace
Is ravish'd, Rhodanus, by thy swift race.[7]

Of the latter.

So have I seen, where those fine turrets rear
Their glittering tops, which fatal lightning fear;
The silent Araris so slowly pass
By Rhodanus, as if of solid glass.
When with a lover's speed, th' impatient flood
There meets her, where the fane[8] of Venus stood.
Yet run unmixed together; till at length
He forces her with long resisted strength.

Maeander and Marsyas were worshipped for gods by the idolatrous Gentiles: and to increase their supersistion, whatsoever was offered to Maeander would not mingle with the streams of Marsyas; and what to Marsyas, was cast up by Maeander. Curtius reports that the river Marsyas falls from the top of a mountain on subjacent rocks[9] with a mighty murmur, and passing from thence, glides on in a quiet current: fained a piper, and being stripped of his skin, to have dissolved into water, because that murmur renders a kind of harmony; the river suddenly changing by his abated violence, as if uncased of his skin, assuming another color, and becoming more crystalline. Marsyas, the inventor of wind instruments, may resemble ambition and vainglory, which delight in loud shouts and applause: but virtue and wisdom have a sweeter touch, though they make not so great a noise in popular opinion.

[7] **By Mycale . . . race:** verses by Claudian, 20.265–69. [8] **fane:** temple. [9] **subjacent rocks:** rocks lying beneath.

PLUTARCH

From Lives of the Noble Grecians and Romans Compared Together

1579

The contest of Apollo and Marsyas had long-lived consequences. As a result of Apollo's victory, prejudice against wind-blown instruments persisted in the Renaissance. In *Il Libro del Cortegiano* (1528, English translation 1588 as *The Book of the Courtier*), for example, Baldassare Castiglione (1478–1529) has his spokesman

Plutarch, *Lives of the Noble Grecians and Romans Compared Together,* trans. Sir Thomas North (London: Thomas Vautroullier and John Wright, 1579), 211–12.

Sir Frederick side with Apollo when it comes to instruments worthy of a courtier's cultivation: "All instruments with frets" — that is all stringed instruments — "are full of harmony, because the tunes of them are very perfect, and with ease a man may do many things upon them that fill the mind with sweetness of music" (101). The rationale for such prejudice can be found in one of the stories that Plutarch tells about Alcibiades (c. 450–404 B.C.E.), the enterprising Athenian general who was a protégé of Socrates. The collection of exemplary biographies put together by the Greek writer Plutarch (first century C.E.) was one of the most widely read books of the sixteenth century. Writing long after Rome had succeeded Athens as the center of Western civilization, Plutarch set the lives of notable Greeks and Romans in parallel, matching up figures with similar careers. Sixteenth-century gentlemen like Sir Thomas North (1535–c. 1603) took Plutarch's biographies to be models of how modern men ought — and ought not — to live their lives. After studying at university, probably at Peterhouse College, Cambridge, North took up law studies at Lincoln's Inn in 1557 but spent most of his career translating classical texts. North's translation of Plutarch's *Lives of the Noble Grecians and Romans Compared Together* (1579), dedicated to Queen Elizabeth, is quite explicit about the collection's ethical program. Whatever the complications of Alcibiades' military career (Plutarch parallels him with Coriolanus, both of whom changed sides and had trouble maintaining their popularity), Alcibiades taught Renaissance gentlemen a straightforward lesson about music: flute-playing is *infra dignitatem,* beneath one's dignity.

The Life of Alcibiades

. . . When he was put to school to learn, he was very obedient to all his masters that taught him anything, saving that he disdained to learn to play of the flute or recorder: saying, that it was no gentlemanly quality. For, said he, to play on the viol with a stick, doth not alter man's favor, nor disgraceth any gentleman: but otherwise, to play on the flute, his countenance altereth and changeth so oft, that his familiar friends can scant know him. Moreover, the harp or viol doth not let[1] him that playeth on them, from speaking, or singing as he playeth: where he that playeth on the flute, holdeth his mouth so hard to it, that it taketh not only his words from him, but his voice. Therefore, said he, let the children of the Thebans[2] play on the flute, that cannot tell how to speak: as for us Athenians, we have (as our forefathers tell us) for protectors and patrons of our country, the goddess Pallas,[3] and the god Apollo: of the which the one in old time (as it is said) brake the

[1] **let:** prevent. [2] **Thebans:** citizens of the city of Thebes in Boeotia, famous for their indolence and sluggishness. [3] **Pallas:** Athena, Minerva in Latin.

flute, and the other pulled his skin over his ears, that played upon a flute. Thus Alcibiades alleging these reasons, partly in sport, and partly in good earnest, did not only himself leave to learn to play on the flute, but he turned his companions' minds also quite from it. For these words of Alcibiades, ran from boy to boy incontinently:[4] that Alcibiades had reason to despise playing on the flute, and that he mocked all those that learned to play of it. So afterwards, it fell out at Athens, that teaching to play of the flute, was put out of the number of honest and liberal exercises, and the flute itself was thought a vile instrument, and of no reputation.

[4] **incontinently:** immediately.

JOHN CASE (ATTRIBUTED)

From The Praise of Music

1586

The varied musics of *Twelfth Night* take their varied places in a grand conception of Music with a capital *M.* Marsyas with his mindless piping stands as the ultimate inspiration for the snatches of catches that Sir Toby and Sir Andrew wail in the night air. Feste's songs, if accompanied by a lute or other stringed instrument, might have carried the force of cosmic harmony. The latter possibility is part of *The Praise of Music,* a volume that collects between two covers just about everything that anybody ever said about music. The book was published anonymously in 1586, but three years later the poet Thomas Watson and the composer William Byrd collaborated on *A Gratification unto Master John Case for His Learned Book Lately Made in Praise of Music.* Case (d. 1600), having been a chorister at Christ Church and New College, Oxford, took degrees at St. John's College, Oxford, but left his fellowship there to tutor Catholic young men in logic and philosophy in his own home. Case's Catholic sympathies may be indicated not only in his connection with Byrd (who remained true to the old faith even though he composed liturgical music for the Church of England) but in the primary goal of *The Praise of Music,* announced in the subtitle: to declare *The Sober and Lawful Use of the Same in the Congregation and Church of God.*

In the three chapters reproduced here Case pursues three concerns relevant to the music in *Twelfth Night.* Chapter 1, "The antiquity and original of music," recognizes the difficulty of writing about music, even the difficulty of reading about it. Something ordinarily understood through the ears is turned into something understood through the eyes. Chapter 3, "The suavity of music," questions just where music resides — in the voice, in the body, in the cosmos, in the soul. The author affirms the last site, since it is in the soul that voice, body, and cosmos come together. Chapter 4 takes up the physical, psychological, and spiritual effects of music on listeners. The polemical purpose of *The Praise of Music* is to justify the inclusion of music in religious worship. The title page carries an epigraph from St. Jerome's commentary on the Psalms: "God is delighted with the morning and evening hymns of the church, in a faithful soul, which rejecting the ceremonies of vain superstition, praiseth Him devoutly." Malvolio, with his antipathy to music in act 2, scene 3, constitutes just the kind of adversary that the author of *The Praise of Music* attempts to persuade.

From *The Praise of Music*

Chapter 1

The antiquity and original of music: first generally, then more particularly set down

It were but lost labor to write anything of music, being an art of more use than credit, more known than acknowledged, were it not that more indifference is to be looked for of the eye, to whose view and oversight she betaketh herself, than hath heretofore been shown by the ear, whose itching sense she hardly[1] contented. But fullness perhaps breeds loathing. And the eye which in a manner hath been kept hungry from these things, may by sight and reading hereof, both satisfy herself, and teach her ungrateful neighbor the ear to think better of so comfortable a treasure. The commendation whereof as it ariseth from many heads, namely her parentage, ancientry, dignity, her both pleasant and profitable service, with other as many and no whit meaner arguments of her praise, all which jointly fill up a perfect measure of more than common honor, so her birth and antiquity maketh not least to the setting forth of her beauty.

And although it is for poor men to reckon[2] their cattle, because rich men's score groweth out of number, and for younglings to account their years, because antiquities wax out of mind, whereupon the Arcadians[3] lest they might come in question of juniority[4] to any other country would needs be elder than the moon. Yet, the casting of her nativity can in no wise prejudice so ancient a science, whose continuance is great but not defined, her birthday ancient, but not dated. For Time cannot say that was before her, or Nature that she wrought without her. To prove this look upon the frame and workmanship of the whole world, whether there be not above, an harmony

[1] **hardly:** scarcely. [2] **reckon:** count. [3] **Arcadians:** inhabitants of a land-locked region of southern Greece, famous as musicians. [4] **juniority:** recentness of foundation.

John Case [attributed], *The Praise of Music: Wherein besides the Antiquity, Dignity, Delectation, and Use Thereof in Civil Matters is also Declared the Sober and Lawful Use of the Same in the Congregation and Church of God* (Oxford: Joseph Barnes, 1586), 1–3, 36, 40–45, 53–54, 56–57, 63–65.

between the spheres, beneath a symbolism[5] between the elements. Look upon a man, whom the philosophers termed a little world, whether the parts accord not one to the other by consent and unity. And who can blame nature in any reason for using her own invention? Doth the nightingale record by art or by nature? Although the Roman taught his crow this one lesson with much ado, "All hail Caesar," and the Carthaginian, his birds hardly enough to sing this one plain song, "Hannon is god," yet it is I am sure besides the custom, and perhaps beyond the cunning of any man to instruct the nightingale in so pleasant and variable notes, being as cunningly delivered as speedily learned. But to leave Nature and come to Art, which then is at her best when she is nearest this mistress, who can be ignorant that Nature hath given her the groundwork, whereon she a long time hath flourished? . . .

Chapter 3

The suavity[6] of music

Music whether it be in the voice only as Socrates thought, or both in the voice and motion of the body as Aristoxenus supposed, or as Theophrastus was of opinion not only in the voice and motion of the body, but also in agitation of the mind, hath a certain divine influence into the souls of men, whereby our cogitations and thought (say Epicurus[7] what he will) are brought into a celestial acknowledging of their natures. For as the Platonics and Pythagorians think, all souls of men are at the recordation[8] of that celestial music, whereof they were partakers in heaven, before they entered into their bodies so wonderfully delighted, that no man can be found so hard hearted which is not exceedingly allured with the sweetness thereof. And therefore some of the ancient philosophers attribute this to a hidden divine virtue, which they suppose naturally to be ingenerated in our minds, and for this cause some other of them as Herophilus and Aristoxenus which was also a musician, thought that the soul was nothing else, but a musical motion, caused of the nature and figure of the whole body, gathering thereof this necessary conclusion, that whereas things that are of like natures, have mutual and easy action and passion between themselves, it must needs be, that musical concent[9] being like that harmonical motion which he calleth the soul, doth most wonderfully allure, and as it were, ravish our senses and cogitations. But this which I have said may seem peradventure to be too

[5] **symbolism:** correspondence. [6] ***suavity:*** sweetness. [7] **Epicurus:** the Greek philosopher Epicurus (c. 340–270 B.C.E.) took a strictly materialist view of human thought and emotion. [8] **recordation:** remembering. [9] **concent:** harmony.

profoundly handled. I will therefore confirm it by natural experience and examples. And first generally, as I said before, there is neither man, nor any other living creature exempt from the participation of the pleasure of music.

As for man let us begin with him even from his cradle and so take a view of his whole life. And we shall see, that even every particular action of his is seasoned with this delight. First in his infancy, while he is yet wholly destitute of reason, we see that the child is stilled and allured to sleep, with the sweet songs and lullabies of his nurse, although the grief of his tender limbs be such as is able to breed impatience in a stronger body. And for this cause is it, that children are so delighted and allured with rattles and bells and such like toys as make a sound. Now as strength and judgement increase in man, so music pleaseth and delighteth him more and more. So that whether he be noble or ignoble, yet the same delight of mind groweth to perfection together with the body. And therefore Aristotle in his *Politics,* counseleth that children be instructed in music, especially if they be of noble parentage, not so much for the profit and commodity thereof, as because it is agreeable to nature being itself both liberal and honest.[10] For in all matters to propose profit as the only end, is neither the part of a liberal nature nor of a gentlemanlike disposition. Again in base and ignoble persons, the very senses and spirits are wonderfully inflamed, with the rural songs of Phyllis and Amaryllis.[11] Insomuch that even the ploughman and carter,[12] are by the instinct of their harmonical souls, compelled to frame their breath into a whistle, thereby not only pleasing themselves, but also diminishing the tediousness of their labors. And therefore most natural is that which Virgil useth in describing of a good housewife:

> The housewife's spinning makes her labor long
> Seem light with singing of some merry song.[13]

As also that other spoken of in the pruner of trees:

> The lopper singing from the craggy rock
> The boughs and leaves beats down with many a knock[14]

And that of the sheep herders:

> Mopsus my friend, seeing our skill is great,
> Thine for the tune, mine for the pleasant rime,
> In the hazel bower why take we not our seat,
> In mirth and singing there spend the time?

[10] **liberal and honest:** free and upright, in the social, moral, pedagogical, and ontological senses of both words. [11] **Phyllis and Amaryllis:** typical names of women in pastoral poetry. [12] **carter:** cart driver. [13] **The housewife's spinning . . . song:** quoting from Virgil, *Georgics* I. [14] **The lopper . . . knock:** quoting from Virgil, *Eclogues* I.

And hence it is, that wayfaring men, solace themselves with songs and ease the wearisomeness of their journey, considering that music as a pleasant companion, is unto them instead of a wagon on the way. And hence it is, that manual laborers, and mechanical artificers of all sorts, keep such a chanting and singing in their shops: the tailor on his bulk, the shoemaker at his last, the mason at his wall, the ship boy at his oar, the tinker at his pan, and the tiler on the housetop. And therefore well sayeth Quintilian, that every troublesome and laborious occupation useth music for a solace and recreation. Whereof that perhaps may be the cause, which Geraldus[15] noteth. The symphony and concert of music, sayeth he, agreeth with the interior parts and affections of the soul. For as there are three parts or faculties of man's soul, the first and worthiest the part reasonable, which is ever chief and never in subjection to the other, the second irascible,[16] which, as it is ruled of the former, so ruleth the latter, and the last concupiscible,[17] which ever obeyeth and never ruleth. So if we compare the symphony of music, with these powers of the soul, we shall find great convenience and affinity between them. . . .

Chapter 4

The effects and operation of music

In the former chapter was gathered a proof and demonstration of the sweetest of music, proceeding from the causes to the effects. Now I mean, by the contrary demonstration, to prove the delectation thereof from the effects to the causes. For it cannot be but that as the convenience and agreement which music hath with our nature is the cause of the delectation thereof, so the pleasure and delectation is also the cause of those effects which it worketh as well in the minds as bodies of them that hear it. Music being in itself wholly most effectual, importeth much of his force and efficacy, even to the peculiar parts and portions thereof. And thereupon ancient writers make the distinction of songs and notes in music, according to the operations which they work in their hearers, calling some of them chaste and temperate, some amorous and light, othersome warlike, others peaceable, some melancholic and doleful, others pleasant and delightful. . . .

So that the effects of music generally are these. To make haste to incite and stir up men's courage, to allay and pacify anger, to move pity and com-

[15] **Geraldus:** Geraldus de Berri, called Geraldus Cambrensis (1146?–1220?), cleric, statesman, and author of itineraries that describe his extensive travels. [16] **irascible:** capable of anger, the second faculty of the soul according to Plato. [17] **concupiscible:** capable of desire, the third faculty of the soul according to Plato.

passion, and to make pleasant and delightsome. Nay yet I will go farther and doubt not but to prove by good authority, that music hath brought mad men to their perfect wits and senses, that it hath cured diseases, driven away evil spirits, yea, and also abandoned the pestilence[18] from men and cities. . . .

I durst in no wise affirm the last effect and operation of this worthy art, were it not that Plato with his credit and authority did embolden me: *"Mutati musica moduli,"* sayeth he, *"status publici mutationem afferunt"* (The changing of musical notes, hath caused an alteration of the common state). The reason hereof can be no other than this: because by this force of music, as well those of less heart and courage, are stirred by, as those of greater stomach weakened and unabled to any excellent enterprise. Whereupon he also inferreth, that such are the manners of young men, as are the notes and tunes they are accustomed to in their tender years.

Now if these my proofs and authorities shall to some . . . unmoveable person either seem too weak or the things attributed to music too hyperbolical, he shall betray either his ignorance in not having read ancient writers, in whom, as of all other sciences, so of this especially, as most admirable, condign[19] praises are comprehended, or else his malice, in derogating from this art, those properties which he can neither deny other men have given, nor convince, ought not by good reason to be attributed thereunto. For as I do not stand on the sufficiency of these allegations, meaning on this part only to show what hath been ascribed unto music in former times, so it is not enough for any malicious Musomastix[20] to take his pen and write I lie, unless he can by sufficient reason declare, that these authors by me cited have erred heretofore, which if he shall not be able to perform, then let him give some reason why music in these days, is not the same it hath been heretofore. Or why music hath rather lost any of her former excellency, than increased in perfection from time to time, considering that time is the perfecter and increaser of all arts. But I will not willingly entangle myself with the brain and fantastical devils of this sort of men. Only I conclude this point, with that common saying of the learned: *"Scientia neminem habet inimicum nisi ignorantem"* (None are so great enemies to knowledge as they that know nothing at all).

[18] **pestilence:** the plague. [19] **condign:** fitting. [20] **Musomastix:** Music Hater.

THOMAS WRIGHT

From The Passions of the Mind in General

1604

A more scientific explanation of the powers of music is offered by Thomas Wright (1561–1623) in his treatise *The Passions of the Mind,* first printed in 1601 and revised in 1604. A brief biography of Wright appears in Chapter 3. The word *passions* in Wright's title is the term that speakers of early modern English used for what we today would call *emotions.* Our word is bound up with modern ideas of a subconscious self "out of" which feelings "move" (*ex + movere*). Wright's word is less psychological than physiological. A model of the human body going back to the Galen (second century C.E.) was, in Shakespeare's time, only just beginning to be modified in response to scientific anatomy. In Galen's construction, the body is a closed system of four basic fluids or humors, the composition of which changes in response to external stimuli like sounds.[1] The following excerpt from *The Passions of the Mind in General* questions how music is able to work its effects on the body. Even Wright, in his attempt to be as rational as possible, entertains the idea that music offers a unique means of harmonizing the body and the cosmos.

But to knit up this discourse there remaineth a question to be answered, as difficult as any whatsoever in all natural or moral philosophy; viz., how music stirreth up these passions, and moveth so mightily these affections. What hath the shaking or artificial crispling of the air (which is in effect the substance of music) to do with rousing up choler, afflicting with melancholy, jubilating the heart with pleasure, elevating the soul with devotion, alluring to lust, inducing to peace, exciting to compassion, inviting to magnanimity? It is not so great a marvel that meat, drink, exercise, and air set passions aloft, for these are divers ways qualified, and consequently apt to stir up humors;[2] but what quality carry simple single sounds and voices to enable them to work such wonders? I had rather in this point read some learned discourse than deliver mine opinion; nevertheless, in such an abstruse difficulty he that speaketh most apparently and probably saith the best; and therefore I will set down those forms or manners of motion which occur to my mind and seem likeliest.

[1] Useful introductions to Galenic ideas about physiology, sensation, and emotion are provided by Siraisi, *Medieval and Early Renaissance Medicine,* 97–114, and Park, "The Organic Soul," 464–84. For a more extended treatment, see James, *Passion and Action,* esp. 1–25.

[2] **humors:** four bodily fluids of blood, yellow bile, black bile, and phlegm.

Thomas Wright, *The Passions of the Mind in General* (1604), ed. William Webster Newbold (New York: Garland Publishing, 1986), 208–10.

The first is a certain sympathy, correspondence, or proportion betwixt our souls and music; and no other cause can be yielded. Who can give any other reason why the loadstone draweth iron but a sympathy of nature? Why the needle, touched but with such a stone, should never leave looking toward the North Pole, who can render other reason than sympathy of nature? If we make a survey of all birds of the air, fishes of the sea, beasts of the land, we shall find every sort affect a proper kind of food; a lion will eat no hay, nor a bull, beef; a horse eateth bread, and a leopard abhorreth it; a kite liveth upon carrion, and a hen cannot endure it; if a man should beat his brain to find out the reason, no better can be given than sympathy of nature. So we may say that such is the nature of our souls as music hath a certain proportionate sympathy with them, as our tastes have with such variety of dainty cates, our smelling, such variety of odors, etc.

The second manner of this miracle in nature some assign and ascribe to God's general providence, who, when these sounds affect the ear, produceth a certain spiritual quality in the soul, the which stirreth up one or other passion, according to the variety of voices or consorts of instruments. Neither this is to be marveled at, for the very same upon necessity we must put in the imagination, the which not being able to dart the forms of fancies, which are material, into the understanding, which is spiritual; therefore where nature wanteth, God's providence supplieth. So corporal music being unable to work such extraordinary effects in our souls, God, by his ordinary natural providence, produceth them. The like we may say of the creation of our souls, for men being able to produce the body but unable to create the soul; man prepareth the matter and God createth the form. So in music men sound and hear, God striketh upon and stirreth up the heart.

The third manner, more sensible and palpable, is this: that the very sound itself, which according to the best philosophy is nothing else but a certain artificial shaking, crispling, or tickling of the air (like as we see in the water crispled, when it is calm and a sweet gale of wind ruffleth it a little; or when we cast a stone into a calm water we may perceive divers warbling natural circles) which passeth through the ears, and by them into the heart, and there beateth and tickleth it in such sort as it is moved with semblable[3] passions. For as the heart is most delicate and sensitive, so it perceiveth the least motions and impressions that may be; and it seemeth that music in those cells playeth with the vital and animate spirits, the only instruments and spurs of passions. In like manner, we perceive by a little tickling of our sides or the soles of our feet how we are moved to laughter; yea, and the very heart-strings seem in some sort to be moved by this almost senseless

[3] **semblable:** similar, like.

motion. And in confirmation hereof we may bring two apt conjectures. The first is, in our own hands or face, the which if we smooth, tickle, press down, nip, heat, or cool we perceive divers sorts and diversities of sensations, and feel ourselves sundry ways affected; if such varieties we find in a thick skin, how much more in a tender heart, far more apter to feel than any member else of our body. The second conjecture is the filing of iron and scraping of trenchers,[4] which many naturally (yea, and almost all men, before they be accustomed unto them) abhor to hear, not only because they are ungrateful to the ear but also for that the air so carved punisheth and fretteth the heart.

The last and best manner I take to be that as all other senses have an admirable multiplicity of objects which delight them, so hath the ear; and as it is impossible to expound the variety of delights or disgusts we perceive by them and receive in them (for who can distinguish the delights we take in eating fish, flesh, fruit, so many thousand sauces and commixtions of spices with fish, flesh, and fruit), so in music divers consorts stir up in the heart divers sorts of joys and divers sorts of sadness or pain, the which, as men are affected, may be diversly applied. Let a good and Godly man hear music and he will lift up his heart to heaven; let a bad man hear the same and he will convert it to lust. Let a soldier hear a trumpet or a drum and his blood will boil and bend to battle; let a clown hear the same and he will fall a dancing; let the common people hear the like and they will fall a gazing or laughing, and many never regard them, especially if they be accustomed to hear them. So that in this, men's affection and dispositions by means of music may stir up divers passions, as in seeing we daily prove the like.

True it is that one kind of music may be more apt to one passion than another, as also one object of sight is more proportionate to stir up love, hatred, or pleasure, or sadness than another. Wherefore the natural disposition of a man, his custom or exercise, his virtue or vice, for most part at these sounds diversificate passions; for I cannot imagine that if a man never had heard a trumpet or drum in his life that he would at the first hearing be moved to wars. Much more might be said in this matter, and yet not all fully satisfy and content a sound judgement; but what occurred unto me in this question I have set down, leaving the choice and approbation, or censure, to them that see more in it than I do.

[4] **trenchers:** metal dishes.

CHAPTER 3

Sexuality

It takes just seven words, about three seconds in time, for the master motive of *Twelfth Night* to be introduced: "If music be the food of *love*" (1.1.1). As early modern speakers and listeners understood the word, "love" could cover quite diverse ideas and feelings.[1] To start at the top, there is *agape,* the love of God for His creation. *Philia,* the love of friends for each other, is rated by Aristotle in the *Nicomachaean Ethics* as the highest of all human bonds. Finally there is *erōs.* Orsino's equation of "love" with food leaves no doubt about which kind of "love" he has in mind at the beginning of *Twelfth Night:*

> If music be the food of love, play on;
> Give me excess of it, that surfeiting,
> The appetite may sicken and so die. (1.1.1–3)

"Appetite" is the key word here. Aristotle's treatise *De Anima* (On the Soul) disposed Shakespeare, his actors, and his audiences to understand desire for another person's body as one particular instance of the soul's two basic responses to external stimuli: either desire or avoidance. Through the senses the soul becomes aware of objects outside the body. Imagination

[1] On the four kinds of love and their interrelated histories in antiquity, the Middle Ages, and the Renaissance, see Singer, *The Nature of Love,* volume 1.

presents an image of such objects to the heart, and the heart's response produces chemical alterations in the body's fluids that early modern men and women knew as "passions." While there was some disagreement on just what the range of these passions might be — Aristotle in the *Nicomachean Ethics* distinguishes eleven — most authorities agreed with Aristotle that all of them are versions of pleasure or pain. Response to a beautiful person is, then, a function of one's soul, an experience of a desire to draw into one's own body the sensuous image of that person's body. *Concupiscence* is Plato's word for this state of feeling — Orsino's "appetite" is a synonym — and it is contrasted with the soul's capacity for "irascibility."[2]

To stay absolutely true to early modern ways of thinking, we should talk about Orsino's love-longing in act 1, scene 1, as an instance of *erōs,* not as a matter of "sexuality." The word "sex" certainly existed in early seventeenth-century English, meaning the configuration of bodily characteristics that distinguish male from female. The term *sexuality,* however, dates from no earlier than the 1830s and 1840s, when it was coined as a biological term for reproductive activity involving anatomical parts identified as male and female, whether that activity occurs in plants, animals, or human beings. As a psychological term, as a word for the interior experience of genital desire, "sexuality" dates only from the second half of the nineteenth century. Later still is the sense of the word as a mode of self-identity. To speak of Orsino's "sexuality" is, then, an anachronism. Be that as it may, Orsino's desires are unmistakably focused on certain body parts. Orsino, whose comment on "Cesario's" girl-like voice we have noted already in Chapter 2, emphasizes the femininity of his new servant's appearance when he sends him/her/him as messenger to Olivia: "It shall become thee well to act my woes," the Duke says,

> She will attend it better in thy youth
> Than in a nuncio's of more grave aspect.
> VIOLA: I think not so, my lord.
> ORSINO: Dear lad, believe it;
> For they shall yet belie thy happy years
> That say thou art a man. Diana's lip
> Is not more smooth and rubious; thy small pipe
> Is as the maiden's organ, shrill and sound,

[2] The eleven passions mentioned by Aristotle in the *Nicomachean Ethics* are appetite, anger, fear, confidence, envy, joy, love, hatred, longing, emulation, and pity, which tend to form opposite pairs (appetite/anger, fear/confidence, envy/joy, love/hatred, emulation/pity) that conform with Aristotle's treatment of the passions in his *Rhetoric:* anger/mildness, love/hatred, fear/confidence, shame/esteem, kindness/unkindness, pity/indignation, envy/emulation. See James, *Passion and Action,* 5.

And all is semblative a woman's part.
I know thy constellation is right apt
For this affair. (1.4.25–34)

"Constellation" here carries its literal sense as an ensemble of stars, with power to influence human events. "Lip," "pipe," and "organ" are not just terms of anatomy: they are explicitly terms of *sexual* anatomy. They refer to parts of the female reproductive apparatus that Orsino is imagining in his mind's eye as well as to parts of the male vocal tract that he is seeing and hearing in the supposed young man in front of him. A vagina has "lips," a "neck" connects the vagina to the womb, "the maiden's organ" may be the recently anatomized clitoris (Park 171–94). (See Figures 15 and 16.) Olivia is no less attentive to the sex-coding of "Cesario's" body. After "Cesario" has departed, Olivia reflects on "Cesario's" reply "I am a gentleman":

I'll be sworn thou art!
Thy tongue, thy face, thy limbs, actions, and spirit
Do give thee fivefold blazon. (1.5.236–38)

We can, then, with some propriety speak of "sexuality" as one of the seventeenth-century contexts for *Twelfth Night,* as long as we realize we are talking about the focus of erotic desire on certain body parts and not about the psychological or political identities of the speakers who feel that desire. That is not to say, however, that early modern ways of articulating erotic experience have nothing to do with our own ideas about sexuality. The distinctive ways in which erotic desire is articulated in *Twelfth Night* serve as a forceful reminder that *erōs* may be a universal instinct but the objects to which *erōs* is directed vary from culture to culture and from historical moment to historical moment.

Will and Passion

→ WILLIAM SHAKESPEARE

From Shake-spear's Sonnets, Never Before Imprinted

1609

What you will: the best possible gloss to the subtitle of *Twelfth Night* is provided by William Shakespeare himself in two of the 154 sonnets published in a quarto edition by the printer Thomas Thorpe in 1609. Shakespeare's connection with this printing project is problematic. By 1609 sonnets were *passé* as a verse form. Most scholars agree that the sonnets must have been written more than a decade earlier. It is possible, however, that Shakespeare was capitalizing on the outmoded features of the genre by writing sonnets that are anything but the conventional complaints of a male lover to his aloof mistress. To begin with, there are three parties to the transactions in Shakespeare's sonnets, not two. As printed by Thorpe, the 154 sonnets fall into two loosely linked narrative groups: 126 sonnets concerning (and in many cases addressed to) "a man right fair" and 28 sonnets concerning (and addressed to) "a woman colored ill." Another major difference from conventional sonnets is the fact that all three parties, the woman included, don't just feel erotic desire; they act on it, each, it seems, with the other two.

Sonnets 135 and 136 are among the sonnets addressed to the so-called dark lady. In their erotic exuberance and arch wit, they resemble other sonnets in the group, such as 127 ("In the old age black was not counted fair"), 128 ("How oft, when thou, my music, music play'st /. . . / Do I envy those jacks"), 130 ("My mistress' eyes are nothing like the sun"), and 132 ("Thine eyes I love, and they, as pitying me, /. . . / Have put on black"). The particular joke in 135 and 136 turns on the word *will,* which, depending on how the reader takes it, not only points to a head-spinning variety of referents but even defies the laws of syntax as it shifts from noun to verb and back again. As a noun, *will* in these sonnets can mean volition, lust, penis, vagina, and the author's nickname Will. As a verb, it can indicate future action. The reader faces the delightful challenge of letting the word mean all those things at once. One result of doing so is to cast doubt on how language can ever hope to pin down *erōs.*

From *Shake-spear's Sonnets, Never Before Imprinted*

135

Whoever hath her wish, thou has thy *Will,*[1]
And *Will* to boot, and *Will* in over-plus.
More than enough am I that vex thee still,
To thy sweet will making addition thus.
Wilt thou whose will is large and spacious,
Not once vouchsafe to hide my will in thine?
Shall will in others seem right gracious,
And in my will no fair acceptance shine?
The sea, all water, yet receives rain still,[2]
And in abundance addeth to his store.

[1] ***Will:*** italics and capitalization follow the 1609 printing, which italicizes and capitalizes some instances of "will" but not others. [2] **still:** continuously.

William Shakespeare, *Shake-spear's Sonnets, Never Before Imprinted* (London: Thomas Thorpe, 1609), I.

So thou being rich in *Will* add to thy *Will*
One will of mine to make thy large *Will* more.
  Let no unkind, no fair beseechers[3] kill;
  Think all but one, and me in that one *Will.*

136

If thy soul check[4] thee that I come so near,
Swear to thy blind soul that I was thy *Will,*
And will thy soul knows is admitted there;
Thus far for love my love-suit sweet fulfill.[5]
Will will fulfill the treasure of thy love,
Ay, fill it full with wills, and my will one.
In things of great receipt[6] with ease we prove
Among a number one is reckoned none.[7]
Then in the number let me pass untold,[8]
Though in thy store's account I one must be.
For nothing[9] hold me, so it please thee hold
That nothing me a something sweet to thee.
  Make but my name thy love, and love that still,[10]
  And then thou lovest me for my name is *Will.*

[3] **beseechers:** suitors. [4] **check:** reproach. [5] **fulfill:** grant (with pun on fill full). [6] **receipt:** capability of receiving. [7] **Among . . . none:** alluding to the common saying "one is no number." [8] **untold:** uncounted. [9] **nothing:** with pun on "no thing," no penis. [10] **still:** always.

Heart, Soul, and Genitalia

To understand early modern notions of erotic desire — what it is, what causes it, how it makes the desiring subject feel, what it causes him or her to do — we need to understand early modern notions about the soul and the emotions. For us, "soul" is a thoroughly spiritual concept. For Shakespeare and his contemporaries, it was as much physical as spiritual. "Soul" was, indeed, the entity that joined body with spirit. It was imagined to have a triple nature: not only "rational" in its capacity to know and to will but "sensible" in its capacity to see, hear, smell, taste, and touch and "vegetable" in its capacity to process food, grow, and reproduce.[1] In such a conception of self, erotic desire begins as sense experience, as a body seen, as a voice heard, as a

[1] These multiple functions are handily summarized from ancient and Renaissance sources in Bamborough, *Little World of Man,* 29–51.

breath smelled, as lips tasted, as flesh touched. All of the senses, let us recall, are engaged in Orsino's description of music as "the food of love": it can be tasted, felt as downward motion, heard with the ears, breathed in like the scent of violets, seen as flowers on a bank (1.1.1–7). When "Cesario" appears before Orsino in act 1, scene 4, the impression the he/she/he makes is likewise synaesthetic. Orsino commends "Cesario's" lips for their color and smoothness to the touch, his/her/his voice for its pitch and clarity (1.4.29–32). Olivia's "five-fold blazon" of "Cesario" may, in turn, find its fiveness in the five senses: in her catalogue of "this youth's perfections" Olivia includes the sight of "Cesario's" face and limbs, the sounds (and perhaps the imagined taste) of his/her/his tongue, the plasticity of his/her/his actions, perhaps even the fragrance of his/her/his "spirit" if we take that word to mean breath as well as vigor (1.5.238–39).

According to Aristotelian and Galenic ideas about the body, external sense experiences like these were then conveyed via an aerated fluid called *spiritus* to the common sense, where the individual sensations were combined and presented to the imagination. Olivia knows precisely what is happening to her:

> Even so quickly may one catch the plague?
> Methinks I feel this youth's perfections
> With an invisible and subtle stealth
> To creep in at mine eyes. (1.5.240–43)

Some theorists referred to this internal image as *species*. Dispersal of the image through the succumbing lover's entire body was accomplished by *spiritus*. Anatomical studies and the philosophical criterion of efficiency led sixteenth- and seventeenth-century thinkers increasingly to question the existence of *species*, but authorities like Helkiah Crooke in *Microcosmographia* (1618) and even Descartes could not give up the idea of the body as a hydraulic system in which *spiritus* does the work of intercommunication among the body's parts.[2] Crooke knew all about the nerves as a network of specialized tissue; what he did not know was the workings of electrical impulses. It was in the heart that sense impressions, brought there by *spiritus*, were converted into passions in *Le Prince d'Amour*, a masque presented by nine law students, disguised as "nine several passions," making their entry out of a giant heart (see Introduction, p. 123).

[2] On Descartes see Charles Taylor, *The Sources of the Self*, 143–58.

THOMAS WRIGHT

From The Passions of the Mind in General *1604*

The entire process whereby perception of a beautiful object becomes a bodily desire is explained by Thomas Wright in *The Passions of the Mind in General:*

> First, then, to our imagination cometh by sense or memory some object to be known, convenient or disconvenient to Nature; the which being known [. . .] in the imagination [. . .] presently the purer spirits flock from the brain by certain secret channels to the heart, where they pitch at the door, signifying what an object was presented, convenient or disconvenient for it. The heart immediately bendeth either to prosecute it or to eschew it, and the better to effect that affection draweth other humors to help him. (Wright 123)

Erotic desire was imagined to rouse one humor in particular: blood. The succumbing lover experiences this visceral bodily response as *passion.* There was some debate among the authorities about how many passions there are, but love makes every list.

Wright (1561–1624) was born into an old Catholic family in York and received a Jesuit education at the English College in Rome. After teaching at the English College at Valladolid in Spain, he returned to England and, with protection from the Earl of Essex, worked openly to secure religious toleration for Catholics in exchange for their political loyalty to the English crown. Part of his plan was to exploit the political threat posed by Puritans. Repeatedly imprisoned at the instigation of Essex's rivals the Cecils, Wright returned to the Continent about 1610 but again returned to England in 1623–24 as a canon to William Bishop, whose presence as Vicar Apostolic was allowed by King James. *The Passions of the Mind in General* (first published in 1601, then in a revised and enlarged edition in 1604) was probably written while Wright was under house arrest with the dean of Westminster in 1597–98.

The Passions of the Mind in General was designed by Wright with the express purpose of helping the reader learn to control the passions, the better to make his or her way in the world. In Wright's scheme reason stands in an uneasy relationship to the passions. Reason ought to direct the passions, but the passions have a friendlier working relationship with the senses. Indeed, the passions can prevent reason from knowing the truth about objects that the body, through the senses, sees and hears. Folk in England, Wright claims, are especially in need of his book, since their openness and forthrightness make them vulnerable to the ploys of foreigners. In their distinctive temper Englishmen are no different from other people. "In traveling in strange countries," Wright observes, the reader

> may discover to what passion the people are most inclined; for as I have seen by experience, there is no nation in Europe that hath not some extraordinary affection either in pride, anger, lust, inconstancy, gluttony, drunkenness,

sloth, or such like passion. Much it importeth in good conversation to know exactly the company's inclination; and his society cannot but be grateful whose passions are moderate and behavior circumspect. (92)

The inhabitants of Illyria, suffice it to say, are prone to falling in love. Two chapters from Wright's *The Passions of the Mind in General* will give today's readers a sense of what people in the early seventeenth century told themselves was happening when they fell in love.

From *The Passions of the Mind in General*

Book 1, Chapter 2

What We Understand by Passions and Affections

Three sorts of actions proceed from men's souls: some are internal and immaterial, as the acts of our wits and wills; others be mere external and material, as the acts of our senses (seeing, hearing, moving, etc.); others stand betwixt these two extremes and border upon them both; the which we may best discover in children, because they lack the use of reason and are guided by an internal imagination, following nothing else but that pleaseth their senses, even after the same manner as brute beasts do; for as we see beasts hate, love, fear, and hope, so do children. Those actions then which are common with us and beasts we call passions and affections, or perturbations, of the mind. *Motus,* saith St. Augustine, *animae quos Graeci pathe apellant ex Latinis quidam ut Cicero 3 Tuscul. perturbationes dixerunt, alii affectiones, alii affectus, alii expressas passiones vocaverunt.* "The motions of the soul, called of the Greeks pathe, some Latins, as Cicero, called them perturbations, others affections, others affects, others more expressly name them passions."[1] They are called passions (although indeed they be acts of the sensitive power or faculty of our soul, and are defined of Damascene *Motio sensualis appetetivae virtutis, ob boni vel mali imaginationem,* "a sensual motion of our appetitive faculty through imagination of some good or ill thing")[2] because when these affections are stirring in our minds they alter the humors of our bodies, causing some passion or alteration in them. They are called perturbations for that (as afterward shall be declared) they trouble

[1] Augustine *De civitate dei,* 9. 4 [Wright's note].
[2] Damascene 2 *De fide orthodoxa,* 2.22 [Wright's note].

Thomas Wright, *The Passions of the Mind in General* (1604), ed. William Webster Newbold (New York: Garland Publishing, 1986), 94–96, 103–05.

wonderfully the soul,[3] corrupting the judgement and seducing the will, inducing, for the most part, to vice, and commonly withdrawing from virtue; and therefore some call them maladies or sores of the soul. They be also named affections, because the soul by them either affecteth some good or, for the affection of some good, detesteth some ill.[4] These passions then be certain internal acts or operations of the soul, bordering upon reason and sense, prosecuting some good thing or flying some ill thing, causing therewithal some alteration in the body.[5]

[6]Here must be noted that albeit these passions inhabit the confines both of sense and reason, yet they keep not equal friendship with both; for passions and sense are like two naughty servants who ofttimes bear more love one to another than they are obedient to their master. And the reason of this amity betwixt the passions and sense I take to be the greater conformity and likeness betwixt them than there is between passions and reason. For passions are drowned in corporal organs and instruments, as well as sense; reason dependeth of no corporal subject, but as a princess in her throne considereth the state of her kingdom. Passions and sense are determined to one thing, and as soon as they perceive their object sense presently receives it and the passions love or hate it; but reason, after she perceiveth her object, she stands in deliberation whether it be convenient she should accept it or refuse it. Besides, sense and passions, as they have had a league the longer, so their friendship is stronger;[7] for all the time of our infancy and childhood our senses were joint friends in such sort with passions, that whatsoever delighted sense pleased the passions, and whatsoever was hurtful to the one was an enemy to the other.[8] And so by long agreement and familiarity the passions had so engaged themselves to sense, and with such bonds and seals of sensual habits confirmed their friendship, that as soon as reason came to possession of her kingdom they began presently to make rebellion; for right reason oftentimes deprived sense of those pleasures he had of so long time enjoyed, as by commanding continency and fasting, which sense most abhorred. Then passions repugned, and very often hailed her by force to condescend to that they demanded; which combat and captivity was well perceived by him who said *Video aliam legem in membris meis repugnantem legi mentis meae et captivantem me in lege peccati,* "I see another law in my members,

[3] Cicero in *Disputationes Tusculanae* 3 [Wright's note].

[4] The definition of Passions [Wright's note].

[5] Zeno apud Cicero *Disputationes Tusculanae* 4: "ita definit[ur] perturbatio ceu pathos aversa a recto ratione contra naturam animi commotio" ("Thus passion is defined as a pathos opposed to right reason and against the nature of the soul") [Wright's note].

[6] Why passions follow rather sense than reason [Wright's note].

[7] Cicero ubi supra (see above) [Wright's note].

[8] Aristotle insinuates, *Ethics,* 3.2 [Wright's note].

repugning to the law of my mind and leading me captive in the law of sin."[9] Whereupon Saint Cyprian said *Cum Avaritia,* etc., "We must contend with avarice, with uncleanness, with anger, with ambition; we have a continual and molestful battle with carnal vices and worldly enticements."[10]

Moreover, after that men by reason take possession over their souls and bodies, feeling this war so mighty, so continual, so near, so domestical that either they must consent to do their enemy's will, or still be in conflict; and withal foreseeing by making peace with them they were to receive great pleasures and delights, the most part of men resolve themselves never to displease their sense or passions, but to grant them whatsoever they demand. What curiosity the eyes will see, they yield unto them; what dainty meats the tongue will taste, they never deny it; what savors the nose will smell, they never resist it; what music the ears will hear, they accept it; and finally, whatsoever by importunity, prayer, or suggestion sensuality requesteth, no sooner to reason the supplication is presented but the petition is granted. Yet if the matter here were ended, and reason yielded but only to the suits of sensuality, it were without doubt a great disorder to see the lord attend so basely upon his servants. But reason, once being entered into league with passions and sense, becometh a better friend to sensuality than the passions were before; for reason straightways inventeth ten thousand sorts of new delights which the passions never could have imagined. And therefore if you ask now who procured such exquisite arts of cookery, so many sauces, so many broths, so many dishes, no better answer can be given than reason, to please sensuality. Who found first such gorgeous attire, such variety of garments, such decking, trimming, and adorning of the body that tailors must every year learn a new trade, but reason to please sensuality. Who devised such stately palaces, such delicious gardens, such precious canopies and embroidered beds, but reason to feed sensuality. In fine, discourse over all arts and occupations and you shall find men laboring night and day spending their wit and reason to excogitate some new invention to delight our sensuality, in such sort as a religious man, once lamenting this ignominious industry of reason employed in the service of sense, wished with all his heart that godly men were but half so industrious to please God as worldly men to please their inordinate appetites. By this we may gather how passions stand so confined with sense and reason that for the friendship they bear to the one they draw the other to be their mate and companion.

[9] Romans 7.23. [Wright's note].
[10] Cyprian *De mortalitate* [Wright's note].

Book 1, Chapter 5

An Explication of the Division of Our Sensitive Appetite into Concupiscibile *and* Irascibile, *That Is, Coveting and Invading*

Before we do declare the number of passions that issue out of our souls, it is necessary to permit a common division of our sensual appetite, found out by experience, allowed of by philosophers, and approved by divines; that is, in *concupiscibile,* which in English may be termed coveting, desiring, wishing, and *irascibile,* that is, anger, invading, or impugning (for so I think it may better be called).[11] These coveting and invading appetites are not two faculties or powers of the soul but one only power and faculty which hath two inclinations; as we have but one power or faculty of seeing but two eyes, one power of hearing with two ears, so we have one sensual appetite with two inclinations, the one to covet, the other to invade.

In the manner of explicating these two inclinations both divines and philosophers dissent; yet two explications there are, as more common, so more probable, and more conform to reason. The first may be declared after this manner:

We see by experience that beasts sometimes have great facility to prosecute or obtain those objects they covet, as for example a horse, the grass which groweth in the pasture where he feedeth; sometimes they have great difficulty, as for the lion to eat a bear; sometimes they have great facility to eschew that evil they hate, a wolf or a fox to escape with his prey from a little cur; other times we prove they have extreme difficulty to avoid it, as a bull to fly from a lion. Now the authors of this explication conclude that the coveting appetite inclineth only to the obtaining of those objects which may easily be come by, and to the eschewing of those that may easily be escaped; the invading appetite only inclineth to the possessing of those objects which may hardly be gotten and hardly escaped.

This explication, in my opinion, as it is more common, so it is more untrue. For who doubteth but many both love and desire (which according to all doctors are operations of the coveting appetite) divers things hard to be compassed, as the two unchaste judges the chaste Susanna; and in beasts we see they often affect, love, and desire that they hardly can purchase. It were folly to think the fox affected, loved, or desired not a goose because she were surely penned up, hardly to be come by; or the wolf desired not the sheep when she is defended with the shepherd's dogs.

[11] Aristotle, *Rhetorica,* 1.10; Hieronymus, 2.10; Damascene, *De fide orthodoxa,* 2.12; Thomas [Aquinas, *Summa Theologine*], 1[a]2[ae].23.1.2 [Wright's note].

Besides, many be angry (which is a passion of the invading appetite) for things they may easily avoid, as the lady which chid her maid because the floor of her chamber was defiled with a drop of candle. Finally, we know God himself to be affected with anger, to whom nothing can be hard or difficile. Many things more might be said concerning this matter, as how the difference of hardly or easily obtaining a thing cannot cause such diversities of inclinations; for so we might say our seeing might be divided, for some things we see with facility, others with difficulty; some sounds we hear easily, others hardly. Moreover, the difficulty of obtaining an object rather deterreth a man from procuring it than inciteth to prosecute it, and therefore consequently it cannot be a cause of distinction. But these arguments and many more for brevity's sake I omit, pretending after another manner to explicate this division.

The other explication, and as easy to be perceived as the precedent, is this: first, as we have insinuated before, God and Nature gave men and beasts these natural instincts or inclinations to provide for themselves all those things that are profitable, and to avoid all those things which are damnifiable; and this inclination may be called *concupiscibilis,* coveting. Yet because that God did foresee that oftentimes there should occur impediments to hinder them from the execution of such inclinations, therefore he gave them an other inclination to help themselves to overcome or avoid those impediments, and to invade or impugn whatsoever resisteth; for the better execution whereof he hath armed all beasts either with force, craft, or flight to eschew all obstacles that may detain them from those things which they conceive as convenient; wherefore to the bull he hath imparted horns, to the boar his tusks, to the lion claws, to the hare her heels, to the fox craft, to men their hands and wit. And for this cause we see the very little children, when any would deprive them of their victuals, for lack of strength to fight they arm themselves with tears. To this explication it seemeth that the names of *irascibilis* and *concupiscibilis* more aptly agree than to the other, because here only *irascibilis* invadeth and impugneth, and not affecteth or desireth, as in the other.

HELKIAH CROOKE

From Microcosmographia: A Description of the Body of Man

1616, 1625

In 1602, when *Twelfth Night* received its first recorded performance, knowledge of the human body was undergoing rapid revision. For nearly fifteen hundred years Europeans had thought about their bodies in the terms given to them by the second-century physician Galen. In Galen's construction, the body was conceived as a container of four basic fluids or "humors" — yellow bile, blood, phlegm, and black bile — each of them seated in a different organ but capable of circulating all over the body. They could also change into one another, depending on ingested food and drink and on stimulation of the senses. Blood, as we have seen, was associated with *erōs*. By 1602 scientific anatomy was challenging Galen's pronouncements. In 1602, however, it was still fourteen years before William Harvey would argue in a lecture that what circulated in the body was not a mixture of humors but blood. It was twelve years later still before Harvey demonstrated his argument in print. Helkiah Crooke's *Microcosmographia* is an encyclopedic work that attempts to collect all the recent findings of scientific anatomy for the use of physicians and the education of learned readers. The full subtitle of *Microcosmographia* declares that the hefty folio volume includes not only *A Description of the Body of Man* but also *The Controversies Thereto Belonging*. What Crooke attempts to do at every turn is to reconcile the evidence of recent anatomical investigations with the received opinions of Galen. Sexual organs present a case in point.

Galen encouraged Shakespeare and his contemporaries to think of male and female sexual organs as being alike: the neck of the womb corresponded to the penis, the ovaries to the testicles. Women's sexual organs were imagined to be merely the inverse of men's, an accident of the relative differences in body heat between men and women produced by differences in humors. The greater heat and dryness of men's bodies caused the sexual organs to protrude, while the greater coolness and wetness of women's bodies caused the sexual organs to remain inside. Illustrations in Crooke's encyclopedia make this scheme graphically clear. (See Figures 15 and 16.) In effect, Galenic medicine posits *one* sex, not two.[1] Everyone starts out as a female, just as "the man right fair" does in Shakespeare's Sonnet 20:

> And for a woman wert thou first created,
> Till Nature, as she wrought thee, fell a-doting,
> And by addition me of thee defeated,
> By adding one thing to my purpose nothing.

[1] A full explanation of this proposition and its influence in European anatomy are provided by Laqueur in *Making Sex*.

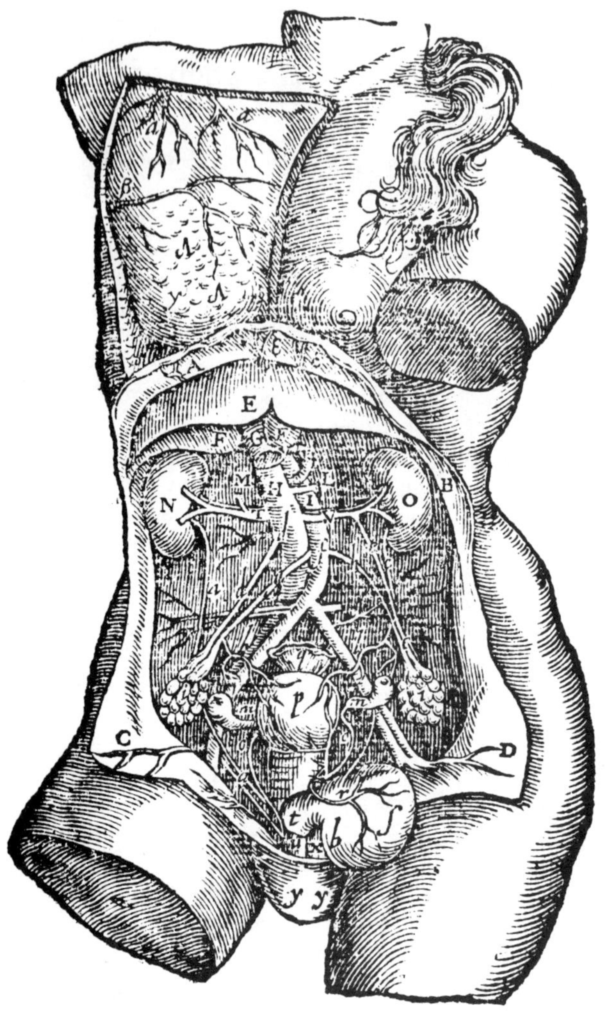

FIGURE 15 *Female Reproductive Organs, from Helkiah Crooke,* Microcosmographia: A Description of the Body of Man *(1625). The womb is designated by the letter* p.

Nature's "addition" comes about through the greater heat of male bodies, an effect that is heightened at puberty, when the testicles develop, the penis becomes enlarged, and body hair begins to appear, most notably in the form of a beard. Stories circulated about how an increase in body heat could turn women into men. Montaigne, for example, on his journey from southwestern France via Germany to Italy stopped off to visit a peasant girl named Marie who, at the age

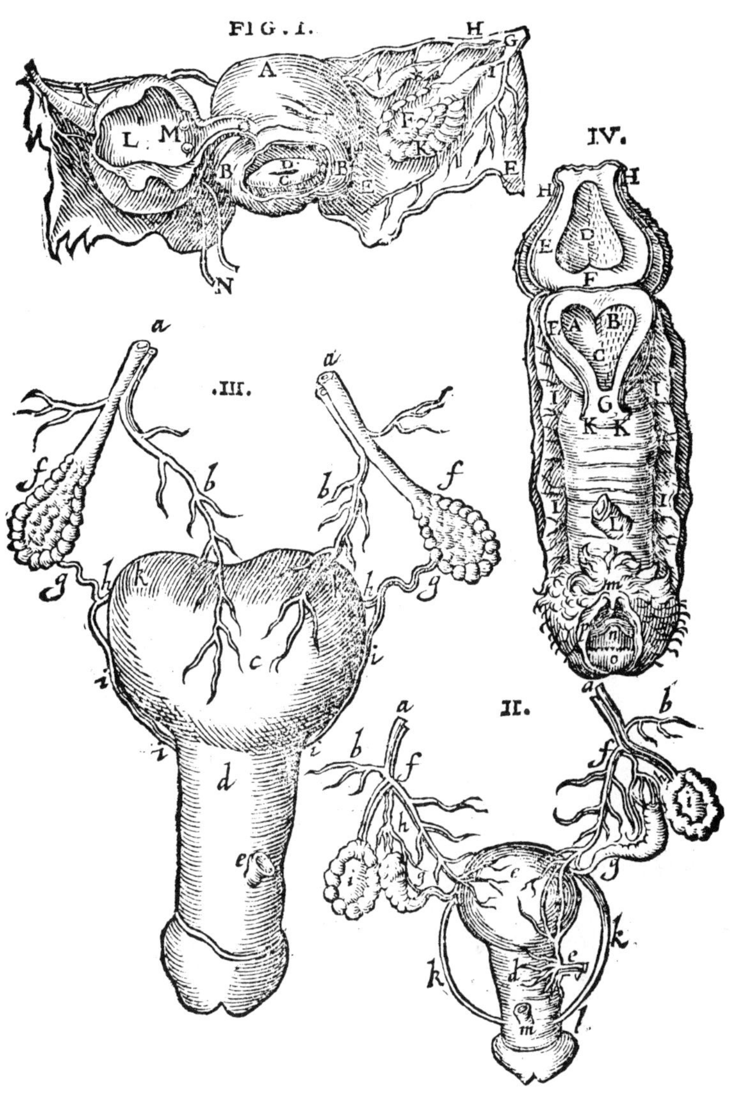

FIGURE 16 *Female Reproductive Organs (Detail) from Helkiah Crooke,* Microcosmographia: A Description of the Body of Man *(1625). Figure III (bottom left) shows "the body or bottom of the womb" (labeled* c*), "the neck of the womb" (labeled* d*), and "the testicles" (labeled* f*). Figure II (bottom right) represents the same organs seen from above. Figure I (top left) dissects the body of the womb; Figure IV (top right), the neck of the womb.*

of fifteen, leaped over a ditch while "rather robustly" chasing some pigs, and "at that very moment the genitalia and male rod came to be developed." She changed her name to Germain. By the time Montaigne visited her, Germain had served in the king's retinue and, though unmarried, sported "a big, very thick beard" (qtd. in Greenblatt 30–52).

In the fourth book of *Microcosmographia,* "Of the natural parts belonging to generation, as well in men as in women," Crooke takes up the challenges posed by modern anatomy to the Galenic model of one sex. Recent dissections and fresh looks at the evidence had brought to light parts of female anatomy — the fallopian tubes are a signal example — that did not correspond to male sexual apparatus. Crooke gives this evidence due weight. Among the questions he takes up in the fourth book is whether there is one sex or two. Although Crooke takes a conservative position on many controversies, on the question of sex he accepts the evidence of modern anatomy. The very fact that he should give such careful consideration to the one-sex model, however, suggests the hold of that model on popular conceptions of the human body.

From *Microcosmographia: A Description of the Body of Man*

How the Parts of Generation in Men and Women Do Differ

Concerning the parts of generation in women, it is a great and notable question whether they differ only in situation from those of men. For the ancients have thought that a woman might become a man, but not on the contrary side a man become a woman. For they say that the parts of generation in women lie hid, because the strength of their natural heat is weaker than in men, in whom it thrusteth those parts outward. Women have spermatical vessels, as well, preparing as leading vessels and testicles which boil the blood, and a kind of yard[2] also, which they say is the neck of the womb if it be inverted. Finally, the bottom of the womb, distinguished by the middle line, is the very same with the cod or scrotum. This Galen[3] often urgeth in diverse of his works, as before is said. So Aegineta, Avicen,[4] Rhasis, and all of the Greek and Arabian families, with whom all anatomists do consent.

[2] **yard:** penis. [3] **Galen:** second-century Greek physician whose writings formed the basis of European medical knowledge through the early seventeenth century. [4] **Avicen:** Avicenna (or Ibn Sina) (980–1037 C.E.), Arabic physician whose writings also informed European medical knowledge.

Helkiah Crooke, *Microcosmographia: A Description of the Body of Man* (1616; London: William Jaggard, 1625), 249–50.

For confirmation also hereof there are many stories current among ancient and modern writers of many women turned into men, some of which we will not here think much to remember. First therefore we read that at Rome when Lucinius Crassus and Cassius Longinus were consuls, the servant of one Cassinus of a maid became a young man, and was thereupon led aside into the desert island of the sooth-sayers. Mutianus Licinious reporteth, that at Argos in Greece, he saw a maid named Arescusa, who after she was married became a man and had a beard and after married another woman by whom she had issue.

Pliny also writeth, that he saw in Africa, P. Cossitius, a citizen of Tisdetra, who of a woman the day before became a man the next day. The hyena, also a cruel and subtle beast, doth every other year change her sex. Of whom, Ovid in the xv. [book] of his *Metamorphosis* sayeth:

> The same hyena which we saw admit the male before,
> To cover now her female mate, we can but wonder for.

Pontanus hath the same of Iphis in an elegant verse:

> Iphis her vow benempt[5] a maid,
> But turned boy her vow she paid.

Of later times. Volateran, a cardinal, sayeth, that in the time of Pope Alexander the Sixth he saw at Rome a virgin, who on the day of her marriage had suddenly a virile member grown out of her body. We read also that there was at Auscis in Vasconia, a man of above sixty years of age, grey, strong, and hairy, who had been before a woman till the age of fifteen years, or till within fifteen years of threescore, yet at length by accident of a fall, the ligaments (sayeth my author) being broken, her privities came outward, and she changed her sex, before which change she had never had her courses.[6] Pontanus witnesseth that a fisherman's wench of Caieta of fourteen years old became suddenly a young springal.[7] The same happened to Emilia the wife of Antony Spensa, a citizen of Ebula, when she had been twelve years a married woman.

In the time of Ferdinand, the first king of Naples, Carlotta and Francisca, the daughters of Ludovick Quarna of Salernum, when they were fifteen years old changed their sex. Amatus Lusitanus testifieth in his *Centuries* that he saw the same at Conibrica, a famous town of Portugal. There standeth upon record in the eighth section of the sixth book of Hippocrates[8] his *Epidemea,* an elegant history of one Phaetusa, who when her husband was banished was so overgrown with sorrow, that before her time

[5] **benempt:** named. [6] **courses:** menstrual periods. [7] **springal:** young man. [8] **Hippocrates:** Greek physician (c. 460–377 B.C.E.) who stressed direct observation.

her courses utterly stopped and her body became manlike and hairy all over, and she had a beard and her voice grew stronger. The same also he recordeth to have happened to Namisia, the wife of Gorgippus in Thaso.

Wherefore say they, if a woman may become a man and her parts of generation which before lay hid within may come forth and hang as men's do, then do women differ from men only in the site or position of their parts of generation.

Notwithstanding all this, against this opinion there are two mighty arguments. One is taken from the αυτοψια [self-evidence] in dissection, another from reason, which two are the philosopher's bloodhounds, by which they track the causes of things.

For first of all, sayeth Laurentius, these parts in men and women differ in number. The small bladders which first Herophylus found and called *varicosos adstites,* that is, the *parastatae,*[9] women have not at all, nor the *prostatae*[10] which are placed at the root of the yard and neck of the bladder, in which seed is treasured up for the necessary uses of nature, although there be some that think that women have them but so small that they are insensible, which is, sayeth he, to beg the question. Again, methinks it is very absurd to say, that the neck of the womb inverted is like the member[11] of a man. For the neck of the womb hath but one cavity, and that is long and large like a sheath to receive the virile member. But the member or yard of a man consisteth of two hollow nerves, a common passage for seed and urine, and four muscles. Neither is the cavity of a man's yard so large and ample as that of the neck of the womb. Add to this, that the neck of the bladder in women doth not equal in length the neck of the womb, but in men it equalleth the whole length of the member or yard. Howsoever therefore the neck of the womb shall be inverted, yet will it never make the virile member. For three hollow bodies cannot be made of one, but the yard consisteth of three hollow bodies, two ligaments arising from bones and the ύρυθρα [urethra] we have before sufficiently showed. If any man instance in the *tentigo*[12] of the ancients, or Fallopius[13] his clitoris, bearing the shape of a man's yard, as which hath two ligaments and four muscles, yet see how these two differ. The clitoris is a small body, not continuated at all with the bladder, but placed in the height of the lap. The clitoris hath no passage for the emission of seed, but the virile member is long and hath a passage in the midst by which it poureth seed into the neck of the womb.

Neither is there, sayeth Laurentius, any similitude between the bottom of the womb inverted, and the scrotum or cod of a man. For the cod is a

[9] ***parastatae:*** epididymis, ducts emptying the testicles. [10] ***prostatae:*** prostate gland. [11] **member:** penis. [12] ***tentigo:*** immoderate tumescence. [13] **Fallopius:** Gabriello Fallopio (1523–1562), anatomist who is credited with "discovering" the clitoris and the fallopian tubes.

rugous[14] and thin skin, the bottom of the womb is a very thick and tight membrane, all fleshy within and woven with manifold fibers.

Finally, the insertion of the spermatic vessels, the different figure of the man's and woman's testicles, their magnitude, substance, and structure or composition do strongly gainsay this opinion.

But what shall we say to those so many stories of women changed into men? Truly I think, sayeth he, all of them monstrous and some not credible. But if such a thing shall happen, it may well be answered that such parties were hermaphrodites, that is, had the parts of both sexes, which because of the weakness of their heat in their nonage[15] lay hid, but broke out afterward as their heat grew unto strength. Or we may safely say, that there are some women so hot by nature that their clitoris hangeth forth in the fashion of a man's member, which because it may be distended and again grow loose and flaccid, may deceive ignorant people. Again, midwives may oft be deceived because of the faulty conformation of those parts, for sometimes the member and testicles are so small and sink so deep into the body that they cannot easily be discerned.

Pinaeus writeth, that at Paris in the year 1577, in the street of S. Dennis, a woman travailed and brought forth a son, which because of the weakness of the infant was suddenly baptized for a daughter and was called Joanna. A few days after, in dressing the infant, the mother perceived it to be a man child, and so did the standers by and they named it John.

As for the authority of Hippocrates, it followeth not that all those women whose voices turn strong or have beards, and grow hairy do presently also change their parts of generation. Neither doth Hippocrates say so, but plainly the contrary. For he addeth, when we had tried all means, we could not bring down her courses, but she perished. Wherefore her parts of generation remained as those of a woman, although her body grew mannish and hairy.

[14] **rugous:** wrinkled. [15] **nonage:** formative years.

Eroticism, Homoeroticism, Paneroticism

The one-sex model helps to explain the appeal of Viola/"Cesario"/Sebastian to the people in Shakespeare's story who see them, hear them speak, and fall in love with them: Orsino, Olivia, Antonio. In their prepubescent youthfulness, brother and sister present the same attractive features of lips, limbs, voice, action, and spirit. In comparison with these features, their genital differences seem, for the time of Twelfth Night at least, unimportant. Act 5 betrays, however, some anxieties about how the illusion of boy-girl can be sustained, once true identities have been revealed in the sunlight of Thirteenth Day. Sebastian, for one, makes a point of Viola's femaleness (and implicitly) his own maleness as he declares to Olivia,

> So comes it, lady, you have been mistook.
> But nature to her bias drew in that.
> You would have been contracted to a maid.
> Nor are you therein, by my life, deceived,
> You are betrothed both to a maid and man. (5.1.244–48)

Orsino catches the point of Sebastian's offer, in his own male right, to marry Olivia. "Be not amazed," Orsino tells Olivia;

> right noble is his blood.
> If this be so, as yet the glass seems true,
> I shall have share in this most happy wreck. (5.1.249–51)

Turning to Viola, he teasingly persists in identifying her as male:

> Boy, thou hast said to me a thousand times
> Thou never shouldst love woman like to me. (5.1.252–53)

When Viola affirms as much, Orsino replies, "Give me thy hand, / And let me see thee in thy woman's weeds" (5.1.257–58).

What would seem to be going on in these exchanges is an affirmation of male/female sexual difference. Sebastian speaks of Nature's "bias" in terms that recall Shakespeare's sonnet 20, as if it were only natural for the unsexed youth to turn into a man. Orsino would seem to be insisting on a similar distinction when he asks Viola to let him see her "in thy woman's weeds." "Bias" in bowling means a ball that hits the desired mark, albeit in a roundabout way (*OED*, "bias," 2a and 2b). Petruchio uses the word in just this way, as he describes to Hortensio how well his plot to tame Kate is working: "Thus the bowl should run, / And not unluckily against the bias" (*The Taming of the Shrew* 4.5.24–25). On the other hand, Orsino does not get to see Viola in her woman's weeds before act 5 comes to an end. Instead, he escorts her offstage:

> Cesario, come —
> For so you shall be, while you are a man;
> But when in other habits you are seen,
> Orsino's mistress and his fancy's queen. (5.1.362–65)

No longer "boy," mind you, but "man." If the sexual sameness of lover and beloved has not been emphasized earlier in the play, it is certainly flirted with in the end. Nature's "bias," after all, may not be that men should marry women but that cooler female bodies will become hotter male bodies. On several fronts *Twelfth Night* invites us to consider early modern ideas about erotic attraction between people possessing the same sexual organs.

→ OVID

From The Heroical Epistles of Publius Ovidius Naso in English Verse

1567

Translated by George Turberville

A listener-spectator attentive to gender has at least three ways of regarding "Cesario" in his/her/his interview with Olivia in act 1, scene 5, of *Twelfth Night:* as a boy actor playing opposite another boy actor, as a fictional female talking to another fictional female, and as fictional female disguised as a boy talking to another fictional female. The second and third of these three frames raise the prospect of female homoerotic flirtation. The scripted dialogue encourages as much:

VIOLA: If I did love you in my master's flame,
With such a suffering, such a deadly life,
In your denial I would find no sense;
I would not understand it.
OLIVIA: Why, what would you?
VIOLA: Make me a willow cabin at your gate
And call upon my soul within the house;
Write loyal cantons of contemnèd love
And sing them loud even in the dead of night;
Hallow your name to the reverberant hills,
And make the babbling gossip of the air
Cry out "Olivia!" O, you should not rest
Between the elements of air and earth
But you should pity me!
OLIVIA: You might do much.

And to leave no question what's on her mind, Olivia immediately asks, "What is your parentage?" (1.5.209–22) — the question with which she begins her love-lorn soliloquy after Viola/"Cesario" has departed (1.5.234).

Just how would the likes of John Manningham have regarded the spectacle of two women speaking love to each other as he watched the play unfold at the Middle Temple in 1602? (On John Manningham and this early performance, see the Introduction.) One answer is to be found in Ovid's *Heroides,* in the verse epistle Ovid imagines the Greek poet Sappho writing to the male lover Phaon, who has just abandoned her for another woman. In the course of her complaints, Sappho recounts the love affairs with "Lesbian lasses" that Phaon made her forego and forget. Phaon was able to win her love, she confesses, precisely because of his androgynous qualities: he was "a beardless youth[. . .]/[. . .] whose tender childish years / allowed his chin no hair." In George Turberville's translation of 1567, Sappho is able to speak unashamedly about her love affairs with girls. Why should that be so? In part, because those affairs are in the past, set at a safe elegiac distance from Sappho's more conventional involvement with

Phaon. In part, too, because it was only well-educated men like John Manningham who were likely to read her complaints in Latin verse or even in Turberville's English translation.[1]

Turberville (c. 1540–c. 1595) was educated at Oxford and apparently had connections with one of the Inns of Court. His *Heroical Epistles of Publius Ovidius Naso in English Verse,* styled "the first fruits of his travail" and dedicated to Lord Thomas Howard, was one of three books of verse that Turberville published in 1567, all of them with a distinctly academic cast. *Epitaphs, Epigrams, Songs, and Sonnets* naturalized the Latin epigram to English; a translation of Mantuan's *Eclogues* provided English versions of texts that were standards in the humanist curriculum. In Turberville's rendition of Ovid, Sappho and her female lovers are objects for the private academic connoisseur, who was, of course, male. By the time Wye Saltonstall took the same heroical epistle in hand in the changed cultural circumstances of 1636, Sappho's sexual escapades had become a source of public embarrassment. In his translation, Saltonstall carefully removes all explicit references to Sappho's erotic history with her own sex. Sophisticated acceptance of Sappho's homoerotic verse in the culture of sixteenth-century humanism gave way to ever increasing anxieties and hostility in the seventeenth century as sexual mores became more regulated and as more and more people, especially women, learned how to read (Andreadis 105–21). The performance of *Twelfth Night* at the Middle Temple in 1602 came precisely at the midpoint between Turberville's license and Saltonstall's prudence.

[1] On the elegiac distancing of lesbian love in Renaissance verse, see Traub, "The (In)Significance of Lesbian Desire," 62–83.

From *The Heroical Epistles of Publius Ovidius Naso in English Verse*

Epistle 17

Sappho to Phaon

Where when thou saw'st at first
   my loving lines with eye,
Thou knowledge hadst from whence they came
   and notice by and by?
Where if thou hadst herein
   not read the author's name

Ovid, *The Heroical Epistles of Publius Ovidius Naso in English Verse,* trans. George Turberville (London: H. Denham, 1567), 109–16.

And Sappho seen, thou hadst not known
  from whom this writing came:
Demand thou wilt perhaps
  what me procured to write,
This kind of verse, that merry tunes,
  and luting do delight?
For that this love of mine
  is doleful and the verse,
Elegia called, a woeful kind
  of meter to rehearse.
No cythron[2] serves a mourning mind,
  whom cruel cares do pierce.
As straw doth kindle soon,
  when Eurus[3] 'gins to drive
The flash into the fertile fields:
  even so I fry alive.
To Ætna Phaon now
  hath ta'en his way in haste:
And me poor wench as great a fire
  as Ætna's flame doth waste.
I can not frame my frets,
  my stubborn strings do jar:
For why? indeed of quiet mind
  such verses tokens are.
Pyrino is forgot,
  ne Dryades do delight
My fancy: Lesbian[4] lasses eke[5]
  are now forgotten quite.
Not Amython I force,
  nor Cydno passing fine:
Nor Atthis, as she did of yore,
  allures these eyes of mine.
Ne yet a hundred more
  whom (shame ylaid[6] aside)
I fancied erst: thou all that love
  from them to thee hast wryed.

. . . .

[2] **cythron:** cittern, a guitar-like instrument. [3] **Eurus:** the east wind. [4] **Lesbian:** from Lesbos, the island where they and Sappho live. [5] **eke:** also. [6] **ylaid:** laid (*y-* is a form of the past participle that was already archaic in 1567).

What wonder if with such
  a beardless youth I were
Attached, whose tender childish years
  allowed his chin no hair?
I dread (Aurora) least
  for Cephalus[7] thou would
Ychosen him: save that thy former rape doth thee withhold.
If Phœbe[8] view him once,
  that all surveys with eye,
My Phaon shall be quickly forced
  in slumber long to lie.
In ivory wagon would
  dame Venus to the stars
Borne him: but that she feared he would
  have coyed[9] the god of wars.[10]
O thou that neither art
  a boy, nor man in sight,
But aptest age: of all thy race
  the most excellent wight,
Come hither, come, and to
  my bosom make retour:[11]
No love I crave in faith of thee
  but thee to love the power.
I write and from my cheeks
  the dewy tears distill:
Behold how many blots they cause
  in Sappho's doleful bill.[12]

. . . .

Ye Lesbian lasses all
  that border on the lake:
And ye that of the Æolian town
  your names are thought to take:
Ye Lesbian lasses (that
  for cause I loved you sore
Breed my defame) unto my harp
  I charge you come no more.

[7] **Cephalus:** with whom Aurora (the dawn) fell in love. [8] **Phoebe:** the Moon, who put Endymion to sleep in order to kiss him. [9] **coyed:** made jealous. [10] **god of wars:** Mars, one of Venus's lovers. [11] **retour:** return. [12] **bill:** letter.

Look what did like you erst,
  of that is Phaon sped:
Alas poor wretch, my Phaon I
  had very near ysaid.
Cause Phaon to retire[13]
  and then your poet will
Revert again: 'tis he that doth
  both make and mar my skill.
. . . .

[13] **retire:** go away.

JOHN DONNE

Sappho to Philaenis

1597–98?

John Donne (1572–1631) enjoys the distinction of being the most frequently copied poet of his day. Rare is the miscellany copied out by Oxford students in the 1620s and 1630s that does not include at least one poem by Donne.[1] By the time his love poems finally appeared in print in 1633, two years after his death, Donne was famous enough that the printer had only to advertise *Poems by J. D.* to sell out the first edition within two years. Donne's other claim to fame was preaching. Taking orders in the Church of England at King James's urging in 1615, Donne was named Dean of St. Paul's Cathedral and penned a series of sermons that are no less astonishingly immediate than his poems. "Sappho to Philaenis" appears with ascriptions to Donne in numerous manuscript collections as well as in the 1633, 1635, and 1639 printed editions of Donne's poems. A possible clue to its date of composition is the appearance in 1597 of Michael Drayton's *England's Heroical Epistles,* a collection modeled on Ovid's *Heroides.* From 1592, when he entered Lincoln's Inn, Donne was active in the literary culture of the inns of court.

In the passage from Turberville's Sappho to Saltonstall's (see p. 204), Donne's Sappho occupies the same middle ground as Shakespeare's Olivia. Donne's Sappho speaks about her erotic desire for another woman with a candor that would become unseemly a generation later. The very fact that a woman should be given an erotic voice is altogether characteristic of the dramatic presence of Donne's love poetry. Two other poems by Donne, "Break of Day" and "Confined Love," likewise have women speakers. Since the critical rediscovery of Donne's poetry in the twentieth century, some readers have taken these women speakers as evidence of Donne's sense of mutuality in love; others have

[1] On the culture of writing and collecting that produced these manuscript miscellanies, see Marotti, *John Donne.*

insisted on his male-centeredness. For readers of the second group, "Sappho to Philaenis" is an exercise in male ventriloquy and male cross-dressing, all done to titillate a male readership. Lincoln's Inn was, to be sure, an all-male milieu, and most known owners of the early-seventeenth-century manuscript collections were men. To what degree, then, is Sappho a desiring female subject in her own right, and to what degree is she the desired object of a reading male? The same questions face the spectator of act 3, scene 1 of *Twelfth Night*.

Sappho to Philaenis

Where is that holy fire which verse is said
To have? Is that enchanting force decay'd?
Verse, that draws nature's works from nature's law,[2]
Thee, her best work, to her work cannot draw.
Have my tears quench'd my old poetic fire?
Why quench'd they not as well that of desire?
Thoughts, my mind's creatures, often are with thee,
But I, their maker, want their liberty.
Only thine image in my heart doth sit,
But that is wax, and fires environ it.
My fires have driven, thine have drawn it hence;
And I am robb'd of picture, heart, and sense.
Dwells with me still mine irksome memory,
Which, both to keep and lose, grieves equally.
That tells me how fair thou'rt: Thou art so fair,
As gods, when gods to thee I do compare,
Are grac'd thereby; and to make blind men see
What things gods are, I say they're like to thee.
For if we justly call each silly[3] man
A little world, what shall we call thee then?
Thou art not soft and clear and straight and fair
As down, as stars, cedars, and lilies are,
But thy right hand and cheek and eye, only
Are like thy other hand and cheek and eye.
Such was my Phao awhile, but shall be never
As thou wast, art, and, O, mayst be ever!

[2] **Verse . . . law:** spells or charms. [3] **silly:** simple.

John Donne, "Sappho to Philaenis," *Poems by J. D., with Elegies on the Author's Death* (London: M. Fleshner for J. Marriott, 1633), 166–68.

Here lovers swear in their idolatry
That I am such, but grief discolors me.
And yet I grieve the less, lest grief remove
My beauty and make me unworthy of thy love.
Plays some soft boy with thee? O, there wants yet
A mutual feeling which should sweeten it.
His chin, a thorny-hairy unevenness
Doth threaten, and some daily change possess.
Thy body is a natural paradise[4]
In whose self, unmanur'd, all pleasure lies,
Nor needs perfection. Why shouldst thou then
Admit the tillage of a harsh, rough man?
Men leave behind them that which their sin shows,
And are as thieves trac'd which rob when it snows.
But of our dalliance no more signs there are
Than fishes leave in streams, or birds in air.
And between us, all sweetness may be had,
All, all that nature yields, or art can add.
My two lips, eyes, thighs, differ from thy two
But so as thine from one another do.
And, O, no more! The likeness being such,
Why should they not alike in all parts touch?
Hand to strange hand, lip to lip, none denies.
Why should they breast to breast, or thighs to thighs?
Likeness begets such strange self-flattery
That touching myself, all seems done to thee.
Myself I'embrace, and mine own hands I kiss,
And amorously thank myself for this.
Me in my glass[5] I call *thee,* but alas,
When I would kiss, tears dim mine eyes and glass.
O, cure this loving madness and restore
Me to me (thee), my half, my all, my more.
So may thy cheeks' red outwear scarlet dye,
And their white, whiteness of the Galaxy;
So may thy mighty, amazing beauty move
Envy'n all women, and in all men, love,
And so be change and sickness far from thee,
As thou by coming near keep'st them from me.

[4] **paradise:** Garden of Eden. [5] **glass:** mirror.

JOHN LYLY

From Gallathea

1588

The flirtation between two girls in John Lyly's court comedy *Gallathea* was designed to please one spectator above all others, and she was not a man. That spectator was Queen Elizabeth, the self-proclaimed Virgin Queen. By the time *Gallathea* was performed before the queen at Greenwich Palace on the night of New Year's day 1588, Elizabeth had long since found in virginity the perfect way to maintain a position of power over male courtiers who were forced to speak the deferential language of courtly love even as they jockied for political power (Montrose 151–78; Jankowski 194–98). In a not dissimilar way, the comedies that Lyly wrote for court consumption in the 1580s engage serious political issues, but in the most witty, whimsical, nonthreatening ways possible. John Lyly (1553/54–1606), grandson of the famous humanist educator William Lily, went up to London after taking degrees at Oxford and in short order had made his reputation by publishing *Euphues: The Anatomy of Wit* (1578). Whatever the book may have lacked in plot it more than made up for in style — and critical success. Lyly's way of carrying balance and antithesis to outrageous extremes became a fad with writers and conversationalists and inspired a sequel in *Euphues His England* (1580). Under patronage of the earl of Oxford, Lyly was granted a lease to a theater fitted up in the former Blackfriars monastery in the City of London (Shakespeare's company later took over the space) and became the impresario of a troupe of boy actors drawn from St. Paul's School and the choir of the Chapel Royal. Under Lyly's direction, the boys performed a series of comedies at court.

Ovid's *Metamorphoses* is the ultimate inspiration behind all of Lyly's dramas of passion and transformation. In the case of *Gallathea,* Lyly has drawn on the mutual love of two girls, Iphis and Ianthe, as recounted in book 9 of *Metamorphoses.* The occasion for their falling in love is provided by a situation out of the legend of Hesione, a virgin whose sacrifice is demanded to appease the angry sea god Neptune. To save their daughters Gallathea and Phyllida from that fate, each of the shepherd fathers in Lyly's play decides to disguise his daughter as a boy. It is in those male costumes that Gallathea and Phyllida meet, take a fancy to one another, and struggle with the incongruity that both seem to be boys, though each suspects the other of being a girl. Venus's convenient transformation of one of the pair into a male — just which one will not be revealed until they arrive at the church door — parallels the discovery in *Twelfth Night* that "Cesario," no less conveniently, is really a girl. In the meantime, however, the audience is treated to the titillation of watching two girls — or rather two girls disguised as boys — fall in love with one another. In anatomical fact both girls *were* boys, since *Gallathea* was acted by the choirboys of St. Paul's School. Lyly's characteristic style of "Euphuism" brings a delight in antithesis that is altogether appropriate to the circumstances in the scene that follows.

From *Gallathea*

Act Three, Scene two

[Enter] Phyllida and Gallathea.

PHYLLIDA: It is pity that Nature framed you not a woman, having[1] a face so fair, so lovely a countenance, so modest a behavior.

GALLATHEA: There is a tree in Tylos whose nuts have shells like fire, and, being cracked, the kernel is but water.[2]

PHYLLIDA: What a toy[3] is it to tell me of that tree, being nothing to the purpose! I say it is pity you are not a woman.

GALLATHEA: I would not wish to be a woman, unless it were because thou art a man.

PHYLLIDA: Nay, I do not wish thee to be a woman, for then I should not love thee, for I have sworn never to love a woman.

GALLATHEA: A strange humor in so pretty a youth, and according to mine, for myself will never love a woman.

PHYLLIDA: It were a shame, if a maiden should be a suitor (a thing hated in that sex), that thou shouldst deny to be her servant.[4]

GALLATHEA: If it be a shame in me, it can be no commendation in you, for yourself is of that mind.

PHYLLIDA: Suppose I were a virgin (I blush in supposing myself one), and that under the habit of a boy were the person of a maid: if I should utter my affection with sighs, manifest my sweet love by my salt tears, and prove my loyalty unspotted and my griefs intolerable, would not then that fair face pity this true heart?

GALLATHEA: Admit that I were as you would have me suppose that you are, and that I should with entreaties, prayers, oaths, bribes, and whatever can be invented in love, desire your favor, would you not yield?

PHYLLIDA: Tush, you come in with "admit."

GALLATHEA: And you with "suppose."

PHYLLIDA: [*aside*] What doubtful[5] speeches be these! I fear me he is as I am, a maiden.

GALLATHEA: [*aside*] What dread riseth in my mind! I fear the boy to be as I am, a maiden.

[1] **having:** refers to *you.* [2] **tree . . . water:** Pliny (12.10) speaks of a tree on the island of Tylos which bears a gourd containing down. [3] **toy:** piece of nonsense. [4] **servant:** professed lover. [5] **doubtful:** (1) ambiguous; (2) giving cause for apprehensions.

John Lyly, *Galathea,* ed. Anne Begor Lancashire (1592; Lincoln: University of Nebraska Press, 1969), 36–39.

PHYLLIDA: [*aside*] Tush, it cannot be; his voice shows the contrary.

GALLATHEA: [*aside*] Yet I do not think it, for he would then have blushed.

PHYLLIDA: Have you ever a sister?

GALLATHEA: If I had but one, my brother must needs have two. But, I pray, have you ever a one?

PHYLLIDA: My father had but one daughter, and therefore I could have no sister.

GALLATHEA: [*aside*] Ay me, he is as I am, for his speeches be as mine are.

PHYLLIDA: [*aside*] What shall I do? Either he is subtle or my sex simple.

GALLATHEA: [*aside*] I have known divers of Diana's nymphs enamored of him, yet hath he rejected all, either as too proud, to disdain, or too childish, not to understand, or for that he knoweth himself to be a virgin.

PHYLLIDA: [*aside*] I am in a quandary. Diana's nymphs have followed him, and he despised them, either knowing too well the beauty of his own face, or that himself is of the same mold. I will once again try him. [*To Gallathea.*] You promised me in the woods that you would love me before all Diana's nymphs.

GALLATHEA: Ay, so you would love me before all Diana's nymphs.

PHYLLIDA: Can you prefer a fond[6] boy as I am before so fair ladies as they are?

GALLATHEA: Why should not I as well as you?

PHYLLIDA: Come, let us into the grove and make much one of another, that cannot tell what to think one of another. *Exeunt.*

[6] **fond:** (1) affectionate; (2) foolish.

→ *From* The Whole Volume of Statutes at Large *1587*

and

SIR EDWARD COKE

From The Third Part of the Institutes of the Laws of England *1644*

The ending of *Twelfth Night* opens out into the world of marriage that John Manningham, witness to the 1602 performance of the play, indicates in his diary that he so eagerly wished to enter. (See the Introduction.) Viola and Sebastian may appear as interchangeable "youths" through most of the play, but at the end they become marriage partners. That would place them well beyond the age of puberty. Although it was legal in early modern England for men to marry at age fourteen and women at age twelve, the vast majority of the population did not marry until they were well into their twenties. Aristocrats might marry early (or, rather, have their marriages arranged for them at an early age), but most members of the audience at the Middle Temple in 1602 would not expect to marry until they had completed their legal studies and had set themselves as financially independent. Parish records indicate that the average age of marriage for the population at large was about twenty-eight years old for men and twenty-five years old for women (Wrightson 68–70). Manningham was thirty when he married Anne Curle, sister of his Middle Temple chambermate, in 1605, three years after he witnessed the performance of *Twelfth Night* (Manningham 268). Sebastian, as we have seen, insists on his own masculinity in act 5, scene 1, when he tells Olivia, "Lady, you have been mistook" (5.1.244). Orsino, having discovered Viola's sex, desires to see her "in thy woman's weeds" (5.1.258), even though Viola herself has referred to her clothes as "my maiden weeds" (5.1.240) — a demure usage she later repeats as "my maid's garments" (5.1.260). For all that, Orsino's addresses her in his last speech as "Cesario," "For so you shall be, while you are a man" (5.1.363). "Man" can, of course, mean "servant," but in the betrothal scene Orsino seems to be masculinizing the erstwhile "youth" in just the way that Sebastian has carefully masculinized himself in Olivia's eyes. If so, *Twelfth Night* ends with the spectacle, inside the fiction, of a man talking love to a man or, outside the fiction, of an adult male actor talking love to a boy.

Such a scene was likely to make Manningham and his peers rather more anxious than Gallathea talking love to Phyllida. More was at stake. A woman might talk love to a woman, because neither of them exercised power within the patriarchal structure of early modern society, nor did their erotic behavior really signify, since no phallus was involved. Sexual acts between males threatened the economy of power in ways that sexual acts between females did not. There were good reasons, therefore, to police such acts. Since Henry VIII's reign, sodomy had been not only a crime but a *capital* crime, a felony that cost the convicted offender his life. An unresvolved question remained, however: just what was sodomy? Traditionally the term *sodomy* had been broad enough to include state-threatening offenses like heresy and treason. Indeed, the criminalization of sodomy in the statute 25 Henry VIII, chapter 6 (1533–34) had been designed to aid Henry VIII in his attack on the Catholic Church by giving the "visitors" he sent around to all the kingdom's monasteries a useful weapon for entrapping monks.[1] Once monastic closures had come about, however, "sodomy" was not a major legal concern in early modern England. As originally passed in 1533–34, the statute was only temporary and had to be renewed several times during the reigns of Henry VIII and Edward VI. Under the Catholic Queen Mary, the law was allowed to lapse. The statute 5 Elizabeth I, chapter 17, reinstated sodomy as a capital offense and made the law perpetual. However, Sir Edward Coke's interpretation of the statute itself and legal precedents in *The Third Part of the Institutes*

[1]On the association of sodomy with heresy and treason, see Bray, 13–32, and Bredbeck, 33–86; on legal discourse about sodomy see Smith, *Homosexual Desire,* 42–44.

of the Laws of England (1644) in effect limits the legal definition of sodomy to forcible rape. The record of actual prosecutions during the reigns of Elizabeth and James bears out Coke's interpretation: prosecutions were extremely rare, successful prosecutions rarer still, and almost always the victim was beneath the age of consent and hence, in the eyes of the law, someone's property. Such a circumstance accords with the prosecution records for rape in general. The law was interested, not in morality, but in civil damages. According to Coke, sodomy between women did not exist. He carefully considers the possibilities of sexual activity between man and man, between man and beast, even between woman and beast, but not between woman and woman. Nor, according Coke, did sodomy extend to consensual relations between adult men that did not involve penetration or ejaculation: "*Emissio seminis* [ejaculation] maketh it not buggery, but is an evidence in case of buggery of penetration." All things considered, Orsino could flirt with "Cesario" as a man without necessarily attracting the attention of the legal system.

From *The Whole Volume of the Statutes at Large*

An Act for the Punishment of the Vice of Buggery (25 Henry VIII, chapter 6, 1533–34)

For as much as there is not yet sufficient and condign[2] punishment appointed and limited by the due course of the laws of this realm, for the detestable & abominable vice of buggery committed with mankind or beast. It may please the king's highness, with the assent of his lords spiritual and temporal, and the commons of this present parliament assembled, that it may be enacted by the authority of the same, that the same offense be from henceforth adjudged felony, and such order and form of process therein to be used against the offenders, as in cases of felony at the common law. And that the offenders being hereof convict by verdict, confession, or outlawry,[3] shall suffer such pains of death and losses, and penalties of their goods, chattels, debts, lands, tenements, and hereditaments, as felons been accustomed to do according to the order of the common laws of this realm. And that no person offending in any such offense, shall be admitted to his clergy.[4] And

[2] **condign:** fitting. [3] **outlawry:** condition of being outside the protection of the law, through flight, banishment, or other means. [4] **admitted to his clergy:** allowed to avoid punishment by demonstrating ability to read Latin (and hence, in the days of the Catholic Church, his being subject to canon law rather than temporal law).

The Whole Volume of Statutes at Large Which at Any Time Heretofore Have Been Extant in Print since Magna Carta until the XXIX Year of the Reign of Our Most Gracious Sovereign Lady Elizabeth . . . (London: Christopher Barker, 1587), 1:637, 2:449.

that justices of peace shall have power and authority within the limits of their commissions and jurisdictions, to hear and determine the said offense, as they use to do in cases of other felonies. This act to endure till the last day of the next parliament.

An Act for the Punishment of the Vice of Buggery (5 Elizabeth I, chapter 17, 1562–63)

Where in the parliament begun at London the third day of November, in the one and twentieth year of the late king of most famous memory King Henry the Eighth, and after by prorogation holden at Westminster, in the five and twentieth year of the reign of the said late king, there was one act and statute made, entitled "An act for the punishment of the vice of buggery," whereby the said detestable vice was made felony, as in the said statute more at large it doth and may appear. Forasmuch as the said statute, concerning the punishment of the said crime and offense of buggery, standeth at this present repealed and void, by virtue of the statute of repeal, made in the first year of the reign of the late Queen Mary: sithens which repeal so had and made, divers evil disposed persons have been the more bold to commit the said most horrible and detestable vice of buggery aforesaid, to the high displeasure of almighty God.

Be it enacted, ordained and established by the queen our sovereign lady, and by the assent of the lords spiritual and temporal, and the commons of this present parliament assembled, and by the authority of the same, that the said statute before mentioned, made in the five and twentieth year of the said late King Henry the Eighth, for the punishment of the said destestable vice of buggery, and every branch, clause, article, and sentence therein contained, shall from and after the first day of June next coming, be revived, and from thenceforth shall stand, remain, and be in full force, strength, and effect forever, in such manner, form, and condition, as the same statute was at the day of the death of the said late King Henry the Eighth, the said statute of repeal made in the said first year of the said late Queen Mary, or any word general or special therein contained, or any other act or acts, thing or things to the contrary notwithstanding.

From *The Third Part of the Institutes of the Laws of England*

Chapter 10

Of Buggery or Sodomy

If any person shall commit buggery with mankind or beast, by authority of parliament this offence is adjudged felony without benefit of clergy. But it is to be known, (that I may observe it once for all) that the statute of 25 H[enry].8.[chapter 6] was repealed by the statute of I Mar[y].[chapter 1] whereby all offences made felony or *premunire* by an Act of Parliament made since I H[enry].8 were generally repealed: but 25 H[enry].8.[chapter 6] is revived by 5 Eliz[abeth].[chapter 17].

Buggery is a detestable and abominable sin, amongst Christians not to be named, committed by carnal knowledge against the ordinance of the Creator and order of nature, by mankind with mankind, or with brute beast, or by womankind with brute beast.

Bugeria is an Italian word, and signifies so much as is before described. *Paederastes* or *paiderastes* is a Greek word, *amator puerorum* [lover of boys], which is but a *species* of buggery: and it was complained of in Parliament, that the Lombards had brought unto the realm the shameful sin of sodomy that is not to be named, as there it is said.[5] Our ancient authors do conclude, that it deserveth death, *ultimum supplicium* [the final punishment], though they differ in the manner of punishment. Britton[6] sayeth, that sodomites and miscreants shall be burnt: and so were the sodomites by Almighty God. Fleta[7] sayeth, *pecorantes & sodomitae in terra vivi confodiantur* [buggerers and sodomites should be buried alive]: and therewith agreeth the *Mirror*,[8] *pur le grand abomination* [concerning the great abomination]; and in another

[5] **as there it is said:** in a marginal note, Coke cites the parliamentary roll 50 Edward 3, number 58: "All the Lombards who use occupations other than that of banker are to leave the land immediately; they practice bad usury, and all sorts of subtle schemes are carried out and kept up by them. Note, most noble sirs, that the land is inhabited by a great number of Lombard bankers and merchants, who cause great harm. The most part of those who are taken for Lombards are Jews, Saracens, and privy spies, and they have brought into the land a most horrible vice that cannot be named. By which the realm cannot but be quickly destroyed if corrective action is not taken at once" (translated from the original in Law French, as printed in *Rolls or Records of Parliament,* 2 [London: n.p., 1767]: 332). [6] **Britton:** thirteenth-century codifier of common laws of England. [7] **Fleta:** thirteenth-century codifier of common laws of England. [8] ***Mirror:*** *The Mirror of Justice,* an early medieval legal text.

Edward Coke, *The Third Part of the Institutes of the Laws of England* (1644), 2nd ed. (London: W. Lee and D. Pakeman, 1660), 58–59.

place he sayeth, *sodomitae est crime de Majestie vers le Roy celestre* [sodomy is a crime of *lese-majeste* against the King of Heaven]. But (to say it once for all) the judgement in all cases of felony is, that the person attainted be hanged by the neck until he or she be dead. But in ancient times in that case, the man was hanged and the woman was drowned, whereof we have seen examples in the reign of R[ichard].I. And this is the meaning of ancient franchises granted *de furca & fossa,* of the gallows and the pit, for the hanging upon the one and drowning in the other: but *fossa* is taken away, and *furca* remains.

Cum masculo non commiscearis coitu foemineo, quia abominatio est. Cum omni pecore non coibis, nec maculaberis cum eo. Mulier non succumbet jumento, nec miscebitur ei, quia scelus est, &c. [Thou shalt not lie with mankind, as with womankind: it is abomination. Neither shalt thou lie with any beast to defile thyself therewith; neither shall any woman stand before a beast to lie down thereto: it is confusion, etc. (Leviticus 18.22–23, King James version).]

The act of 25 H[enry].8.[chapter 6] hath adjudged it felony, and therefore the judgement for felony doth now belong to this offence, *viz.* to be hanged by the neck till he be dead. He that readeth the preamble of this act, shall find how necessary the reading of our ancient authors is. The statute doth take away the benefit of clergy from the delinquent. But now let us peruse the words of the said description of buggery.

Detestable and abominable. These just attributes are found in the act of 25 H[enry].8.[chapter 6].

Amongst Christians not to be named. These words are in the usual indictment of this offence, and are in effect in the Parliament Roll of 50 E[dward].3.

By carnal knowledge, &c. The words of the indictment be, *contra ordinationem Creatoris & naturae ordinem, rem habuit veneream, dictumque puerum carnaliter cognovit, &c.* [against the ordinance of the Creator and the order of Nature, he had sexual intercourse and had carnal knowledge of the said boy]. So as there must be *penetratio,* that is, *res in re* [the thing in the thing], either with mankind or with beast, but the least penetration maketh it carnal knowledge. See the indictment of Stafford, which was drawn by great advice, for committing buggery with a boy; for which he was attainted and hanged.

The sodomites came to this abomination by four means, *viz.* by pride, excess of diet, idleness, and contempt of the poor. *Otiosus nihil cogitat, nisi de ventre & venere* [the idle think of nothing but the belly and fornication]. Both the agent and consentient are felons: and this is consonant to the law of God, *Qui dormierit cum masculo coitu foemineo, uterque operatus est nefas, & morte moriatur* [If a man also lie with mankind, as he lieth with a woman, both of them have committed an abomination: they shall surely be put to death . . . (Leviticus 20.13, KJV)]. And this accordeth with the ancient rule of law, *agentes & consentientes pair poena plecentur* [the doers and those consenting to the doing alike deserve punishment].

Emissio seminis [ejaculation] maketh it not buggery, but is an evidence in case of buggery of penetration: and so in rape the words be also *carnaliter cognovit* [had carnal knowledge], and therefore there must be penetration: and *emissio seminis* without penetration maketh no rape. *Vide* in the Chapter of Rape [which follows next]. If the party buggered be within the age of discretion, it is no felony in him, but in the agent only. When any offence is felony either by the common law, or by statute, all accessories both before and after are incidently included. So if any be present, abetting and aiding any to do the act, though the offence be personal, and to be done by one only, as to commit rape, not only he that doth the act is a principal, but also they that be present, abetting and aiding the misdoer, are principals also; which is a proof of the other case of sodomy.

Or by woman. This is within the purview of this act of 25 H[enry].8.[chapter 6]. For the words be, *if any person, &c.* which extend as well to a woman as to a man, and therefore if she commit buggery with a beast, she is a person that commits buggery with a beast, to which end this word [*person*] was used. And the rather, for that somewhat before the making of this act, a great lady had committed buggery with a baboon, and conceived by it, &c.

There be four sins in Holy Scripture called *clamantia peccata,* crying sins[,] whereof this detestable sin is one, expressed in this *distichon,*

Sunt vox clamorum, vox sanguinis, & Sodomorum,
Vox oppressorum, merces detenta laborum.

[They are the voice of shouts, the voice of blood, and of sodomites, the voice of the oppressed, when punishment is withheld.]

MICHEL DE MONTAIGNE

From Essays

1603
Translated by John Florio

One signal difficulty with the policing of sodomy in sixteenth- and seventeenth-century England was the fact that public ways of demonstrating friendship between men — kissing, embracing, sharing effusive compliments — could also be interpreted as signs of sodomy (Bray 40–61). (See Figure 17.) In *The En-*

FIGURE 17 *Acquaintance, from Richard Brathwait,* The English Gentleman *(1630).*

glish Gentleman (1630), an advice book on how to be one, Richard Brathwait amplifies the feelings implied in the title page illustration of two men embracing: "Acquaintance is in two bodies individually incorporated, and no less selfly than sociably united. Two twins cannot be more naturally near than these be affectionately dear, which they express in hugging one another and showing the consenting consort of their mind" (Brathwait "Draught of the Frontispiece"). Such opinions confirm Aristotle's argument in the *Nicomachaean Ethics* that friendship between men is the highest of human ties. True friendship, Aristotle maintains, can occur only between equals. Any disparity between one party and the other means that one of them *needs* something from the other. Hence, sons cannot be friends with their fathers, lovers with their mistresses, or wives with their husbands. Male friendship is, indeed, the basis on which civil society is founded. Cicero in his treatise *De Amicitia* (On Friendship) gave Aristotle's arguments particularly influential confirmation.

When Michel de Montaigne turned to the subject of friendship in his essays, he had, then, a long tradition of received opinion to guide him in his thinking. True to form, however, Montaigne was unwilling to accept these opinions at face value; he insisted on testing them against his own experience. Taught Latin, not French, as a child, Montaigne (1533–1592) spent his life reading the classics and testing their precepts against his own observations of the world. Most of those observations were gathered close to home, near Bordeaux in southwestern France, where Montaigne served from 1557 to 1570 as a councillor in the Parliament of Bordeaux and from 1580 to 1585 as mayor of Bordeaux for two terms. He did, however, undertake a two-year trip to Italy via Germany, Switzerland, and other parts of France. His *Essays* (first edition 1580) appealed to skeptical sensibilities of the late sixteenth century. Included in the skepticism that Montaigne brings to received opinions about friendship is the question whether husbands can be friends with their wives. Montaigne entertains the possibility of just how strong such a bond would be but reluctantly dismisses it, largely on grounds of women's upbringing in a patriarchal culture.

The most important relationship Montaigne has experienced, as his essay makes clear, is his friendship with Etienne de La Boétie, a writer, recently deceased, whom the twenty-six-year-old Montaigne had met in 1559, six years before his own marriage at age thirty-two. The terms that Montaigne finds to describe that relationship illustrate the ambiguity of kisses, embraces, and exchanges of compliments. On the one hand, Montaigne is careful to distinguish friendship from sodomy — "this other Greek license," as he calls it in reference to the Athens of Socrates. On the other hand, he can speak of his friendship with Etienne de La Boétie in graphically physical terms, describing how his feelings, "having seized all my will, induced the same to plunge and lose itself in his, which likewise having seized all his will, brought it to lose and plunge itself in mine, with a mutual greediness." Readers since the eighteenth century have been anxious to write off such physical images as just so much rhetoric, as if the very power of those images did not reside in their erotic force. With reference to the homoerotic images in Shakespeare's sonnet 20, for example, Edmund Malone observed, "Such addresses to men, however indelicate, were customary in our author's time, and neither imported criminality nor were esteemed indecorous."[1] Such a formulation attempts to clarify what Renaissance writers left ambiguous: the relationship between male friendship and male

[1]Edmund Malone was responding to his fellow editor George Steevens, who said of sonnet 20, "It is impossible to read this fulsome panegyric, addressed to a male object, without an equal mixture of disgust and indignation." The exchange of opinions is quoted in Pequigney, 30–31.

homoeroticism. Certainly John Florio, in his translation of 1603, leaves all of Montaigne's ambiguities intact. Florio's translation reached a wide readership — including, it seems, William Shakespeare, who alludes in *The Tempest* to Montaigne's essay "Of Cannibals."

From *Essays*

Book 1, Chapter 27

Of Friendship

Considering the proceeding of a painter's work I have, a desire hath possessed me to imitate him: He maketh choice of the most convenient place and middle of every wall, there to place a picture, labored with all his skill and sufficiency; and all void places about it he filleth up with antic boscage or grotesco works;[2] which are fantastical pictures, having no grace, but in the variety and strangeness of them. And what are these my compositions in truth, other than antic works, and monstrous bodies, patched and huddled up together of divers members, without any certain or well ordered figure, having neither order, dependency, or proportion, but casual and framed by chance?

> A woman fair for parts superior,
> Ends in a fish for parts inferior. [Horace, *De Arte Poetica* 4]

Touching this second point I go as far as my painter, but for the other and better part I am far behind: for my sufficiency reacheth not so far, as that I dare undertake, a rich, a polished, and according to true skill, and art-like table.[3] I have advised myself to borrow one of Steven de la Boitie, who with this kind of work shall honor all the world. It is a discourse he entitled, *Voluntary Servitude,* but those who have not known him, have since very properly rebaptized the same, *The against one.* In his first youth he writ, by way of essay, in honor of liberty against tyrants [. . .]. To which his pamphlet I am particularly most bound, forsomuch as it was the instrumental means of our first acquaintance. For it was showed me long time before I saw him; and gave me the first knowledge of his name, addressing, and thus nourishing that unspotted friendship, which we (so long as it pleased God) have so sincerely, so entire and inviolably maintained between us, that truly a man

[2] **antic, boscage, or grotesco works:** fanciful designs made up of intertwined lines ("antic" or "antique"), stylized foliage ("boscage"), or strange creatures ("grotesco" or "grotesque").
[3] **table:** free-standing painting on canvas or wood panel.

Michel de Montaigne, *Essays,* trans. John Florio (London: V. Sims for E. Blount, 1603), 89–93.

shall not commonly hear of the like; and amongst our modern men no sign of any such is seen. So many parts are required to the erecting of such a one, that it may be counted a wonder, if fortune once in three ages contract the like. There is nothing to which nature hath more addresed us than to society. And Aristotle sayeth, that perfect law-givers have had more regardful care of friendship than of justice. And the utmost drift of its perfection is this. For generally, all those amities which are forged and nourished by voluptuousness or profit, public or private need, are thereby so much the less fair and generous, and so much the less true amities, in that they intermeddle other causes, scope, and fruit with friendship, than itself alone [. . .].

To compare the affection toward women unto it, although it proceed from our own free choice, a man cannot, not may it be placed in this rank. Her fire, I confess it

(Nor is that goddess ignorant of me,
Whose bitter-sweets with my cares mixed be.)

to be more active, more fervent, and more sharp. But it is a rash and wavering fire, waving and divers: the fire of an ague subject to fits and stints, and that hath but slender hold-fast of us. In true friendship, it is a general and universal heat, and equally tempered, a constant and settled heat, all pleasure and smoothness, that hath no pricking or stinging in it, which the more it is in lustful love, the more is it but a ranging and mad desire in following that which flies us,

Ev'n as the huntsman doth the hare pursue,
In cold, in heat, on mountains, on the shore,
But cares no more, when he her taken espies,
Speeding his pace, only at that which flies. [Ariosto, *Orlando Furioso* 10.7]

As soon as it creepeth into the terms of friendship, that is to say, in the agreement of wills, it languisheth and vanisheth away: enjoying doth lose it, as having a corporal end, and subject to satiety. On the other side, friendship is enjoyed according as it is desired, it is neither bred, nor nourished, nor increaseth but in jovissance,[4] as being spiritual, and the mind being refined by use and custom. Under this chief amity, these fading affections have sometimes found place in me, lest I should speak of him, who in his verses speaks but too much of it. So are these two passions entered into me in knowledge one of another, but in comparison never: the first flying a high, and keeping a proud pitch, disdainfully beholding the other to pass her points far under it. Concerning marriage, besides that it is a covenant which had nothing free but the entrance, the continuance being forced and con-

[4] **jovissance:** joy.

strained, depending elsewhere than from our will, and a match ordinarily concluded to other ends: A thousand strange knots are therein commonly to be unknit, able to break the web, and trouble the whole course of a lively affection; whereas in friendship, there is no commerce or business depending on the same, but itself. Seeing (to speak truly) that the ordinary sufficiency of women, cannot answer this conference and communication, the nurse of this sacred bond: nor seem their minds strong enough to endure the pulling of a knot so hard, so fast, and durable. And truly, if without that, such a genuine and voluntary acquaintance might be contracted, where not only minds had this entire jovissance, but also bodies, a share of the alliance, and where a man might wholly be engaged: It is certain, that friendship would thereby be more complete and full: But this sex[5] could never yet by any example attain unto it, and is by ancient schools rejected thence.

And this other Greek license[6] is justly abhorred by our customs, which notwithstanding, because according to use it had so necessary a disparity of ages, and difference of offices between lovers, did no more sufficiently answer the perfect union and agreement, which here we require: *Quis est enim iste amor amicitiæ? cur neque deformem adolescentem quisquam amat, neque formosum senem?* (For, what love is this of friendship? why doth no man love either a deformed young man, or a beautiful old man?) (Cicero, *Tusculanae Disputations* 4). For even the picture the Academy[7] makes of it, will not (as I suppose) disavow me, to say thus in her behalf: That the first fury, inspired by the son of Venus in the lover's heart, upon the object of tender youth's-flower, to which they allow all insolent and passionate violences, an immoderate heat may produce, was simply grounded upon an external beauty; a false image of corporal generation: for in the spirit it had no power, the sight whereof was yet concealed, which was but in his infancy, and before the age of budding. For, if this fury did seize upon a base-minded courage, the means of its pursuit, [were] riches, gifts, favor to the advancement of dignities, and such like vile merchandise, which they reprove. If it fell into a most generous mind, the interpositions were likewise generous: Philosophical instructions, documents to reverence religion, to obey the laws, to die for the good of his country: examples of valor, wisdom and justice. The lover endeavoring and studying to make himself acceptable by the good grace and beauty of his mind (that of his body being long since decayed), hoping by this mental society to establish a more firm and permanent bargain. When this pursuit attained the effect in due season, (for by not requiring in a lover, he should bring leisure and discretion in his enterprise, they

[5] **this sex:** i.e., women. [6] **this other Greek license:** pederasty. [7] **the Academy:** the school of Socrates.

require it exactly in the beloved; forasmuch as he was to judge of an internal beauty, of a difficile knowledge, and abstruse discovery) [then] by the interposition of a spiritual beauty was the desire of a spiritual conception engendered in the beloved. The latter was here chiefest; the corporal, accidental and second, altogether contrary to the lover. And therefore do they prefer the beloved, and verify that the gods likewise prefer the same: and greatly blame the poet Aeschylus, who in the love between Achilles and Patroclus ascribeth the lover's part unto Achilles, who was in the first and beardless youth of his adolescence, and the fairest of the Grecians. After this general community, the mistress, and worthiest part of it, predominant and exercising her offices (they say the most availful commodity did thereby redound both to the private and public). That it was the force of countries received the use of it, and the principal defense of equity and liberty: witness the comfortable loves of Hermodius and Aristogiton. Therefore name they it sacred and divine, and it concerns not them whether the violence of tyrants, or the demissness[8] of the people be against them: To conclude, all can be alleged in favor of the Academy, is to say, that it was a love ending in friendship, a thing which hath no bad reference unto the Stoical definition of love: *Amorem conatum esse amicitiæ faciendæ ex pulchritudinis specie* (That love is an endeavour of making friendship, by the show of beauty) (Cicero, *Tusculanae Disputations*).

I return to my description in a more equitable and equal manner. *Omnino amicitiæ corroboratis jam confirmatisque ingeniis et ætatibus judicandæ sunt* (Clearly friendships are to be judged by wits, and ages already strengthened and confirmed) (Cicero, *De Amicitia*). As for the rest, those we ordinarily call friends and amities, are but acquaintances and familiarities, tied together by some occasion or commodities, by means whereof our minds are entertained. In the amity I speak of, they intermix and confound themselves one in the other with so universal a commixture, that they wear out, and can no more find the seam that hath conjoined them together. If a man urge me to tell wherefore I loved him, I feel it cannot be expressed, but by answering; Because it was he, because it was myself. There is beyond all my discourse, and besides what I can particularly report of it, I know not what inexplicable and fatal power, a mean and mediatrix of this indissoluble union. We sought one another, before we had seen one another, and by the reports we heard one of another; which wrought a greater violence in us, than the reason of reports may well bear: I think by some secret ordinance of the heavens, we embraced one another by our names. And at our first meeting, which was by chance at a great feast, and solemn meeting of a whole township, we found

[8] **demissness:** submissiveness.

ourselves so surprised, so known, so acquainted, and so combinedly bound together, that from thenceforward, nothing was so near unto us, as one unto another. He writ an excellent Latin satire; since published; by which he excuseth and expoundeth the precipitation of our acquaintance, so suddenly come to her perfection; Sithence it must continue so short a time, and begun so late (for we were both grown men, and he some years older than myself) there was no time to be lost. And it was not to be modeled or directed by the pattern of regular and remiss friendship, wherein so many precautions of a long and preallable[9] conversation are required. This hath no other idea than of itself, and can have no reference but to itself. It is not one especial consideration, nor two, nor three, nor four, nor a thousand: It is I wot not what kind of quintessence, of all this commixture, which having seized all my will, induced the same to plunge and lose itself in his, which likewise having seized all his will, brought it to lose and plunge itself in mine, with a mutual greediness, and with a semblable concurrance. I may truly say, lose, reserving nothing unto us, that might properly be called our own, nor that was either his, or mine. . . . It is not in the power of the world's discourse to remove me from the certainty I have of his intentions and judgements of mine: no one of its actions might be presented unto me, under what shape soever, but I would presently find the spring and motion of it. Our minds have jumped so unitedly together, they have with so fervent an affection considered of each other, and with like affection so discovered and sounded, even to the very bottom of each other's heart and entrails, that I did not only know his, as well as mine own, but I would (verily) rather have trusted him concerning any matter of mine, than myself. Let no man compare any of the other common friendships to this.

[9] **preallable:** preliminary.

FRANCIS BEAUMONT

From Salmacis and Hermaphroditus

1602

In the very year that *Twelfth Night* was acted at the Middle Temple there appeared from the press of John Hodgets a long narrative poem inspired by Ovid's *Metamorphoses* that seems to capture the paneroticism that suffuses Shakespeare's play. Not attributed to Francis Beaumont until it was included in editions of his poems printed in 1640 and 1653, the original 1602 printing of *Salmacis and Hermaphroditus* comes equipped with commendatory verses that imply a clubby all-male readership very much like the young men assembled in

Middle Temple Hall in February the same year. When *Salmacis and Hermaphroditus* first appeared, Francis Beaumont (1584–1616) was just beginning a writing career that later coupled him with John Fletcher as the leading playwrights of the King's Men after Shakespeare began to provide fewer scripts for the acting company in 1610 or so.

Salmacis and Hermaphroditus took its place in a tradition of Ovidian narrative poems that included Christopher Marlowe's *Hero and Leander* (published 1598) and William Shakespeare's *Venus and Adonis* (1593). Like Marlowe's poem, like Shakespeare's, like the *Metamorphoses* that inspired the whole tradition, Beaumont's poem concerns the transformative force of *erōs,* its power to turn Jupiter into a bull, Daphne into a laurel tree, Actaeon into a stag, Adonis into a flower, or, in the case of Salmacis and Hermaphroditus, a pair of male and female lovers into a one-sexed body. (See Figure 18.) Erudite voyeurism provides the main motive for all these Ovidian poems. The reader is assumed to be learned enough to know the myth from classical sources, sensitive enough to revel in the author's luscious picture-painting, amorous enough to enjoy watching other people make love — and witty enough to share the author's ironic detachment about the whole thing. Inns-of-court men, especially, seem to have enjoyed this particular readerly role.

In the license it gives to erotic desire, the imaginative world of *Salmacis and Hermaphroditus* resembles the dukedom of Illyria. The prefatory address, "Author to the Reader," seems to presume a male reader even as it teases him that reading the poem will turn him into a girl: "I hope my poem is so lively writ, / That thou wilt turn half maid with reading it." Certainly the reader's own sex is left ambiguous as both male and female objects of desire are offered up for

FIGURE 18 *Salmacis and Hermaphroditus, from G. A. Bredero,* Thronus Cupidinis *(1620).*

delectation. Salmacis and Hermaphroditus are each described in a blazon of beauty like Olivia devotes to "Cesario," but the real object of erotic interest in the poem is Hermaphroditus. It is his description that begins the poem, in sexually ambiguous terms strikingly like those in which Orsino and Olivia describe "Cesario." Hermaphroditus's appeal combines the best features of both sexes:

> His cheek was sanguine, and his lip as red
> As are the blushing leaves of the rose spread.
>
> . . . .
>
> His leg was straighter than the thigh of Jove:
> And he far fairer than the god of love.

Which sex is assumed in the reader who observes these beauties? Two perspectives are offered here, just as they are in Shakespeare's *Venus and Adonis:* one masculine (the viewpoint of the narrator) and one feminine (that of the female subject who pursues the unwilling male object of desire). The reader gets to enjoy the pleasures of Hermaphroditus's fair flesh by remaining a man or becoming a woman, as he pleases. Since the poem's two objects of erotic interest, Salmacis and Hermaphroditus, are fused into one sex at the end, the reader, rendered "half maid" by what he has read, is invited to keep his own sexual identity in play. The androgynous enticements of *Salmacis and Hermaphroditus* suggest that *Twelfth Night,* performed the same year for the same people who were reading Beaumont's poem, is neither homoerotic in its appeal, nor heteroerotic, but *pan*erotic.

From *Salmacis and Hermaphroditus*

My wanton lines do treat of amorous love,
Such as would bow the hearts of gods above:
Then Venus, thou great Citherean queen,
That hourly trips on the Idalian green,
Thou laughing Erycina, deign to see
The verses wholly consecrate to thee;
Temper them so within thy Paphian shrine,[1]
That every lover's eye may melt a line;
Command the god of love,[2] that little king,
To give each verse a slight touch with his wing,
That as I write, one line may draw the other,

[1] **Citherean . . . Erycina . . . Paphian shrine:** epithets and places associated with Venus. [2] **the god of love:** Cupid.

Francis Beaumont, *Salmacis and Hermaphroditus* (London: John Hodgets, 1602), Sigs. B1–B3, C3–C3v, D3v–E4.

And every word skip nimbly o'er another.
There was a lovely boy the nymphs had kept,
That on the Idan mountain oft had slept,
Begot and born by powers that dwelt above,
By learned Mercury of the queen of love:
A face he had that showed his parents' fame,
And from them both conjoined, he drew his name:
So wondrous fair he was, that (as they say)
Diana being hunting on a day,
She saw the boy upon a green bank lay him,
And there the virgin-huntress meant to slay him,
Because no Nymph did now pursue the chase:
For all were struck blind with the wanton's face.
But when that beauteous face Diana saw,
Her arms were numbed, and she could not draw;
Yet did she strive to shoot, but all in vain,
She bent her bow, and loosed it straight again.
Then she began to chide her wanton eye,
And fain would shoot, but durst not see him die.
She turned and shot, and did of purpose miss him,
She turned again, and did of purpose kiss him.
Then the boy ran: for (some say) had he stayed,
Diana had no longer been a maid.
Phoebus[3] so doted on this roseate face,
That he hath oft stole closely from his place,
When he did lie by fair Leucothoe's side,
To dally with him in the vales of Ide:
And ever since this lovely boy did die,
Phoebus each day about the world doth fly,
And on the earth he seeks him all the day,
And every night he seeks him in the sea:
His cheek was sanguine, and his lip as red
As are the blushing leaves of the rose spread:
And I have heard, that till this boy was born,
Roses grew white upon the virgin thorn,
Till one day walking to a pleasant spring,
To hear how cunningly the birds could sing,
Laying him down upon a flowery bed,
The roses blushed and turned themselves to red.

[3] **Phoebus:** Apollo.

The rose that blushed not, for his great offense,
The gods did punish, and for impudence
They gave this doom that was agreed by all;
The smell of the white rose should be but small.
His hair was bushy, but it was not long,
The nymphs had done his tresses mighty wrong:
For as it grew, they pulled away his hair,
And made habiliments[4] of gold to wear.
His eyes were Cupid's: for until his birth,
Cupid had eyes, and lived upon the earth,
Till on a day, when the great queen of love
Was by her white doves drawn from heaven above,
Unto the top of the Idalian hill,
To see how well the nymphs their charge fulfill,
And whether they had done the goddess right,
In nursing of her sweet Hermaphrodite:
Whom when she saw, although complete and full,
Yet she complained, his eyes were somewhat dull:
And therefore, more the wanton boy to grace,
She pulled the sparkling eyes from Cupid's face,
Faining a cause to take away his sight,
Because the ape would sometimes shoot for spite.
But Venus set those eyes in such a place,
As graced those clear eyes with a clearer face.
For his white hand each goddess did him woo:
For it was whiter than the driven snow:
His leg was straighter than the thigh of Jove:
And he far fairer than the god of love.
When first this well-shaped boy, beauty's chief king,
Had seen the labor of the fifteenth spring,
How curiously it painted all the earth,
He 'gan to travel from his place of birth,
Leaving the stately hills where he was nursed,
And where the nymphs had brought him up at first:
He loved to travel to the coasts unknown,
To see the regions far beyond his own,
Seeking clear watery springs to bathe him in:
(For he did love to wash his ivory skin)
The lovely nymphs have oft times seen him swim,

[4] **habiliments:** wearings.

And closely stole his clothes from off the brim,
Because the wanton wenches would so fain
See him come naked to ask his clothes again.
He loved besides to see the Lycian grounds,
And know the wealthy Carians' utmost bounds.
Using to travel thus, one day he found
A crystal brook, that trilled along the ground,
A brook, that in reflection did surpass
The clear reflection of the clearest glass.[5]
About the side there grew no foggy reeds,
Nor was the fount compassed with barren weeds:
But living turf grew all along the side,
And grass that ever flourished in his pride.
Within this brook a beauteous nymph did dwell,
Who for her comely feature did excel;
So fair she was, of such a pleasing grace,
So straight a body, and so sweet a face,
So soft a belly, such a lusty thigh,
So large a forehead, such a crystal eye,
So soft and moist a hand, so smooth a breast,
So fair a cheek, so well in all the rest,
That Jupiter would revel in her bower,
Were he to spend again his golden shower:[6]
Her teeth were whiter than the morning's milk,
Her lip was softer than the softest silk,
Her hair as far surpassed the burnished gold,
As silver doth excel the basest mold.

. . . .

Oft in the water did she look her face,
And oft she used to practise what quaint grace
Might well become her, and what comely feature
Might be best fitting so divine a creature.
Her skin was with a thin veil overthrown,
Through which her naked beauty clearly shone.
She used in this light raiment as she was,
To spread her body on the dewy grass:
Sometimes by her own fountain as she walks,

[5] **glass:** mirror. [6] **golden shower:** Jupiter seduced Danaë by turning himself into a shower of golden coins.

She nips the flowers from off the fertile stalks,
And with a garland of the sweating vine,
Sometimes she doth her beauteous front entwine:
But she was gath'ring flowers with her white hand,
When she beheld Hermaphroditus stand
By her clear fountain, wond'ring at the sight,
That there was any brook could be so bright:
For this was the bright river where the boy[7]
Did die himself, that he could not enjoy
Himself in pleasure, nor could taste the blisses
Of his own melting and delicious kisses.
Here did she see him, and by Venus' law,
She did desire to have him as she saw.

. . . .

There was he come to seek some pleasing brook.
No sooner came he, but the Nymph was struck:
And though she hastened to embrace the boy,
Yet did the nymph awhile defer her joy,
Till she had bound up her loose flagging hair,
And ordered well the garments she did wear,
Faining her count'nance with a lover's care,
And did deserve to be accounted fair.
And thus much spake she while the boy abode:
"O boy, most worthy to be thought a god,
Thou mayest inhabit in the glorious place
Of gods, or mayest proceed from human race:
Thou mayest be Cupid, or the god of wine,
That lately wooed me with the swelling vine:
But whosoe'r thou art, O happy he,
That was so blest, to be a sire to thee;
Thy happy mother is most blest of many,
Blest thy sisters, if her womb bear any,
Both fortunate, and O thrice happy she,
Whose too much blest breasts gave suck to thee:
If any wife with thy sweet bed be blest,
O, she is far more happy than the rest;
If thou hast any, let my sport be stolen,
Or else let me be she, if thou hast none."

[7] **the boy:** Narcissus.

. . . .

Her radiant beauty and her subtle art
So deeply struck Hermpahroditus' heart,
That she had won his love, but that the light
Of her translucent eyes did shine too bright:
For long he looked upon the lovely maid,
And at the last Hermaphroditus said,
"How should I love thee, when I do espy
A far more beauteous nymph hid in thy eye?
When thou dost love, let not that nymph be nigh thee;
Nor when thou wooest, let that same nymph be by thee:
Or quite obscure her from thy lover's face,
Or hide her beauty in a darker place."
By this, the nymph perceived he did espy
None but himself reflected in her eye,
And, for himself no more she meant to show him,
She shut her eyes and blindfold thus did woo him:
"Fair boy, think not thy beauty can dispense
With any pain due to a bad offense;
Remember how the gods punished that boy[8]
That scorned to let a beauteous nymph enjoy
Her long wished pleasure; for the peevish elf,
Loved of all others, needs would love himself.
So mayest thou love, perhaps thou mayest be blest,
By granting to a luckless nymph's request:
Then rest awhile with me amid these weeds.
The sun that sees all, sees not lovers' deeds;
Phoebus is blind when love-sports are begun,
And never sees until their sports be done:
Believe me, boy, thy blood is very staid,
That art so loath to kiss a youthful maid.
Were thou a maid, and I a man, I'll show thee,
With what a manly boldness I could woo thee:
Fairer than love's queen, thus I would begin,
Might not my over-boldness be a sin,
I would entreat this favor, if I could,
Thy roseate cheek a little to behold:
Then would I beg a touch, and then a kiss,
And then a lower, yet a higher bliss:

[8] **that boy:** Narcissus.

Then would I ask what Jove and Leda did,
When like a swan the crafty god was hid?
What came he for? why did he there abide?
Surely I think he did not come to chide:
He came to see her face, to talk, and chat,
To touch, to kiss: came he for nought but that?
Yes, something else: what was it he would have?
That which all men of maidens ought to crave."
This said, her eyelids wide she did display:
But in this space the boy was run away:
The wanton speeches of the lovely lass
Forced him for shame to hide him in the grass.
When she perceived she could not see him near her,
When she had called, and yet he could not hear her,
Look how when Autumn comes, a little space
Paleth the red blush of the Summer's face,
Tearing the leaves the Summer's covering,
Three months in weaving by the curious spring,
Making the grass his green locks go to wrack,
Tearing each ornament from off his back;
So did she spoil the garments she did wear,
Tearing whole ounces of her golden hair:
She thus deluded of her longed bliss,
With much ado at last she uttered this:
"Why were thou bashful, boy? Thou hast no part
Shows thee to be of such a female heart."

. . . .

This said, hid in the grass she did espy him,
And stumbling with her will, she fell down by him,
And with her wanton talk, because he wooed not,
Begged that, which he poor novice understood not:
And, for she could not get a greater bliss,
She did entreat at least a sister's kiss.

. . . .

But then the boy did struggle to be gone,
Vowing to leave her and that place alone.
But then bright Salmacis began to fear,
And said, "Fair stranger, I will leave thee here
Amid these pleasant places all alone."
So turning back, she fained to be gone;
But from his sight she had no power to pass,

Therefore she turned, and hid her in the grass,
When to the ground bending her snow-white knee,
The glad earth gave new coats to every tree.
He then supposing he was all alone,
(Like a young boy that is espied of none)
Runs here, and there, then on the banks doth look,
Then on the crystal current of the brook,
Then with his foot he touched the silver streams,
Whose drowsy waves made music in their dreams,
And, for he was not wholly in, did weep,
Talking aloud and babbling in their sleep:
Whose pleasant coolness when the boy did feel,
He thrust his foot down lower to the heel:
O'ercome with whose sweet noise, he did begin
To strip his soft clothes from his tender skin,
When strait the scorching sun wept tears of brine,
Because he durst not touch him with his shine,
For fear of spoiling that same iv'ry skin,
Whose whiteness he so much delighted in;
And then the moon, mother of mortal ease
Would fain have come from the Antipodes,[9]
To have beheld him naked as he stood,
Ready to leap into the silver flood;
But might not: for the laws of heaven deny,
To show men's secrets to a woman's eye:
And therefore was her sad and gloomy light
Confined unto the secret-keeping night.
When beauteous Salmacis awhile had gazed
Upon his naked corps, she stood amazed,
And both her sparkling eyes burnt in her face,
Like the bright sun reflected in a glass:
Scarce can she stay from running to the boy,
Scarce can she now defer her hoped joy;
So fast her youthful blood plays in her veins,
That almost mad, she scarce herself contains.
When young Hermaphroditus as he stands,
Clapping his white side with his hollow hands,
Leapt lively from the land, whereon he stood,
Into the main part of the crystal flood.

[9] **the Antipodes:** the opposite ends of the earth.

Like iv'ry then his snowy body was,
Or a white lily in a crystal glass.
Then rose the water-nymph from where she lay,
As having won the glory of the day,
And her light garments cast from off her skin.
"He's mine," she cried; and so leapt spritely in.
The flattering ivy who did ever see
Enclasp the huge trunk of an aged tree,
Let him behold the young boy as he stands,
Enclasped in wanton Salmacis' hands,
Betwixt those iv'ry arms she locked him fast,
Striving to get away, till at the last,
Fondling, she said, "Why striv'st thou to be gone?
Why shouldst thou so desire to be alone?
Thy cheek is never fair, when none is by:
For what is red and white, but to the eye?
And for that cause the heavens are dark at night,
Because all creatures close their weary sight;
For there's no mortal can so early rise,
But still the morning waits upon his eyes.
The early-rising and soon-singing lark
Can never chant her sweet notes in the dark;
For sleep she ne'er so little or so long,
Yet still the morning will attend her song.
All creatures that beneath bright Cynthia[10] be,
Have appetite unto society;
The overflowing waves would have a bound
Within the confines of the spacious ground,
And all their shady currents would be placed
In hollow of the solitary vast,
But that they loath to let their soft streams sing,
Where none can hear their gentle murmuring."
Yet still the boy regardless what she said,
Struggled apace to overswim the maid.
Which when the Nymph perceived, she 'gan to say,
"Struggle thou may'st, but never get away.
So grant, just gods, that never day may see
The separation twixt this boy and me."
The gods did hear her prayer and feel her woe;

[10] **Cynthia:** Diana, so-called from Mount Cynthos on her native island of Delos.

And in one body they began to grow.
She felt his youthful blood in every vein;
And he felt hers warm his cold breast again.
And ever since was woman's love so blest,
That it will draw blood from the strongest breast.
Nor man nor maid now could they be esteemed:
Neither, and either, might they well be deemed,
When the young boy Hermaphroditus said,
With the set voice of neither man nor maid,
"Swift Mercury, thou author of my life,
And thou my mother Vulcan's lovely wife,[11]
Let your poor offspring's latest breath be blest,
In but obtaining this his last request,
Grant that whoe'er heated by Phoebus' beams,
Shall come to cool him in these silver streams,
May nevermore a manly shape retain,
But half a virgin may return again."
His parents harkened to his last request,
And with that great power they the fountain blest.
And since that time who in that fountain swims,
A maiden smoothness seizeth half his limbs.

[11] **Vulcan's lovely wife:** Venus.

CHAPTER 4

Clothing and Disguise

In the course of act 5 the entire cast of *Twelfth Night* — everyone but the ship's captain who has rescued Viola — finds his or her way to the stage. Olivia in her mourning clothes, Orsino in a lover's dishabille, Feste in his Fool's garb, Sir Andrew and Sir Toby in their revelers' gear, the priest in his robes, Antonio in his captain's clothes: they make up a carnivalesque conglomeration. Amid all the variety there is one glaring anomaly that arrests everyone's attention. *Enter Sebastian.* Orsino — looking at "Cesario" looking at Sebastian looking at Orsino looking at everyone else — speaks for all: "One face, one voice, one habit, and two persons, / A natural perspective, that is and is not!" (5.1.SD before 200, 200–01). A "perspective," an optical illusion. No, a "*natural* perspective," an illusion created by Nature. However diverse the rest of the cast may be, each is his or her own *person.* "Cesario" and Sebastian, sharing the same physiognomy, the same voice, the same "habits" or clothing, call into question the easy equation among face, voice, clothing, and identity on which all the other cast members can rely.

"Person" is the operative word in that question. In early modern English it could mean four things: a physical body (*OED,* "person" 3.4), an individual acting in some capacity (*OED* 2.2a), a personage to be reckoned with (*OED* 2.2b), or an actor in a play (*OED* 1.1). In calling the cast's attention to the "two persons" before them, Orsino seems to have in mind the first meaning, person as physical body, but all the other meanings of "person" unfold in the course of the scene. To everyone but herself, Viola's person has been that of a servant. To herself, she has been acting the sister to Sebastian. Through their betrothals both Viola and Sebastian become personages. And, of course, they along with everyone else onstage are actors in a play.

It is the disjunction between appearance and personhood that makes the final scene so arresting. Witness audience member John Manningham's description of *Twelfth Night* in his diary: "a play called '~~Mid~~ Twelve Night, or What You Will,' much like 'The Comedy of Errors' or 'Menaechmi' in Plautus." The plot of Plautus's *Menaechmi,* the inspiration for Shakespeare's *The Comedy of Errors,* turns on a pair of twin brothers, separated at birth, who happen to turn up in the same place at the same time, to everyone's consternation — including their own. The appeal of this confusion is universal enough for twins to have their own reference number, T685, in Stith Thompson's *Motif-Index of Folk-Literature,* a compilation based on narratives from all over the world. *Twelfth Night* adds to the usual confusion by giving these seemingly identical twins different body parts underneath their clothes. Costume is the key to the comedy's existential confusions. A look at Edward Alleyn and Philip Henslowe's inventory of theatrical properties (see p. 244) will reveal how important costumes were to the business of putting on a play. According to Henslowe's financial records, costumes constituted, in fact, the single most expensive consideration in mounting a production. Partly that can be explained by the generally greater cost of hard goods in early modern commerce compared with human services, but mostly it is the result of using real clothes, including the cast-off clothing of gentlemen. (Concerning this point see the Introduction.) On the stage and on the street, therefore, the same garments were being used — and for the same purpose of making the wearer's identity instantly knowable.

One trouble with the theater, or so it seemed to literal-minded foes like Phillip Stubbes and William Prynne (see Chapters 5 and 6), was that the clothing *never* matched the wearer's identity, since the actors playing kings and dukes were legally no more than some nobleman's servants. And, to hear the anti-theatricalist tell it, actors liked to wear their fine clothes outside the theater as well as within. Stephen Gosson in *The School of Abuse* (1579) is outraged that "the very hirelings of some of our players . . . jet under gentleman's noses in suits of silk, exercising themselves to prating on the stage, and common scoffing when they come abroad, where they look askance over the shoulder at every man, of whom the Sunday before they begged an alms" (Gosson C6). In dressing above their station, actors were flouting a series of royal proclamations that attempted to regulate precisely who could wear what fabrics in what yardages with what accoutrements. A disjunction between clothing and true identity was, therefore, at the very heart of playacting. *Twelfth Night* capitalizes on that disjunction.

By dressing in clothes like her brother's and posing as a servant, Viola carries out an act of deconstruction more than three centuries before the word was invented: she puts a ≠ between sartorial signifer and signified person, and she does so with respect not only to social class but to gender. Her action is even more radical than that. "She," in the original production, was not really a "she," after all, but a boy actor in the Lord Chamberlain's Men. As we have seen in Chapter 3, Shakespeare delights in playing up that fact, just as he always does when a boy actor playing a girl dresses as a boy. Viola's disguise raises two questions of identity that extend to other characters as well.

With respect to social rank, other characters are in equally ambiguous positions. With their honorific titles, *Sir* Toby and *Sir* Andrew can lay claim to a gentlemanly status that does not match their actions or (in many productions) their clothing. Maria, often miscast as a maid in productions today, is in fact a kind of lady-in-waiting, an attendant "gentlewoman," as Olivia hails her in 1.5.127. Malvolio may give these gentlefolk a dressing down; as for himself, he daydreams about dressing up. Once he has married Olivia, he will order his servants about while dressed in his "branched velvet gown," winding up his watch, playing with "some rich jewel" for which he has cast aside his steward's chain (2.5.39, 49–50).

With respect to gender, Viola's change of costume from female to male has its counterpart in Orsino's effeminate pose as a languishing lover. In act 1, scene 1, he is all appetite. He has given up the reasonableness that was supposed to make men *men.* Orsino's behavior in act 1, scene 1, seems calculated in some respects to illustrate Nicholas Breton's character of "An Effeminate Fool." Such a man

> loves nothing but gay, to look in a glass, to keep among wenches, and to play with trifles; to feed on sweetmeats and to be danced in laps, to be embraced in arms, and to be kissed on the cheek; to talk idly, to look demurely, to go nicely, and to laugh continually; to be his mistress's servant and her maid's master, his father's love and mother's none-child; to play on a fiddle and sing a love-song. (Breton 274–75)

The selections in this chapter have been chosen to address both sorts of questions raised by costume and disguise in *Twelfth Night:* questions of social rank and questions of gender, with special attention to the phenomenon of boy actors playing women's parts.

→ *From* Of Excess of Apparel

1563

The liturgy of the Church of England, as codified in *The Book of Common Prayer* in 1559, called for a sermon to be preached during The Order for the Administration of the Lord's Supper, or Holy Communion. It was to come just after the congregation had heard readings from the scriptures and had affirmed their belief by pronouncing the creed and just before they presented their tithes and offerings and began the series of prayers that led up to the service of communion itself. In keeping with Protestant ideas about communion, the reading of the scriptures and the preaching of the sermon were, temporally in the service and physically on the page, the central events in the service. In an attempt to assure uniformity of belief in the newly reestablished Church of England, the authorities issued two collections of prepared homilies that could be read aloud. The second of these collections, possibly edited by John Jewel (1522–1571), Bishop of Salisbury and diligent propagandist for the Church of England, includes a homily "Of Excess of Apparel," an excerpt from which appears here. Dressing according to one's means and social station is set forth as a principle ordained by God.

. . . He that is ashamed of base and simple attire, will be proud of gorgeous apparel, if he may get it. We must learn therefore of the Apostle St. Paul both to use plenty, and also to suffer penury,[1] remembering that we must yield accounts, of those things which we have received, unto Him who abhorreth all excess, pride, ostentation, and vanity, who also utterly condemneth and disalloweth whatsoever draweth us from our duties towards God, or diminisheth our charity towards our neighbors and children, whom we ought to love as ourselves. The fourth and last rule is, that every man behold and consider his own vocation, inasmuch as God hath appointed every man his degree and office, within the limits whereof it behooveth him to keep himself. Therefore all may not look to wear like apparel, but everyone according to his degree, as God hath placed him. Which, if it were observed, many one doubtless should be compelled to wear a russet coat,[2] which now ruffleth in silks and velvets, spending more by the year in sumptuous apparel, than their fathers received for the whole revenue of their lands. But alas nowadays how many may we behold occupied in pampering the flesh, taking on care at all, but only how to deck themselves, setting their affection altogether on worldly bravery,[3] abusing God's goodness, when He

[1] **penury:** poverty. [2] **russet coat:** common brown coat. [3] **bravery:** audacity, showiness.

The Second Tome of Homilies (London: R. Jugge and J. Cawood, 1563), II4v–II6.

sendeth plenty, to satisfy their wanton lusts, having no regard to the degree[4] wherein God hath placed them?

The Israelites were contented with such apparel as God gave them, although it were base and simple. And God so blessed them, that their shoes and clothes lasted them forty years, yea, and those clothes which their fathers had worn, their children were contented to use afterward. But we are never contented and therefore we prosper not, so that most commonly he that ruffleth in his sables, in his fine furred gown, corked slippers, trim buskins,[5] and warm mittens, is more ready to chill for cold, than the poor laboring man, which can abide in the field all day long, when the north wind blows, with a few beggarly clouts[6] about him. We are loath to wear such as our fathers have left us, we think not that sufficient or good enough for us. We must have one gown for the day, another for the night, one long, another short, one for winter, another for summer, one through-furred,[7] another but faced, one for the working day, another for the holiday, one of this color, another of that color, one of cloth, another of silk or damask. We must have change of apparel, one afore dinner, another after, one of the Spanish fashion, another Turkey, and to be brief, never content with sufficient.

Our Savior Christ bade His disciples they should not have two coats, but the most men, far unlike to His scholars, have their presses[8] so full of apparel, that many know not how many sorts they have. Which thing caused Saint James to pronounce this terrible curse against such wealthy worldlings: "Go to, ye rich men, weep and howl on your wretchedness that shall come upon you, your riches are corrupt, and your garments are moth-eaten, ye have lived in pleasure on the earth, and in wantonness, ye have nourished your hearts, as in the day of slaughter." Mark, I beseech you, Saint James calleth them miserable, notwithstanding their richness and plenty of apparel, forasmuch as they pamper their bodies, to their own destruction. What was the rich glutton better for his fine fare and costly apparel? Did not he nourish himself to be tormented in hell fire? Let us learn therefore to content ourselves, having food and raiment, as Saint Paul teacheth, lest desiring to be enriched with abundance, we fall into temptations, snares, and many noisome lusts, which drown men in perdition and destruction.

Certainly, such as delight in gorgeous apparel, are commonly puffed up with pride, and filled with diverse vanities. So were the daughters of Zion and people of Jerusalem, whom Isaiah the prophet threateneth, because they walked with stretched-out necks and wandering eyes, mincing as they went,

[4] **degree:** social rank. [5] **buskins:** foot-coverings reaching to the calf or knee. [6] **clouts:** patches, rags. [7] **through-furred:** completely fur-lined. [8] **presses:** cabinets for storing clothing and linen.

and nicely[9] treading with their feet, that Almighty God would make their heads bald and discover their secret shame. In that day, saith he, shall the Lord take away the ornament of the slippers, and the cauls,[10] and the round attires, and the sweet balls, and the bracelets, and the attires of the head, and the slops,[11] and the head bands, and the tablets,[12] and the ear-rings, the rings, and the mufflers, the costly apparel, and the veils and wimples,[13] and the crisping pin,[14] and the glasses,[15] and the fine linen, and the hoods, and the lawns.[16] So that Almighty God, would not suffer His benefits to be vainly and wantonly abused, no not of that people whom He most tenderly loved, and had chosen to Himself before all other. No less truly is the vanity that is used among us in these days. For the proud and haughty stomachs[17] of the daughters of England, are so maintained with diverse disguised sorts of costly apparel, that as Tertullian an ancient father saith, there is left no difference in apparel between an honest matron and a common strumpet.[18] Yea many men are become so effeminate, that they care not what they spend in disguising themselves, ever desiring new toys,[19] and inventing new fashions. Therefore a certain man that would picture every countryman in his accustomed apparel, when he had painted other nations, he pictured the English man all naked, and gave him cloth under his arm, and bade him make it himself as he thought best, for he changed his fashion so often, that he knew not how to make it.

Thus with our fantastical devices, we make ourselves laughingstocks to other nations, while one spendeth his patrimony upon pounces and cuts,[20] another bestoweth more on a dancing shirt, than might suffice to buy him honest and comely apparel for his whole body. Some hang their revenues about their necks, ruffling in their ruffs, and many a one jeopardeth his best joint,[21] to maintain himself in sumptuous raiment. And every man, nothing considering his estate and condition, seeketh to excel other in costly attire. Whereby it commeth to pass, that in abundance and plenty of all things, we yet complain of want and penury, while one man spendeth that which might serve to supply the necessities of other.

There hath been very good provision made against such abuses, by diverse good and wholesome laws, which if they were practiced as they ought to be of all true subjects, they might in some part serve to diminish this raging and riotous excess in apparel. But alas, there appeareth amongst

[9] **nicely:** fastidiously. [10] **cauls:** netted caps. [11] **slops:** loose-fitting outer garments. [12] **tablets:** flat pieces of jewelry. [13] **wimples:** garments that completely enclose the head and neck. [14] **crisping pin:** hair-curler. [15] **glasses:** mirrors. [16] **lawns:** apparel made from fine linen. [17] **stomachs:** desires. [18] **strumpet:** prostitute. [19] **toys:** trifles. [20] **pounces and cuts:** cutwork. [21] **jeopardeth his best joint:** jeopardizes his inheritance.

us little fear and obedience either of God, or man. Therefore must we needs look for God's fearful vengeance from heaven, to overthrow our presumption and pride, as He overthrew Herod, who in his royal apparel, forgetting God, was smitten of an angel, and eaten of by worms. By which terrible example, God hath taught us that we are but worms' meat, although we pamper ourselves never so much in gorgeous apparel.

EDWARD ALLEYN AND PHILIP HENSLOWE

An Inventory of Costumes

c. 1600

Nothing could stand in sharper contrast to the strictures of the homily against excess of apparel than the sumptuousness of some sixty-five costumes owned by the Lord Admiral's Men around 1600. This inventory forms part of the business papers kept by the theatrical impresario Philip Henslowe (d. 1616) during the 1590s. It was possibly Henslowe who erected the Curtain playhouse in Shoreditch, north of the London city walls, a year or so after James Burbage had erected the Theater in the same locale. About ten years later Henslowe inaugurated a shift in theatrical activity to the South Bank when he erected the Rose playhouse. James Burbage's sons Richard and Cuthbert followed suit in 1599 when they dismantled the timbers of the Theater, transported them to the South Bank, and had them reassembled as the Globe. Our knowledge of the 1599 Globe is dependent in large part on the builder's contract that Henslowe drew up for the Fortune playhouse shortly thereafter. The Fortune contract specifies that certain dimensions should be the same as those of the Globe. Throughout the 1590s, Shakespeare and his fellow actors were sometimes collaborators with Philip Henslowe's actors and sometimes rivals. From 1590 to 1594 an amalgamation of Lord Strange's Men and the Lord Admiral's Men performed jointly under Henslowe's management. The company included several men who, in 1594, broke away to form the Lord Chamberlain's Men. William Shakespeare's name does not appear among those in the amalgamated company, although Henslowe's records indicate they performed a play called "Harry the Sixth" (*Henry VI, Part 2* or *3*?) in 1592.

The surviving papers do not constitute a complete, continuous record, but Henslowe provides a day-by-day accounting of the theater business in the 1590s: outlays for costumes and properties, payments to script writers, purchases of musical instruments, and the box office take on a given day. One thing that these financial accounts make absolutely clear is that costumes formed the single most expensive factor in the production of a play. Playbooks were important, but Henslowe invested more money in apparel than in scripts. It was a double investment, since Henslowe realized a tidy profit by hiring out the costumes when they were not in use for play productions. He could do so because the costumes were real clothes, often the cast-off clothes of noble personages.[1] Among Henslowe's papers is an inventory, drawn up probably about 1600, of costumes used by the Lord Admiral's Men in their productions at the Rose theater. The document is in the hand of Edward Alleyn (1566–1626), Henslowe's son-in-law and one of the most famous actors of his day. Alleyn's success with the troupes that Henslowe managed, like Shakespeare's with the Lord Chamberlain's Men, was not only artistic but financial. Alleyn used his profits to found a school at Dulwich, the College of God's Gift, in whose keeping Henslowe's papers survive. The inventory breaks down the company's costumes into garment types (cloaks, gowns, fantasy-suits, vests and jackets, knee-breeches in the French style, and knee-breeches in the Venetian style). Within these categories some indication is given as to which sort of character might wear the garment in question (a boy, a cardinal, a woman, an angel, a horseman), sometimes a particular character is specified (Harry VIII's gown, Pan's gown, the Moor's coat, Faustus's jerkin and cloak, the Guise's apparel, Priam's hose), sometimes a particular actor seems to be named (Daniel's gown, Will Summers's coat, Cavendish's gold-paned black-striped French hose), but the emphasis falls much more often on the color, the fabric, and the trimmings. These, as we shall see, are the very things that royal proclamations attempted to control.

An Inventory of Costumes

Cloaks

1. a scarlet cloak with 2 broad gold laces, with gold buttons of the same down the sides
2. a black velvet cloak
3. a scarlet cloak laid down with silver lace and silver buttons
4. a short velvet cap cloak embroidered with gold and gold spangles
5. a watchet[2] satin cloak with 5 gold laces
6. a purple satin [cloak] welted with velvet and silver twist
7. a black tufted cloak
8. a damask cloak guarded[3] with velvet

[1] On Henslowe's records generally see Foakes and Rickert's edition of *Henslowe's Diary*, especially xlii–xliii; on costumes in particular, see Gurr, 193–200. [2] **watchet:** light blue. [3] **guarded:** ornamented.

Edward Alleyn and Philip Henslowe, An Inventory of Costumes Belonging to the Lord Admiral's Men, c. 1600, transcribed in R. A. Foakes and R. T. Rickert, eds., *Henslowe's Diary* (Cambridge: Cambridge University Press, 1961), 291–94.

9. a long black taffeta cloak
10. a colored bugle[4] [cloak] for a boy
11. a scarlet [cloak] with buttons of gold, faced with blue velvet
12. a scarlet [cloak] faced with black velvet
13. a stammel[5] cloak with gold lace
14. black bugle cloak

Gowns

1. Harry the VIII['s] gown
2. the black velvet gown with white fur
3. a crimson robe striped with gold, faced with ermine
4. one of wrought cloth of gold
5. one of red silk with gold buttons
6. a cardinal's gown
7. women's gowns

8, 9. 1 black velvet [gown] embroidered with gold

10. 1 cloth-of-gold [gown], Cavendish his stuff
11. 1 black velvet [gown] laced and drawn out with white sarsenet[6]
12. a black silk [gown] with red flush[7]
13. a cloth-of-silver [gown] for Pan
14. a yellow silk gown
15. a red silk gown
16. angel's silk [gown]
17. 2 blue calico gowns

Antic[8] Suits

1. a coat of crimson velvet cut in panes[9] and embroidered with gold
2. 1 cloth-of-gold coat with green bases[10]
3. 1 cloth-of-gold coat with orange tawny bases
4. 1 cloth-of-silver coat with blue silk and tinsel[11] bases
5. 1 blue damask coat, the Moor

[4] **bugle:** beadwork. [5] **stammel:** coarse woolen, usually dyed red. [6] **sarsenet:** very fine and soft silk. [7] **flush:** (presumably) plush trim. [8] **antic:** fantastic, bizarre, grotesque. [9] **panes:** inset fabric of contrasting color. [10] **bases:** skirts. [11] **tinsel:** silk or wool fabric interwoven with thread of gold or silver.

6. a red velvet horseman's coat
7. a yellow taffeta [coat]
8. cloth-of-gold horseman's coat
9. cloth-of-baudkin[12] horseman's coat
10. orange tawny horseman's coat of cloth laced
11. Daniel's gown
12. blue embroidered bases
13. Will Summers' coat
14. white embroidered bases
15. gilt leather coat
16. 2 head-tires set with stones

Jerkins and doublets[13]

1. a crimson velvet case[14] with gold buttons and lace
2. a crimson satin case laced with gold lace all over
3. a doublet cut diamond,[15] laced with gold lace and spangles
4. a doublet of black velvet cut on silver tinsel
5. a ginger-colored doublet
6. 1 white satin [jerkin or doublet] cut on white
7. black velvet [jerkin or doublet] with gold lace
8. green velvet [jerkin or doublet]
9. black taffeta [jerkin or doublet] cut on black velvet, laced with bugle
10. black velvet plain [jerkin or doublet]
11. old white satin [jerkin or doublet]
12. red velvet [jerkin or doublet] for a boy
13. a carnation velvet [jerkin or doublet] laced with silver
14. a yellow spangled case
15. red velvet [jerkin or doublet] with blue satin sleeves and case
16. cloth-of-silver jerkin
17. Faustus' jerkin, his cloak

[12] **cloth-of-baudkin:** brocade. [13] **jerkins and doublets:** close-fitting jackets and torso garments with or without sleeves. [14] **case:** pair (or perhaps a type of doublet or jerkin). [15] **cut diamond:** cut in a diamond pattern.

French Hose[16]

1. blue velvet [hose] embroidered with gold panes, blue satin scalings[17]
2. [hose with] silver panes, laced with carnation satin, laced over with silver
3. the Guise's [hose]
4. [hose with] rich panes with long stockings
5. [hose with] gold panes with black-striped scalings of canish[18]
6. [hose with] gold panes with velvet scalings
7. [hose with] gold panes with red-striped scalings
8. [hose of] black bugle
9. [hose with] red panes for a boy, with yellow scalings
10. Priam's hose
11. spangled hose

Venetians[19]

1. a purple velvet [venetian] cut in diamonds, laced, and spangles
2. red velvet [venetian] laced with gold spangles
3. a purple velvet [venetian] embroidered with silver cut on tinsel
4. green velvet [venetian] laced with gold, Spanish
5. black velvet [venetian]
6. cloth-of-silver [venetian]
7. green-striped satin [venetian]
8. cloth-of-gold [venetian] for a boy

[16] **French Hose:** breeches reaching to the knees, worn with stockings below the knees. [17] **scalings:** (uncertain; clearly a feature of panes, or inset fabric). [18] **canish:** (uncertain; perhaps another reference to Cavendish). [19] **Venetians:** hose or breeches in the style of Venice.

Social Rank

A Proclamation Enforcing Statutes and Proclamations of Apparel

1597

That clothing was an index to the wearer's social status was not just a custom in Shakespeare's England; it was the law. Statutes passed by Parliament during the reigns of Henry VIII (1533 and 1542) and Philip and Mary (1555) were still on the books, though hopelessly outdated with respect to rising prices and changing fashions. Those earlier statutes were reaffirmed, extended, and brought up to date in nine royal proclamations during the course of Elizabeth's reign (1558–1603). These so-called sumptuary laws (from Latin *sumptus,* "expense") were designed to regulate costs, but they had the effect of maintaining — or attempting to maintain — the existing social order. Government control of what people could wear ended in 1604 — much earlier than elsewhere in Europe — but only because Parliament rejected bills that would have given regulatory power solely to the crown (Hooper 433–49; Young 161–70; Jardine 141–68; Jones and Stallybrass). The original act of 1533 divides people of the realm into twelve ranks, each distinguished from the next by precisely graded fabrics, yardage, colors, and adornments. The shift from a feudal economy to a capitalist economy in the course of the sixteenth century meant that more and more people had the cash to buy clothes that once belonged to a privileged few. Elizabeth's royal proclamations become ever more urgent, culminating in the next to last, reprinted here. If the proclamation is to be believed, extravagant taste in clothing had led to the decay of hospitality, even to robbery. The range of costumes that one might have seen on London's streets in Shakespeare's youth are paraded in Figure 19. Figure 20 shows the table of men's ranks and men's clothing that accompanied the proclamation of July 6, 1597. The table of women's ranks and women's clothing runs to two broadside pages.

FIGURE 19 *English Apparel, from Abraham de Bruyn,* Omnium Gentium Habitus *(1581).*

A Proclamation Enforcing Statutes and Proclamations of Apparel

[Greenwich, 6 July 1597, 39 Elizabeth I]

Whereas the Queen's majesty, for avoiding of the great inconvenience that grow and daily doth increase within this her realm by the inordinate excess in apparel, hath in her princely wisdom and care for reformation thereof by sundry former proclamations straightly charged and commanded those in authority under her to see her laws provided in that behalf duly executed.

Whereof notwithstanding, partly through their negligence and partly by the manifest contempt and disobedience of the parties offending, no reformation at all hath followed; her majesty, finding by experience that by clemency (whereunto she is most inclinable so long as there is any hope of redress) this increasing evil hath not been cured, hath thought fit to seek to remedy the same by correction and severity to be used against both these kinds of offenders in regard to the present difficulties of this time wherein the decay and lack of hospitality appears in the better sort in all countries, principally occasioned by the immeasurable charges and expenses which they are put to in superfluous appareling their wives, children, and families; the confusion also of degrees in all places being great where the meanest are as richly appareled as their betters, and the pride that such inferior persons take in their garments driving many for their maintenance to robbing and stealing by the highway. And yet in her gracious disposition, being willing to have that course of punishment to be the last mean of reformation, did in the end of this last term of the Holy Trinity in her highness' Court of Star

---

A Proclamation Enforcing Statutes and Proclamations of Apparel (London: Christopher Barker, 1597).

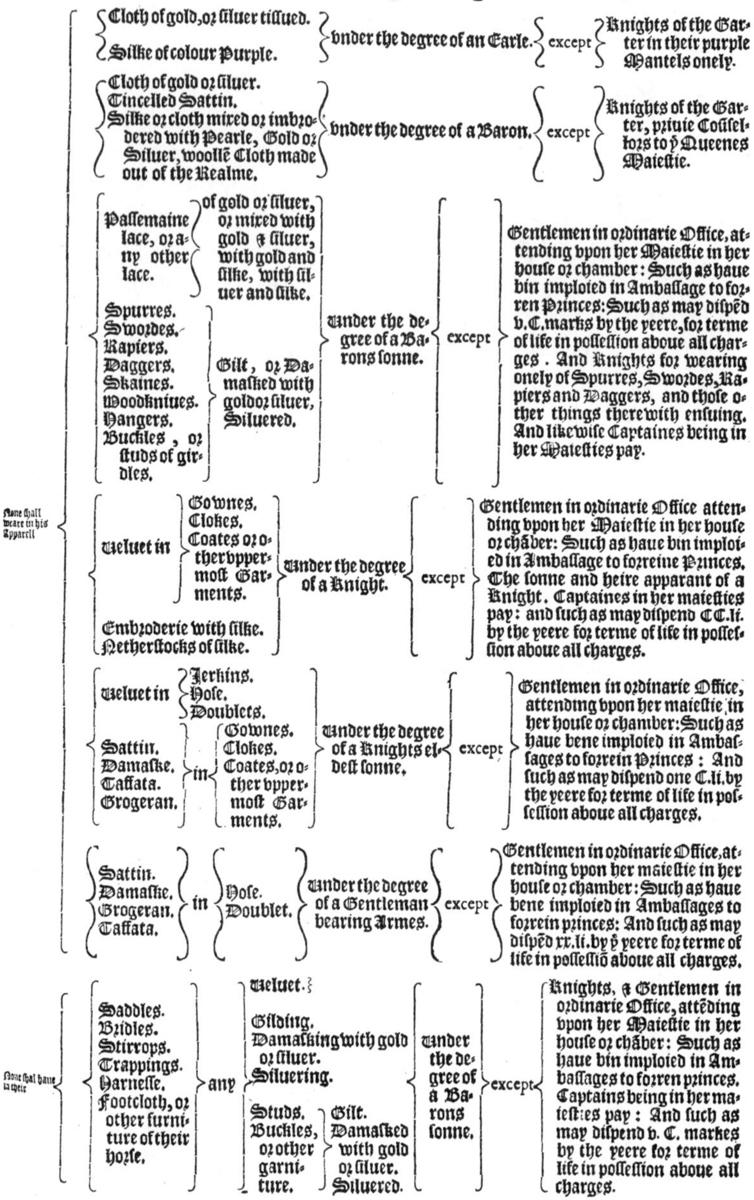

That is to say: For Mens Apparell.

Her Maiestie doeth straightly charge and commaund, That

None shall weare in his Apparell

Apparel		Under the degree of		Exceptions
Cloth of gold, or siluer tissued. Silke of colour Purple.		vnder the degree of an Earle.	except	Knights of the Garter in their purple Mantels onely.
Cloth of gold or siluer. Tincelled Sattin. Silke or cloth mixed or imbrodered with Pearle, Gold or Siluer, woollē Cloth made out of the Realme.		vnder the degree of a Baron.	except	Knights of the Garter, priuie Counsellors to ỹ Queenes Maiestie.
Passemaine lace, or any other lace.	of gold or siluer, or mixed with gold & siluer, with gold and silke, with siluer and silke.	Vnder the degree of a Barons sonne.	except	Gentlemen in ordinarie Office, attending vpon her Maiestie in her house or chamber: Such as haue bin imploied in Ambassage to forren Princes: Such as may dispēd v. C. marks by the yeere, for terme of life in possession aboue all charges. And Knights for wearing onely of Spurres, Swordes, Rapiers and Daggers, and those other things therewith ensuing. And likewise Captaines being in her Maiesties pay.
Spurres. Swordes. Rapiers. Daggers. Skaines. Woodkniues. Hangers. Buckles, or studs of girdles.	Gilt, or Damasked with gold or siluer, Siluered.			
Veluet in	Gownes. Clokes. Coates or other vppermost Garments.	Vnder the degree of a Knight.	except	Gentlemen in ordinarie Office attending vpon her Maiestie in her house or chāber: Such as haue bin imploied in Ambassage to forreine Princes. The sonne and heire apparant of a Knight. Captaines in her maiesties pay: and such as may dispend CC. li. by the yeere for terme of life in possession aboue all charges.
Embroderie with silke. Netherstocks of silke.				
Veluet in	Jerkins. Hose. Doublets.	Vnder the degree of a Knights eldest sonne.	except	Gentlemen in ordinarie Office, attending vpon her maiestie in her house or chamber: Such as haue bene imploied in Ambassages to forrein Princes: And such as may dispend one C. li. by the yeere for terme of life in possession aboue all charges.
Sattin. Damaske. Taffata. Grogeran. in	Gownes. Clokes. Coates, or other vpper most Garments.			
Sattin. Damaske. Grogeran. Taffata. in	Hose. Doublet.	Vnder the degree of a Gentleman bearing Armes.	except	Gentlemen in ordinarie Office, attending vpon her maiestie in her house or chamber: Such as haue bene imploied in Ambassages to forrein princes: And such as may dispēd xx. li. by ỹ yeere for terme of life in possessiō aboue all charges.

None shal haue in their

Apparel			Under the degree of		Exceptions
Saddles. Bridles. Stirrops. Trappings. Harnesse. Footcloth, or other furniture of their horse.	any	Veluet. Gilding. Damasking with gold or siluer. Siluering.	Vnder the degree of a Barons sonne.	except	Knights, & Gentlemen in ordinarie Office, attēding vpon her Maiestie in her house or chāber: Such as haue bin imploied in Ambassages to forren princes. Captains being in her maiesties pay: And such as may dispend v. C. markes by the yeere for terme of life in possession aboue all charges.
		Studs. Buckles, or other garniture. — Gilt. Damasked with gold or siluer. Siluered.			

FIGURE 20 *Who Can Legally Wear What, from* A Proclamation Enforcing Statutes and Proclamations of Apparel *(1597).*

Chamber[1] at an assembly of divers lords of her Privy Council,[2] and most of the judges being justices of Assize, in the open hearing of many justices of the peace of all the parts of the realm and of a multitude of her majesty's subjects there present, by way of admonition signify her princely determination to have (specially at this time) for many urgent considerations this intolerable abuse and unmeasurable disorder reformed. And albeit her highness knows how she might justly make great profit as well by the executions of her laws standing in force for the penalties already due as also against both the said kinds of offenders for their manifest contempt against her majesty's said proclamations; yet her majesty, not respecting her advantages in these cases but seriously intending the reformation of the abuses and the common good and benefit of all her loving subjects by these most royal and gracious proceedings, hath not only added by these presents such favorable tolerations and qualifications to such points of the former laws now standing in force as by alteration of time may seem in some part hard to be exactly observed, but also hath commanded the due execution of those parts of those laws that be most agreeable to this time and easy and necessary to be observed, without charging either kind of the said offenders for any offense already past, unless it be against such as shall hereafter offend or not observe the special parts and branches of the laws now standing in force and articles hereafter following, according to such toleration and moderation thereof as is hereafter expressed and set down;

That is to say for men's apparel her majesty doth straightly charge and command that:

None shall wear in his apparel cloth of gold or silver tissued, silk of color purple under the degree of an earl, except Knights of the Garter in their purple mantles only;

Cloth of gold or silver, tinseled satin, silk or cloth mixed or embroidered with pearl, gold, or silver, wool cloth made out of the realm, under the degree of a baron, except Knights of the Garter, Privy Councilors to the Queen's majesty;

Passement lace[3] or other lace of gold or silver or mixed with gold and silver, with gold and silk, with silver and silk; spurs, swords, rapiers, daggers, skeans, woodknives, hangers, buckles, or studs of girdles gilt or damasked with gold or silver, silvered, under the degree of a baron's son, except gentlemen in ordinary office attending upon her majesty in her house or chamber, such as have been employed in embassage to foreign princes, such as may dispend 500 marks by the year for term of life in possession above all

[1] **Court of Star Chamber:** court of law founded on royal prerogative and not bound by common law. [2] **Privy Council:** immediate circle of advisers. [3] **passement lace:** lace made of gold or silver thread.

charges, and knights for wearing only of spurs, swords, rapiers, and daggers and those other things therewith ensuing, and likewise captains being in her majesty's pay;

Velvet in gowns, cloaks, coats, or other uppermost garments, embroidery with silk, netherstocks of silk, under the degree of a knight, except gentlemen in ordinary office attending upon her majesty in her house or chamber, such as have been employed in embassages to foreign princes, the son and heir apparent of a knight, captains in her majesty's pay, and such as may dispend £200 by the year for term of life in possession above all charges;

Velvet in jerkins, hose, doublets; satin, damask, taffeta, grosgrain in gowns, cloaks, coats, or other uppermost garments, under the degree of a knight's eldest son, except gentlemen in ordinary office attending upon her majesty in her house or chamber, such as have been employed in embassages to foreign princes, and such as may dispend £100 by the year for term of life in possession above all charges;

Satin, damask, grosgrain, taffeta in hose, doublet, under the degree of a gentleman bearing arms, except gentlemen in ordinary office attending upon her majesty in her house or chamber, such as have been employed in embassages to foreign princes, and such as may dispend £20 by the year for term of life in possession above all charges.

None shall have in their saddles, bridles, stirrups, trappings, harness, footcloth, or other furniture of their horse any velvet, gilding, damasking with gold or silver, silvering, studs, buckles, or other garniture gilt, damasked with gold or silver, silvered, under the degree of a baron's son, except knights and gentlemen in ordinary office attending upon her majesty in her house or chamber, such as have been employed in embassages to foreign princes, captains being in her majesty's pay, and such as may dispend 500 marks by the year for term of life in possession above all charges.

None shall wear in their apparel any caps, hats, hatbands, capbands, garters, boothose, silk netherstocks trimmed with gold, silver, or pearl, enameled chains, buttons, aglets, except men of the degrees above mentioned, the gentlemen attending upon the Queen's person in her highness' privy chamber or in the office of cupbearer, carver, skewer, esquire for the body, gentlemen ushers, or esquires of the stable;

Satin, damask, silk camlet, or taffeta in gown, coat, hose, or uppermost garments; fur whereof the kind groweth not within the Queen's dominions except foins,[4] gray genets,[5] and bodge,[6] except the degrees and persons above mentioned, and men that may dispend £100 by the year and so valued in the subsidy book;

[4] **foins:** weasels or polecats. [5] **genets:** civet-cats. [6] **bodge:** badgers.

Hat, bonnet, girdle, scabbards of swords, daggers, and etc., shoes, and pantofles[7] of velvet, except the degrees and persons above named, and the son and heir apparent of a knight;

Silk, other than satin, damask, taffeta,[8] camlet,[9] in doublets, and sarcenet, camlet, or taffeta in facing of gowns and cloaks and in jackets, jerkins, coifs, purses being not of color of scarlet, crimson, or blue, fur of foins, gray genets, or other as the like groweth not in the Queen's dominions, except men of the degrees and persons above mentioned, son of a knight, or son and heir apparent of a man of 300 mark land by year so valued in the subsidy books, and men that may dispend £40 by the year so valued *ut supra.*[10]

None shall wear spurs, swords, rapiers, daggers, skeans, woodknives, or hangers, buckles of girdles gilt, silvered, or damasked, except knights and barons' sons and other of higher degree or place, and gentlemen in ordinary office attendant upon the Queen's majesty's person, which gentlemen so attendant may wear all the premises saving gilt, silvered, or damasked spurs.

None shall wear in their trappings or harness of their horse any studs, buckles, or other garniture gilt, silvered, or damasked, nor stirrups gilt, silvered, or damasked, nor any velvet in saddles or horse trappers, except the persons next before mentioned and others of higher degrees, and gentlemen in ordinary *ut supra.*

Note that the Lord Chancellor, Treasurer, President of the council, Privy Seal may wear any velvet, satin, or other silks except purple, furs except black genets.

These may wear as they have heretofore used, viz., any of the King's Council, Justices of either Bench, Barons of the Exchequer, Master of the Rolls, sergeants at law, Masters of the Chancery, of the Queen's council, apprentices at law, physicians of the King, Queen, and Prince, mayors and other head officers of any town corporate, Barons of the Five Ports, except velvet, damask, satin of the color crimson, violet, purple, blue.

Note that her majesty's meaning is not by this order to prohibit in any person the wearing of silk buttons, the facing of coats, cloaks, hats, and caps, for comeliness only with taffeta, grosgrain, velvet, or other silk as is commonly used.

For women's apparel her majesty doth straightly charge and command that:

None shall wear in her apparel cloth of gold or silver tissued, silk of color purple, under the degree of a countess, except viscountesses to wear cloth of gold or silver tissued in their kirtles[11] only;

[7] **pantofles:** slippers. [8] **taffeta:** light, thin silk. [9] **camlet:** rich fabric woven of silk and camel's hair. [10] ***ut supra:*** as above. [11] **kirtles:** gowns

Cloth of gold, cloth of silver, tinseled satin, satins branched with silver or gold, satins striped with silver or gold, taffetas branched with silver or gold, taffetas with gold or silver grounds, tinseled taffetas tufted or plain, tinseled cypresses, cypresses flourished with silver or gold, gold or silver camlets, networks wrought with silver or gold, tabinet branched or wrought with silver or gold, or any other silk or cloth mixed or embroidered with pearl, gold, or silver, under the degree of a baroness, except the wives of barons' eldest sons, and barons' daughters to wear cloth of gold and silver only in their kirtles and linings of their garments, and knights' wives to wear cloth of silver in their kirtles only;

Embroideries of gold or silver, passement lace or any other lace of gold or silver or mixed with gold and silver, with gold and silk, with silver and silk; cowls, attires, or other garnishings for the head trimmed with pearl, under the degree of a baron's eldest son's wife, except barons' daughters, the wives of knights of the Order of the Garter or of Privy Councilors, the ladies and gentlewomen of the privy chamber, the maidens of honor, and such whose husbands may dispend 500 marks by the year for term of life in possession above all charges;

Velvet in gowns, cloaks, safeguards, or other uppermost garments; embroidery with silk; ncthcrstocks of silk, under the degree of a knight's wife, except gentlewomen of the privy chamber, the maidens of honor, and such whose husbands or themselves may dispend £200 by the year for term of life in possession above all charges;

Velvet in kirtles, petticoats, satin in gowns, cloaks, safeguards, or other uppermost garments, under the degree of a knight's eldest son's wife, except gentlewomen in the privy chamber, the maidens of honor, gentlewomen attendant upon countesses, viscountesses, or ladies of the like or higher degree, and such whose husbands or themselves may dispend £100 by the year for term of life in possession above all charges;

Satin in kirtles; damask, tufted taffeta, plain taffeta, grosgrain in gowns, under the degree of a gentleman's wife bearing arms, except gentlewomen attendant upon knights' wives or ladies of the like or higher degree, and such whose husbands or themselves may dispend £40 by the year for term of life in possession above all charges.

Gentlewomen attendant upon duchesses, marquises, countesses may wear in their liveries given by their mistresses as the wives of those that may dispend £100 by the year and are so valued *ut supra.*

Gentlewomen attendant upon viscounts' wives and barons' wives may wear in their liveries as the daughters of such as may dispend 300 marks by the year, and as the wives of those that may dispend £40, valued *ut supra.*

None shall wear any velvet, tufted taffeta, satin, or any gold or silver in their petticoats, except wives of barons, knights of the order, or councilors; ladies and gentlewomen of the privy chamber and bed chamber; and the maidens of honor;

Damask, taffeta, or other silk in their petticoats, except knights' daughters and such as be matched with them in the former article, who shall not wear a guard of any silk upon their petticoats;

Velvet, tufted taffeta, satin, nor any gold or silver in any cloak or safeguard, except the wives of barons, knights of the order, or councilors, ladies and gentlewomen of the privy chamber and bed chamber, and the maidens of honor, and all degrees above them;

Damask, taffeta, or other silk in any cloak or safeguard, except knights' wives and the degrees and persons above mentioned.

No person under the degrees above specified shall wear any guard or welt[12] of silk upon any petticoat, cloak, or safeguard.

All which articles, clauses, and premises her majesty straightly commandeth to be from henceforth exactly and duly observed in all points; and the parties offending to be further punished as violators and contemners of her royal and princely commandment by this her highness' proclamation expressed and published.

[12] **guard or welt:** ornament or border.

→ **ROBERT GREENE**

From A Quip for an Upstart Courtier *1592*

Among the claims to fame of playwright, romance-writer, and pamphleteer Robert Greene (1558–1592) is his attack in *Greene's Groatsworth of Wit* (1592) on a certain "Johannes *fac totum*" who "is in his own conceit the only Shake-scene in a country." This fellow who thinks he can do everything (*fac totum*) is "an upstart Crow, beautified with *our* feathers" — the "our" in this case being university-educated playwrights like Christopher Marlowe, Thomas Lodge, George Peele, and Greene himself (Green F1v). Greene may have had a point. The device of a boy actor playing a girl dressing up as a boy was first used by Shakespeare in *The Two Gentlemen of Verona* (1590?), probably in the same season that Greene made capital of the device in *James IV,* written for a rival company. Feathers are precisely the issue in Greene's satirical pamphlet *A Quip for an Upstart Courtier,* written the same year as his quip for an upstart crow. The jest at the courtier's expense is a dialogue between Velvet Britches and Cloth Britches as to who has the stronger claim to "frank tenement," the right to dwell, in England. (See Figure 21.) Outrageously large breeches, or "hose" as they were generally called in early modern English, were singled out for special attention in many of the sumptuary laws, in part to protect English-produced goods against foreign imports. The excerpt below narrates the first meeting of Velvet Britches and Cloth Britches and the setting up of the debate between them. During the 1599–1600 season Shakespeare's company mounted a production of a now-lost script entitled *Cloth Britches and Velvet Hose* (Knutson 182).

FIGURE 21 *Velvet Britches (left) and Cloth Britches (right), from Robert Greene,* A Quip for an Upstart Courtier *(1592).*

From *A Quip for an Upstart Courtier*

As thus I walked forward seeking up the hill, I was driven half into a maze, with the imagination of a strange wonder which fell out thus: Methought I saw an uncouth headless thing come pacing down the hill, stepping so proudly with such a geometrical grace, as if some artificial braggart had resolved to measure the world with his paces: I could not descry it to be a man, although it had motion, for that it wanted a body, yet, seeing legs and hose,[1] I supposed it to be some monster nourished up in those deserts. At last, as it drew more nigh unto me, I might perceive that it was a very, passing costly pair of Velvet-Breeches, whose panes,[2] being made of the chiefest Neapolitan stuff, was drawn out with the best Spanish satin, and marvellous curiously over whipped with gold twist, interseamed with knots of pearl; the nether-stock[3] was of the purest Granado silk; no cost was spared to set out these costly Breeches, who had girt unto them a rapier and dagger gilt, point pendant, as quaintly as if some curious Florentine had tricked them up to square it up and down the streets before his mistress. As these Breeches were exceeding sumptuous to the eye, so were they passing pompous in their gestures, for they strutted up and down the valley as proudly as though they had there appointed to act some desperate combat.

Blame me not if I were driven into a muse with this most monstrous sight, to see in that place such a strange headless courtier jetting up and down like the usher of a fence-school[4] about to play his prize, when I deem never in any age such a wonderful object fortuned unto any man before. Well, the greater dump[5] this novelty drove me into, the more desire I had to see what event would follow. Whereupon, looking about to see if that any more company would come, I might perceive from the top of the other hill another pair of Breeches more soberly marching, and with a softer pace, as if they were not too hasty, and yet would keep promise nevertheless at the place appointed.

As soon as they were come into the valley, I saw they were a plain pair of Cloth-Breeches, without either welt or guard,[6] straight to the thigh, of white kersey,[7] without a slop,[8] the nether-stock of the same, sewed too above the knee, and only seamed with a little country blue, such as *in diebus illis*[9] our great grandfathers wore, when neighborhood and hospitality had

[1] **hose:** breeches reaching to the knee. [2] **panes:** inlaid panels of contrasting fabric. [3] **nether-stock:** stockings. [4] **fence-school:** fencing school. [5] **dump:** melancholy musing. [6] **welt or guard:** border or ornament. [7] **kersey:** coarse woolen cloth. [8] **slop:** loose-fitting outer garment. [9] ***in diebus illis:*** in those days.

Robert Greene, *A Quip for an Upstart Courtier* (London: John Wolfe, 1602), sigs. B3–B4v.

banished pride out of England: nor were these plain Breeches weaponless, for they had a good sower bat[10] with a pike in the end, able to lay on load enough, if the heart were answerable to the weapon: and upon this staff, pitched down upon the ground, Cloth-Breeches stood solemnly leaning, as if they meant not to start, but to answer to the uttermost whatsoever in that place might be objected.

Looking upon these two, I might perceive the pride of the one, and homely resolution of the other, that this their meeting would grow to some dangerous conflict; and therefore, to prevent the fatal issue of such a pretended quarrel, I stepped between them both; when Velvet-Breeches greeted Cloth-Breeches with this salutation: "Proud and insolent peasant, how darest thou, without leave or low reverence, press into the place whether I am come for to disport myself? Art thou not afraid thy high presumption should summon me to displeasure, and so force me draw my rapier, which is never unsheathed but it turns into the scabbard with a triumph of mine enemy's blood? Bold bayard,[11] avaunt; beard me[12] not to my face, for this time I pardon thy folly and grant thy legs leave to carry away thy life."

Cloth-Breeches, nothing amazed at this bravado, bending his staff as if he meant (if he were wronged) to bestow his benison, with a scornful kind of smiling, made this smooth reply: "Marry gip, Goodman Upstart, who made your father a gentleman? Soft fire makes sweet malt, the curstest cow hath the shortest horns, and a brawling cur, of all, bites the least. Alas! good sir, are you so fine that no man may be your fellow? I pray you, what difference is between you and me, but in the cost and the making? Though you be never so richly daubed with gold and powdered with pearl, yet you are but a case for the buttocks, and a cover for the basest part of a man's body, no more than I; the greatest pre-eminence is in the garnishing, and thereof you are proud ; but come to the true use we were appointed to, my honor is more than thine, for I belong to the old ancient yeomanry, yea, and gentility, the fathers, and thou to a company of proud and unmannerly upstarts, the sons." . . .

"The right and title in this country, base brat (quoth Velvet-Breeches) now authority favors me, I am admitted Viceroy, and I will make thee do me homage, and confess, that thou holdest thy being and residence in my land from the gracious favor of my sufferance;" and with that he laid on the hilts of his rapier, and Cloth-Breeches betook him to his staff, when I, stepping betwixt them, parted them thus: "Why, what mean ye; will you decide your

[10] **sower bat:** strong club. [11] **bayard:** bay horse. [12] **beard me:** insult me by plucking my beard, offending my manhood.

controversy by blows, when you may debate it by reason? This is a land of peace, governed by true justiciaries[13] and honorable magistrates, where you shall have equity without partiality, and therefore listen to me, and discuss the matter by law; your quarrel is, Whether of you are most ancient and most worthy? You, sir, boast of your country and parentage, he of his native birth in England; you claim all, he would have but his own: both plead an absolute title of residence in this country; then must the course between you be trespass or disseison[14] of frank tenement; you Velvet-Breeches, in that you claim the first title, shall be plaintiff, and plead a trespass of disseison done you by Cloth-Breeches; so shall it be brought to a jury, and tried by a verdict of twelve or four and twenty.

[13] **justiciaries:** justices of the peace. [14] **disseison:** legal dispossession.

I. T. (OR J. T.)

From The Haven of Pleasure, Containing a Free Man's Felicity and a True Direction How to Live Well

1596

It is leg fashions that Maria and her cohorts use to dupe Malvolio into making a fool of himself. When Maria's forged letter recommends yellow stockings and cross-gartering, Malvolio shows himself to be as quick as the next man in imagining that clothes will make the man: "I will be strange, stout, in yellow stockings and cross-gartered, even with the swiftness of putting on" (2.5.136–37). "Stout" changes the deferential steward into a stalwart hero. The ostentatiousness of cross-gartering can be glimpsed in Figure 22. The garters holding up the wearer's stockings are crisscrossed behind the knees and fashioned into outsized rosettes on the front. What Malvolio *should* be wearing as "a kind of puritan" (2.3.115) is spelled out in *The Haven of Pleasure.* The little book is one in a series of advice manuals published in the 1590s and early decades of the seventeenth century with a specifically nonaristocratic, probably mercantile, often Puritan readership in view — the bourgeois equivalent of Castiglione's *The Book of the Courtier.* What the author, I. T. (or J. T.), counsels is a moderation in dress. Scripture is cited to demonstrate the vanity of dress, while the explicit reference to women suggests that concern with dress is both feminine and effeminating. The bottom line, so to speak, in the chapter following is money: the likes of yellow stockings and cross-garters are to be condemned because they lead to financial ruin.

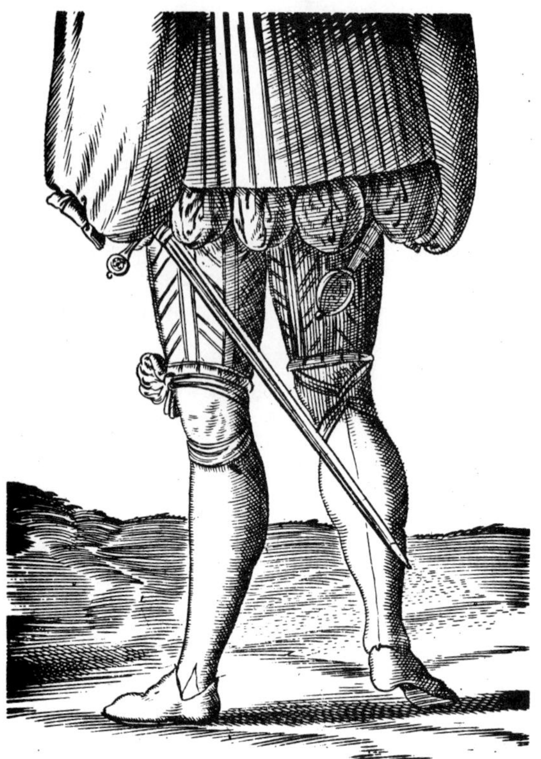

FIGURE 22 *Cross-Gartering, from Abraham de Bruyn,* Omnium Gentium Habitus *(1581).*

Chapter 34

Keep a Mean in Attire

Now as in the making of banquets thriftiness and temperance in diet is to be regarded, so in apparel and decking the body, a measure must be regarded. For if nothing be made for pride and vain glory, but all things cut according to the use and necessity of this life, so that if comeliness and not an over-curious fineness be added, I judge it to be every way tolerable. But seeing that women desire to be decked and trimmed above all other crea-

I. T. [or J. T.], *The Haven of Pleasure, Containing a Free Man's Felicity and a True Direction How to Live Well* (London: P. Short, 1596), 68–69.

tures, who apparel themselves gorgeously, to the end they may seem fair and beautiful to men, the apostle Peter warneth matrons that they bestow not too much cost on their world of furniture,[1] nor prostitute or set themselves to sale to such as may see them, nor to use curled and crisped hair, gold, precious stones, chains, and bracelets. But with modest attire, sober and not over-curious apparel, to please their husbands, by seeking to get their favors and good wills, as those noble ladies, Rachel, Sarah, Rebecca, and Susanna,[2] did. But there are many in ours and our forefather's time who appareling themselves with gorgeous apparel, and that after the foreign and new cut, painting themselves like pageants, have brought themselves to beggary and extreme poverty, who are then flouted of[3] such as helped them to spend their patrimonies, and of them also who by deceit, guile, craft, cunning, and fraud, have so scraped their wealth from them that they have not so much as a farthing to bestow on the relief of the poor that are brought to extreme penury and want. So that seeing there are so many prodigal spenders, wasters, and consumers of their own goods and hunters after other men's, is it any marvel to see so many bankrupts and desperate debtors in all places, not only of the base and common sort of people, but also of gentlemen, noblemen, and such as carry the port of kings? Who deceiving the fatherless and the widows have so stripped them of all their money, that they are never paid again during their lives, much less satisfied after their death, because they have laid more to pawn than their souls, which are condemned by their creditors. So that a while after their deaths, their goods are all set out to sale and the creditors strive who shall give most.

[1] **furniture:** things provided for oneself, in this case clothing and garnishments.
[2] **Rachel . . . Susanna:** exemplary women of the Old Testament and the Apocrypha.
[3] **flouted of:** insulted by.

Gender

Clothing comes from the same Germanic root as *clay (Klaith)*: both are things that "stick." In early modern England, however, clay had more fixity than clothing, even with respect to body parts.

SIR PHILIP SIDNEY

From Arcadia

1581

Intimations in *The Haven of Pleasure* that clothing can undo distinctions in gender as well as social class become an explicit source of pleasure in Sir Philip Sidney's *Arcadia* as well as in dozens of other romance narratives written in the fifty years before *Twelfth Night* and in the fifty years after. As we have seen in Chapter 1, a suspension of ordinary constraints, including constraints on gender behavior, was one of the things that made romance narratives so appealing. Sidney's *Arcadia* provides a signal instance. For four centuries Sir Philip Sidney (1554–1586) has enjoyed a reputation as the consummate Renaissance man. He received a classical education, he served his country on diplomatic missions abroad, while traveling in Italy he was painted by Veronese, he wrote a sonnet cycle, against literal-minded philistines he formulated a *Defense of Poesy,* he died a hero's death in the religious wars in the Netherlands against perceived Spanish tyranny. This reputation emerged soon after his death at age thirty-two, thanks in part to the literary ministrations of his friend Fulke Greville and his sister Mary Herbert, Countess of Pembroke. In his own lifetime his career was beset with political frustrations, he was not able to marry the lady addressed in his sonnets, and none of his works was printed while he was alive.

It was for his sister Mary and her friends that Sidney wrote the first version of *Arcadia,* a narrative in five books or "acts" with interspersed poetry, in 1581. A revised version, written in 1583–84, got as far as the middle of the third book. This incomplete revision was printed in 1590 and then again in 1593 with the last three books of the earlier version added to complete the story. Both versions concern the adventures of two young princes, Musidorus and Pyrocles, whose adventures at the court of Arcadia's ruler, Basilius, require them to disguise themselves as a shepherd and as an Amazon. Pyrocles' disguise as "Cleophila" is the occasion, in both versions, for sundry characters to fall in love with him/"her," just as Viola's disguise as "Cesario" piques the interests of both Orsino and Olivia. The erotic appeal of such a costume change is a major theme in both versions of *Arcadia.* The excerpt below, from the original version, catches the erotic *frisson* experienced by Musidorus as he helps his friend into women's clothes. We take up the story just at the point where Pyrocles has confessed to Musidorus that he has fallen in love with the beautiful Philoclea and that he intends to pursue her by disguising himself as a woman. Musidorus's initial reaction is horror. He fears that by putting on women's clothes Pyrocles will, in effect, *become* a woman:

> for to take this woman's habit, without you frame your behavior accordingly, is wholly vain; your behavior can never come kindly [i.e., naturally] from you but as the mind is proportioned unto it. So that you must resolve, if you will play your part to any purpose, whatsoever peevish imperfections are in that

sex, to soften your heart to receive them — the very first down step to wickedness. (19)

Pyrocles' reassurances at last bring Musidorus around.

From *Arcadia*

And thus remained they a time, till at length Musidorus, embracing him, said, "And will you thus shake off your friend?"

"It is you that shake off me," said Pyrocles, "being, for my unperfectness, unworthy of your friendship."

"But this," said Musidorus, "shows you much more unperfect, to be cruel to him that submits himself unto you. But since you are unperfect," said he, smiling, "it is reason you be governed by us wise and perfect men. And that authority will I begin to take upon me with three absolute commandments: the first, that you increase not your evil with further griefs; the second, that you love Philoclea with all the powers of your mind; and the last commandment shall be that you command me to do you what service I can towards the attaining of your desires."

Pyrocles' heart was not so oppressed with the two mighty passions of love and unkindness but that it yielded to some mirth at this commandment of Musidorus that he should love Philoclea. So that, something clearing his face from his former shows of grief, "Well," said he, "dear cousin, I see by the well choosing of your commandments that you are far fitter to be a prince than a councillor. And therefore I am resolved to employ all my endeavor to obey you, with this condition: that the commandments you command me to lay upon you shall only be that you continue to love me, and look upon my imperfections with more affection than judgement."

"Love you," said he, "alas how can my heart be separated from the true embracing of it without it burst by being too full of it? But," said he, "let us leave off these flowers of new-begun friendship; and since you have found out that way as your readiest remedy, let us go put on your transforming apparel. For my part, I will ever remain hereabouts, either to help you in any necessity or, at least, to be partaker of any evil may fall unto you."

Philip Sidney, *Arcadia* (1581), ed. Jean Robertson as *The Countess of Pembroke's Arcadia* (*The Old Arcadia*) (Oxford: Clarendon Press, 1973), 25–28.

Pyrocles, accepting this as a most notable testimony of his long-approved friendship, and returning to Mantinea where, having taken leave of their host (who, though he knew them not, was in love with their virtue), and leaving with him some apparel and jewels, with opinion they would return after some time unto him, they departed thence to the place where he had left his womanish apparel which, with the help of his friend, he had quickly put on in such sort as it might seem love had not only sharpened his wits but nimbled his hands in anything which might serve to his service. And to begin with his head, thus was he dressed: his hair (which the young men of Greece ware very long, accounting them most beautiful that had that in fairest quantity) lay upon the upper part of his forehead in locks, some curled and some, as it were, forgotten, with such a careless care, and with an art so hiding art, that he seemed he would lay them for a paragon whether nature simply, or nature helped by cunning, be the more excellent. The rest whereof was drawn into a coronet of gold, richly set with pearls, and so joined all over with gold wires, and covered with feathers of divers colors, that it was not unlike to a helmet, such a glittering show it bare, and so bravely it was held up from the head. Upon his body he ware a kind of doublet[1] of sky-color satin, so plated over with plates of massy gold that he seemed armed in it; his sleeves of the same, instead of plates, was covered with purled lace. And such was the nether part of his garment; but that made so full of stuff, and cut after such a fashion that, though the length fell under his ankles, yet in his going[2] one might well perceive the small of the leg which, with the foot, was covered with a little short pair of crimson velvet buskins,[3] in some places open (as the ancient manner was) to show the fairness of the skin. Over all this he ware a certain mantle of like stuff, made in such manner that, coming under his right arm, and covering most part of that side, it touched not the left side but upon the top of the shoulder where the two ends met, and were fastened together with a very rich jewel, the device whereof was this: an eagle covered with the feathers of a dove, and yet lying under another dove, in such sort as it seemed the dove preyed upon the eagle, the eagle casting up such a look as though the state he was in liked him, though the pain grieved him. Upon the same side, upon his thigh he ware a sword (such as we now call scimitars), the pommel[4] whereof was so richly set with precious stones as they were sufficient testimony it could be no mean personage that bare it. Such was this Amazon's attire: and thus did Pyrocles become Cleophila — which name for a time hereafter I will use, for I myself feel such compassion of his passion that I find even part of his fear lest his name should be uttered before fit time

[1] **doublet:** close-fitting jacket. [2] **going:** walking. [3] **buskins:** foot-coverings reaching to the calf or knee. [4] **pommel:** rounded knob.

were for it; which you, fair ladies that vouchsafe to read this, I doubt not will account excusable. But Musidorus, that had helped to dress his friend, could not satisfy himself with looking upon him, so did he find his excellent beauty set out with this new change, like a diamond set in a more advantageous sort. Insomuch that he could not choose, but smiling said unto him:

"Well," said he, "sweet cousin, since you are framed of such a loving mettle, I pray you, take heed of looking yourself in a glass lest Narcissus's fortune fall unto you. For my part, I promise you, if I were not fully resolved never to submit my heart to these fancies, I were like enough while I dressed you to become a young Pygmalion."[5]

"Alas," answered Cleophila, "if my beauty be anything, then will it help me to some part of my desires; otherwise I am no more to set by it than the orator by his eloquence that persuades nobody."

"She is a very invincible creature, then," said he, "for I doubt me much, under your patience, whether my mistress, your mistress, have a greater portion of beauty."

"Speak not that blasphemy, dear friend," said Cleophila, "for if I have any beauty, it is the beauty which the imagination of her strikes into my fancies, which in part shines through my face into your eyes."

"Truly," said Musidorus, "you are grown a notable philosopher of fancies."

"Astronomer," answered Cleophila, "for they are heavenly fancies."

[5] **Pygmalion:** mythical sculptor who fell in love with the female statue he had created.

From Hic Mulier, or The Man-Woman

and

From Haec-Vir, or The Womanish Man *1620*

An altogether unromantic view of women dressing as men and men as women is taken by the anonymous author (or perhaps authors) of two pamphlets that appeared in 1620. The printer's right to *Hic Mulier* was entered into the Stationers' Register seven days before his right to *Haec-Vir,* suggesting either that the second's reply to the first was written in great speed or else that the printer knew from the beginning that controversy always sells. (See the title pages in Figures 23 and 24.) Both pamphlets proceed from the original meaning of the word *gender* as a *grammatical* relationship of noun and modifier. As a noun belonging to the feminine declension, the Latin word *mulier* (woman) ought to take the feminine demonstrative *haec* (this). Similarly, as a noun belonging to the masculine declension, *vir* (man) ought to take the masculine *hic* (this). Behind the grammar

HIC MVLIER:

OR,

The Man-Woman:

Being a Medicine to cure the Coltiſh Diſeaſe of *the Staggers in the Maſculine-Feminines* of our Times.

Expreſt in a briefe Declamation.

Non omnes poſſumus omnes.

Miſtris, will you be trim'd or truſſ'd?

London printed for *I.T.* and are to be ſold at Chriſt Church gate. 1620.

FIGURE 23 *The Man-Woman at His/Her Toilette, from* Hic Mulier, or The Man-Woman *(1620).*

rule is the assumption that the noun, by nature, is what it is and that is that. Applied to persons, the rule requires that the body be either male or female and that modifiers in the form of clothing agree in gender. Contemporary English fashions, or so the pamphlets allege, have flouted this "natural" agreement. *Hic Mulier* is a monologue by an unnamed speaker who harangues women who dress like men and act like men. Wearing yellow on white comes in for particular ridicule. (Take note, Malvolio.) In *Haec-Vir,* such women get to make a reply in a dialogue that Hic-Mulier carries on with her counterpart Haec-Vir, the representative of men who adorn themselves like women and comport themselves like women.

From *Hic Mulier*

Hic Mulier, how now? Break Priscian's[1] head at the first encounter? But two words, and they false Latin?[2] Pardon me good Signior Construction, for I will not answer thee as the Pope did, that I will do it in despite of the grammar. But I will maintain, if it be not the truest Latin in our kingdom, yet it is the commonest. For since the days of Adam, women were never so masculine. Masculine in their genders and whole generations, from the mother, to the youngest daughter. Masculine in number, from one to multitudes. Masculine in case, even from the head to the foot. Masculine in mood, from bold speech, to impudent action. And masculine in tense, for, without redress, they were, are, and will be still most masculine, most mankind, and most monstrous. Are all women then turned masculine? No, God forbid, there are a world full of holy thoughts, modest carriages, and severe chastity. To these let me fall on my knees and say, "You, O you women, you good women, you that are in the fullness of perfection. You that are the crowns of nature's work, the complements of men's excellencies, and the seminaries of propagation. You that maintain the world, support mankind, and give life to society. You, that are armed with infinite power of virtue, are castles impregnable, rivers unsailable, seas immoveable, infinite treasures, and invincible armies, that are helpers most trusty, sentinels most careful, signs deceitless, plain ways failess, true guides dangerless, balms that instantly cure, and honors that never perish. O do not look to find your names in this declamation, but with all honor and reverence do I speak to you. You are Seneca's[3] graces, women, good women, modest women, true women, ever young, because ever virtuous, ever

[1] **Priscian:** Latin grammarian (fl. 500 C.E.). [2] **false Latin:** *hic* (this) is masculine, *mulier* (woman) is feminine; according to the rules of Latin grammar they ought to agree in gender. [3] **Seneca:** Roman moral philosopher and tragic playwright (4 B.C.E.–65 C.E.).

Anonymous, *Hic Mulier, or The Man-Woman* (London: John Trundle, 1620), A3–B2, C2v.

chaste, ever glorious. When I write of you, I will write with a golden pen on leaves of golden paper. Now I write with a rough quill and black ink on iron sheets, the iron deeds of an iron generation."[4]

Come then, you masculine women, for you are my subject, you that have made Admiration an ass and fooled him with a deformity never before dreamed of, that have made yourselves stranger things then ever Noah's Ark unloaded, or Nile engendered,[5] whom to name, he that named all things, might study an age to give you a right attribute, whose like are not found in any antiquary's study, in any seaman's travel, nor in any painter's cunning. You that are stranger than strangeness itself, whom wise men wonder at, boys shout at, and goblins themselves start at. You that are the gilt dirt,[6] which embroiders playhouses, the painted statues which adorn caroches,[7] and the perfumed carrion that bad men feed on in brothels. 'Tis of you, I entreat, and of your monstrous deformity. You that have made your bodies like antic boscage or grotesco work,[8] not half man, half woman, half fish, half flesh, half beast, half monster, but all odious, all devil, that have cast off the ornaments of your sexes, to put on the garments of shame, that have laid by the bashfulness of your natures, to gather the impudence of harlots, that have buried silence, to revive slander, that are all things but that which you should be, and nothing less than friends to virtue and goodness, that have made the foundation of your highest detested work, from the lowest despised creatures that record can give testimony of, the one cut from the commonwealth at the gallows; the other is well known. From the first you got the false armory of yellow starch, for to wear yellow on white, or white upon yellow, is by the rules of heraldry baseness, bastardy, and indignity, the folly of imitation, the deceitfulness of flattery, and the grossest baseness of all baseness, to do whatsoever a greater power will command you. From the other, you have taken the monstrousness of your deformity in apparel, exchanging the modest attire of the comely hood, caul,[9] coif,[10] handsome dress or kerchief, to the cloudy ruffianly broad-brimmed hat, and wanton feather, the modest upper parts of a concealing straight gown, to the loose lascivious civil embracement of a French doublet, being all unbuttoned to entice, all of one shape to hide deformity, and extreme short-waisted to give a most easy way to every luxurious action. The glory of a fair large hair, to the shame of most ruffianly short locks, the side thick gathered, and close guarding safe-

[4] **gold pen . . . iron generation:** with an allusion to the Golden Age as the first, the Iron Age as the last, with Silver and Bronze in between. [5] **Nile engendered:** the crocodiles of the Nile River were supposed to be generated out of the river's mud. [6] **gilt dirt:** dirt covered with a thin veneer of gold. [7] **caroches:** coaches. [8] **antic boscage or grotesco work:** fanciful designs of intertwined lines ("antic" or "antique"), stylized foliage ("boscage"), or strange creatures ("grotesco" or "grotesque"). [9] **caul:** netted cap. [10] **coif:** close-fitting cap covering the top, back, and sides of the head.

guards, to the short, weak, thin, loose, and every-hand-entertaining short bases.[11] For needles, swords, for prayer books, bawdy jigs, for modest gestures, giant-like behaviors, and for women's modesty, all mimic and apish incivility. These are your founders, from these you took your copies, and, without amendment, with these you shall come to perdition. . . .

Why, did ever these mermaids, or rather mermonsters, that wear the car-man's block,[12] the Dutchman's feather Upsy-van-Muffe,[13] the poor man's pate polled by a treen dish,[14] the French doublet trussed with points,[15] to Mary Ambray's light nether skirts,[16] the fool's baldric,[17] and the devil's poniard.[18] Did they ever know comeliness, or modesty? Fie, no, they never walked in those paths. For these, at the best, are sure rags of gentry, torn from better pieces for their food stains, or else the adulterate branches of rich stocks, that taking too much sap from the root, are cut away, and employed in base uses. Or, if not so, they are the stinking vapors drawn from dunghills, which nourished in the higher regions of the air, become meteors and false fires blazing and flashing therein, and amazing men's minds with their strange proportions, till the substance of their pride being spent, they drop down again to the place from whence they came, and there rot and consume unpitied, and unremembered.

And questionless it is true, that such were the first beginners of these last deformities, for from any purer blood would have issued a purer birth. There would have been some spark of virtue, some excuse for imitation. But this deformity hath no agreement with goodness, nor no difference against the weakest reason. It is all base and barbarous. Base, in respect it offends man in the example and God in the most unnatural use. Barbarous, in that it is exorbitant from nature, and antithesis to kind,[19] going astray, with ill-favored affectation, both in attire, in speech, in manners, and, it is to be feared, in the whole courses and stories of their actions. What can be more barbarous, than with the gloss of mumming art, to disguise the beauty of their creation? To mold their bodies to every deformed fashion, their tongues to vile and horrible profanations, and their hands to ruffianly and uncivil actions? To have their gestures as pie-bald,[20] and as motley various as their disguises, their souls fuller of infirmities than a horse or prostitute, and

[11] **bases:** skirts. [12] **car-man's block:** carter's hat-fashion. [13] **Upsy-van-Muffe:** made-up Dutch name suggesting "upsy Dutch" ("excessively"), said of drinking. [14] **pate . . . dish:** close haircut styled by putting a wooden dish over the head and cutting around the edges. [15] **doublet . . . points:** close-fitting jacket double laced with needlepoint trim. [16] **Mary . . . skirts:** the thin (or nonexistent) underskirts worn by Mary Ambray, the heroine of a famous ballad who dressed as a man and fought as a soldier. [17] **baldric:** richly ornamented belt or girdle worn cross-wise on the torso. [18] **poniard:** dagger. [19] **kind:** natural species. [20] **pie-bald:** of two colors.

HÆC-VIR:
OR
The VVomanish-Man:

Being an Anſwere to a late Booke intituled *Hic-Mulier*.

Expreſt in a briefe Dialogue betweene *Hæc-Vir* the Womaniſh-Man, and *Hic-Mulier* the Man-Woman.

London printed for *I.T.* and are to be ſold at Chriſt Church gate. 1620.

FIGURE 24 *The Man-Woman and the Womanish Man in Dialogue, from* Haec-Vir, or The Womanish Man *(1620).*

their minds languishing in those infirmities? If this be not barbarous, make the rude Scythian, the untamed Moor, the naked Indian, or the wild Irish, lords and rulers of well governed cities. . . .

It is an infection that emulates the plague, and throws itself amongst women of all degrees, all deserts, and all ages. From the Capitol to the cottage, are some spots or swellings of this disease, yet evermore the greater the person is, the greater is the rage of his sickness, and the more they have to support the eminence of their fortunes, the more they bestow in the augmentation of their deformities. Not only such as will not work to get bread, will find time to weave herself points to truss[21] her loose breeches. And she that hath pawned her credit to get a hat, will sell her smock to buy a feather. She that hath given kisses to have her hair shorn, will give her honesty to have her upper parts put into a French doublet. To conclude, she that will give her body to have her body deformed, will not stick to give her soul to have her mind[22] satisfied.

But such as are able to buy all their own charges, they swim in the excess of these vanities, and will be man-like not only from the head to the waist, but to the very foot, and in every condition. Man in body by attire, man in behavior by rude compliment, man in nature by pursuing revenge, man in wearing weapons, man in using weapons, and in brief, so much man in all things, that they are neither men, nor women, but just good for nothing. . . .

To you therefore that are fathers, husbands, or sustainers of these new hermaphrodites, belongs the cure of this impostume. It is you that give fuel to the flames of their wild indiscretion. You add the oil which makes their stinking lamps defile the whole house with filthy smoke, and your purses purchase their deformities at rates, both dear and unreasonable. Do you but hold close your liberal hands, or take a strict account of the employment of the treasure you give to their necessary maintenance, and these excesses will either cease, or else die smothered in prison in the tailor's trunks for want of redemption.

[21] **truss:** lace up. [22] **mind:** fancy.

From *Haec-Vir*

THE SPEAKERS:

HAEC-VIR: The Womanish Man
HIC-MULIER: The Man-Woman

HAEC-VIR: Most redoubted and worthy sir, for less than a knight I cannot take you, you are most happily given unto mine embrace.

Haec-Vir, or The Womanish Man (London: John Trundle, 1620), A3–A4, C2–C3.

HIC-MULIER: Is she mad? Or doth she mock me? Most rare and excellent lady, I am the servant of your virtues and desire to be employed in your service.

HAEC-VIR: Pity of patience, what doth he behold in me, to take me for a woman? Valiant and magnanimous sir, I shall desire to build the tower of my fortune upon no stronger foundation than the benefit of your grace and favor.

HIC-MULIER: O! Proud to ever be your servant.

HAEC-VIR: No, the servant of your servant.

HIC-MULIER: The tithe[23] of your friendship, good lady, is above my merit.

HAEC-VIR: You make me rich beyond expression. But fair knight, the truth is I am a man and desire but the obligation of your friendship.

HIC-MULIER: It is ready to be sealed and delivered to your use. Yet, I would have you understand that I am a woman.

HAEC-VIR: Are you a woman?

HIC-MULIER: Are you a man? O Juno Lucina[24] help me.

HAEC-VIR: Yes I am.

HIC-MULIER: Your name, most tender piece of masculine.

HAEC-VIR: No stranger either in court, city, or country. But what is yours, most courageous counterfeit of Hercules and his distaff?[25]

HIC-MULIER: Near akin to your goodness and compounded of fully as false Latin. The world calls me, Hic-Mulier.

HAEC-VIR: What, Hic-Mulier, the Man-Woman? She that like a larum-bell at midnight hath raised the whole kingdom in arms against her? Good stand, and let me take a full survey, both of thee and all thy dependents.

HIC-MULIER: Do freely. And when thou hast daubed me over, with the worldly colors thy malice can grind, then give me leave to answer for myself, and I will say thou art an accuser just and indifferent. Which done, I must entreat you to sit as many minutes, that I may likewise take your picture, and then refer to censure, whether of our deformities is most injurious to nature, or most effeminine to good men, in the notoriousness of the example. . . .

To see one of your gender either show himself, in the midst of his pride or riches, at a playhouse, or public assembly how, before he dare enter, with the Jacob's staff[26] of his own eyes and his pages', he takes a full survey of himself, from the highest sprig in his feather, to the lowest spangle that shines in his shoestring. How he prunes and picks himself like a hawk set a weathering, calls every several garment to auricular confession, making

[23] **tithe:** tenth part. [24] **Juno Lucina:** the goddess of childbirth. [25] **Hercules . . . distaff:** Hercules exchanged clothes with Omphale and took up her spinning. [26] **Jacob's staff:** pilgrim's staff.

them utter both their mortal great stains, and their venial and less blemishes, though the mote[27] be much less than an atom. Then to see him pluck and tug everything into the form of the newest received fashion. And by Durer's rules[28] make his leg answerable to his neck, his thigh proportionable with his middle, his foot with his hand, and a world of such idle disdained foppery. To see him thus patched up with symmetry, make himself complete, and even as a circle, and lastly, cast himself amongst the eyes of the people, as an object of wonder, with more niceness[29] than a virgin goes to the sheets of her first lover, would make patience herself mad with anger. . . .

Now since according to your own inference, even by the laws of nature, by the rules of religion, and the customs of all civil nations, it is necessary there be a distinct and special difference between man and woman, both in their habit and behaviors, what could we poor weak women do less, being far too weak by force to fetch back those spoils you have unjustly taken from us, than to gather up those garments you have proudly cast away, and therewith to clothe both our bodies and our minds, since no other means was left us to continue our names, and to support a difference? For to have held the way in which our forefathers first set us, or to have still embraced the civil modesty, or the gentle sweetness of our soft inclinations, why, you had so far encroached upon us, and so over-bribed the world, to be deaf to any grant of restitution, that as at our creation, our whole sex was contained in man our first parent, so we should have had no other being, but in you, and your most effeminate quality. Hence we have preserved, though to our own shames, those manly things which you have forsaken, which would you again accept, and restore to us the blushes we laid by, when first we put on your masculine garments, doubt not but chaste thoughts and bashfulness will again dwell in us, and our palaces being newly gilt, trimmed, and re-edified, draw to us all the graces, all the muses.

[27] **mote:** particle, in contrast to the "beam" in the eye of the critic (cf. Matthew 7.3 and Luke 6.41). [28] **Durer's rules:** Albrecht Dürer (1471–1528), German artist famous for his writings on perspective. [29] **niceness:** fastidiousness.

→ Eight Accounts of Boy Actors *1583–1630*

The physical persons that focused anxieties about clothing and disguise with special intensity were boy actors. Take for example the boy actor who played Viola. He was neither the personage of gentle rank that Viola claims to be — "my state is well: / I am a gentleman" (1.5.235–36) — nor was he a girl.

Anyone made anxious by the first discrepancy could cite the Proclamation of 1597 or either of the statutes from the reigns of Henry VIII and Philip and Mary. Anyone made anxious by the second could cite Deuteronomy 22.5. Between an injunction not to avoid helping one's brother raise up an ox or an ass that has stumbled and one not to steal a bird's nest with mother and young comes this commandment: "The woman shall not wear that which pertaineth unto the man, neither shall a man put on woman's raiment, for all that do so are abomination unto the Lord thy God." A marginal gloss in the Geneva Bible (1560) adds, "For that were to alter the order of nature and to despite God" (90). Feminist criticism, deconstruction, and queer studies have, in recent years, given new prominence to the early modern controversy over boy actors playing women's roles. Where earlier historians of theater were content to assume that boys-as-women were simply a custom, many recent critics have taken anti-theatricalists like Philip Stubbes at face value and contended that boys-as-women were provocations to homoerotic fantasy.[1] A look at the range of ways in which Shakespeare's contemporaries talked about boy actors suggests, however, that the issue at hand was not an either/or matter. A variety of reactions was possible, ranging from homosexual panic to religious objections to appreciation of artistry to seeming indifference to amused ridicule. It all depended on who was doing the looking and the writing. Just what kind of play was being performed seems also to have been a factor. In comic situations like that in which the boy actor playing Viola/"Cesario" finds himself/herself/"himself," Shakespeare never fails to call attention to the discrepancy between body and costume. Other examples are Julia in *The Two Gentlemen of Verona,* Sly's wife in *The Taming of the Shrew,* Portia and Nerissa in *The Merchant of Venice,* Rosalind in *As You Like It,* and Imogen in *Cymbeline.* The boy actor playing Desdemona in *Othello* seems not to have raised the same questions, to judge at least by Henry Jackson's account of seeing Shakespeare's company perform the play at Oxford in 1610. Jackson's description is in Latin, and he seems quite content to accept "Desdemona" as a feminine noun in all its modifiers. Let us survey how boys in women's clothes struck a diverse group of sixteenth- and seventeenth-century witnesses, looking at the matter from diverse vantage points.

[1] See, for example, Jardine, *Still Harping,* 9–36; Levine; Howard, 418–29; Garber; and Orgel, 53–82.

Eight Accounts of Boy Actors

Puritan polemicist Philip Stubbes (fl. 1583–91) assumes in *The Anatomy of Abuses* (1583) that erotic titillation is the very reason that people go to plays — and that the fundamental appeal of boy actors is homoerotic:

> . . . mark the flocking and running to Theaters and Curtains,[1] daily and hourly, night and day, time and tide, to see plays and interludes; where such wanton gestures, such bawdy speeches, such laughing and fleering,[2] such kissing and bussing, such clipping and culling,[3] such winking and glancing of wanton eyes, and the like, is used, as is wonderful to behold. Then, these goodly pageants being done, every mate sorts to his mate, every one brings another homeward of their way very friendly, and in their secret conclaves (covertly) they play the sodomites, or worse. And these be the fruits of plays and interludes for the most part.

The academic writer John Rainolds (1549–1607) is no less certain that boy actors break biblical edicts and inflame pagan lusts. In *The Overthrow of Stage Plays* (1599) he cites Deuteronomy 22.5, forbidding "a man to put on woman's raiment":

> . . . if we mark with judgement and wisdom, first, how this precept is referred by learned divines to the commandment "Thou shalt not commit adultery," some expressly making it a point annexed thereto, some impliedly, in that either they knit it to modesty, a part of temperance, or note the breach of it as joined with wantonness and impurity: next, among the kinds of adulterous lewdness how filthy and monstrous a sin against nature men's natural corruption and viciousness is prone to; the Scripture witnesseth it in Canaanites, Jews, Corinthians, other in other nations, and

[1] **Theaters and Curtains:** At the time Stubbes was writing, the Theater and the Curtain, north of the city walls, were the two most prominent public playhouses. [2] **fleering:** grinning or coarse laughter. [3] **clipping and culling:** fondling and holding in the arms.

Philip Stubbes, *The Anatomy of Abuses in Ailgna* (1583), ed. F. J. Furnivall (London: New Shakespeare Society, 1877–79), 144–45; John Rainolds, *The Overthrow of Stage Plays* (Middelburg: R. Schilders, 1599), 8–11; Thomas Platter, *Travels in England 1599,* trans. Clare Williams (London: Jonathan Cape, 1937), 166; Thomas Heywood, *An Apology for Actors* (London: Nicholas Okes, 1612), C3v; Henry Jackson, quoted in Geoffrey Tillotson, "*Othello* and *The Alchemist* at Oxford in 1610," *The Times Literary Supplement,* 20 July 1933: 494; Thomas Coryate, *Coryate's Crudities* (London: William Stansby, 1611), 247–48; George Sandys, *A Relation of a Journey Begun Anno Domini 1610,* 2nd ed. (London: W. Barrett, 1615), 246–47; Mary Wroth, *The First Part of the Countess of Montgomery's Urania,* ed. Josephine A. Roberts (Binghamton, NY: Medieval and Renaissance Texts and Studies, 1995), 73; Wroth, *The Second Part of the Countess of Montgomery's Urania,* ed. Josephine A. Roberts, Suzanne Gossett, and Janel Mueller (Tempe, AZ: Renaissance English Text Society, 1999), 41, 159–60.

> one with special caution, "*Nimium est quod intelligitur*":[4] thirdly, what sparkles of lust to that vice the putting of women's attire on men may kindle in unclean affections, as Nero showed in Sporus, Heliogabalus in himself;[5] yea certain, who grew not to such excess of impudency, yet arguing the same in causing their boys to wear long hair like women: if we consider these things, I say, we shall perceive that he, who condemneth the female whore and male, and, detesting specially the male by terming him a dog, rejecteth both their offerings with these words that "they both are abomination to the Lord thy God," might well control likewise the means and occasions whereby men are transformed into dogs, the sooner to cut off all incitements to that beastly filthiness, or rather more than beastly.

Thomas Platter (1574–1628), a Swiss tourist who saw *Julius Caesar* at the Globe in the very year Rainolds's book was published, observes men dressed in women's clothes on the stage and simply records it as a custom, no more, no less: "When the play was over, they danced very marvelously and gracefully together as is their wont, two dressed as men and two as women." The actor and playwright Thomas Heywood takes the same line in his book *An Apology for Actors,* written in retaliation against the likes of Stubbes and Rainolds: "To see our youths attired in the habit of women, who knows not what their intents be? Who cannot distinguish them by their names, assuredly knowing they are but to represent such a lady, at such a time appointed?" Indeed, Henry Jackson (1586–1662), a member of the audience when Shakespeare's troupe performed *Othello* at Oxford in September 1610, fails even to notice the gender of the actor playing Desdemona. To Jackson, Desdemona is simply Desdemona: "not only by their speech but by their deeds they drew tears — But indeed Desdemona, killed by her husband, although she always acted the matter very well, in her death moved us still more greatly; when lying in bed she implored the pity of those watching with her countenance alone."

If Jackson was aware at all that Desdemona was a boy in women's clothes, the fact seems to have registered only to the degree that the boy actor was very good at his art. Two English travelers who happened to see women playing women's parts in Italy confirm that interest in the boys as dramatic artists. Thomas Coryate (1577?–1617), catching a play at Venice in the course of a tour through France, Italy, Switzerland, Germany, and Holland in 1608, was frankly surprised that Italian actresses could portray female roles as well as boy actors back home; George Sandys (1578–1644), stopping at Messina in Sicily on the way home from the Middle East in 1611, thought that the women performers he saw there lacked art. Here is Coryate on Venice:

[4] ***Nimium est quod intelligtur:*** "A great deal is known." [5] **Nero . . . himself:** Suetonius (second century C.E.) in his *Lives of the Caesars* makes much of Nero's "wedding" to the boy Sporus and Heliogabalus's varied lusts.

> I was at one of their playhouses where I saw a comedy acted. The house is very beggarly and base in comparison of our stately playhouses in England: neither can their actors compare with us for apparel, shows and music. Here I observed certain things that I never saw before. For I saw women act, a thing that I never saw before, though I have heard that it hath been sometimes used in London, and they performed it with as good a grace, action, gesture, and whatsoever convenient for a player, as ever I saw any masculine actor.

What mainly occupied Coryate's attention were not the women on stage but the women in the audience, the "noble and famous courtesans" who attended the performance in masks. George Sandys was impressed with most things about Messina — but not with women performing women's parts in plays:

> Every evening they solace themselves along the Marine (a place left throughout between the city wall and the haven) the men on horseback, and the women in large carosses,[6] being drawn with the slowest procession. There is to be seen the pride and beauties of the city. There have they their playhouses, where the parts of women are acted by women, and too naturally passionated;[7] which they forbear not to frequent upon Sundays.

The final vantage point on boy actors is supplied by a woman. Several times during the two parts of her romance narrative *Urania* (part one published 1621, part two continued in manuscript 1622–30), Lady Mary Wroth (c. 1586–c. 1640) invokes boy actors as exemplars of exaggerated feminine wiles. Where Coryate and Sandys saw art, she saw artificiality. In part one, a disillusioned lover watches his former mistress try to seduce a stranger:

> He plotted to undo her, and watched the opportunity, which he obtained by his diligent prying; that, bringing him to discover her going into her cabinet with this stranger, pretending there to show him some jewels. They were no sooner within the room (she having put the door a little to, not closed), but her enraged enemy came, and finding means of discerning what was to be seen, lost it not, but stood still looking in. She (whose thoughts carried her to higher points than care) took no heed of that which most concerned her: for there he saw her with all passionate ardency, seek, and sue for the stranger's love; yet he unmoveable, was no further wrought, than if he had seen a delicate play-boy act a loving woman's part, and knowing him a boy, liked only his action.

[6] **carosses:** coaches. [7] **too naturally passionated:** played with emotions that are too natural.

Men watching a play, Wroth implies, make a distinction between the action and the actor. The action may provoke an erotic response, but not the boy actor. In part two of *Urania* (1622–30) "play-boys" figure twice. In the first instance, one of the male protagonists describes to the lady Pamphilia how outrageously his aunt is behaving:

> my aunt's raging, raving, extravagant discursive language is most apparently and understandingly discerned flat madness. If you did, madam, but see her speak, you would say you never saw so direct a mad woman. Such gestures and such brutish demeanor, fittinger[8] for a man in woman's clothes acting a Sybilla[9] than a woman. . . .

The second reference associates "play-boys" specifically with guile. A female narrator is telling a male listener about a notorious libertine woman:

> Having spent all her husband's estate and her own, she was forced to leave that country and came unluckily hither, leaving the silly[10] man at home without mean or honor but the memory and sight of a ruined estate, and only by her. Hither she came under color of retiring, but alas, it is as hard for her to live privately as without sin: which she cannot do, having ever been the greatest libertine the world had of female flesh, and above any that fictions can set forth or truths manifest. A woman dangerous in all kinds, flattering and insinuating abundantly, winning by matchless enticing, and as soon cast off, but with hazard sufficient to the forsaken or the forsaker; her trains[11] far exceeding her love and as full of falsehood as of vain and endless expressions, being for her overacting fashion, more like a play-boy dressed gaudily up to show a fond loving woman's part, than a great lady, so busy, so full of talk, and in such a set formality, with so many framed looks, feigned smiles, and nods, with a deceitful downcast look, instead of purest modesty, and bashfulness, too rich jewels for her rotten cabinet to contain, sometimes a little (and that while painful) silence as wishing, and with gestures, as longing to be moved to speak again, and seeming so loathe, as supplications must be as it were made to hear her tongue once more ring chimes of false beguilings, and entrapping charms, wit being overworn by her far nicer, and more strange, and so much the more prized, enchanting inventions, so as her charming fancies, and her alluring dallyings[12] make True Wit a fool in such a school, and Base Foulness, and Luxury the jailers of her house, and unfortunate prisoners.

Boy's body, women's clothes: how that combination struck early modern playgoers seems to have depended very much on who was doing the looking.

[8] **fittinger:** more fit. [9] **Sybilla:** a Sibyl or prophetess, as in a pageant or a masque. [10] **silly:** simple. [11] **trains:** treachery, guile. [12] **dallyings:** flirtations.

CHAPTER 5

Household Economies

Along with Viola/"Cesario," we in the audience come to know Illyria through our admittance to two households, Duke Orsino's and Lady Olivia's. Neither household conforms to conventional expectations back in England. Orsino's establishment seems curiously empty of people, especially for the household of a nobleman. Before "Cesario" arrives, only two attending gentlemen, Valentine and Curio, put in speaking appearances. Their very names suggest that they are psychological appendages of Orsino, given over as he is to love and to the cares (Latin *curiae*) of love. Orsino and his feelings fill the house from front to back, from tower to cellar. Olivia's household is something else again. It is full of people, and a diverse set of people at that. Olivia herself may be assuming a pose of mourning for her brother every bit as intense as Orsino's pose of love-longing for her, but her retinue hardly seems mournful: it includes a motley assortment, in more ways than one. The particolored costume worn by her fool Feste seems to the perfect badge for the rest of the household: the gentlewoman Maria whose behavior seems anything but gentle, Olivia's tippling uncle Sir Toby Belch, his boon companion Sir Andrew Aguecheek, the willing gamester "Signor Fabian" (2.5.1), and, most incongruously amid this crew, Olivia's dour steward Malvolio. Sir Toby's very first line is a questioning of decorum, with respect to all three of its classical aspects: time, place, and persons.

"What a plague means my niece to take the death of her brother thus? I am sure care's an enemy to life" (1.3.1–2). For his part, Sir Toby flouts all expectations of decorous behavior.

It is, above all, the decorum of time that Sir Toby, a denizen of Twelfth Night Illyria, refuses to observe. As Maria quips, "By my troth, Sir Toby, you must come in earlier o' nights. Your cousin, my lady, takes great exceptions to your ill hours" (1.3.3–4). Sir Toby functions in *Twelfth Night* as a Lord of Misrule, as the merry monarch outlawed by the masters of the Middle Temple in 1584. Richard Martin, Le Prince d'Amour in 1597–98, and his crony John Davies were real-life equivalents of Sir Toby in 1591, when they both participated in riots protesting the outlawing of lords of misrule at Christmas (Manningham 311). The two noble households of Illyria are, then, symbolic places on the order of the allegorical houses in Edmund Spenser's *The Faerie Queene* (1590–96). Orsino's palace shapes up as the House of Love; Olivia's, as the House of Misrule. Knowing something about households in early modern England can help us appreciate the parallels and the divergences that these two houses present vis-à-vis the other households involved in the performance of *Twelfth Night* at the Middle Temple in 1602: the Middle Temple as an all-male academic community, the (play)household of Shakespeare and his fellow actors, the "household" of Illyria as a fictional place, and the "household" of Britain as a nation.

The word that can help us get our bearings is *economy.* It is derived, in fact, from the Greek word for "household," *oikos,* combined with the Greek verb "to manage," *nemein:* hence *oikonomos,* steward, and *oikonomia,* household management. In all its manifestations economy consists of three key ideas: (1) individual items arranged in (2) a certain order within (3) a closed system of possibilities. A person writing up an account in the seventeenth century specified each entry in the account book as an "item." In a household economy these items are not just money and material goods, but people. A household economy involves the positioning of people in certain ways vis-à-vis each other. Implicit in all economies is an issue of control: who is disposing of goods and people? who is in charge? Within all six of the households of *Twelfth Night* control is a function of gender, age, and social rank. The play's free ways with decorum, however, call these distinctions into question. Class, cash, gender, and gentility are related in complicated ways.

The two real-life households involved in the play's first recorded performance, the Middle Temple as audience and the Lord Chamberlain's Men as actors, present the most straightforward cases. Both were all-male institutions in which power was distributed according to age. Both the lawyers and the actors saw themselves as "fellows," but some were ranked higher than others. Students like John Manningham, who recorded the performance in his diary, were under the authority of the Masters of the Bench, just as the boy actor who played Viola/"Cesario" was under the authority of company shareholders like William Shakespeare. Orsino's household is arranged in much the same way: Orsino is the master, "Cesario" his young gentleman-servant. Youths of gentle status often took service in a nobleman's household in just the way that apprentices took service with master craftsmen (Ben-Amos 84–108).

Olivia's estate presents a more complicated case, since Olivia is a woman, her steward is a man, and her householders include down-at-the-heels gentlefolk who behave in anything but gentle ways. In making Olivia out to be a "lady-widow," Manningham is trying to make sense of the anomaly that she is head of the house. Generally in early modern England only widows enjoyed the same control over property as men. Before she was married, a woman's property belonged to her father; after she was married, to her husband. The script of *Twelfth Night,* at least the version printed in the First Folio in 1623, quite clearly presents Olivia as being in mourning for her brother, not for a dead husband. She is a free agent. Olivia's various suitors offer different ways of imposing economic regularity on Olivia's anomalous household. Malvolio, the erstwhile steward, imagines himself, three months after marriage, as master of the house, "sitting in my state . . . calling my officers about me, in my branched velvet gown; having come from a daybed where I have left Olivia sleeping" (2.5.36–40). Marriage of Olivia to Orsino would preserve the proprieties of social rank, but under English law all of her goods would become his. What will happen when Olivia, after the play, marries her partner of choice, Sebastian? Legally the youthful gentleman will become master of everything, just as Manningham so often fantasizes through the advantageous marriages he records in his diary. But Sebastian has been presented as a *boy,* as the visual and vocal twin of his sister Viola/"Cesario." Who, then, will regulate the household, Sebastian or Olivia? That question is left as open-ended as just what kind of household Orsino and "Cesario"/Viola will form, an all-male equivalent of the Middle Temple, or a model home out of Puritan advice-givers like William Perkins. Neither? Or both? At issue in all these arrangements, perhaps, is the economy of Britain itself, ruled, for a few more months at least, by a woman.[1] *Twelfth Night* was performed at the Middle Temple on February 2, 1602; Elizabeth died on March 23, 1603.

[1] Some of the same anxieties about Elizabeth that Louis Montrose has found in *A Midsummer Night's Dream* (1595) may be still at work in *Twelfth Night.* See Montrose, 151–78.

Decorum

A visit to the bookstalls in St. Paul's churchyard in 1602 would have turned up "self-help" books in numbers quite proportionate to what bookstores display today. Baldassare Castiglione's *Il Libro del Cortegiano,* first published in Italian in 1528 and "Englished" by Sir Thomas Hoby as *The Book of the Courtier* in 1576, is the first and most famous of a long series of conduct books that were addressed to readers far beyond the confines of the court. Giovanni della Casa's *Galateo* [. . .] *Or Rather a Treatise of the Manners and Behaviors It Behooveth a Man to Use and Eschew in His Familiar Conversation* (Italian printing 1558, English translation 1576) and Stephano Guazzo's *Civil Conversation* (Italian printing 1574, English translation 1581) broadened Castiglione's range of social reference to include would-be gentlemen. Readers further down the social scale could find instruction in books like Anthony Skoloker's *The Ordinary for All Faithful Christians* (1549), I. T.'s (or J. T.'s) *Haven of Pleasure, Containing a Free Man's Felicity and a True Direction of How to Live Well* (1596), Robert Cleaver's *A Godly Form of Household Government* (1598), William Perkins's *Christian Economy* (1602), and William Gouge's *Of Domestical Duties* (1622). Common to all these writers is a concern with decorum, with behavior that is calculated for the social context in which one finds oneself. The activity of interacting with other people was understood by Shakespeare and his contemporaries to be "conversation," in the literal sense of the word as to turn (*vertere*) with (*con*) other people. Hence the titles of the treatises by della Casa and Guazzo. Talk is only one part of a whole range of behaviors that define the individual person as an "item" in the economy of society.

→ **STEPHANO GUAZZO**

From Civil Conversation

1581

Translated by George Pettie

The "civil" in Guazzo's title *Civil Conversation* refers to the city (*civis*) and to the various institutions that constitute urban society. Chief among those institutions is the family. Stephano Guazzo (1530–1593) was born into a family that served the dukes of Mantua. Stephano followed his father as a member of the ducal treasury and went on to perform diplomatic work in Spain and France, eventually becoming the duke's ambassador to Pope Pius V. After retiring from

Stephano Guazzo, *Civil Conversation,* trans. George Pettie (London: T. Dawson for Richard Watkins, 1581), 45–48.

state service, he founded an academy of like-minded gentlemen in his home town of Casale in the Monferrato. Some of the members of the *Illustrati,* as the members of the academy called themselves, figure as spokesmen in Guazzo's treatise on cultivated behavior. Guazzo's experience as a courtier shapes his view of society as an inherently hierarchical structure. The bonds between members of the social order are, in Guazzo's view, "chains" that tie those in inferior positions to those higher up. The chains can be seen as iron or as golden, depending on one's point of view — and social station. Guazzo's interlocutor in this excerpt is Annibale, who takes an altogether more sceptical view of service as the currency in the social economy of early modern society. Annibale implies that all men would like to be free agents; Guazzo assumes that all men are inescapably implicated in master/servant relationships. In the end, the two spokesmen reach a meeting of the minds — but only by agreeing that gentlemen accept and exploit the social hierarchy, while "the baser sort of servants" resist it.

GUAZZO: We are at that point, as far as I can see, to make an end of this day's discourse, seeing we have no more to speak of, but of the conversation between the master and the servant, yet I am afeard lest it be grievous unto you to spend the time here to your loss, which in other places you might bestow to your gain.

ANNIBALE: I frequent other places to pleasure others, and there indeed I spend the time, but I am with you for mine own pleasure, and therefore here I get the time. Wherefore let us go forward cheerfully, for if my servant be no more grieved to attend me without,[1] than I am to be here within, it is not possible to find a master and servant better content than we are.

GUAZZO: I will answer for your man, that he is content where he is at present, for he is with our servants, where they pass the time together in three things, which they take singular pleasure in.

ANNIBALE: What be those?

GUAZZO: In drinking, playing, and speaking ill.

ANNIBALE: Those things cannot be done, but to the disprofit and dispraise of the masters.

GUAZZO: Though they should want those three, yet I dare warrant you, your man is content, in that he is out of your sight.

ANNIBALE: I believe it without an oath. But whereof think you proceedeth that discontentment of servants?

GUAZZO: Of the lack of love, for if they loved their master, they would love his presence, and would come to be continually in his sight.

[1] **without:** outside the room in which the speakers are situated.

ANNIBALE: And whereof may we think that lack of love in servants proceedeth?

GUAZZO: Perchance of the difference of life, of minds, and of manners, which is between them. What say you of it?

ANNIBALE: I am of the opinion likewise, but the very servitude itself may also be a cause of this lack of love (that I may not say hatred) of the servants towards the masters, for that men serve commonly rather of necessity, than of free will. For so much as a man knowing himself to be born free, when he putteth himself in service, he forceth his nature, and though voluntarily he maketh himself a prisoner, yet it is not to be said, that he is content with it, or that he hateth not him which keepeth him in subjection. There is no doubt of it, but though he have with his mouth promised and sworn fidelity to his master, yet nevertheless, in heart he rebelleth against his service. And therefore it is no marvel though he fly his presence, and like better to be his servant afar off, than to do him service hard by. For so long as he is out of his master's sight, he forgetteth in a manner that he is a servant, and he thinketh he hath recovered his liberty, whereas contrariwise, when he cometh before his master, he holdeth down his head, and persuadeth himself he returneth to the collar like a dog, that for a time hath been let loose.

GUAZZO: It were good here that we came to the distinction of servants, for that which you say of servants which fly their master's presence, is not general, and is to be understood of the nature of vile and base servants, not of the good and such as are gentlemen, who for the most part, are never well, but when they are in their master's presence, and serve him lovingly and willingly. Whereupon it is said, that the gentleman loveth, and the slave feareth.

ANNIBALE: In the distinction which may be made between gentlemen courtiers which serve princes, and the base sort, which serve gentlemen, is, that the chains or fetters of the baser sort, are of iron, and those of the gentlemen, of gold.

GUAZZO: I hold well with that difference, and I make good moreover, that the chains of gold, bind more strongly than those of iron, but I think you will not say that gentlemen, and common servingmen, serve with one mind, or propose to themselves one self[2] end of their service.

ANNIBALE: I say unto you, that common servingmen hate both their master and the chain, where the other love their masters, but cannot away with[3] the chain.

[2] **self:** single. [3] **away with:** do away with.

GUAZZO: I cannot see how it can be said, that gentlemen cannot away with the chain, seeing they seek not entertainment[4] upon constraint or necessity, as the baser sort do, but are naturally given that way, not pitching their mark at vile gain, as the other do, but at honor and renown. I will not speak of others, but of myself only, assuring you, that the duke my master, seeing that I am unfit to serve him, by reason of my sickness, hath appointed me a better pension to live by hereafter in my house, than I had heretofore when I followed his court. Yet for all that (to confess unto you my ambition) I reason this with myself, that when I shall live at rest at my father's house, I shall be no more than others of my neighbors are, and I shall take myself to be as unprofitable to the world, whereas being about that prince, I am in case every hour to pleasure a number of persons, to get friends daily, and to make myself honored of the most honorable in the court, by reason whereof, I curse my infirmity, which will not suffer me long to be bound to this chain of gold, which I like above all things in the world.

ANNIBALE: All men indued with noble minds, are in love with that chain, not for itself, but for the honor which is annexed unto it. And I remember I have heard your brother say, that he loved my lady his mistress well, but he could not well away with service, and I can tell you, he had shrunk his head out of the collar of those insupportable pains long before that princess died, if her exceeding bounty and extraordinary favors towards him, had not kept him from it. And in truth that constraint to eat, to speak, and to go, by the mouth, by the tongue, and by the feet of others, that estate never to have rest either of body or mind, to lose one's self in the service of his master, to be short, those incommodities, vexations, troubles, and annoys, rehearsed in a letter of yours, whereof you have endured in your own person a great part, fill up the cup with so bitter a potion, that the smell of it, yea, the very remembrance of it, offendeth nature.

GUAZZO: You know well, that a man winneth not the wager without running.

ANNIBALE: Yet you know there are many which run, but only one winneth, and for one which you see recompensed for his service, you shall hear a number complain, that they have consumed their goods, and hazarded their lives in the service of princes, without gaining other thing than a miserable old age, with too late repentance, and few there are of them, which are not made to burst either with travail,[5] or with grief. That gold

[4] **entertainment:** being retained. [5] **travail:** labor.

chain never liked me, and I have always counted all service unsure and miserable, unless it were one kind of service, of a Spanish gentleman, who after he had long time served his king, made himself a monk, writing forthwith to the king, that he was preferred to the service of a greater Prince than he was, of whom he looked for better wages, than he had received at his master's hands. These servants which enter into the ministry and service of God, do no doubt love well both the master and the chain, and they are only they, amongst all others which rule in serving. But for that our purpose is to speak of this earthly and uncertain service, returning to gentlemen servingmen, I grant, that for the most part, they love their masters, to whom they are like, in life, in mind, and in manners, and therefore they think themselves happy, when they are in their presence, and when they have occasion offered to do them some acceptable service. And as the baser sort of servants, withdraw themselves so much as they may, out of their master's sight, to the end, they may not be set about[6] anything, so contrarily, the better sort, think themselves in great favor, if they be oftener employed by their masters, than their fellows are.

GUAZZO: It is for no other cause that princes are said to be better served than we are, but for that their servants are gentlemen, and ours are otherwise.

[6] **set about:** ordered to do.

WILLIAM VAUGHAN

From The Golden Grove Moralized in Three Books

1600

William Vaughan gives the idea of conversation a macrocosmic application in his book *The Golden Grove . . . A work very necessary for all such as would know how to govern themselves, their houses, or their country* (1600). Vaughan (1577–1641) was a twenty-three-year-old law student when he completed *The Golden Grove,* his first published work. He named it for his ancestral home in Carmarthen in Wales. "The Golden Grove" eventually became a place-name in Newfoundland when Vaughan sponsored a colonizing expedition and went there for a spell himself. His last published work, *The Golden Fleece* (1626), assembles at Apollo's court a group of historical characters who present bills of complaint against the evils of the age and predict the rediscovery of universal happiness when the golden fleece, lost in ancient times, is found again in Newfoundland. In *The Golden Grove,* Vaughan argues that the principles for governing of the commonwealth at large are the very principles for governing one's behavior as an individual. Chapters in *The Golden Grove* attacking intemperance, lechery, gluttony, and drunkenness become the foundation on which Vaughan constructs principles for the "conservation" of the entire country. The word *conservation* is itself a household word, suggesting the preservation of perishable foodstuffs. Vaughan's guidelines for individual behavior indicate the degree to which Lady Olivia's self-indulgent household could be seen as the very anti-type of right government.

CHAPTER 30

Of Temperance and Continence

All virtues do make a commonwealth happy and peaceable, but temperance alone is the sustainer of civil quietness, for it taketh care that the realm be not corrupted with riot and wanton delights, whereby diverse states have been cast away. This is that virtue which hindereth dishonest actions, which restraineth pleasures within certain bounds, and which maketh men to differ from brute beasts. Moreover, this is that herb, which Mercury gave to Ulysses, lest he should taste of the enchantress's cup[1] and so with his fellows be transformed into a hog, and this is that virtue which great men ought specially to embrace, that by their example the common sort might become temperate. For this is the reason why so many nowadays live riotously like beasts, namely because they see noblemen and magistrates, that govern the commonwealth, to lead their lives wantonly, as Sardanapalus[2] did. Therefore let noblemen be temperate, and spend less in shows and apparel, that they make keep better hospitality than they do, and benefit the poor. Let them, I say, imitate those famous wights,[3] who voluntarily resigned up their large portions in this world, that they might live the more contentedly. Amurath the second, Emperor of the Turks, after he had gotten infinite victories, became a monk of the straightest sect amongst them in the year of our Lord 1449. Charles the 5, Emperor of Germany gave up his empire into the hands of the Prince's electors, and withdrew himself in the year 1557 into a monastery. The like of late did the tyrant his son King Philip of Spain. What shall I say of Daniel, and his three companions Ananias, Azarias, and Mishael? Did they not choose to sustain themselves with pulse,[4] whenas they might have had a portion of the king's meat? Seeing therefore by these examples we perceive, how great the force of temperance is over the greedy

[1] **enchantress's cup:** the potion with which Circe turned men into beasts (*Odyssey* 10). [2] **Sardanapalus:** Assurbanipal (668–c. 625 B.C.E.), king of Syria. [3] **wights:** human beings, persons. [4] **pulse:** beans and peas.

William Vaughan, *The Golden Grove Moralized in Three Books* (London: Simon Stafford, 1600), G4–H1, BB5–BB5v.

affections of the mind, let us devoutly love her, and through her love, observe a mean in our pleasures and sorrows.

Chapter 31

Of Intemperance, and Incontinence

Intemperance is an overflowing in pleasures, desperately constraining all reason, in such sort, that nothing is able to stay him from the execution of his lusts. For that cause there is a difference between it and incontinence, namely that an incontinent man knoweth full, that the sin which he commits is sin and he intended not to follow it, but being overmastered by his lordly perturbations, he yieldeth in a manner against his will thereunto, whereas the intemperate man sinneth of purpose, esteeming it a goodly thing, and never repents him once of his wickedness. Wherehence I conclude, that an intemperate man is incurable, and far worse than the incontinent. For the incontinent man, being persuaded with wholesome counsels, will be sorry for his offense, and will strive to overcome his passion. But to make both, as well the intemperate man, as the incontinent hateful unto us, let us call to mind, how they do nothing else, but think on their present provender and rutting. Also, we must consider how that intemperance is that google-eyed[5] Venus, which hindreth honest learning, which metamorphoseth a man into a beast, and which transformeth simple wretches into toss-potted[6] asses. Wherefore I wish all men of what quality soever they be, to take heed of this vice, lest they either be accounted beasts, or alive be reckoned among the number of the dead.

[There is no Chapter 32]

Chapter 33

Of Lechery

Lechery is a short pleasure, bringing in long pain, that is, it expelleth virtue, shorteneth life, and maketh the soul guilty of abominable sin. This vice, I fear me, is too rife here in England, for how many Ursulas have we like that princely Ursula, who with eleven thousand virgins more in her company being taken by the paynim[7] fleet, as they were sailing into Little Britain,[8] for the defense of their chastities, were all of them most tyrannically martyred? Instead of Ursulas, I doubt, we have courtesans, and whorish droyes,[9] who

[5] **google-eyed:** featured with large, rolling eyes. [6] **toss-potted:** free-drinking. [7] **paynim:** pagan. [8] **Little Britain:** Brittany. [9] **droyes:** drudges.

with their brayed[10] drugs, periwigs, farthingales,[11] false bodies,[12] trunk sleeves,[13] Spanish white,[14] pomatoes,[15] oils, powders, and other glozing[16] fooleries too long to be recounted, do disguise their first natural shape, only sophisticatedly to seem fair unto the outward view of tame and indiscrete woodcocks. Yet notwithstanding, let a man behold them at night or in the morning, and he shall find them more ugly and loathsome than before. And I cannot so well liken them, as to millers' wives, because they look as though they were beaten about their faces with a bag of meal. But what ensueth after all these artificial inventions? The vengeance of God. Instead of sweet savor, there shall be stink, instead of a girdle, a rent, instead of dressing the hair, baldness, instead of a stomacher,[17] a girding of sack cloth, and burning, instead of beauty. What shall I do then, asketh the honest man? How shall I discern a chaste woman from a bawdy trull,[18] a diligent housewife, from an idle drone? If she be fair, she is most commonly a common quean.[19] If she be foul, then is she odious. What shall I do? This thou shalt do, O honest man, choose thee not a wife above thine estate, nor under, lest the one be too haughty, or the other displease thee. Rather harken unto a witty virgin, born of virtuous and witty parents, correspondent unto thee both in birth and degree, and no doubt but with thy good admonitions thou shalt have her tractable. No woman is so flinty, but fair words and good usage will in time cause her to relent, and love thee as she should, above all other. In fine, respect not dowry, for if she be good, she is endowed well.

Chapter 34

Of Gluttony and Drunkenness

Of gluttony there be four kinds. The first happeneth, when a man causeth his meat to be made ready before due and ordinary time for pleasure, and not for necessity. The second, when a man curiously hunteth after diversities and dainty meat. The third, when he eateth more than sufficeth nature. The last, when we eat our meat too greedily and hungrily, like unto dogs.

Now to come to drunkenness, I find that there be three sorts thereof. The first, when we being very thirsty, not knowing the force of the drink, do unwittingly drink ourselves drunk, and this can be no sin. The second, when we understand that the drink is immoderate, and for all that, we respect not our weak nature, which unawares becommeth cup-shot,[20] and this is a kind

[10] **brayed:** powdered. [11] **farthingales:** hoops for spreading skirts. [12] **bodies:** bodices. [13] **trunk sleeves:** baggy sleeves. [14] **Spanish white:** finely powdered chalk. [15] **pomatoes:** pomades, ointments. [16] **glozing:** glazing, painting over. [17] **stomacher:** waistcoat. [18] **trull:** low prostitute. [19] **quean:** whore. [20] **cup-shot:** drunk.

of sin. The third, when we obstinately do persevere in drinking, and this certainly, is a grievous and intolerable sin.

Chapter 35

The Discommodities of Drunkenness

The discommodities of drunkenness are many. First, it displeaseth God. Secondly, it is indecent and filthy. For doth not a drunken man's eyes look red, bloody, and staring? Doth not his tongue falter? Doth not his breath stink? Is not his nose fiery and worm-eaten? Are not his wits dead according to that [saying] "When the ale is in, wit is out"? Doth not his body shiver? In brief, what doth not drunkenness signify? It discloseth secrets, it maketh the unarmed man to thrust himself into the wars, and causeth the careful mind to become quite void of care. The third discommodity of drunkenness is that it shorteneth life, defaceth beauty, and corrupteth the whole world. For how can it otherwise be, when God blesseth not the meat and drink within our bodies? Fourthly, drunkenness is the cause of the loss of time. Fifthly, hell gapeth and openeth her mouth wide, that the multitude and wealth of them that delight therein, may go down into it. For proof whereof, I will declare one notable example, taken out of *The Anatomy of Abuses.* About twenty years since, there dwelt eight men, citizens and citizens' sons of Swaden, a city of Germany, who upon a Sunday morning, agreed to go into a tavern, and coming to the house of one Antoine Hage, an honest man, and zealously given, they called for wine. The good man told them that they should have none before sermon time was past, and persuaded them to go hear the word preached. But they (save one Adam Giebens, who advised them to hear the sermon for fear of God's wrath) denied, saying that they loathed that kind of exercise. The good host neither giving them any wine himself, nor permitting any other, went to the sermon. Who being gone, they fell to cursing, and wishing that he might break his neck before he returned. Whereupon the devil appeared unto them in the shape of a young man, bringing in his hand a flagon of wine and drink unto them, saying, "Good fellows, be merry, for you shall have wine enough, and I hope you will pay me well." Then they inconsiderately[21] answered that they would pay him, or else they would gauge[22] their necks, yea, their bodies and souls, rather than to fail. Thus they continued swilling and bibbing so long till they could scant see one another. At the last, the devil, their tapster, told them that they must needs pay their shot, whereat their hearts waxed cold.

[21] **inconsiderately:** without considering the situation. [22] **guage:** risk.

But he comforting them, said, "Be of good cheer, for now must you drink boiling lead, pitch, and brimstone with men in the pit of hell for evermore." Hereupon he made their eyes appear like fire, and in breadth as broad as a saucer, and ere they could call for grace and mercy the devil prevented them and break their necks asunder. The other Adam Giebens, who counseled them before to hear God's word, having some sparks of faith within him, was preserved from death, by the great mercy of God.

After this sort God punished drunkenness, to the terror of all such as delight therein. God grant that men hereafter may beware, how they play the drunkards. For doubtless, although he bears with our quaffers[23] here in England, yet notwithstanding, he hath prepared heavy punishments for them in the world to come. . . .

Chapter 59

Of the Conservation of a Commonwealth

There be many means to preserve a commonwealth, but above the rest these ten are of most efficacy. The first, and chiefest, is to live uprightly in the fear of God. The second, to make no delay in executing of attainted and condemned persons. The third, to suffer every man to enjoy his own and not lavishly to spend and take the private inhabitant's goods. The fourth, to have a great regard of mischiefs and evils at the first budding, how small soever it be. For the corruption that creepeth in by little and little is no more perceived, than small expenses be, the often disturbing whereof undoeth the substance of a house. And as great rain and horrible storms proceed from vapors and exhalations that are not seen, so alteration and changes breed in a commonwealth of light and trifling things, which no man would judge to have such an issue. The fifth means is, that magistrates behave themselves mildly and modestly towards their inferiors. The sixth, that princes be not partial in their subjects' factions. The seventh, the prince and his council must not give ear to every tale and crafty device, for it may be, that the enemy hath his intelligence in the realm. The eighth, to cast out heretics and schismatics[24] from among the people. The ninth, to muster and train the people once a month in martial[25] affairs. The tenth, to discard stage plays, usury, extortion, bribes, and such like abominable vices.

[23] **quaffers:** drinkers. [24] **schismatics:** sectarians, division-makers. [25] **martial:** military.

Traditional Hospitality

The presence of Malvolio in the midst of Lady Olivia's remarkably profligate household points up a fundamental conflict in ideas of household economy during Shakespeare's lifetime. Traditional notions of how a noble person should run his house entailed an open door at holiday times to all the people round about (Palmer). Hospitality was very much part of *noblesse oblige,* as Ben Jonson's poem "To Penshurst" makes clear. Satirical complaints like *Grievous Groans for the Poor* and the character of "Hospitality" in Donald Lupton's *London and the Country Carbonadoed and Quartered* testify to the widespread perception that such traditional customs were no longer being kept up. The often cited reason for the lapse was the replacement of feudal landowners whose titles went back centuries by *nouveaux riches* who had earned their wealth in trade. Where the traditional feudal economy had stressed generosity, the new capitalist economy stressed thrift. The traditional view is represented, ironically enough, by an "Exhortation to the Rich of This World" in one of the earliest conduct books published in England for ordinary folk, Anthony Skoloker's *The Ordinary for All Faithful Christians* (1549?). (See Figure 25.) Beneath the image of a rich man with open arms appear a series of admonitions, including "A wicked eye spareth bread, and there is scantness upon his table" (L3v).

→ **BEN JONSON**

To Penshurst

c. 1610

Among the poems collected by Ben Jonson in *The Forest* and printed in the first folio of Jonson's collected works in 1616 is this celebration of Penshurst Place, the ancestral home of the Sidney family in the Medway River valley of Kent. During the course of his long career as a writer, Jonson (1573–1637) wrote scripts for the public theaters, provided ideas and speeches for masques at court, naturalized into English many of the major verse forms of Latin literature, and issued critical pronouncements that anticipated the future direction of literary theory. His classical tragedy *Sejanus* joined the repertory of Shakespeare's company the year after *Twelfth Night* was performed at the Middle Temple. For the King's Men, Jonson also wrote *Volpone* (1606) and *The Alchemist* (1610), comedies that are still often produced today. In his poem "To Penshurst," Jonson effectively inaugurated the genre of country house poem that Aemilia Lanier ("The Description of Cookham," 1611) and Andrew Marvel ("Upon Appleton House, To My Lord Fairfax," 1650–52) also cultivated.

FIGURE 25 *The Rich of This World, from Anthony Skoloker,* The Ordinary for All Faithful Christians *(1549?).*

Unlike many monumental houses built by the nobility in the sixteenth century, Penshurst in Jonson's time preserved its medieval great hall, a large open room where the nobleman, his family, and all his retainers could eat together under one capacious hammer-beam roof. (The great hall still forms the centerpiece of the house today.) Like older seats of the nobility, and unlike some newer country houses, Penshurst was located in close proximity to the village where the workers of the nobleman's lands lived.[1] Jonson's interest in Penshurst is not confined to the physical house and its setting in the country. The core of the poem is the kind of life the Sidneys live in the house — a life that includes open hospitality at holiday times. Jonson specifically mentions harvest-home, but Twelfth Night was another occasion when country house owners opened their doors to their neighbors.

[1] On the social implications of these architectural and geographical arrangements see Girouard, 81–118.

To Penshurst

Thou art not, PENSHURST, built to envious show
Of touch[2] or marble; nor canst boast a row
Of polish'd pillars, or a roof of gold:
Thou hast no lantern,[3] whereof tales are told;
Or stair, or courts; but stand'st an ancient pile,
And these grudg'd at, art reverenced the while.
Thou joy'st in better marks, of soil, of air,
Of wood, of water; therein thou art fair.
Thou hast thy walks for health, as well as sport:
Thy mount, to which thy Dryads[4] do resort,
Where Pan and Bacchus their high feasts have made,
Beneath the broad beech, and the chestnut shade;
That taller tree, which of a nut was set,
At his great birth, where all the Muses met.[5]
There, in the writhed bark, are cut the names
Of many a sylvan, taken with his flames;
And thence the ruddy satyrs oft provoke
The lighter fauns, to reach thy lady's oak.[6]
Thy copse too, named of Gamage,[7] thou hast there,
That never fails to serve thee season'd deer,
When thou wouldst feast, or exercise thy friends.
The lower land, that to the river bends,
Thy sheep, thy bullocks, kine,[8] and calves do feed;
The middle grounds thy mares and horses breed.
Each bank doth yield thee conies,[9] and the tops
Fertile of wood, Ashore and Sydney's copses,
To crown thy open table, doth provide
The purpled pheasant, with the speckled side:
The painted partridge lies in ev'ry field,
And for thy mess is willing to be kill'd.
And if the high-swoln Medway fail thy dish,

[2] **touch:** black marble. [3] **lantern:** cupola. [4] **Dryads:** wood spirits. [5] **taller . . . met:** Sir Philip Sidney, born at Penshurst on November 30, 1554; an oak is said to have been planted from an acorn on that day. [6] **thy lady's oak:** an old tradition records that the Countess of Leicester, wife of Sir Philip Sidney's brother Sir Robert, first felt the pangs of childbirth under the oak. [7] **copse . . . Gamage:** grove named for Barbara Gamage, the countess of Leicester, Sir Robert Sidney's wife. [8] **kine:** cows. [9] **conies:** rabbits.

Ben Jonson, "To Penshurst" (before 1612), in *The Works of Benjamin Jonson* (London: Will Stansby, 1616), 818–21.

Thou hast thy ponds, that pay thee tribute fish,
Fat aged carps that run into thy net,
And pikes, now weary their own kind to eat,
As loth the second draught or cast to stay,
Officiously[10] at first themselves betray.
Bright eels that emulate them, and leap on land,
Before the fisher, or into his hand.
Then hath thy orchard fruit, thy garden flowers,
Fresh as the air, and new as are the hours.
The early cherry, with the later plum,
Fig, grape, and quince, each in his time doth come:
The blushing apricot, and woolly peach
Hang on thy walls, that every child may reach.
And though thy walls be of the country stone,
They're rear'd with no man's ruin, no man's groan;
There's none, that dwell about them, wish them down;
But all come in, the farmer and the clown;
And no one empty-handed, to salute
Thy lord and lady, though they have no suit.
Some bring a capon, some a rural cake,
Some nuts, some apples; some that think they make
The better cheeses, bring them; or else send
By their ripe daughters, whom they would commend
This way to husbands; and whose baskets bear
An emblem of themselves in plum, or pear.
But what can this (more than express their love)
Add to thy free provisions, far above
The need of such? whose liberal board doth flow,
With all that hospitality doth know!
Where comes no guest, but is allow'd to eat,
Without his fear, and of thy lord's own meat:
Where the same beer and bread, and self-same wine,
That is his lordship's, shall be also mine.
And I not fain to sit (as some this day,
At great men's tables) and yet dine away.
Here no man tells[11] my cups; nor standing by,
A waiter, doth my gluttony envy:
But gives me what I call, and lets me eat,
He knows, below, he shall find plenty of meat;

[10] **Officiously:** dutifully. [11] **tells:** keeps count of.

Thy tables hoard not up for the next day,
Nor, when I take my lodging, need I pray
For fire, or lights, or livery;[12] all is there;
As if thou then wert mine, or I reign'd there;
There's nothing I can wish, for which I stay.
That found king JAMES, when hunting late, this way,
With his brave son, the prince; they saw thy fires
Shine bright on every hearth, as the desires
Of thy Penates[13] had been set on flame,
To entertain them; or the country came,
With all their zeal, to warm their welcome here.
What (great, I will not say, but) sudden cheer
Didst thou then make 'em! and what praise was heap'd
On thy good lady,[14] then! who therein reap'd
The just reward of her high housewifery;
To have her linen, plate, and all things nigh,
When she was far; and not a room, but drest,
As if it had expected such a guest!
These, Penshurst, are thy praise, and yet not all.
Thy lady's noble, fruitful, chaste withal.
His children thy great lord[15] may call his own,
A fortune, in this age, but rarely known.
They are, and have been taught religion; thence
Their gentler spirits have suck'd innocence.
Each morn, and even, they are taught to pray,
With the whole household, and may, every day,
Read in their virtuous parents' noble parts,
The mysteries of manners, arms, and arts.
Now, Penshurst, they that will proportion thee
With other edifices, when they see
Those proud ambitions heaps, and nothing else,
May say, their lords have built, but thy lord dwells.

[12] **livery:** provision, allowance. [13] **Penates:** guardian deities. [14] **thy good lady:** Barbara Gamage, countess of Leicester, who was away from home when King James appeared. [15] **thy great lord:** Sir Robert Sidney, Sir Philip's brother.

From Grievous Groans for the Poor *1621*

A shift from the kind of hospitality celebrated by Ben Jonson in "To Penshurst" to the thrifty self-interest encouraged by capitalism can be witnessed in this rabble-rousing pamphlet, published in 1621 and sometimes attributed to Thomas Dekker (1570?–1632). In an appeal for organized aid to the poor, the author looks back nostalgically to a time when the poor could depend on their landlords for food and gifts at holiday times. One cause of the changed conditions was the forced removal of agricultural workers from lands that once had been leased out in parcels but was now being enclosed for the landowner's own use. Workers who had once lived on the land, in close proximity to the landowner, found themselves with nowhere to go and no means of supporting themselves. The process of enclosing common land for private use had begun before the sixteenth century but reached crisis proportions in the 1590s and first two decades of the 1600s, when the repeal of earlier anti-enclosure legislation, a steep rise in rents and leases, and a series of bad harvests exacerbated the plight of landless workers. The result, in some places, were riots. Several recent researchers have suggested connections among land enclosures and other forms of coercing the human items in the country's economy.[1] A connection between the decorum of traditional hospitality and the decorum of traditional dress is made explicit in a royal proclamation of 1597, which attributes to the extravagant dress of "the better sort" nothing short of "the decay and lack of hospitality . . . principally occasioned by the immeasurable charges and expenses which they are put to in superfluous appareling of their wives, children, and families." (See Chapter 4.)

The Poor Without Release

Look with hearts of charity and eyes of pity unto the distressed estate of the poor, good Christians, for first, although the commons[2] with common commodities in some town be worth an hundred or two hundred pounds a year, or more, yet, the poor of the same town, unto the third part of the town in number, shall not be thereby relieved, to the value of forty shillings in a year. So are the commons surcharged by the rich and the profit of their town lands employed to bear other common charges withal.

And how may I complain therewith of the decay of hospitality in our land, whereby many poor souls are deprived of that relief which they

[1] See Burt and Archer, especially the essays by Siemon, 17–33, and Carroll, 34–47. [2] **commons:** common land, supposed to be available for use to all local inhabitants.

Grievous Groans for the Poor (London: Michael Sparke, 1621), C3–C3v.

have had heretofore? The time hath been, that men have hunted after worship and credit by good housekeeping and therein spent great part of their revenues. But now commonly, the greater part of their livings is too little to maintain us and our children in the pomp of pride. Yea, and yet all is well if we may maintain that, though no hospitality be maintained there withal.

DONALD LUPTON

From London and the Country Carbonadoed and Quartered into Several Characters

1632

By the 1630s, when Donald Lupton (d. 1676) turned ten days of leisure time as a soldier into personified speeches by some of London's landmarks and caricatures of some of England's social types, "merry" was becoming a politically loaded word. Leah Marcus in *The Politics of Mirth* and Ronald Hutton in *The Rise and Fall of Merry England* offer two different versions of the same story: communal celebrations of the ritual year in the England of the 1520s became increasingly politicized in the course of the sixteenth century, reaching crisis level in the 1630s and 1640s as Protestant extremists and politicians with new ideas about decorum mounted an ultimately fatal attack on church ales at Whitsuntide, Robin Hood plays on May Day, and Lords of Misrule at Christmas, as well as music, dancing, and sports on Sunday afternoons (Marcus; Hutton 62–64, 260–62). Hutton's documentation of this process in dozens of church wardens' accounts from all over the country suggests that "Merry England" was not a survival from the pagan past, as many zealots believed at the time, but a creation of the fifteenth and early sixteenth centuries, when a fashion for ceremonial display, economic prosperity, and religious belief all encouraged communal celebrations of holidays.

The demise of "Merry England" in the 1640s and 1650s was likewise the result of a number of converging factors: the enclosure of open fields, the displacement of a land-based feudal economy by a money-based capitalist economy, an increasing gap between the well-to-do and the rest of the populace, changing ideas of decorum, and the final triumph of Protestant antipathy to Catholic ritual. The original performances of *Twelfth Night* in 1602 come squarely in the middle of the battle for Merry England. Like Lupton's personfied figure of Hospitality, Shakespeare's Sir Toby Belch has about him an air of nostalgic caricature — an air he shares with his predecessor on Shakespeare's stage, Sir John Falstaff. The jolly trencherman of *Henry IV, Parts 1 and 2* belongs as much to the fifteenth century as he does to the Eastcheap of Shakespeare's own day.

From *London and the Country Carbonadoed and Quartered into Several Characters*

Hospitality

This true noble-hearted fellow is to be dignified and honored, wheresoever he keeps house: it's thought that pride, puritans, coaches and covetousness hath caused him to leave our land: there are six upstart tricks come up in great houses of late which he cannot brook:[1] Peeping windows for the ladies to view what doings there are in the hall, a buttery hatch[2] that's kept locked, clean tables, and a French cook in the kitchen, a porter that locks the gates in dinner time, the decay of black-jacks[3] in the cellar, and blue-coats[4] in the hall:[5] he always kept his greatness by his charity: he loved three things, an open cellar, a full hall, and a sweating cook: he always provided for three dinners, one for himself, another for his servants, the third for the poor: anyone may know where he kept house, either by the chimney's smoke, by the freedom at gate, by want of whirligig jacks[6] in the kitchen, by the fire in the hall, or by the full furnished tables: he affects not London, Lent, lackeys, or bailiffs, there are four sorts that pray for him, the poor, the passenger, his tenants, and servants: he is one that will not hoard up all, nor lavishly spend all, he neither racks nor rakes his neighbors, they are sure of his company at church, as well as at home, and gives his bounty as well to the preacher, as to others whom he loves for his good life and doctrine: he had his wine came to him by full butts,[7] but this age keeps her wine cellar in little bottles. Lusty able men well maintained were his delight, with whom he would be familiar: his tenants knew when they saw him, for he kept the old fashion, good, commendable, plain: the poor about him wore [clothes] upon their backs; but now since his death, landlords wear and waste their tenants upon their backs in French, or Spanish fashions. Well, we can say that once

[1] **brook:** tolerate. [2] **buttery hatch:** door to the keeping room for beer and other provisions. [3] **black-jacks:** large leather jugs for beer. [4] **blue-coats:** almsmen, charity seekers. [5] **hall:** great hall. [6] **whirligig jacks:** continuously busy servants. [7] **butts:** large barrels.

Donald Lupton, *London and the Country Carbonadoed and Quartered into Several Characters* (London: Nicholas Oakes, 1632), 100–04.

such a charitable practitioner there was, but now he's dead, to the grief of all England: And tis shrewdly suspected that he will never rise again in our climate.

Puritan Ideals

As early as the 1540s, when an English translation of Anthony Skoloker's *The Ordinary for All Faithful Christians* (originally printed in Dutch) appeared on the London bookstalls, religious-minded merchants and craftsmen had their own counterparts to Castiglione's *The Book of the Courtier*. By the 1620s there were many such books, including *The Haven of Pleasure, Containing a Free Man's Felicity and a True Direction How to Live Well* (1596) by one I. T. (or possibly J. T.) and *Christian Economy, or A Short Survey of the Right Manner of Erecting and Ordering a Family* (1608) by William Perkins. Where Castiglione cites Plato, I. T. and Perkins are more apt to cite the Bible. Not surprisingly, the codes of behavior advocated in these books for the middling sort are grounded in economic metaphors. *The Haven of Pleasure* and *Christian Economy* can help us understand Malvolio's parsimony, calculation, and disdain for Twelfth Night revelry.

→ I. T. (OR J. T.)

From The Haven of Pleasure, Containing a Free Man's Felicity and a True Direction How to Live Well

1596

Castiglione's advice to the courtier on conspicuousness in dress, magnificence in manner, and largess in entertainment become in I. T.'s counsel a calculated moderation in food, drink, dress, and the spending of money. As the steward (*oikonomos*) to Lady Olivia's household, Malvolio seems to have been schooled by the likes of I. T. not only in his management of money but in his expectations about decorum. When Maria joins Sir Toby and Sir Andrew in shrugging off Malvolio's rebuke during the midnight revels, the steward chooses his words precisely: "Mistress Mary, if you prized my lady's favor at anything more than contempt, you would not give means for this uncivil rule" (2.3.100–01). "Uncivil" places the affair within the interlocking frames of Guazzo's *Civil Conversation*, while "rule" invokes measurement and written precepts as well as the now obsolete meaning of behavior in general.

CHAPTER 25

Of the Care and Government of a House

Touching that which appertaineth to economy, that is, the government of a house, which as Tully[1] sayeth, is the servant and handmaid of the body to strengthen and adorn it, it behooveth every man to be wise and painful in it, that the increase if it be referred to the necessary use and commodity of this life, and not to prodigality and delicacy, not to great cheer and unmeasurable making of banquets, which wasteth wealth and consumeth it, be it never so great. Wherefore in decking the table and making good cheer, good husbandry and moderation of diet ought chiefly to be regarded, and all provocation of gluttony and lust to be earnestly avoided, and to be short, all banqueting dishes and junkets[2] which are wont to be brought in at the end of the feast when every man's stomach is satisfied, whereby we are afresh provoked to eat. This prodigality and excess, besides the spending of a man's wealth and the bringing of many diseases, when the wine beginneth to warm us it stirreth us to wantonness, moveth the loins to lechery, and maketh the secret and hidden parts of man and woman to be affected to lust, whereby we begin to itch or, that I may use the Apostle's words,[3] to burn, that is to be more forcibly provoked to venery.[4] Wherefore Paul would have us do nothing to increase the lusts of the flesh, but to refer and do all things to the necessity and use of nature, and not to wantonness and pleasure, which is hurtful both to body and mind. For there is no man that doth so much oppose himself against the sense of nature that he could endure his own body to be hated, but rather as Paul sayeth, he nourisheth it and cherisheth it, as Christ doth his church. By which example, the Apostle would have husbands to love their wives and care for them as he would do for his own body, performing those things to them, as that Christ doth to his well beloved spouse, the church. But in guiding a house well, and in seeking the augmentation and increase of it, to the end all things may be done without shame, thou must so order everything, that thou neither incur the name of prodigal and wasteful spender, nor of too covetous and near a niggard.[5] For as thou must increase thy stock with good husbandry, and augment thy wealth with sparing, so must thou not bring it to such a strait, that thou defraud thy nature of her right, nor pinch thy family with want and necessity,

[1] **Tully:** Marcus Tullius Cicero (105 B.C.E.–43 C.E.), Roman philosopher and rhetorician. [2] **junkets:** sweetmeats, cakes, or confections. [3] **the Apostle's words:** Paul in 1 Corinthians 7.9. [4] **venery:** deeds of lust. [5] **near a niggard:** stingy, a miser.

I. T. [or J. T.], *The Haven of Pleasure, Containing a Free Man's Felicity and a True Direction How to Live Well* (London: P. Short, 1596), 44–46, 48.

like the filthy and greedy snudges[6] of this world. Nor yet be like to those bankrupt belly gods, which spend their gains and patrimony prodigally, inviting they care not what spendthrift companions to associate them, till all be spent. But, as Terence[7] sayeth, he must needs spend that gaineth. So, as Plautus[8] sayeth, "There is no gain where expenses exceed." And as the Dutchman sayeth, "Stelt u teringhe naer u neringhe." I may say, in converting it to our English proverb, "Cut your coat according to your cloth." Whereby it appeareth, that we must moderate our expenses and square them out according to our gains, lest we waste our wealth and patrimony with too much prodigality. Wherefore the duty of a painful housekeeper is to bring out his provision as time requireth and to store himself again when occasion is proffered. For as the proverb sayeth, "Sow thrift in thy ground and thou shalt reap it." But it shall not be much from our purpose, nor from the profit of our commonwealth, nor from the preservation of our substance, if we allege a law that Amasis king of the Egyptians published and Solon the lawgiver of the Lacedemonians used, wherein it was decreed, as Herodotus[9] witnesseth, that all men, as well born at home as strangers, should once a year show to the rulers of their provinces by what they lived, and by what means they got their maintenance. And such as could not render a reason of this, nor approve their lives to be lawful and honest, were executed. By the severity of which commandment they bridled the idle persons from filching and stealing, unto which pass are also brought such as spend their patrimonies in dicing, whoring, and drinking. . . .

Paul also the Apostle is a severe looker to men's duties, who commandeth that we shake off the drowsy evil of idleness and slothfulness to take some pains in our handicrafts or occupations, whereby we may maintain our family, which he would have so severely looked unto, that he would have him eat nothing that laboreth not at all, nor looketh to the maintenance of himself and his family, but like a drone bee lives of the sweat of other men's brows, may stealeth away the fruits of other men's labors, living in the alms and liberality of other men, occupying themselves about niceness and curiosity. To which sharp and severe rule, Paul also reclaimeth thieves, which filch and steal away other men's goods. From which he not only warneth them to abstain, but that they should spend upon and relieve the poor with that which they had gained with their honest labor. So that if any ignominy or discredit come unto them by doing of wicked and infamous crimes, they should take it away by requiting it again with good deeds to the poor and

[6] **snudges:** misers. [7] **Terence:** Latin comic playwright (c. 185–c. 160 B.C.E.). [8] **Plautus:** Latin comic playwright (c. 254–c. 184 B.C.E.). [9] **Herodotus:** Greek historian (c. 485–c. 425 B.C.E.)

needy, as Zacheus[10] did, who having got great wealth by usury, divided it afterward unto the poor, so that he blotted out the faults of his former life with good deeds and recompense made by virtuous living. To wit, he altered and changed his old affections and shook off the naughtiness and ill custom of his nature.

[10] **Zacheus:** rich tax-collector who, after an encounter with Christ, gave half his goods to the poor and promised to restore, four for one, anything he had extorted (Luke 19.8).

WILLIAM PERKINS

From Christian Economy *1608*

Books like *The Haven of Pleasure* were not usually reprinted, but William Perkins (1558–1602) acquired an authority throughout the seventeenth century that was backed up by some fifty works printed between 1590 and 1665, many of them in multiple editions. No fewer than ten collected editions of his works appeared in English, three in Latin, and one in Dutch. Individual titles were also translated into Spanish, Welsh, and Irish. What recommended these books to such a wide reading public was Perkins's logical, uncompromising directness in presenting the tenets of Protestant dogma, a quality that also distinguished Perkins's preaching. His book *The Reformed Catholic* (1597), for example, drew the boundary lines between Catholic and Protestant belief so precisely that it was impossible for more moderate-minded readers to waffle. As an undergraduate at Cambridge in the late 1570s, Perkins was, by his own account, anything but a model Christian. His reckless behavior, profanity, and drunkenness came to an abrupt end, however, when Perkins heard a woman on the street point him out to her child as "drunken Perkins." As a fellow of St. John's College, Cambridge, and as a preacher Perkins soon became notorious for his outspoken resistance to all vestiges of Catholic ritual. Archbishop Richard Bancroft (see p. 334) included Perkins among the Puritans singled out by name in *Dangerous Positions* (1593).[1]

Perkins's focus in *Christian Economy* is squarely on the family as the cornerstone of the commonwealth at large. Every one of Perkins's major points is carefully grounded in scripture, in the written word of God. The families, established and incipient, in *Twelfth Night* all fail to meet Perkins's criteria. For a start, Perkins makes no allowance for the gender confusions that attend the wooing of "Cesario"/Viola by Orsino and Olivia. The first requirement to make persons "fit for marriage" is "distinction of the sex." Nor does Perkins consider the anomaly of a "lady-widow" like Olivia marrying someone like Sebastian

[1] On Perkins's influence, see Mallette.

who, if he truly looks like his sister, is "not yet old enough for a man, nor young enough for a boy" (1.5.122). Perkins's ideal household is ruled over by a husband/father/master. In the absence of such a person, Perkins details the duties of "the Master of the Family, or Goodman of the House," who fills the role of husband/father/master even if he is not called to that role by marriage or paternity. Below that presiding figure are the wife or mistress, children, and servants, all related to one another by mutual obligations and expectations. An image of such a household appears in Skoloker's *Ordinary for All Faithful Christians* (1549), under the heading "How youth shall obey their elders, honoring them in the fear of the Lord" (K). (See Figure 26.) In a series of receding planes one sees busy children and servants as they wait on the master and mistress, dining at a table toward the rear. How altogether different is the topsy-turvy household of the Lady Olivia, where, despite Malvolio's best efforts, it remains unclear just who is in charge.

FIGURE 26 *How Youth Shall Obey Their Elders, from Anthony Skoloker,* The Ordinary for All Faithful Christians *(1549?).*

From *Christian Economy*

Chapter 1

Of Christian Economy and of the Family

Christian economy is a doctrine of the right ordering of the family.

The only rule of ordering the family is the written word of God. By it David resolved to govern his house, when he sayeth, "I will walk in the uprightness of my heart in the midst of my house" (Psalm 101.2). And Solomon affirmeth, that through wisdom an house is built, and with understanding it is established (Proverbs 24.3).

A family is a natural and simple society of certain persons, having mutual relation one to another, under the private government of one. Their persons must be at the least three, because two cannot make a society. And above three under the same head, there may be a thousand in one family, as it is in the households of princes and men of state in the world. . . .

Chapter 5

Of the Choice of Persons Fit for Marriage

For the making of a contract, two things are requisite: first the choice, and then the consent of the parties.

Choice is an enquiry after persons marriageable.

Persons marriageable are such as be fit and able for the married state.

This fitness or ability is known and discerned by certain signs, which are either essential to the contract or accidental.

An essential sign is that without which the contract in hand becomes a mere nullity. And of this sort there are principally five.

The first is the distinction of the sex, which is either male or female. The male is man of a superior sex, fit for procreation. The female is woman of an inferior sex, fit to conceive and bear children: "The man ought not to cover his head, for as much as he is the image and glory of God, but the woman is the glory of the man" (1 Corinthians 2:7), "I permit not the woman to teach, neither to usurp authority over the man, but to be in silence" (1 Timothy 2:12). By this distinction is condemned, that unnatural and monstrous sin of uncleanness between parties of the same sex, commonly termed sodomy, as

---

William Perkins, *Christian Economy* (first printed 1608), in *Collected Works* (Cambridge: Legge, 1618), 3: 669, 673, 691–93, 696–700.

also the confusion of the kinds[1] of creatures, when one kind commits filthiness and abomination with another.

The second sign, is, the just and lawful distance of blood.

Distance of blood is then just and lawful, when neither of the persons that are to be married, do come near to the kindred of their flesh, or to the flesh of their flesh, for so the scripture speaketh: "No man shall come near to any of the flesh of his flesh" or to "the kindred of his flesh" (Leviticus 18:6). Where it is to be observed, that by a man's flesh, is meant that substance which is of himself, or whereof himself consisteth. And by "the flesh of his flesh," that which next and immediately issueth out of that flesh whereof he consisteth. Whereupon it followeth, that the touching or coming near of flesh to flesh is not spoken of strangers, but of those that are of kindred. . . .

Chapter II

Of the Husband

Married folks are either husband or wife.

The husband is he which hath authority over the wife. Hereupon in Scripture he is called "the guide of her youth" (Proverbs 2:17), and they twain being but one flesh, he is also the head over his wife.

The duties of the husband towards the wife, are these:

I. To love her as himself: "Let every one love his wife even as himself" (Ephesians 5:33), "Afterward Isaac brought her unto the tent of Sarah his mother; and he took Rebecca, and she was his wife, and he loved her: so Isaac left mourning for his mother" (Genesis 24:67). Note how the love of the husband to the wife mitigates sorrow for the death of the mother.

He is to show this love in two things. First, in protecting her from danger: "And unto Sarah he said, 'Behold, I have given 1000 shekels of silver unto thy brother: behold, he is covering of thine eyes amongst all that are with thee. Let it be known amongst all, and be thou instructed'" (Genesis 20:16), "David's two wives were taken prisoners also, Abinoam the Israelite, and Abigail the wife of Nabal the Carmelite. . . . Then David asked counsel of the Lord, saying, 'Shall I follow after this company? shall I overtake them?' And He answered him, 'Follow, for thou shalt surely overtake them, and recover all'" (1 Samuel 30:5, 8). Secondly, in regarding her estate as his own, and providing maintenance for her, both for his life time, and as much as he may, for time to come after his death: "So ought men to love their wives and their own bodies: he that loveth his wife loveth himself. For no

[1] **kinds:** natural species.

man ever yet hated his own flesh, but nourisheth it, etc." (Ephesians 5:28–29), "If he take him another wife, he shall not diminish her food, her raiment, and recompense of her virginity" (Exodus 21:10), "Unto whom he said, 'Who art thou?' Which said, 'I am Ruth thine handmaid, spread therefore the wing of thy garment over thine handmaid: for thou art the kinsman'" (Ruth 3:9).

II. To honor his wife: "Giving honor to the woman" (1 Peter 3:7).

This honor stands in three things. First, in making account of her as his companion, or yoke-fellow. For this cause, the woman when she was created was not taken out of the man's head because she was not made to rule over him, nor out of his feet because God did not make her subject to him as a servant, but out of his side, to the end that man should take her as his mate. Secondly, in a wise and patient bearing or covering of her infirmities, as anger, waywardness, and such like, in respect of the weakness of her sex: "Giving honor to the woman as unto the weaker vessel, seeing ye are heirs together of the grace of life, that your prayers be not hindered" (1 Peter 3:7). Thirdly, by suffering himself sometimes to be admonished or advised by her. It was God's commandment to Abraham concerning Sarah his wife, "Let it not be grievous in thy sight, for the child, and for thy bondwoman: in all that Sarah shall say unto thee, hear her voice: for in Isaac shall thy seed be called" (Genesis 21:12). Thus Elkanah was willing to subscribe unto his wife Anna's advice for her tarrying at home till the child was weaned: "And Elkanah her husband said unto her, 'Do what seemeth thee best: tarry until thou hast weaned him: only the Lord accomplish His word'" (1 Samuel 1:23). Hereupon the heathen philosopher [Aristotle] said that "the master of the family exerciseth (after a sort) a power tyrannical over his servants, a power regal over his children, because kings are fathers of their commonweals, but in respect of his wife, he exerciseth a power aristocratical, not after his own will, but agreeable to the honor and dignity of married estate" [*Nicomachean Ethics* 8], and consequently, that he ought not in modesty to challenge the privilege of prescribing and advertizing[2] his wife in all matters domestical, but in some to leave her to her own will and judgment. . . .

[*Question:*] It is alleged, husbands are commanded so to love their wives, as Christ doth his church. Now Christ chastiseth his church with strokes, and therefore so may the husband his wife. *An*[*swer*]: As Christ doth entirely love his church, so he may also chastise the same, because he is not only the husband, but absolute lord and king of his church, so is not the husband absolute over the wife.

[2] **advertizing:** warning, advising.

[*Question:*] But his authority over his wife, is after a sort civil, as is the authority of the magistrate over his people? *Ans*[*wer:*] It is not so. For the magistrate hath in his hand the power of the sword, by which power he inflicteth punishment in case of offense. But the husband can challenge to himself no such power. Yea it is flatly forbidden in the civil law, that he should scourge or strike his wife.

Nevertheless, if she grow to extremities, and be desperately perverse, so as there be no hope of amendment, then the magistrate may be informed, who to prevent scandals, and to provide for public peace, both ought and may assign unto her necessary correction and punishment according to her desert. Now the husband that hath a wife so stubborn and peevish, must bear it, if it may be borne, as the portion of his cross laid upon him by God. And in this case if he be impatient, he may in some sort be pardoned and pitied, but he is not wholly to be excused.

Chapter 12

Of the Wife

The wife is the other married person, who being subject to her husband, yieldeth obedience unto him.

Touching the subjection of this wife, the word of God mentioneth it in sundry places: "The woman which is in subjection to the man, is bound by the law to the man while he liveth" (Romans 7:2), "As the church is in subjection to Christ, even so let the wives be to their husbands in everything" (Ephesians 4:24), "Wives, submit yourselves unto your husbands, as it is comely in the Lord" (Colossians 3:18), "I permit not a woman to usurp authority over the man" (1 Timothy 2:12). And it was a law established by God immediately after the fall: "Unto the woman he said, 'I will greatly increase, etc. and thy desire shall be subject to thine husband, and he shall rule over thee'" (Genesis 3:16). Indeed the daughter according to the civil law, even when she is married is in the power of her father, and not of her husband. But this is directly against the Law of Moses, and crosseth the law of nature (Leviticus 22:12–13, Numbers 30:13).

Now the duties of the wife are principally two.

The first, is to submit herself to her husband, and to acknowledge and reverence him as her head in all things: "Likewise Abimelech said unto Sarah, 'Behold thy brother' (that is, thy husband whom thou callest thy brother) 'is the veil of thine eyes to all that are with thee'" (Genesis 20:16), as if he should say, "Thy husband is thy head, and hath power over thee, and thou oughtest to reverence him." For of ancient times, the wife was covered with a veil in the presence of her husband, in token of subjection unto him. Thus Rebecca in the sight of Isaac took a veil, "and covered her head therewith" (Genesis 24:65). "The man is the woman's head" (1 Corinthians 5:22). "Wives, submit yourselves unto your husbands, as unto the Lord, for the husband is the wife's head, even as Christ is the head of the church" (Ephesians 5:22). The reason hereof is good. For the wife enjoyeth the privileges of her husband, and is graced by his honor and estimation amongst men. His nobility maketh her noble, though otherwise she is base and mean. As contrariwise, his baseness and low degree causeth her, though she be by birth noble and honorable, to be by estate base and mean.

The second duty is to be obedient unto her husband in all things, that is, wholly to depend upon him, both in judgment and will. For look as the Church yields obedience to Christ her head, and yields herself to be commanded, governed, and directed by him, so ought the woman to the man. So Sarah is said to obey Abraham, and to give him the means of obedience, "She called him Lord, or Sir" (2 Peter 3:6). Hence it followeth, that the woman is not to take liberty of wandering, and straying abroad from her own house, without the man's knowledge and consent: "Then she called to her husband and said, 'Send with me, I pray thee, one of the young men, and one of the asses, for I will make haste to the man of God, and come again'" (2 Kings 4:22). Again, that she is to follow her husband when he flitteth or departeth from place to place, unless he forsake either her or Christ. To this purpose Paul saith, he "had power to lead about a wife, being a sister, as well as the rest of the apostles" (1 Corinthians 9:5). Thus Sarah went with Abraham into Egypt (Genesis 12:11) and out of Egypt (Genesis 13:1) and to "Gerar to sojourn there" (Genesis 20:1–3). Thus the wives of Jacob departed with him from their father Laban (Genesis 31:17).

Contrary to these duties, are the sins of wives. To be proud, to be unwilling to bear the authority of their husbands, to chide and brawl with bitterness, to forsake their houses, etc.: "A continual dropping in the day of rain, and a contentious woman are alike" (Proverbs 27:15), "He that hideth her, hideth the wind; and she is as the oil in his right hand, that uttereth[3] itself" (Proverbs 27:16), "Then Zipporah said, 'O bloody husband, because of the circumcision'" (Exodus 4:26). It was the fault of the Levite's concubine, "who played the whore, and went away from him unto her father's house to Bethlehem Judah, and there continued the space of four months" (Judges 19:2). It was the sin of Queen Vashti, who "refused to come at the king's word, which he had given in charge to the eunuchs: therefore the king was very angry, and his wrath kindled in him" (Esther 1:12). Lastly, to be a cause

[3] **uttereth:** passes forth.

of grief to their kindred. Thus the proud wives of Esau, the daughters of the Hittites, were a grief of mind to Isaac and Rebecca (Genesis 26:35 and 27:46). . . .

Chapter 15

Of the Master

Next unto parents and children, whereby the family is increased, is a second sort of couples, which are helps thereunto. And they are masters and servants.

The master is a member in the family, which hath power, and beareth rule over the servant. And his duty stands principally in three things.

First, to make a good choice of his servants, which is then done, when he inquireth first after such as fear God, and be willing to serve him. Paul makes the service and fear of God the main ground of true obedience in servants. . . .

Secondly, to enjoin them labor, and not to require more of them than their strength will bear. The master is to rule over the servant in justice. And then is his commandment unjust, when it will not stand with the course of nature, with the ability of his servant, or with the word of God. Therefore he is to require labor at their hands proportionable to their strength, and yield them sometimes intermission and rest. . . .

Thirdly, to recompense the diligence and pains of his servant, and that three ways.

First, by giving him his due of meat and drink for the present. . . .

Secondly, by paying him his hire in the end of his service. . . .

Here three caveats are to be observed. I. That the wages be proportionable to the work. II. That it be paid in due time, without deferring. So the master of the vineyard, when even[4] was come, called his servants together to give them their hire (Matthew 20:8). III. That the servant be not defrauded of any part of his due. For this is a crying sin. . . .

Thirdly, if the servant in time of his service be sick, the master's care must be by all means possible to procure his recovery. Equity must be the rule in these cases. . . .

[4] **even:** evening.

Chapter 17

Of the Master of the Family, or Goodman of the House

Thus much touching the diverse and several combinations or couples belonging to the state economical. From which do arise two persons of a mixed or compounded nature and condition, commonly called the goodman and the goodwife of the house.

The goodman or master of the family, is a person, in whom resteth the private and proper government of the whole household, and he comes not unto it by election, as it falleth out in other states, but by the ordinance of God, settled even in the order of nature. The husband indeed naturally bears rule over the wife, parents over their children, masters over their servants. But that person, who by the providence of God hath the place of an husband, a father, a master in his house, the same also by the light of nature hath the principality and sovereignty therein, and he is paterfamilias, the father and chief head of the family. To him therefore the true right and power over all matters domestical, of right appertaineth. The duties of the master of the family are specially five.

I. To bear the chief stroke, and to be the principal agent, director, and furtherer of the worship of God within his family. . . .

II. To bring his family to the church or congregation on the Sabbath day. To look that they do religiously there behave themselves, and after the public exercises ended and the congregation is dismissed, to take account of that which they have heard, that they may profit in knowledge and obedience. . . .

III. To provide for his family meat, drink, and clothing, and that they may live a quiet and peaceable life. . . .

IV. To keep order and to exercise discipline in his house, and that in this manner. In case of offense, when a capital crime is committed, which incurreth public censure he is not to punish it himself, but to bring the offender to the civil magistrate, to inform of his fault, that he may have his desert. It was a course established by the judicial law, which God gave unto Moses for his direction in causes criminal among the Israelites. . . .

If the fault be of an inferior nature, and lesser in comparison, the master of the family ought to proceed by private censure upon the delinquent party, sometimes by admonition, otherwhiles by correction, and chastisement, according to the quality of the offense, and the condition and state of the person. . . .

When admonitions and corrections will not prevail, the party must be brought before the ministers and governors of the church, that they may censure him. . . .

V. To give entertainment to those that are strangers, and not of the family, if they be Christians, and believers, but specially to the ministers of the word. . . .

Chapter 18

Of the Mistress of the Family or Goodwife of the House

The goodwife or mistress of the house is a person which yieldeth help and assistance in government to the master of the family. For he is, as it were, the prince and chief ruler. She is the associate, not only in office and authority, but also in advice, and counsel unto him. . . .

Her duty is two-fold.

First, to govern the house, as much as concerneth her, in her place. . . . And that she doeth three ways. I. By exercising herself in some profitable employments, for the good of her charge. . . . II. By appointing her maids their work and overseeing them therein. . . . III. By ordering her children and servants in wisdom, partly by instruction, partly by admonition, when there is need. . . .

The second duty is to give the portion of food unto her family or cause it to be given in due season.

Alternative Households

Educational institutions were understood to be households. Thus, all the people gathered in Middle Temple Hall on February 2, 1602 — John Manningham, his fellow law students, the masters who taught them and governed them — constituted a household. They shared the same physical quarters for months at a time, they dined together, they worshiped together, they celebrated holidays together. (For them, *Twelfth Night* was a household entertainment.) In many ways this group of younger and older men embodied the very hierarchical structure that authorities like Perkins saw as the basis of a family. The court gathered about Le Prince d'Amour during Christmas 1597–98, with its reigning monarch and attendant officers, was typical of the mock courts assembled on such festive occasions. When "a comedy of errors (like to Plautus his *Menaechmus*)" was performed at Gray's Inn during Christmas 1594, the presiding monarch was the Prince of Purpool — Purpool being a London neighborhood adjacent to the school.[1]

[1] See the account in *Gesta Grayorum*.

Schools and colleges did the like. The one consideration that made these households different from those described in Puritan conduct books was the absence of women. The household of the Middle Temple was an all-male household. From the vantage point of Middle Temple Lane, women were physically marginal figures: they lodged somewhere else, under the protection of fathers or masters, or they plied their trade in houses of prostitution grouped in certain places beyond the Temple gates. Hence the fascination with things feminine in souvenir pamphlets like *Gesta Grayorum* and *Le Prince d'Amour* — and in plays performed for all-male households on such occasions, notably Shakespeare's *Twelfth Night.* A recurrent concern in all these pamphlets and plays is how to integrate the household's masculine identity with the desired feminine other. The ending of *Twelfth Night* suggests that ambiguity was a particularly attractive alternative.

Schools, colleges, and the inns of court differed from the apprenticeship system in their gender exclusivity. Typically a young man of seventeen years or so who wished to learn a trade got himself apprenticed to a recognized master in that trade. In the course of the seven years it took (in theory at least) to become a master in one's own right the apprentice typically became a member of his master's household. In exchange for lodging and food the apprentice provided services while he was learning his craft (Ben-Amos 84–108). The master's household was likely, just as Perkins describes it, to include a wife. Acting companies were, like the inns of court, all-male institutions. They were made up of men only, with boy actors occupying, for all practical purposes, the place of apprentices. Boy actors boarded with the adult actors, but not every adult actor belonged to a normative household with wife, children, and servants. Shakespeare was one of these odd men out. Leaving his family back in Stratford, he rented quarters in London for most of his professional career. Several of his fellow actors did, in fact, make up alternative households of their own, living together as they worked together (Masten 28–62). From the standpoint of Perkins, both the Middle Temple and the Lord Chamberlain's Men shape up as (play)households. Their coming together on February 2, 1602, represented a mirroring of certain features of each other's social identities. With respect to gender, both of them constituted alternative households that bore a problematic relation to the ideal household described by Perkins.

A range of viewpoints on these alternative households can be witnessed in the two texts excerpted below: William Prynne's attack on the licentiousness of actors' living arrangements in *Histrio-Mastix, The Players' Scourge or the Actors' Tragedy* (1633) and the coexistence of two households, professional and domestic, as witnessed in the last will and testament of Shakespeare's fellow actor Augustine Phillips (1605).

WILLIAM PRYNNE

From Histrio-Mastix, The Players' Scourge or Actors' Tragedy

1633

In the paper attack on the theaters, William Prynne (1600–1669) arrived late, but with much more ammunition than his predecessors. Prynne's *Histrio-Mastix: The Players' Scourge or Actors' Tragedy, Divided into Two Parts, Wherein It Is Largely Evidenced, by Divers Arguments, by the Concurring Authorities and Resolutions of Sundry Texts of Scripture, of the Whole Primitive Church, Both Under the Law of God and Gospel, of 55 Synods and Councils, of 71 Fathers and Christian Writers, Before the Year of Our Lord 1200, of Above 150 Foreign and Domestic Protestant and Popish Authors Since, of 40 Heathen Philosophers, Historians, Poets of Many Heathen, Many Christian Nations, Republics, Emperors, Princes, Magistrates, of Sundry Apostolical, Canonical, Imperial Constitutions, and of Our Own English Statutes, Magistrates, Universities, Preachers, That Popular Stage Plays (the Very Pomps of the Devil, Which We Renounce in Baptism, If We Believe the Fathers) Are Sinful, Heathenish, Lewd, Ungodly Spectacles, and Most Pernicious Corruptions [. . .]* and so on for 85 more words on the title page alone (1633) is one the heftiest quarto-size books printed in England before 1642. It runs to more than a thousand pages. One of about two hundred books and pamphlets published by the Puritan propagandist during his long career, *Histrio-Mastix* presents every possible argument against stage plays. In this selection, Prynne attacks the irregular living habits of actors.

What the conditions, lives, and qualities of stage-players have been in former ages, let Cyprian, Nazianzen, Chrisostom, Augustine, Nicholaus Cabasila, Cornelius Tacitus, Marcus Aurelius, with others, testify. The first of these[1] informs us that "Stageplayers are the masters, not of teaching, but of destroying youth, insinuating that wickedness into others, which themselves have sinfully learned." Whence he writes to Eucratius, to excommunicate a player who trained up youths for the stage, affirming that "it could never stand with the majesty of God, nor the discipline of the gospel, that the chastity and honor of the church should be defiled with so filthy, so infamous a contagion." The more than sodomitical uncleanness of players' lives, he farther thus deciphers. "O," writes he, "that thou couldst in that sublime watch-tower insinuate thine eyes into these players' secrets, or set open the

[1] **the first of these:** St. Cyprian (200–258 C.E.), one of the fathers of the early Christian church.

William Prynne, *Histrio-Mastix, The Players' Scourge or Actors' Tragedy . . .* (London: Michael Sparke, 1633), 135–39.

closed doors of their bedchambers, and bring all their innermost hidden cells unto the conscience of thine eyes. Thou shouldst then see that which is even a very sin to see. Thou mightest behold that, which these groaning under the burthen of their vices, deny that they have committed, and yet hasten to commit. Men rush on men with outrageous lusts. They do those things which can neither please those who behold them, nor yet themselves who act them. The same persons are accusers in public, guilty in secret, being both censurers and nocents[2] against themselves. They condemn that abroad, which they practice at home. They commit that willingly, which when they have committed, they reprehend. I am verily a liar, if those who are such abuse not others. One filthy person defameth others like himself, thinking by this means to escape the censure of those who are privy to his sin, as if his own conscience were not sufficient both to accuse him and condemn him." Thus far Saint Cyprian. . . .

Such were the lives, the insolencies, the exorbitancies of stage-players in former times. What the lives, the qualities of our own domestic actors are, or have been heretofore, two several acts of Parliament, which adjudge and style them rogues, together with two penitent reclaimed play-poets of our own (who were thoroughly acquainted with their practices and persons too) will at large declare. The first of these two play-poets,[3] who out of conscience renounced his profession, and then wrote against the abominations of our stage-plays, writes thus of stage-players: "As I have had a saying to these versifying play-makers, so likewise must I deal with shameless enactors. When I see by them young boys, inclining of themselves to wickedness, trained up in filthy speeches, unnatural and unseemly gestures, to be brought up by these schoolmasters, in bawdry and in idleness, I cannot choose but with tears and grief of heart lament. O with what delight can the father behold his son bereft of shamefastness, and trained up to impudency? How prone are they of themselves and apt to receive instruction of their lewd teachers, which are the schoolmasters of sin in the school of abuse? What do they teach them, I pray you, but to foster mischief in their youth that it may always abide with them, and in their age bring them sooner unto Hell? And as for these stagers themselves, are they not commonly such kind of men in their conversation, as they are in profession? Are they not as variable in heart as they are in their parts? Are they not as good practicers of bawdry, as enactors? Live they not in such sort themselves, as they give precepts unto others? Doth not their talk on the stage, declare the nature of their disposition? Doth not the ploughman's tongue talk of his plough, the

[2] **nocents:** harmful persons. [3] **first . . . play-poets:** the anonymous author of *The Blast of Retreat from Plays and Theaters* (1588).

seafaring man's of his mast, cable, and sail, the soldier's of his harness, spear and shield, and bawdy mates' of bawdy matters? Ask them, if in the laying out of their parts, they choose not those parts which are most agreeable to their inclination, and that they can best discharge. And look what every of them doth most delight in, that he can best handle to the contentment of others. If it be a roisting,[4] bawdy, or lascivious part, wherein are unseemly speeches, and that they make choice of them as best answering, and proper to their manner of play, may we not say by how much the more he exceeds in his gesture, he delights himself in his part? And by so much it is pleasing to his disposition and nature? If (it be his nature) to be a bawdy player, and he delight in such filthy and cursed actions, shall we not think him in his life to be more disordered and to abhor virtue?"

[4] **roisting:** reveling, swaggering.

AUGUSTINE PHILLIPS

Last Will and Testament

1605

What part Shakespeare's fellow actor Augustine Phillips (d. 1605) may have played in *Twelfth Night* is not known, but when he joined the Lord Chamberlain's Men in 1594 he brought a store of acting experience with Lord Strange's Men, including the period when that company was amalgamated with the Lord Admiral's Men. In the course of his career he got to work therefore with the two most famous actors of his age, Edward Alleyn and Richard Burbage. By 1596 Phillips was one of eight principal shareholders in the Lord Chamberlain's Men.[1] His last will and testament, executed on May 4, 1605, attests to his financial success as a shareholder. In addition to the expected legacies to his wife, daughters, mother, brothers, sisters, and nephews, Phillips leaves sizeable sums to his fellow actors, including William Shakespeare, as well as money, clothing, and a bass viol to his former apprentice Samuel Gilborne and a lute and a bandore to his current apprentice, James Sands. Phillips's will suggests that, in effect, he belonged to *two* households, one domestic and one professional, one conventional and one not.

[1] On Phillips's career, see Gurr, 33–44.

In the name of God, amen. The fourth day of May Anno Domini 1605 and in the years of the reign of our sovereign Lord James by the grace of God King of England, Scotland, France, and Ireland the Third, and Scotland the eighth and thirtieth, I, Augustine Phillips, of Mortlake in the County of Surrey, Gent[leman], being at this present sick and weak in body, but of good and perfect mind and remembrance, thanks be given unto Almighty God, do make ordain and dispose this present testament and last will in manner and form following.

That is to say, first and principally I commend my soul into the hands of Almighty God my maker, savior, and redeemer, in whom and by the merits of the second person Jesus Christ, I trust and believe assuredly to be saved, and to have full and clear remission and forgiveness of my sins. And I commit my body to be buried in the chancel of the parish church of Mortlake aforesaid. And after my body buried and funeral charges paid, then I will that all such debts and duties as I owe to any person or persons of right or in conscience shall be truly paid. And that done, then I will that all and singular my goods, chattels,[2] plate, household stuff, jewels, ready money, and debts shall be divided by my executrix and overseers of this my last will and testament into three equal and indifferent parts and portions whereof one equal part I give and bequeath to Anne Phillips, my loving wife, to her own proper use and behoof,[3] one other part thereof to and amongst my three eldest daughters Magdalene Phillips, Rebecca Phillips, and Anne Phillips, equally amongst them to be divided portion and portion like, and to be paid and delivered unto them as they and every of them shall accomplish and come to their lawful ages of twenty and one years or at their days of marriage, and every of them to be others' heir of their said parts and portions if any of them shall fortune to die before their said several ages of twenty and one years or days of marriage. And the other part thereof I reserve to my self and to my executrix to perform my legacies hereafter following.

Item, I give and bequeath to the poor of the parish of Mortlake aforesaid, five pounds[4] of lawful money of England, to be distributed by the church wardens of the same parish within twelve months after my decease.

Item, I give and bequeath to Agnes Bennett, my loving mother, during her natural life, every year yearly the sum of five pounds of lawful money of England, to be paid her at the four usual feasts or terms in the year by my executrix out of any part and portion reserved by this my present will.

[2] **chattels:** moveable goods. [3] **behoof:** benefit. [4] **five pounds:** about $3,750 U.S.

Augustine Phillips, Last Will and Testament (1605), in E. A. J. Honigmann and Susan Brock, eds., *Playhouse Wills, 1558–1642* (Manchester: Manchester University Press, 1993), 72–74.

Item, I give to my brothers William Webb and James Webb, if they shall be living at my decease, to either of them the sum of ten pounds a piece of lawful money of England, to be paid unto them within three years after my decease.

Item, I give and bequeath to my sister Elizabeth Gough, the sum of ten pounds of lawful money of England to be paid her within one year after my decease.

Item, I will and bequeath unto Miles Borne and Phillips Borne, two sons of my sister Margery Borne, to either of them ten pounds a piece of lawful money of England to be paid unto them when they shall accomplish the full age of twenty and one years.

Item, I give and bequeath unto Timothy Withorne, the sum of twenty pounds of lawful money of England to be paid unto him within one year after my decease.

Item, I give and bequeath unto and amongst the hired men of the company which I am of, which shall be at the time of my decease the sum of five pounds of lawful money of England, to be equally distributed amongst them.

Item, I give and bequeath to my fellow William Shakespeare, a thirty-shillings piece in gold. To my fellow Henry Condell, one other thirty-shillings piece in gold. To my servant Christopher Beeson, thirty shillings in gold. To my fellow Lawrence Fletcher, twenty shillings in gold. To my fellow Robert Armin, twenty shillings in gold. To my fellow Richard Coweley, twenty shillings in gold. To my fellow Alexander Cook, twenty shillings in gold. To my fellow Nicholas Tooley, twenty shillings in gold.

Item, I give to the preacher which shall preach at my funeral, the sum of twenty shillings.

Item, I give to unto Samuel Gilborne, my late apprentice, the sum of forty shillings and my mouse-colored velvet hose[5] and a white taffeta doublet,[6] a black taffeta suit, my purple cloak, sword and dagger, and my bass viol.

Item, I give to James Sands, my apprentice, the sum of forty shillings and a cithern,[7] a bandore,[8] and a lute, to be paid and delivered unto him at the expiration of his term of years in his indenture or apprenticehood.

Item, my will is that Elizabeth Phillips, my youngest daughter, shall have and quietly enjoy for term of her natural life, my house and land in Mortlake, which I lately purchased to[9] me, Anne my wife, and to the said Elizabeth, for term of our lives in full recompense and satisfaction of her part and portion which she may in any wise challenge or demand of, in, and to any of my goods and chattels whatsoever. And I ordain and make the said Anne

[5] **hose:** breeches reaching to the knee. [6] **doublet:** padded jacket. [7] **cithern:** stringed instrument similar to a guitar. [8] **bandore:** stringed instrument similar to a guitar or lute. [9] **to:** in the names of.

Phillips, my loving wife, sole executrix of this my present testament and last will, provided all ways that if the said Anne my wife do at any time marry after my decease, that then and from thenceforth she shall cease to be any more or longer my executrix, of this my last will and testament or any ways intermeddle with[10] the same. And the said Anne to have no part or portion of goods and or chattels to me or my executors, reserved or appointed, by this my last will and testament. And that then and from thenceforth, John Heminges, Richard Burbage, William Sly, and Timothy Withorne[11] shall be fully and wholly my executors of this my last will and testament, as though the said Anne had never been named. And of the execution of this my present testament and last will, I ordain and make the said John Heminges, Richard Burbage, William Sly, and Timothy Withorne overseers of this my present testament and last will. And I bequeath unto the said John Heminges, Richard Burbage, and William Sly, to either of them my said overseers, for their pains herein to be taken a bowl of silver of the value of five pounds apiece.

In witness thereof to this my present testament and last will, I, the said Augustine Phillips, have put my hand and seal the day and year above written.

A. Phillips

Sealed and delivered by the said Augustine Phillips as his last will and testament in the presence of us,

Robert Goffe
William Shepherd

[10] **intermeddle with:** have anything to do with. [11] **John Heminges . . . Timothy Withorne:** all members of Phillips's acting company, the King's Men.

CHAPTER 6

Puritan Probity

When Maria describes Malvolio as "a kind of puritan" (2.3.115), she assumes a capital *P* (at least in the original printing of the text in the folio of 1623) but qualifies the definitiveness of that label with the phrase "a kind of." What did it mean in 1602 to be a Puritan — or at least to be *called* one? Maria immediately provides a list of synonyms: (1) "a time-pleaser," (2) "an affectioned ass, that cons state without book and utters it by great swaths," (3) "the best persuaded of himself, so crammed, as he thinks, with excellencies, that it is his grounds of faith that all that look on him love him" (2.3.120–24). Reform of religion by "purifying" the Church of England is not the main thing on Maria's mind, despite her swipe at Malvolio's "faith." Instead, Maria identifies the Puritan in Malvolio as a matter of social ambition and exaggerated self-worth.

The chronicler John Stow (1525?–1605) claims that "Puritan" was the name that several congregations of Anabaptists in London gave themselves in the 1560s, but the earliest recorded uses of the word are all derogatory. (See *OED*, "puritan," A.1.) The label became attached to the Protestant reformers who published *An Admonition to Parliament* in 1572 and called for the abolition of bishops and a return to the principles of church government implied by Paul's epistles in the New Testament. Since the existing episcopal form of church government was under the control of the crown, there was a political element to the so-called Puritans' demands. To change church government would be to alter the balances of power among king, nobility, and commoners. The need for such changes might seem especially apparent to individuals whose wealth and social standing came through capitalist trade rather than feudal land-owning. Social and economic factors were as much a part of *An Admonition to Parliament* as biblical precedents.[1] The Puritan ideals of household government that we surveyed in Chapter 5 were products of these social and economic shifts. The issues that Malvolio brings to a head are thus religious, economic, social, and political in nature, all at the same time. Treated with ridicule in *Twelfth Night* in 1602, those issues conspired to produce the English Revolution of 1640. Laughter at Malvolio was *nervous* laughter.

Malvolio enters *Twelfth Night* as Feste's *bête noir* — with an emphasis on the *noir.* Black is, in fact, very much on everyone's mind in act 1, scene 5, when Feste tries to tease Olivia into giving up her unseasonably long mourning for her dead brother. He presumes to call *her* the fool. Why? Her brother's soul is in heaven, Feste observes: "The more fool, madonna, to mourn for your brother's soul, being in heaven. Take away the fool, gentlemen." Visibly amused or not, Olivia immediately turns to her steward Malvolio: "What think you of this fool, Malvolio? Doth he not mend?" That gives Malvolio his cue to berate Feste as a "barren rascal" who can be funny only when other people laugh and "minister occasion to him." Olivia's reply fixes Malvolio in the audience's imagination: "Oh, you are sick of self-love, Malvolio, and taste with a distempered appetite. To be generous, guiltless, and of free disposition is to take those things for birdbolts that you deem cannon bullets" (1.5.56–58, 65, 71–73). Generous, guiltless, and of free disposition are the very things Malvolio (*mal* + *volere* in Italian means "to wish ill") are not. Olivia's reference to his "distempered appetite" suggests he suffers from an imbalance of bodily humors, with black bile in predominance.

It is later in the play, in the scene of midnight revelry, that the label of "Puritan" is put on Malvolio's disposition. The second half of the play seems to query whether the label fits. Malvolio's self-love has already been remarked by Olivia. His opportunism as a time-pleaser soon becomes apparent when he is so easily duped into imagining himself as Olivia's husband and master of her household. Religious dogma might seem to be less an issue, but Maria's references to "bọok," "utter," and "grounds of faith" allude to the Puritan sect's insistence on the written word of God as the

[1] The multiplicity of historical factors behind puritanism can be surveyed in Haller; Hill; Elton; and Todd.

guide to doctrine and behavior. It is a misconstrued letter, after all, that does the presumptious steward in.[2] However astute he may be about "matters of state" when other people are around, Malvolio in private stands as signal proof of Ulysses' observation that "one touch of nature makes the whole world kin" (*Troilus and Cressida* 3.3.169). "By my life, this is my lady's hand," Malvolio exclaims as he takes the letter in hand. He uses an exegete's ingenuity to spell out just which of her body parts best serves his purposes: "These be her very c's, her u's, and her t's; and thus makes she her great P's" (2.5.71–72). So far, so funny. More problematic, to some viewers' eyes at least, is the extremity to which Maria and her cohorts carry their revenge when they lock Malvolio up and try to convince him he is mad. Also troubling to many viewers is Malvolio's refusal of community in the play's last scene. He stalks off swearing, "I'll be revenged on the whole pack of you!" (5.1.355). In historical hindsight, it is a chilling moment. Forty years after the first recorded performance of *Twelfth Night,* the likes of Malvolio succeeded in having the theaters closed and the actors dispersed to more godly ways of making a living.

One group of Puritan dissenters may have left for New England, but during the first decades of the seventeenth century the sect exerted increasing political force at home in England. A number of factors besides the appeal of their doctrine combined to augment their strength, not the least of which was the perfect fit between successful business practices and Puritan principles of literacy, hard work, self-discipline, and strong families. At least as they are portrayed onstage in plays of the early seventeenth century, Puritans are almost always successful merchants. To playwrights they constituted a recognized type, ripe for ridicule. Thanks to the Puritans' devotion to the written word, such stereotypes did not go unchallenged. The number of books published by Puritan writers was huge, as we have seen already with William Prynne and William Perkins. Among these books are reasoned expositions of Puritan doctrine that help us appreciate the excesses of caricatures like Malvolio. The selections that follow begin with a representative stereotype, the character of "A Puritan" printed in later editions of Sir Thomas Overbury's poem *A Wife.* To the social frame set in place in Chapter 5, further selections then add three more frames — religious, economic, and political — for locating puritanism in the culture of early modern England and Malvolio in the design of *Twelfth Night.*

[2] On this point, see Simmons, "A Source for Shakespeare's Malvolio."

SIR THOMAS OVERBURY

From A Wife . . . Whereunto Are Added Many Witty Characters

1614

One of the distinctive genres of the early seventeenth century was books of characters, collections of brief verbal descriptions (usually five hundred words or less) of recognized social types. In their reduction of human complexities to a few quick strokes of the pen, such descriptions would be called caricatures today. The seventeenth-century term *character* plays on the original sense of the word as a written sign (from the Greek *charassein,* to make sharp or engrave) whereby a person might be known. Our more abstract sense of *character* has lost this metonymy. In seventeenth-century character books, Puritans make a regular appearance alongside stage-players. Among the most pointed characters of a Puritan is one added to the fifth edition of Sir Thomas Overbury's *A Wife . . . Whereunto Are Added Many Witty Characters and Conceited News, Written by Himself and Other Learned Gentlemen His Friends* (1614). Although it is questionable whether "A Puritan" is by Overbury or by one of his friends, the point of view from which the caricature is drawn is pointedly that of a learned gentleman who sets himself up as the opposite of a Puritan. After taking a degree at Oxford in 1598, Sir Thomas Overbury (1581–1613) studied law at the Middle Temple. His literary talents were approved by no less a critic than Ben Jonson, but Overbury's main ambitions were political. Having served for a time as an ambassador, he ended his political career — and his life — by openly opposing the marriage of Robert Carr, one of James I's favorites, to Lady Frances Howard. To a gentleman like Overbury, "A Puritan" is perversity personified. Whatever most men approve, a Puritan condemns.

A Puritan

Is a diseased piece of Apocrypha,[1] bind him to the Bible, and he corrupts the whole text; ignorance, and fat feed, are his founders, his nurses, railings, rabbis, and round breeches:[2] his life is but a borrowed blast of wind; for between two religions, as between two doors, he is ever whistling. Truly whose child he is, is yet unknown; for willingly his faith allows no father, only thus far his pedigree is found, Bragger and he flourished about a time first; his fiery zeal keeps him continual costive,[3] which withers him into his

[1] **Apocrypha:** non-canonical books of the Bible. [2] **round breeches:** priests. [3] **costive:** constipated.

Sir Thomas Overbury, *A Wife . . . Whereunto Are Added Many Witty Characters* (London: Lawrence Lisle, 1614), F1–F1v.

own translation, and till he eat a schoolman,[4] he is hidebound; he ever prays against non-residents,[5] but is himself the greatest discontinuer, for he never keeps near his text: anything that the law allows, but marriage and March beer,[6] he murmurs at: what it disallows, and holds dangerous, makes him a discipline. Where the gate stands open, he is ever seeking a stile: and where his learning ought to climb, he creeps through; give him advice, you run into "traditions," and urge a modest course, he cries out "councils."[7] His greatest care, is to condemn obedience, his last care to serve God, handsomely and cleanly. He is now become so cross a kind of teaching, that should the Church enjoin clean shirts, he wore lousy;[8] more sense than single prayers is not his, nor more in those, than still the same petitions; from which he either fears a learned faith, or doubts God understands not at first hearing. Show him a ring, he runs back like a bear; and hates square dealing as allied to caps. A pair of organs blow him out o' the parish, and are the only glister pipes[9] to cool him. Where the meat is best, there he confutes most; for his arguing is but the efficacy of his eating, good bits he holds breeds good positions, and the Pope he best concludes against in plum broth.[10] He is often drunk, but not as we are, temporally, nor can his sleep then cure him, for the fumes of his ambition make his very soul reel, and that small beer that should allay him (silence) keeps him more surfeited, and makes his heat break out in private houses. Women and lawyers are his best disciples, the one next fruit, longs for forbidden doctrine, the other to maintain forbidden titles, both which he sows amongst them. Honest he dare not be, for that loves order; yet if he can be brought to ceremony, and made but master of it, he is converted.

[4] **schoolman:** medieval scholastic. [5] **non-residents:** priests who do not live in the parishes to which they are assigned, but pass the duties to others. [6] **March beer:** strong ale. [7] **"councils":** legislative sessions at which issues of doctrine are decided. [8] **lousy:** full of vermin, dirty. [9] **glister pipes:** clyster pipes, enemas. [10] **plum broth:** thick soup made with beef and fruits, traditionally a Christmas dish.

Religion

WILLIAM BRADSHAW

From English Puritanism

1605

The counter to caricatures like that in Overbury's *A Wife* came from Puritans themselves. William Bradshaw (1571–1618) was in a good position to write such a book, since he was moderate in his religious views and counted among his friends and admirers prominent authorities within the Church of England, such as Joseph Hall (1574–1656), an emissary of King James, bishop of first Exeter and then Norwich, and the originator of the character book in English. Bradshaw's *English Puritanism,* published anonymously in Holland in 1605, was reissued in a Latin translation in 1610 and was republished in English in 1640 and 1641, just as Puritan forces were on the verge of taking over the government of England. The very first words in Bradshaw's treatise are an acknowledgment that the written word of God stands as the ultimate authority over all religious practices. On the subject of church government, however, Bradshaw does not cite scripture. He believes in local government by congregations themselves, but defers to duly constituted civil authority. Hence the moderateness of Bradshaw's position and his success as an apologist for Puritan doctrine on forms of worship. Several of Bradshaw's points of doctrine bear on Malvolio's case: Puritans, says Bradshaw, abhor idolatrous rites and ceremonies (of which Twelfth Night customs were, in many people's eyes, an example), refuse to allow their tithe money to be used to maintain the lavish display of their social superiors in religious ceremonies, insist that "interpreting the written word of God" is the most important function of a pastor or minister, maintain that tradesmen and craftsmen have more right to be church leaders than "persons both ignorant of religion and all good letters," and believe that in judging a person's behavior judicial authorities should not "proceed to molest any man upon secret suggestions, private suspicion, or uncertain fame" or "scorn, deride, taunt, and revile him with odious and contumelious speeches."

To the indifferent[1] reader:

It cannot be unknown unto them that know anything that those Christians in this realm which are called by the odious and vile name of Puritans, are accused by the prelates to the king's majesty and the state to maintain

[1] **indifferent:** unprejudiced.

William Bradshaw, *English Puritanism* (1605), ed. Lawrence A. Sasek, in *Images of English Puritanism* (Baton Rouge: Louisiana State University Press, 1989), 81–94.

many absurd, erroneous, schismatical, and heretical opinions, concerning religion, church government and the civil magistracy. Which hath moved me to collect (as near as I could) the chiefest of them, and to send them naked to the view of all men that they may see what is the worst that the worst of them hold. It is not my part to prove and justify them. Those that accuse and condemn them must in all reason and equity prove their accusation, or else bear the name of unchristian slanderers. I am not ignorant that they lay other opinions (yea some clean contradictory to these) to the charge of these men, the falsehood whereof we shall (it is to be doubted) have more and more occasion to detect. In the meantime all enemies of divine truth shall find, that to obscure the same with calumniations and untruths, is but to hide a fire with laying dry straw or tow upon it. But thou mayest herein observe, what a terrible popedom and primacy these rigid Presbyterians desire. And with what painted bugbears and scarecrows, the prelates[2] go about to fright the states of this kingdom withal. Who will no doubt one day see, how their wisdoms are abused. Farewell.

Chapter 1

Concerning Religion or the Worship of God in General

Imprimis, They hold and maintain that the word of God contained in the writings of the prophets and apostles, is of absolute perfection, given by Christ the head of the church, to be unto the same, the sole canon and rule of all matters of religion, and the worship and service of God whatsoever. And that whatsoever done in the same service and worship cannot be justified by the said word, is unlawful. And therefore that it is a sin, to force any Christian to do any act of religion or divine service, that cannot evidently be warranted by the same.

2. They hold that all ecclesiastical actions invented and devised by man, are utterly to be excluded out of the exercises of religion. Especially such actions as are famous and notorious mysteries of an idolatrous religion, and in doing whereof, the true religion is conformed (whether in whole or in part) to idolatry and superstition.

3. They hold that all outward means instituted and set apart to express and set forth the inward worship of God, are parts of divine worship and that not only all moral actions but all typical rites and figures ordained to shadow forth in the solemn worship and service of God, any spiritual or

[2] **prelates:** priests of the Church of England.

religious act or habit in the mind of man, are special parts of the same, and therefore that every such act ought evidently to be prescribed by the word of God, or else ought not to be done. It being a sin to perform any other worship to God, whether external or internal, moral or ceremonial, in whole or in part, than that which God himself requires in his word.

4. They hold it to be gross superstition, for any mortal man to institute and ordain as parts of divine worship, any mystical rite and ceremony of religion whatsoever, and to mingle the same with the divine rites and mysteries of God's ordinance. But they hold it to be high presumption to institute and bring into divine worship such rites and ceremonies of religion, as are acknowledged to be no parts of divine worship at all, but only of civil worship and honor. For they that shall require to have performed unto themselves a ceremonial obedience, service and worship, consisting in rites of religion to be done at that very instant that God is solemnly served and worshiped, and even in the same worship make both themselves and God also an idol. So that they judge it a far more fearful sin to add unto, and to use in the worship and service of God or any part thereof such mystical rites and ceremonies as they esteem to be no parts or parcels of God's worship at all, than such as in a vain and ignorant superstition, they imagine and conceive to be parts thereof.

5. They hold that every act or action appropriated and set apart to divine service and worship, whether moral or ceremonial, real or typical, ought to bring special honor unto God and therefore that every such act ought to be apparently commanded in the word of God, either expressly, or by necessary consequent.

6. They hold that all actions whether moral or ceremonial appropriated to religious or spiritual persons, functions, or actions, either are or ought to be religious and spiritual. And therefore either are or ought to be instituted immediately by God, who alone is the author and institutor of all religious and spiritual actions, and things, whether internal or external, moral or ceremonial.

Chapter 2

Concerning the Church

1. They hold and maintain that every company, congregation or assembly of men, ordinarily joining together in true worship of God, is a true visible church of Christ; and that the same title is improperly attributed to any other convocations, synods, societies, combinations, or assemblies whatsoever.

2. They hold that all such churches or congregations, communicating after that manner together, in divine worship, are in all ecclesiastical matters equal, and of the same power and authority, and that by the word and will of God they ought to have the same spiritual privileges, prerogatives, officers, administrations, orders, and forms of divine worship.

3. They hold that Christ Jesus hath not subjected an church or congregation of His, to any other superior ecclesiastical jurisdiction, than unto that which is within itself. So that if a whole church or congregation shall err, in any matters of faith or religion, no other churches or spiritual church officers have (by any warrant from the word of God) power to censure, punish, or control the same: but are only to counsel and advise the same, and so to leave their souls to the immediate judgement of Christ, and their bodies to the sword and power of the civil magistrate, who alone upon earth hath power to punish a whole church or congregation.

4. They hold that every established church or congregation ought to have her own spiritual officers and ministers, resident with her, and those such, as are enjoined by Christ in the New Testament and no other.

5. They hold that every established church ought (as a special prerogative wherewith she is endowed by Christ) to have power and liberty to elect and choose their own spiritual and ecclesiastical officers, and that it is a greater wrong to have any such force upon them against their wills, than if they should force upon men wives, or upon women husbands, against their will and liking.

6. They hold that if in this choice any particular churches shall err, that none upon earth but the civil magistrate hath power to control or correct them for it, and that though it be not lawful for him to take away this power from them, yet when they or any of them, shall apparently abuse the same, he stands bound by the law of God, and by virtue of his office (grounded upon the same,) to punish them severely for it, and to force them under civil mulcts[3] to make better choice. . . .

9. They hold that though one church is not to differ from another in any spiritual, ecclesiastical, or religious matters whatsoever, but are to be equal and alike, yet that they may differ and one excel another in outward civil circumstances, of place, time, person etc. So that although they hold that those congregations of which kings and nobles make themselves members, ought to have the same ecclesiastical officers, ministry, worship, sacraments, ceremonies, and form of divine worship, that the basest congregation in the country hath, and no other, yet they hold also that as their persons in civil

[3] **mulcts:** fines or penalties.

respects excel, so in the exercises of religion in civil matters they may excel other assemblies. Their chapels, and seats may be gorgeously set forth with rich arras and tapestry, their fonts may be of silver, their communion tables of ivory and if they will covered with gold. The cup out of which they drink the sacramental blood of Christ may be of beaten gold set about with diamonds. Their ministers may be clothed in silk and velvet, so themselves will maintain them in that manner, otherwise, they think it absurd and against common reason, that other base and inferior congregations must by ecclesiastical tithes, and oblations[4] maintain, the silken and velvet suits and lordly retinue of the ministers and ecclesiastical officers of princes and nobles

10. They hold that the laws, orders, and ecclesiastical jurisdiction of the visible churches of Christ, if they be lawful and warrantable by the word of God, are no ways repugnant to any civil state whatsoever, whether monarchical, aristocratical, or democratical, but do tend to the further establishing and advancing, of the rights and prerogatives of all and every of them. And they renounce and abhor from their souls all such ecclesiastical jurisdiction or policy, that is any way repugnant and derogatory to any of them, especially to the monarchical state, which they acknowledge to be the best kind of civil government for this kingdom. . . .

Chapter 3

Concerning the Ministers of the Word

1. They hold that the pastors of particular congregations are, or ought to be the highest spiritual officers in the church, over whom, (by any divine ordinance) there is no superior pastor but only Jesus Christ; and that they are led by the spirit of Antichrist, that arrogate or take upon themselves to be pastors of pastors. . . .

6. They hold that the highest and supreme office and authority of the pastor, is to preach the gospel solemnly and publicly to the congregation, by interpreting the written word of God, and applying the same by exhortation and reproof unto them. They hold that this was the greatest work that Christ and his apostles did, and that whosoever is thought worthy and fit to exercise this authority, cannot be thought unfit and unworthy to exercise any other spiritual or ecclesiastical authority whatsoever.

7. They hold that the pastor or minister of the word, is not to teach any doctrine unto the church, grounded upon his own judgement or opinion, or upon the judgement or opinion of any or all the men in the world. But only

[4] **oblations:** offerings.

that truth, that he is able to demonstrate and prove evidently, and apparently, by the word of God soundly interpreted, and that the people are not bound to believe any doctrine of religion or divinity whatsoever, upon any ground whatsoever, except it be apparently justified by the word, or by necessary consequent deduced from the same.

8. They hold that in interpreting the scriptures, and opening the sense of them, he ought to follow those rules only that are followed in finding out the meaning of other writings, to wit, by weighing the propriety of the tongue wherein they are written, by weighing the circumstance of the place, by comparing one place with another, and by considering what is properly spoken, and what tropically[5] or figuratively. And they hold it unlawful for the pastor to obtrude upon his people a sense of any part of the divine word, for which he hath no other ground but the bare testimonies of men, and that it is better for the people to be content to be ignorant of the meaning of such difficult places, than to hang their faith in any matter in this case upon the bare testimony of man.

9. They hold that the people of God ought not to acknowledge any such for their pastors as are not able by preaching, to interpret and apply the word of God unto them in manner and form aforesaid. And therefore that no ignorant and sole reading priests are to be reputed the ministers of Jesus Christ, who sendeth none into his ministry and service, but such as he adorneth in some measure with spiritual gifts. And they cannot be persuaded that the faculty of reading in one's mother tongue the scriptures etc. which any ordinary Turk or infidel hath, can be called in any congruity of speech a ministerial gift of Christ. . . .

Chapter 4

Concerning the Elders

1. For as much as through the malice of Satan, there are and will be in the best churches many disorders and scandals committed, that redound to the reproach of the gospel and are a stumbling block to many both without and within the church, and sith they judge it repugnant to the word of God, that any minister should be a sole ruler and as it were a Pope so much as in one parish, (much more that he should be one over a whole diocese, province or nation) they hold that by God's ordinance the congregation should make choice of other officers, as assistants unto the ministers in the spiritual regiment of the congregation who are by office jointly with the ministers of the

[5] **tropically:** as a trope, or figure of speech.

word to be as monitors and overseers of the manners and conversation[6] of all the congregation, and one of another: that so everyone may be more wary of their ways, and that the pastors and doctors may better attend to prayer and doctrine, and by their means may be made better acquainted with the estate of the people, when others' eyes besides their own shall wake, and watch over them.

2. They hold that such only are to be chosen to this office, as are the gravest, honestest, discreetest, best grounded in religion, and the ancientest professors thereof in the congregation, such as the whole congregation do approve of and respect, for their wisdom, holiness, and honesty, and such also (if it be possible) as are of civil note and respect in the world, and able (without any burden to the church) to maintain themselves, either by their lands, or any other honest civil trade of life. Neither do they think it so much disgrace to the policy of the church, that tradesmen and artificers,[7] (endowed with such qualities as are above specified) should be admitted to be overseers of the church as it is that persons both ignorant of religion and all good letters, and in all respects for person, quality, and state, as base and vile, as the basest in the congregation, should be admitted to be pastors and teachers of a congregation. And if it be apparent that God (who always blesseth his own ordinances) doth often even in the eyes of kings and nobles, make honorable the ministers and pastors of his churches upon which he hath bestowed spiritual gifts and graces though for birth, education, presence, outward state, and maintenance they be most base and contemptible, so he will as well in the eyes of all holy men, make this office, which is many degrees inferior to the other, precious, and honorable, even for the divine calling and ordinance sake.

Chapter 5

Concerning the Censures of the Church

1. They hold that the spiritual keys of the church are by Christ, committed to the aforesaid spiritual officers and governors, and unto none other: which keys they hold that they are not to be put to this use, to lock up the crowns, swords or scepters, of princes and civil states, or the civil rights, prerogatives, and immunities, of civil subjects in the things of this life, or to use them as picklocks to open withal, men's treasuries and coffers, or as keys of prisons, to shut up the bodies of men; for they think that such a power and authority

[6] **conversation:** social relations. [7] **artificers:** craftsmen.

ecclesiastical is fit only for the Antichrist of Rome and the consecrated governors of his synagogues, who having no word of God which is the sword of the spirit, to defend his and their usurped jurisdiction, over the Christian world, doth unlawfully usurp the lawful civil sword and power of the monarchs and princes of the earth, thereby forcing men to subject themselves to his spiritual vassalage and service and abusing thereby the spiritual keys and jurisdiction of the church.

2. They hold that by virtue of these keys, they are not to make any curious inquisitions into the secret or hidden vices or crimes of men, extorting from them a confession of those faults that are concealed from themselves and others: or to proceed to molest any man upon secret suggestions, private suspicion, or uncertain fame, or for such crimes as are in question whether they be crimes or no; but they are to proceed, only against evident and apparent crimes, such as are either granted to be such of all civil honest men: or of all true Christians, or at least such, as they are able, by evidence of the word of God, to convince to be sins, to the conscience of the offender; as also such as have been either publicly committed, or having been committed in secret, are by some good means brought to light, and which the delinquent denying, they are able by honest, and sufficient testimony to prove against him.

3. They hold that when he that hath committed a scandalous crime cometh before them and is convinced of the same, they ought not (after the manner of our ecclesiastical courts) scorn, deride, taunt, and revile him, with odious and contumelious[8] speeches, eye him with big and stern looks, procure proctors to make personal invectives against him, make him dance attendance from court day to court day, and from term to term, frowning at him in presence, and laughing at him behind his back: but they are (though he be never so obstinate and perverse) to use him brotherly, not giving the least personal reproaches, or threats, (but laying open unto him the nature of his sin by the light of God's word) are only by denouncing the judgments of God against him, to terrify him, and so to move him to repentance.

4. They hold that if the party offending be their civil superior, that then they are to use even throughout the whole carriage of their censure, all civil compliments, offices, and reverence due unto him, that they are not to presume to convent him before them, but are themselves to go in all civil and humble manner unto him, to stand bare before him, to bow unto him, to give him all civil titles belonging unto him; and if he be a king and supreme ruler, they are to kneel down before him, and in the humblest manner to

[8] **contumelious:** contemptuous, insolent.

censure his faults; so that he may see apparently that they are not carried with the least spice of malice against his person, but only with zeal of the health and salvation of his soul. . . .

Chapter 6

Concerning the Civil Magistrate

1. They hold that the civil magistrate as he is a civil magistrate hath and ought to have supreme power over all the churches within his dominions, in all causes whatsoever. And yet they hold that as he is a Christian he is a member of some one particular congregation, and ought to be as subject to the spiritual regiment thereof prescribed by Christ in his word, as the meanest subject in the kingdom, and they hold that this subjection is no more derogatory to his supremacy, than the subjection of his body in sickness to physicians, can be said to be derogatory thereunto.

2. They hold that those civil magistrates are the greatest enemies to their own supremacy, that in whole or in part, communicate the virtue and power thereof, to any ecclesiastical officers. And that there cannot be imagined by the wit of man a more direct means to checkmate the same, than to make them lords and princes upon earth, to invest them with civil jurisdiction and authority, and to conform the state and limits of their jurisdiction to the state of kings, and bounds of kingdoms.

3. They hold that there should be no ecclesiastical officer in the church so high, but that he ought to be subject unto, and punishable by the meanest civil officer in a kingdom, city, or town, not only for common crimes, but even for the abuse of their ecclesiastical offices, yea they hold that they ought to be more punishable than any other subject whatsoever, if they shall offend against either civil or ecclesiastical laws.

4. They hold that the civil magistrate is to punish with all severity the ecclesiastical officers of churches, if they shall intrude upon the rights and prerogatives of the civil authority and magistracy, and shall pass those bounds and limits that Christ hath prescribed unto them in his word.

5. They hold that the Pope is that Antichrist, and therefore that Antichrist because being but an ecclesiastical officer he doth in the height of the pride of his heart make claim unto and usurp the supremacy of the kings and civil rulers of the earth. And they hold that all defenders of the popish faith, all endeavors of reconcilement with that church, all plotters for toleration of the popish religion, all countenancers and maintainers of seminary priests and professed Catholics, and all deniers that the Pope is that Antichrist are secret enemies to the king's supremacy.

6. They hold that all archbishops, bishops, deans, officials, etc. have their offices and functions only by will and pleasure of the king and civil states of this realm, and they hold that whosoever holdeth that the king may not without sin remove these offices out of the church, and dispose of their temporalities and maintenance according to his own pleasure, or that these offices are *jure divino,* and not only or merely *jure humano:*[9] that all such deny a principal part of the king's supremacy.

7. They hold that not one of these opinions can be proved to be contrary to the word of God, and that if they might have leave that they are able to answer all that hath been written against any one of them.

[9] *jure divino . . . jure humano:* under divine law . . . under human law.

RICHARD BANCROFT

From A Survey of the Pretended Holy Discipline *1593*

Malvolio never shows himself more the Puritan than when he "cons state without book" — that is to say, memorizes the "text" of his betters' behavior — and analyzes the forged letter from Olivia phrase by phrase and letter by letter. William Bradshaw's deference to "the absolute perfection" of the written word of God in *English Puritanism* helps us to frame Malvolio's *logophilia,* his love of The Word, as part of the satire. Lest we have doubts, Richard Bancroft in his *A Survey of the Pretended Holy Discipline* (1593) singles out Puritan misinterpretation of the Bible for pointed condemnation. Bancroft (1544–1610) emerged from a Puritan-influenced education at Cambridge to a career as a vigorous defender of the Church of England — a career that led to his becoming Archbishop of Canterbury, the primate of the Church of England, in 1604 and Chancellor of the University of Oxford in 1608. In the course of this career Bancroft became ever more severe in his response to Puritanism. When a series of anti-episcopal pamphlets began to appear from the pen of "Martin Marprelate," it was supposedly Bancroft who came up with the idea of replying in like satirical vein and enlisted the talents of Thomas Nash and others. *A Survey of the Pretended Holy Discipline* is Bancroft's own response to a manifesto of Puritan principles in a treatise "Of Discipline" that William Perkins, among others, had authored. (On Perkins see Chapter 5.) Concerning Puritan justifications for their practices, Bancroft observes, "There was never anything hitherto so fondly devised but the authors of it did ever pretend they had scripture for it." To justify his desire to become master of Lady Olivia's household, Malvolio becomes a textual scholar who tops them all.

Unto these caterbrawls[1] and pitiful distractions, I might add a great heap of other confusions, all of them proceeding from such intolerable presumption, as is used in the behalf of that minion, by the perverting and false interpretation of the sacred scriptures. But I have been too tedious already in this matter, and therefore to grow towards an end of it. Of all the places of Scripture, which they pretend, to make for such parts of their discipline, as is disliked by the Church of England, as either for their Jewish Sanhedrin,[2] their parish bishops,[3] their unpriestly aldermen, with their priestly functions,[4] their Genevian presbyteries, or elderships.[5] Of all the places of scripture, I say, which they bring for that purpose, I profess unto you, as in the presence of God, that I cannot find any one, but by one means or other, they have cast such a color upon it, as was never known in the church of Christ, amongst all the ancient godly fathers, from the apostles' times, till these our troublesome and presumptuous days.

Well, it is not enough for men to allege scriptures, except they bring the true meaning of the scriptures. For as Saint Augustine sayeth, heresies and erroneous opinions do not otherwise spring and grow up, *"nisi dum scriptura bona intelliguntur non bene et quod in eis non bene intelligitur, etiam temere and audaciter asseritur"* (but when the good scriptures are not well understood, and because that which is not well understood in them is, notwithstanding, rashly and boldly affirmed to be the meaning of them). There was never anything hitherto so fondly devised, but the authors of it did ever pretend they had scripture for it. For else, sayeth Saint Jerome, the garrulity of such persons, *"non haberet fidem"* (would never have won any credit). All sects and schisms have risen, for the most part, upon discontentment. And this a man may observe, in the writings of the ancient fathers, that as many men do marry, and so beget children before they know how to keep them, so commonly it hath fallen out in new and strange opinions. Through pride and vanity, they have been rashly begotten, before the authors of them did know how to maintain them. Marry, when once they had engaged their credits, by broaching[6] of this and that, then they ever labored, not to submit themselves and their opinions unto the truth, but *"sed ut sibi scripturas ipsi subicerent"* ("but," as Augustine sayeth, "that they might bring the scriptures, to be in subjection to them"). Of the which kind of men, Saint Hilary, also speaking,

[1] **caterbrawls:** rollicking dances. [2] **Sanhedrin:** body of men with judicial as well as religious powers. [3] **parish bishops:** Puritans wished to invest church government, not in the episcopal council of bishops, but in local churches. [4] **unpriestly . . . functions:** laymen in the reformed church who exercise authority reserved to priests in the Church of England. [5] **Genevian . . . elderships:** church government by presbyters (literally, "elder men"). [6] **broaching:** introducing into conversation.

Richard Bancroft, *A Survey of the Pretended Holy Discipline* (London: John Wolfe, 1593), 414–16.

sayeth, that they interpret the scriptures, *"pro voluntatis sue sensu"* (according to such a sense as may serve their turns, etc.) Which is, as the same Hilary showeth in another place, *"non expectare"* (not to expect) for the understanding of those things, which are spoken in the scriptures, out of the words themselves, *"sed imponere"* (but to impose) a meaning upon them, *"non refirre sed adferre"* (not to deliver the true sense of them, but to bring a sense of their own), not a yielding to the words, but a kind of compulsion, enforcement, or violence offered, to make that to seem to be contained in them, *"quod ante lectionem presumpserit intelligendum"* (which they presumed should be understood by them before they read them).

Whosoever do deal with the scriptures in this sort, well they may speak proud things, exalt themselves, promise mountains, brag of the prophets, of Christ, of his apostles, and *verisimilia mentiri,*[7] as many such men in former times have done. Whereby for a season some may be deceived, but yet as Saint Cyprian sayeth, *"mendacia non diu fallunt"* (it [mendacity] will come to pass, as always it hath done hitherto), that after a short time the covering of their devices, with so many slights and falsehoods, groweth to be detected. And then they are paid to their utter discredit, the wages and full hire of such unrighteous dealing.

[7] ***verisimilia mentiri:*** seemingly true lies.

Economics

ROBERT CLEAVER AND JOHN DOD

From A Godly Form of Household Government *1614*

William Harrison, writing in 1577, divided his fellow Englishmen into four "sorts" or "orders": (1) nobility and other gentlemen whose wealth is in land, (2) inhabitants of cities and towns who earn their living by plying a trade or practicing a profession, (3) yeomen farmers who own or lease the land they work, and (4) laborers who own nothing themselves and sell their services to others.[1] If Puritanism found a particularly secure base among the third sort of people, among merchants and professionals, it was because the principles of righteousness happened to be good for business. More than three centuries before Max Weber argued that connection in *The Protestant Ethic and the Rise of Capitalism,* Robert Cleaver and John Dod were illustrating the point in one of the all-time best-sellers of early modern England. *A Godly Form of Household Government: For the Ordering of Private Families According to the Direction of God's Word,* orig-

[1] William Harrison, *The Description of England,* ed. George Edelen (Ithaca: Cornell University Press, 1968), 94.

inally authored by Cleaver alone, went through two printings in its first edition in 1598, followed by later reprintings in 1600, 1603, 1610, and 1612 and, with additions by John Dod, in 1614, 1621, and 1624. The book was at the peak of its popularity during the very years when *Twelfth Night* was being acted. While Orsino was reading Italian romances Malvolio was reading *A Godly Form of Household Government.* Malvolio's behavior illustrates many of the major arguments of Cleaver and Dod's book, with respect not only to household management but to the virtues of hard work in contrast with gentlemanly sloth. Everyone, Cleaver and Dod maintain, needs a vocation. Just what is Sir Toby's vocation? Or Sir Andrew's? Cleaver and Dod also counsel their readers to go for the main chance when opportunity presents itself. Malvolio does just that — and forgets all about the evils of gentlemanly sloth as he imagines himself the lord of Lady Olivia's manor, languishing in his dressing gown (2.5.39).

From *A Godly Form of Household Government*

A household is as it were a little commonwealth, by the good government whereof, God's glory may be advanced, and the commonwealth, which standest of several families, benefitted; and all that live in that family receive much comfort and commodity. . . .

That every man must apply himself to some study and calling, is so known, that it needeth no proof: "In the sweat of thy brows thou shalt eat thy bread etc." [Genesis 3:19]. Which condemneth all such as live off the labors of other men, and themselves take no pains or travail, do no good in the world, benefit not human society any way, but devour the good creatures of the earth, which indeed belong to them that take all the pains. In this rank do a number of Gentiles[2] in the world march, devising gay toys, which might well be spared, who are but unprofitable burdens of the earth, that fill up number like ciphers,[3] who glory in their shame, that is, in their ease, pleasures, and bravery,[4] whereof (if they knew thereto a man was born) they would be ashamed.

These be they for whose maintenance in their jollity, a number are fain to toil very hardly, fare meanly, and spend their strength to the very skin and bones, and yet can get but a slender recompence, through their unmerciful exactions. But enough of them: to return. The good government of a house must be none of these; but he must have a calling that is good, honest, and

[2] **Gentiles:** irreligious people. [3] **ciphers:** zeroes. [4] **bravery:** bravado, ostentation.

Robert Cleaver and John Dod, *A Godly Form of Household Government: For the Ordering of Private Families According to the Direction of God's Word* (London: Thomas Man, 1614), sigs. A7, D7v–D8v, E4v–E5v.

lawful, not only gainful to himself, but also holy and profitable to the society of mankind: For thus much doth Saint Paul comprehend within the compass of his words, (Ephes[ians] 24:28), "But let him labor the thing that is good."

It is not enough to have a calling though it be never so good, but it must be followed: So as it may bring in maintenance, for thee and thine, such as is meet for thy estate.[5]

But how must it be followed? First, with diligence: for as Solomon saith, (Prover[bs] 18[:9]) "He that carrieth himself slothfully, or loosely in his business, is the brother of a great waster." That is, he is another waster: and doth as much as unthrift, or spend-good.

To diligence belongeth the blessing: (Prov[erbs].10:4) "The hand of the diligent maketh rich" and (chap[ter] 12.:11) "He that tilleth his land shall be satisfied with meat." Yea, and a large blessing: "The soul of the diligent shall be fatted," that is, he shall have abundantly. And lest that any should say, that in some calling a man may well thrive, but not in mine, it is said, (Prov[erbs] 14:23) "In all labor," that is, diligent following thy calling. Moreover, this diligence will bring a man to renown: (Prov[erbs] 22:29) "Thou seest that a diligent man in his business standeth before kings, etc." . . .

It is not wisdom to carry a higher port and countenance in the world than a man's ability will warrant. Such shall be envied: so long as they do bear it out by the hard edge, they shall be laid at for charges, and if through necessity in the end they be fain to yield, they shall be scorned of their enviers, and little pitied of all others. Wherefore it is wisdom rather to bear a low sail, and to keep within compass, and rather to come short of that thou mightest do, remembering that which is: (Pro[verbs] 12:9) "He that is despised, and is his own man, is better than he that boasteth himself, and lacks bread."

Again, as they which love to perk aloft, and do desire to be carried with a full sail by the wind (a) of ambition, and (b) vainglory, rather than to have sea room, do oftentimes rush upon the rocks of want, and there stick till they sink: so they, which in fear of such rocks choose to ride with half or quarter sail, where they have not room at will, are most safe from danger, and may more conveniently provide against a tempest. Yea, they may so sail, that when God shall remove them hence, they shall not be constrained to leave their children to the wide world, which thing nature bindeth a man to have a care of.

Another rule may be drawn out of that which is Prov[erbs] 10:5, "A wise son gathereth in summer: but he that sleepeth in harvest is the son of confusion." Where he teacheth, that when a man spieth an opportunity of honest

[5] **estate:** social rank

gain and commodity, he is to follow that while the time serveth: but he that for a small matter, letteth slip occasions, and reckoneth of his time, and that time, this day, and that day, thinking then to have more fit opportunity, that will bring all to nothing.

The Politics of Mirth

To the audience gathered in Middle Temple Hall on February 2, 1602, it was not Malvolio's self-love, opportunism, or literal-mindedness that most marked him as "a kind of purtian" but his antipathy to revelry. Sir Toby's retort to Malvolio's scoldings says it all: "Dost thou think because thou art virtuous, there shall be no more cakes and ale?" (2.3.95–96). The traditional pastimes of "merry old England," as we have seen in Chapter 5, became a flash point in the standoff between Puritans and more moderate adherents of the Church of England. Most festivals that brought communities together for feasting, games, dancing, and play watching were, like Twelfth Night, tied to the Catholic liturgical calendar. Hence the suspicions of Protestants. Under the young Edward VI, Protestant extremists succeeded in getting many of these traditional activities banned. The restoration of the activities under the Catholic Queen Mary was followed by a policy of moderation and local choice during the long reign of Elizabeth.

An evocation of these communal celebrations can be found in an anonymous broadside ballad printed in 1569, "Good Fellows Must Go Learn to Dance" (see Figure 27). The occasion at hand is a "bride-ale," a gathering of all and sundry in which *bride* and *ale* have not yet merged into our own blander word *bridal.* The woodcut in the upper left features an outsized "canikin," labeled in vertical type, for quaffing outsized portions of ale. Drinking, dancing, and jokes about the bridegroom's anxieties are the subjects the purchaser of the broadside sheet is invited to sing about. As usual with broadside ballads, no tune is printed, since the purchaser is supposed to know the tune from hearing it, just as he or she is supposed to know drinking, dancing, and joking from doing them with his or her own body. The ballad ends with an affirmation of neighborliness:

> Draw to dancing, neighbors all,
> good fellowship is best-a.
> It skills not if we take a fall
> in honoring this fest-a.

Against such occasions, Puritan writers throughout Elizabeth's reign grumbled in print. With Puritan sentiment ever more insistent, the Stuart

A Newe Ballade intytuled/

Good Fellowes must go learne to Daunce.

GOod fellowes must go learne to daunce,
the brydeall is full nere a:
There is a brall come out of Fraunce,
the tryxt ye harde this yeare a.
For I must leape and thou must hoppe,
and we must turne all thre a:
The fourth must bounce it lyke a toppe,
and so we shall a gree a.
I praye thee Mynstrell make no stoppe,
for we wyll merye be a.

The Brydegrome would giue twentie pounde,
the mariage daye were paste a:
ye knowe whyles louers are vnbounde,
the knotte is slypper faste a.
A better man maye come in place,
and take the Bryde awaye a.
God send our wilkin better grace,
our pretie Tom doth saye a.
God Vycar aske the banes apace,
and haste the mariage daye a.

A bande of belles in Bauderycke wyse,
woulde decke vs in our kynde a:
A shurte after the Morrice guyse,
to flounce it in the wynde a.
A wyffler for to make the waye,
and maye brought in with all a:
Is brauer then the Sunne I saye,
and passeth round or brall a.
For we wyll tripe so tricke and gaye,
that we wyll passe them all a.

Drawe to dauncinge neyghboures all
good fellowshyppe is best a:
It skylles not yf we take a fall,
in honoringe this feste a.
The Brpde wyll thanke vs for oure glee,
the worlde wyll vs beholde a:
O where shall all this dauncinge bee,
in Kent or at cotsolde a.
Oure Lorde doth knowe then axe not mee,
and so my tale is tolde a.

ADewe sweete harte, a dewe
Syth we must parte,
To lose the loue of you,
It greues my harte.
Once againe come kysse me
syth I so long must mys thee
[..]inge harte shall wyshe thee,
To ease me of my smarte.
And thoughe I nowe do leaue thee,
It wyll I not deceaue thee,
But come againe and wedde thee,
Euen for thy iust desarte.

Syr Launcelotte comes againe syr,
So men do saye:
Tom tosse wyll sayle to Spayne sir,
By Tyborne awaye.
Subtoll simme wyll haue her.
Thoughe wyttie watte do craue her,
yet cuttinge clowne shall saue her,
Unlesse he lose his praye.
And though ye be so wyle ye,
And she do loke so hyle ye:
At length she wyll begyle ye,
An[illegible]he best ye maye.

I[illegible]is so coye sir,
Sh[illegible]be solde,
W[illegible]s her ioye sir,
T[illegible]tolde:
Ra[illegible] wyll not blade it,
Jack[illegible]r wyll not swade it,
The Wyllbowes are not made it,
Therof ye maye be bolde.
Although ye now haue cought her,
ye wyll repent here after,
For farder ye haue sought her,
Then I haue thought ye would.

Finis.

Imprinted at London, in Fletestrete at the signe of the Faucon, by wylliam Gryffith, and are to be solde at his shoppe in S. Dunstones Churchyearde. 1569.

FIGURE 27 *A Broadside Bride-Ale: "Good Fellows Must Go Learn to Dance" (1569).*

monarch James I found it necessary to defend the pastimes traditional on Sunday afternoons in a proclamation that came to be known as "The King's Book of Sports." When Charles I reissued the statement in 1633, a crisis of major proportions ensued. Archbishop William Laud (1573–1645) required ministers to read the document aloud from their pulpits. For reformist-minded ministers, this order from above came to stand for royal prerogative over individual conscience. Reactions to the 1633 reissue of "The King's Book of Sports" resulted in Laud's downfall and, ultimately, the beheading of Charles I. In the meantime, as Leah Marcus has shown, poets and playwrights had entered the fray in poems, masques, and playscripts. *Twelfth Night* takes its place as an early salvo on the side of merrymaking.

PHILIP STUBBES

From The Anatomy of Abuses in Ailgna *1583*

It is a supreme irony that Philip Stubbes, inveterate opponent of plays on the public stage, should be the author of one of the most-quoted phrases about the stage in all of early modern culture: "these goodly pageants being done, every mate sorts to his mate, everyone brings another homeward of their way very friendly, and in their secret conclaves they play the sodomites, or worse" (see p. 349). As we have seen in Chapter 3, it is partly with thanks to Stubbes that historians of sexuality have ransacked playscripts that might otherwise have rested in dusty oblivion. In fact, little else is known about Stubbes (fl. 1583–91) apart from his now most famous work, *The Anatomy of Abuses in Ailgna* (1583) and his economium of his wife Katharine, *A Crystal Glass for Christian Women* (1591). Modern readers who know Stubbes only through quotations of his more outrageous fulminations may be surprised to learn that *The Anatomy of Abuses* is cast as a rather lively Ciceronian dialogue between the stay-at-home Spudeus and the traveler Philoponus, who has just returned from Ailgna (Anglia spelled backward). The excerpts printed here include the opening of the dialogue and the sections on stage plays and Lords of Misrule.

It is probably a distortion of hindsight to think that Stubbes appealed only to religious extremists. One of the emblems in Geoffrey Whitney's *A Choice of Emblems* (1586) warns a broad readership of the dangers of drinking and gaming. (See Figure 28.) *"Ludus, luctus, luxus"* ("gaming, bereavement, debauchery") reads the heading over the woodcut of a table of drinkers and gamblers. The first stanza of the verse beneath spells out the moral:

> Behold the fruits of drunkenness and play.
> Here Courage brawls with Cutthroat for a cast,

Ludus, luctus, luxus. 17

BEHOVLDE the fruites of dronkenneſſe, and plaie:
Here corage, brawles with Cutthroate for a caſte,
And ofte in fine, if that they lacke to paie,
They ſweare it out, or blade it at the laſte:
This, frendſhippe breakes: this, makes vs laugh'd to ſcorne,
And beggerie giues, to thoſe that riche are borne.

The Lapithans, by drinke weare ouerthrowne,
The wiſeſt men, with follie this inflames:
What ſhoulde I ſpeake, of father NOAH aloane,
Or bring in LOTT, or HOLOFERNES names:
This SIMON, and his ſonnes, did ouerthrowe,
And BENEDAB, made flee before his foe.

And he that lik'd to ſpende his time at dice,
This lawe in Rome, SEVERVS did prouide:
That euerie man, ſhoulde deeme him as a vice,
And of his Landes, an other ſhoulde bee guide:
Like Lawes beſide, did diuers more deuiſe,
And wiſedome ſtill, againſte ſuche vnthriftes cries.

Tunc ſumus incauti, ſtudioq; aperimur ab ipſo,
Nudaq; per luſus pectora noſtra patent.
Ira ſubit deforme malum, lucriq; Cupido
Iurgiaq;, & rixæ, ſollicitusq; dolor,
Crimina dicuntur, reſonat clamoribus æther,
Inuocat iratos & ſibi quiſque deos.

FIGURE 28 *Gaming, Bereavement, Debauchery, from Geoffrey Whitney,* A Choice of Emblems *(1586).*

And oft, in fine, if that they lack to pay,
They swear it out, or blade it at the last.
    This friendship breaks; this makes us laughed to scorn,
    And beggary gives to those that rich are born.

For all his extremities, Stubbes touches on anxieties about drink, gaming, and debauchery that ran deep in early modern culture.

From *The Anatomy of Abuses in Ailgna*

SPUDEUS: God give you good morrow, Master Philoponus.

PHILOPONUS: And you also, good brother Spudeus.

SPUDEUS: I am glad to see you in good health, for it was bruited[1] abroad everywhere in our country (by reason of your discontinuance, I think) that you were dead long ago.

PHILOPONUS: Indeed, I have spent some time abroad, elsewhere than in my native country, I must needs confess, but how false that report is (by whomsoever it was first rumored, or how far so ever it be dispersed) your present eyes can witness.

SPUDEUS: I pray you, what course of life have you lead in this your long absence forth of your own country?

PHILOPONUS: Truly brother, I have led the life of a poor traveler in a certain famous island, once named Ainabla, after Ainatirb, but now presently called Ailgna,[2] wherein I have lived these seven winters and more, traveling from place to place, even all the land over indifferently.

SPUDEUS: That was to your no little charges, I am sure.

PHILOPONUS: It was so, but what then? I thank God I have achieved it, and by His divine assistance prosperously accomplished it, His glorious name worthy of all magnificence be eternally praised therefore.

SPUDEUS: And to what end did you take in hand this great travel, if I may be so bold as to ask?

PHILOPONUS: Truly, to see fashions, to acquaint myself with the natures, qualities, properties, and conditions of all men, to break myself to the world, to learn nurture, good demeanor, and civil behavior; to see the goodly situation of cities, towns, and countries, with their prospects and commodities; and finally to learn the state of all things in general, all

[1] **bruited:** rumored. [2] **Ainabla . . . Ainatirb . . . Ailgna:** Albania, Britania, Anglia (all spelled backward).

Philip Stubbes, *The Anatomy of Abuses in Ailgna* (1583), ed. F. J. Furnivall (London: New Shakespeare Society, 1877–79), 21–24, 140–50.

which I could never have learned in one place. For who so sitteth at home, ever commorant[3] or abiding in one place, knoweth nothing in respect of him that traveleth abroad. And he that knoweth nothing is like a brute beast, but he that knoweth all things (which thing none doth but God alone) he is a god amongst men. And seeing there is a perfection in knowledge as in everything else, every man ought to desire that perfection. For in my judgment there is as much difference (almost) betwixt a man that hath traveled much, and him that hath dwelt ever in one place (in respect of knowledge and science of things), as is between a man living, and one dead in grave. And therefore I have had a great felicity in traveling abroad.

SPUDEUS: Seeing that by divine providence we are here met together, let us (until we come to the end of our purposed journey) use some conference of the state of the world now at this day, as well to recreate our minds, as to cut off the tediousness of our journey.

PHILOPONUS: I am very well content so to do, being not a little glad of your good company, for *comes facundus in via, pro vehiculo est* (a good companion to travel withal, is instead of a wagon or chariot). For as the one doth ease the painfulness of the way, so doth the other alleviate the irksomeness of the journey intended.

SPUDEUS: But before I enter combat with you (because I am a country man, rude and unlearned, and you, a civilian indued[4] with great wisdom, knowledge, and experience), I most humbly beseech you that you will not be offended with me, though I talk with you somewhat grossly, without either polished words, or filed[5] speeches, which your wisdom doth require, and my insufficiency and inability is not of power to afford.

PHILOPONUS: Your speeches (I put you out of doubt) shall not be offensive to me if they be not offensive to God first.

SPUDEUS: I pray you, what manner of country is that Ailgna where you say you have traveled so much?

PHILOPONUS: A pleasant and famous island immured about with the sea, as it were with a wall, wherein the air is very temperate, the ground fertile, and abounding with all things, either necessary to man or needful for beast.

SPUDEUS: What kind of people are they that inhabit there?

PHILOPONUS: A strong kind of people, audacious, bold, puissant,[6] and heroical, of great magnanimity, valiancy, and prowess, of an incomparable feature, of an excellent complexion, and in all humanity inferior to none under the sun.

[3] **commorant:** dwelling. [4] **indued:** endowed. [5] **filed:** polished. [6] **puissant:** powerful.

SPUDEUS: This people, whom God hath thus blessed, must needs be a very godly people, either else they be mere ingrate[7] to God, the author of all grace, and of these their blessings especially.

PHILOPONUS: It grieveth me to remember their lives, or to make mention of their ways, for notwithstanding that the Lord hath blessed that land with the knowledge of his truth above all other lands in the world, yet is there not a people more abrupt,[8] wicked, or perverse living upon the face of the earth.

SPUDEUS: From whence spring all these evils in man? For we see everyone is inclined to sin naturally, and there is no flesh which liveth and sinneth not.

PHILOPONUS: All wickedness, mischief, and sin (doubt you not, brother Spudeus) springeth of our ancient enemy the devil, the inveterate corruption of our nature, and the intestine[9] malice of our own hearts, as from the originals of all uncleanness and impurity whatsoever. But we are now new creatures and adoptive children created in Christ Jesus to do good works, which God hath prepared for us to walk in. Wherefore we ought to have no fellowship with the works of darkness, but to put on the armor of light, Christ Jesus, to walk in newness of life, and to work our salutation in fear and trembling, as the Apostle[10] saith. And our savior Christ biddeth us so work as our works may glorify our heavenly Father. But (alas!) the contrary is most true, for there is no sin that was ever broached in any age, which flourisheth not now. And therefore the fearful day of the Lord cannot be far off; at which day all the world shall stand in flashing fire. And then shall Christ our savior come marching in the clouds of heaven, with his taratantara[11] sounding in each man's ear, "Arise, you dead, and come to judgement!" And then shall the Lord reward every man after his own works. But how little this is esteemed of and how smally regarded, to consider, it grieveth me to the very heart, and there is almost no life in me.

. . . .

Of Stage Plays, and Interludes, with Their Wickedness.

PHILOPONUS: All stage plays, interludes,[12] and comedies are either of divine or profane matter. If they be of divine matter,[13] then are they most

[7] **mere ingrate:** altogether ungrateful. [8] **abrupt:** probably a misprint for "corrupt." [9] **intestine:** inherent. [10] **Apostle:** Paul, several of whose phrases are quoted here. [11] **taratantara:** trumpet sounds. [12] **interludes:** plays, so named because originally they occurred in the midst of other entertainments. [13] **divine matter:** alluding to plays dramatizing the Bible, traditionally acted on the Feast of Corpus Christi in June and officially suppressed in the 1570s as holdovers from Catholicism.

intolerable, or rather sacrilegious. For that the blessed word of God is to be handled reverently, gravely, and sagely, with veneration to the glorious majesty of God, which shineth therein, and not scoffingly, floutingly,[14] and jibbingly,[15] as it upon stages in plays and interludes, without any reverence, worship, or veneration to the same. The word of our salvation, the price of Christ His blood, and the merits of His passion, were not given to be derided and jested at, as they be in these filthy plays and interludes on stages and scaffolds, or to be mixed and interlaced with bawdry, wanton shows, and uncomely gestures, as is used (every man knoweth) in these plays and interludes. In the first of John we are taught that the word is God, and God is the word. Wherefore, whosoever abuseth word of our God on stages and plays and interludes, abuseth the majesty of God in the same, maketh a mocking stock of him, and purchaseth to himself eternal damnation. And no marvel, for the sacred word of God, and God Himself, is never to be thought of, or once named, but with great fear, reverence, and obedience to the same. All the holy company of heaven, angels, archangels, cherubins, seraphins, and all other powers whatsoever, yea, the devils themselves (as James saith) do tremble and quake at the naming of God, and at the presence of His wrath. And do these mockers and flouters of His majesty, these dissembling hypocrites, and flattering gnats think to escape unpunished? Beware, therefore, you masking players, you painted sepulchers, you double-dealing ambodexters,[16] be warned betimes, and, like good computists,[17] cast your accompts[18] before, what will be the reward thereof in the end, lest God destroy you in His wrath. Abuse God no more, corrupt His people no longer with your dregs, and intermingle not His blessed word with such profane vanities. For at no hand it is not lawful to mix scurrility with divinity, not divinity with scurrility.

Theopompus[19] mingled Moses' law with his writings, and therefore the Lord stroke him mad. Theodictes[20] began the same practice, but the Lord struck him blind for it. With many others, who, attempting the like devises, were all overthrown, and died miserably. Besides, what it is their judgment in the other world, the Lord only knoweth. Upon the other side, if their plays be of profane matters, then tend they to the dishonor of God and nourishing of vice, both which are damnable. So that whether they be the one or the other, they are quite contrary to the word

[14] **floutingly:** jeeringly. [15] **jibbingly:** jokingly. [16] **ambodexters:** two-handed people, people who try to combine the sacred and the profane. [17] **computists:** accountants. [18] **accompts:** accounts. [19] **Theopompus:** Greek historian (c. 375–c. 325 B.C.E.), student of Isocrates. [20] **Theodictes:** (fl. fourth century B.C.E.), Greek orator, poet and tragic playwright; also a student of Isocrates.

of grace and sucked out of the devil's teats[21] to nourish us in idolatry, heathenry, and sin. And therefore they, carrying the note, or brand, of God His curse upon their backs, which way soever they go, are to be hissed out of all Christian kingdoms, if they will have Christ to dwell amongst them.

SPUDEUS: Are you able to show, that ever any good men, from the beginning, have resisted plays and interludes?

PHILOPONUS: Not only the word of God doth overthrow them, adjudging them and the maintainers of them to hell, but also all holy councils and synods, both general, national, and provincial, together with all writers, both divine and profane, ever since the beginning, have disallowed them and writ (almost) whole volumes against them.

The learned father Tertullian, in his book *De Speculo* [On Shows], saith that plays were consecrate to that false idol Bacchus, for that he is said to have found out and invented strong drink.

Augustinus, [in] *De civit[ate] Dei* [On the City of God], saith that plays were ordained by the devil and consecrate to heathen gods to draw us from Christianity to idolatry and Gentilism.[22] And in another place, *"pecunias histrionibus dare vitium est innane, non virtus"* (to give money to players is a grievous sin).

Chrisostom calleth those plays *festa sathani,* feasts of the devil. Lactantius, an ancient learned father, saith, *"Histrionum impudissimi gestus, nihil aliud nisi libidinem movent"* (The shameless gestures of players serve to nothing so much as to move the flesh to lust and uncleanness). And therefore in the 30th Council of Carthage and Synod of Laodicea, it was decreed that no Christian man or woman should resort to plays and interludes, where is nothing but blasphemy, scurrility, and whoredom maintained. Scipio, seeing the Romans bent to erect theaters and places for plays, dehorted[23] them from it with the most prudent reasons and forcible arguments. Valerius Maximus saith, plays were never brought up *sine regni rubore,* without shame to the country. Arist[otle] debarreth youth access to plays and interludes, lest they, seeking to quench the thirst of Venus, do quench it with a pottle[24] of fire. Augustus banished Ovid for making books of love, interludes, and such other amorous trumpery.

Constantius ordained that no player should be admitted to the table of the Lord. Then, seeing that plays were first invented by the devil, practiced by the heathen Gentiles, and dedicated to their false idols, gods, and goddesses, as the house, stage, and apparel to Venus, the music to

[21] **teats:** nipples. [22] **Gentilism:** the religion of the Gentiles (the original Christians were Jews). [23] **dehorted:** dissuaded. [24] **pottle:** half-gallon pot.

Apollo, the penning to Minerva and the Muses, the action and pronunciation to Mercury and the rest, it is more than manifest that they are no fit exercises for a Christian man to follow. But if there were no evil in them save this, namely, that the arguments of tragedies is anger, wrath, immunity,[25] cruelty, injury, incest, murder, and such like, the persons or actors are gods, goddesses, furies, fiends, hags, kings, queens, or potentates; of comedies the matter and ground is love, bawdry, cosenage,[26] flattery, whoredom, adultery; the persons or agents, whores, queans,[27] bawds,[28] scullions,[29] knaves, courtesans, lecherous old men, amorous young men, with such like of infinite variety — if, I say, there were nothing else but this, it were sufficient to withdraw a good Christian from the using of them. For so often as they go to those houses where players frequent, they go to Venus' palace and Satan's synagogue to worship devils and betray Christ Jesus.

SPUDEUS: But notwithstanding, I have heard some hold opinion that they be as good as sermons and that many a good example may be learned of them.

PHILOPONUS: Oh blasphemy intolerable! Are filthy plays and bawdy interludes comparable to the word of God, the food of life, and life itself? It is all one, as if they had said bawdry, heathenry, paganry, scurrility, and devilry itself is equal with the word of God or that the devil is equivalent with the Lord.

The Lord our God hath ordained His blessed word and made it the ordinary mean of our salvation. The devil hath inferred the other as the ordinary mean of our destruction. And will they yet compare the one with the other? If he be accursed that calleth light darkness and darkness light, truth falsehood and falsehood truth, sweet sour and sour sweet, then, *a fortiori*,[30] is he accursed that saith that plays and interludes be equivalent with sermons. Besides this, there is no mischief which these plays maintain not. For do they not nourish idleness? And *otia dant vitia*, idleness is the mother of vice. Do they not draw the people from hearing the word of God, from godly lectures and sermons? For you shall have them flock thither, thick and threefold, when the church of God shall be bare and empty. And those that will never come at sermons will flow thither apace. The reason is, for that the number of Christ His elect is but few and the number of the reprobate is many. The way that leadeth to life is narrow, and few tread that path. The way that leadeth to death is broad, and many find it. This showeth they are not of God who refuse to

[25] **immunity:** exemption from the law. [26] **cosenage:** cheating. [27] **queans:** low prostitutes. [28] **bawds:** pimps. [29] **scullions:** domestic servants of the lowest order. [30] ***a fortiori:*** all the more certainly.

hear His word (for he that is of God heareth God His word, saith our savior Christ), but of the devil, whose exercises they go to visit. Do they not maintain bawdry, insinuate foolery, and renew the remembrance of heathen idolatry? Do they not induce whoredom and uncleanness? Nay, are they not rather plain[31] devourers of maidenly virginity and chastity? For proof whereof, but mark the flocking and running to Theaters and Curtains,[32] daily and hourly, night and day, time and tide, to see plays and interludes. Where such wanton gestures, such bawdy speeches, such laughing and fleering,[33] such kissing and bussing, such clipping and culling,[34] such winking and glancing of wanton eyes and the like is used as is wonderful to behold. Then, these goodly pageants being done, every mate sorts to his mate, everyone brings another homeward of their way very friendly and in their secret conclaves (covertly) they play the sodomites, or worse. And these be the fruits of plays and interludes for the most part. And whereas you say there are good examples to be learned in them, truly so there are. If you will learn falsehood. If you learn cosenage. If you will learn to deceive. If you will learn to play the hypocrite, to coggle,[35] lie, and falsify. If you will learn to jest, laugh, and fleer, to grin, to nod, and mow.[36] If you will learn to play the vice, to swear, tear,[37] and blaspheme both heaven and earth. If you will learn to become a bawd, unclean, and to devirginate maids, to deflower honest wives. If you will learn to murder, slay, kill, pick, steal, rob, and rove. If you will learn to rebel against princes, to commit treasons, to consume treasures, to practice idleness, to sing and talk of bawdy love and venery.[38] If you will learn to deride, scoff, mock and flout, to flatter and smooth.[39] If you will learn to play the whore-master, the glutton, drunkard, or incestuous person. If you will learn to become proud, haughty, and arrogant. And finally, if you will learn to condemn God and all His laws, to care neither for heaven or hell, and to commit all kind of sin and mischief, you need to go to no other school. For all these good examples may you see painted before your eyes in interludes and plays. Wherefore that man who giveth money for the maintenance of them must needs incur the damage of *praemunire*,[40] that is eternal damnation, except they repent. For the Apostle biddeth us beware, lest we communicate with other men's sins, and this their doing is not only to communicate with other men's sins and maintain evil to the destruction of themselves and many others, but also a maintaining

[31] **plain:** outright. [32] **Theaters and Curtains:** The Theater and the Curtain were two playhouses situated north of the city walls of London. [33] **fleering:** grinning or coarse laughter. [34] **clipping and culling:** embracing and fondling in the arms. [35] **coggle:** wobble. [36] **mow:** make mouths or grimaces. [37] **tear:** rant. [38] **venery:** deeds of lust. [39] **smooth:** smooth-talk. [40] ***praemunire:*** penalty for failure to heed an official summons.

of a great sort of idle lubbers and buzzing dronets,[41] to suck up and devour the good honey whereupon the poor bees should live.

Therefore I beseech all players and founders of plays and interludes, in the bowels of Jesus Christ, as they tender their salvation of their souls and others to leave off that cursed kind of life, and give themselves to such honest exercises and godly mysteries as God hath commanded them in his word to get their livings withal. For who will call him a wise man that playeth the part of a fool and a vice? Who can call him a Christian who playeth the part of a devil, the sworn enemy of Christ? Who can call him a just man that playeth the part of a dissembling hypocrite? And to be brief, who can call him a straight-dealing man who playeth a cosener's trick? And so of all the rest. Away therefore with this so infamous an art! For go they never so brave, yet are they counted and taken but for beggars. And is it not true? Live they not upon begging of everyone that comes? Are they not taken by the laws of the realm for rogues and vagabonds? I speak of such as travel the countries[42] with plays and interludes, making an occupation of it and ought so to be punished if they had their deserts. But hoping that they will be warned now at the last, I will say no more of them, beseeching them to consider what a fearful thing it is to fall into the hands of God, and to provoke His wrath and heavy displeasure against themselves and others, which the Lord of His mercy turn from us!

SPUDEUS: Of what sort be the other kinds of plays, which you call lords of misrule? For methink[s] the very name itself carryeth a taste of some notorious evil.

Lords of Misrule in Ailgna

PHILOPONUS: The name, indeed, is odious both to God and good men, and such as the very heathen people would have blushed at once to have named amongst them. And if the name importeth some evil, then what may the thing itself be, judge you? But because you desire to know the manner of them, I will show you as I have seen them practiced myself. First, all the wild heads of the parish, conventing[43] together, chose them a grand captain (of all mischief) whom they ennoble with the title of "my lord of misrule" and him they crown with great solemnity, and adopt for their king. This king anointed chooseth forth twenty, forty, threescore or a

[41] **lubbers . . . dronets:** clumsy oafs and drone bees. [42] **countries:** counties, regions of England. [43] **conventing:** meeting, gathering.

hundred lusty guts, like to himself, to wait upon his lordly majesty, and to guard his noble person. Then, everyone of these his men, he investeth with his liveries of green, yellow, or some other light wanton color. And as though that were not (bawdy) gaudy enough, I should say they bedeck themselves with scarves, ribbons, and laces hanged all over with gold rings, precious stones, and other jewels. This done, they tie about either leg 20 or 40 bells with rich handkerchiefs in their hands, and sometimes laid across over their shoulders and necks, borrowed for the most part of their pretty mopsies and loving bessies,[44] for bussing them in the dark. Thus all things set in order, then have they their hobbyhorses, dragons and other antics,[45] together with their bawdy pipers and thundering drummers to strike up the devil's dance[46] withal. Then, march these heathen company towards the church and churchyard, their pipers piping, their drummers thundering, their stumps dancing, their bells jingling, their handkerchiefs swinging about their heads like madmen, their hobbyhorses and other monsters skirmishing amongst the rout. And in this sort they go to the church (I say) and into the church (though the minister be at prayer and preaching) dancing and swinging their handkerchiefs over their heads in the church like devils incarnate, with such a confused noise that no man can hear his own voice. Then, the foolish people they look, they stare, they laugh, they fleer, and mount upon forms[47] and pews to see these goodly pageants solemnized in this sort. Then, after this, about the church they go again and again and so forth into the churchyard, where they have commonly their summer halls, their bowers, arbors, and banqueting houses set up, wherein they feast, banquet and dance all that day and peradventure all the night too. And thus these terrestrial furies spend that Sabbath day.

They have also certain papers, wherein is painted some babblery[48] or other of imagery work and these they call my lord of misrule's badges. These they give to everyone that will give money for them to maintain them in their heathenry, devilry, whoredom, drunkenness, pride, and what not. And who will not be buxom[49] to them and give them money for these their devil[ish] cognizances, they are mocked and flouted at not a little. And so assotted[50] are some that they not only give them money to maintain their abomination withal, but also wear their badges and cognizances in their hats or caps openly. But let them take heed, for these are badges, seals, brands, and cognizances of the devil, whereby he knoweth

[44] **mopsies . . . bessies:** country girls. [45] **hobby-horses, dragons . . . antics:** animal costumes worn by men. [46] **devil's dance:** Stubbes is describing morris dancing. [47] **forms:** benches. [48] **babblery:** foolish writing. [49] **buxom:** compliant, jolly. [50] **assotted:** blockheaded, foolish.

his servants and clients from the children of God. And so long as they wear them, *sub vexillo diaboli militant contra dominum et legem suam* (they fight under the banner and standard of the devil against Christ Jesus and all His laws). Another sort of fantastical fools bring to these hellhounds (the lord of misrule and his accomplices) some bread, some good ale, some new cheese, some old, some custards, and fine cakes, some one thing, some another. But if they knew that as often as they bring anything to the maintenance of these execrable pastimes, they offer sacrifice to the devil and Satan, they would repent and withdraw their hands, which God grant they may!

SPUDEUS: This is a horrible profanation of the Sabbath (the Lord knoweth) and more pestilent than pestilence[51] itself. But what? Be there any abuses in their May games like unto these?

PHILOPONUS: As many as in the other. The order of them is thus: against May, Whitsunday, or other time, all the young men and maids, old men and wives run gadding overnight to the woods, groves, hills, and mountains where they spend all the night in pleasant pastimes. And in the morning they return, bringing with them birch and branches of trees, to deck their assemblies withal. And no marvel, for there is a great lord present amongst them, as superintendent and lord over their pastimes and sports, namely Satan, prince of hell. But the chiefest jewel they bring from thence is their maypole, which they bring home with great veneration as thus. They have twenty or forty yoke of oxen, every ox having a sweet nosegay of flowers placed on the tips of his horses. And these oxen draw home this maypole (this stinking idol rather) which is covered all over with flowers and herbs, bound round about with strings from the top to the bottom, and sometime painted with variable colors, with two or three hundred men, women, and children, following it with great devotion. And thus being reared up with handkerchiefs and flags hovering on the top, they straw the ground round about, bind green boughs about it, set up summer halls, bowers, and arbors hard by it. And then fall they to dance about it, like as the heathen people did at the dedication of the idols, whereof this is a perfect pattern, or rather the thing itself. I have heard it credibly reported (and that *viva voce*)[52] by men of great gravity and reputation, that of forty, threescore, or a hundred maids going to the wood overnight, there have scarcely the third part of them returned home again undefiled. These be the fruits which these cursed pastimes bring forth. Neither the Jews, the Turks, Saracens, nor pagans,

[51] **pestilence:** the plague. [52] ***viva voce:*** in a loud voice.

nor any other nations, how wicked or barbarous soever, have ever used such devilish exercises as these. Nay, they would have been ashamed once to have named them, much less have used them. Yet we, that would be Christians, think them not amiss. The Lord forgive us and remove them from us!

JAMES I AND CHARLES I

The King's Majesty's Declaration to His Subjects concerning Lawful Sports to be Used *1618, 1633*

Returning from a visit to Scotland in 1617, King James I halted in Lancashire, a county notorious for its Catholic recidivism, and received there a petition from a group of common people complaining that they were being prevented from dancing, sports, and church-ales on Sundays. James's response was to issue on May 20, 1618, a *Declaration to His Subjects concerning Lawful Sports to be Used on the Sabbath Day,* starting a chain of events that eventually led to the beheadings of Archbishop Laud in 1645 and of Charles I in 1649. In granting his subjects the right to most of their traditional Sunday-afternoon recreations — bowling is curiously prohibited — James recognized the political cast of the whole affair. He complains in the proclamation that the realm is "much infested with Papists and Puritans, who both have maliciously traduced and calumniated those our just and honorable proceedings." His mention of Papists is politic but superfluous, since it was the supposedly Catholic laxity of such practices on the Sabbath that Puritans excoriated. Whatever benefits it may have had for the common folk of Lancashire, "The King's Book of Sports," as it came to be known, helped to ally episcopal with royalist on the one hand and Puritan with parliamentary on the other.

When Charles I reissued his father's proclamation in 1633, he did so as part of a campaign against local insubordination to crown rule. Just the year before two chief justices had affirmed local court rulings forbidding dancing, sports, and church-ales on Sundays — and had ordered the ministers of every parish to read the court order twice a year. Charles I's response, likely suggested by Archbishop Laud, was to reissue "The King's Book of Sports" and to require ministers to read *it* from their pulpits instead. Resentment ran deep, many ministers refused to obey, and in 1643 the so-called Long Parliament (it sat from 1640 to 1653) passed an ordinance forbidding the traditional recreations and ordering that all copies of "The King's Book of Sports" be seized and publicly burned (Henderson 539–53). Here follows, in its entirety, one of the most controversial books ever published in England.

The King's Majesty's Declaration to His Subjects concerning Lawful Sports to be Used

¶ BY THE KING.

Whereas upon Our return the last year out of Scotland, We did publish our pleasure touching the recreations of our people in those parts under our hand: For some causes us thereunto moving, we have thought good to command these our directions then given in Lancashire with a few words thereunto added, and most appliable to these parts of our realms, to be published to all our subjects.

Whereas we did justly in our progress through Lancashire, rebuke some Puritans and precise[1] people, and took order that the like unlawful carriage should not be used by any of them hereafter, in the prohibiting and unlawful punishing of our good people for using their lawful recreations, and honest exercises upon Sundays and other holidays, after the afternoon sermon or service: We now find that two sorts of people wherewith that country is much infected, (we mean Papists and Puritans) have maliciously traduced and calumniated those our just and honorable proceedings. And therefore lest our reputation might upon the one side (though innocently) have some aspersion laid upon it, and that upon the other part our good people in that country be misled by the mistaking and misinterpretation of our meaning: We have therefore thought good hereby to clear and make our pleasure to be manifested to all our good people in those parts.

It is true that at our first entry to this crown, and kingdom, we were informed, and that too truly, that our country of Lancashire abounded more in popish recusants[2] than any county of England, and thus hath still continued since to our great regret, with little amendment, save that now of late, in our last riding through our said county, we find both by the report of the judges, and of the bishop of that diocese, that there is some amendment now daily beginning, which is no small contentment to us.

The report of this growing amendment amongst them, made us the more sorry, when with our own ears we heard the general complaint of our people, that they were barred from all lawful recreation, and exercise upon the Sunday's afternoon, after the ending of all divine service, which cannot

[1] **precise:** strict. [2] **popish recusants:** Catholics who refused to attend the Church of England.

The King's Majesty's Declaration to His Subjects Concerning Lawful Sports to be Used (London: Robert Barker, 1633).

but produce two evils: the one, the hindering of the conversion of many, whom their priests will take occasion hereby to vex, persuading them that no honest mirth or recreation is lawful or tolerable in our religion, which cannot but breed a great discontentment in our people's hearts, especially of such as are peradventure upon the point of turning; the other inconvenience is, that this prohibition barreth the common and meaner sort[3] of people from using such exercises as may make their bodies more able for war, when we or our successors shall have occasion to use them. And in place thereof sets up filthy tiplings and drunkenness, and breeds a number of idle and discontented speeches in their alehouses. For when shall the common people have leave to exercise, if not upon the Sundays and holidays, seeing they must apply their labor, and win their living in all working days?

Our express pleasure therefore is, that the laws of our kingdom, and canons of our church be as well observed in that county, as in all other places of this our kingdom. And on the other part, that no lawful recreation shall be barred to our good people, which shall not tend to the breach of our aforesaid laws, and canons of our church: which to express more particularly, our pleasure is, that the bishop, and all other inferior churchmen, and churchwardens, shall for their parts be careful and diligent, both to instruct the ignorant, and convince and reform them that are misled in religion, presenting them that will not conform themselves, but obstinately stand out to our judges and justices: whom we likewise command to put the law in due execution against them.

Our pleasure likewise is, that the bishop of that diocese take the like straight order with all the Puritans and Precisians[4] within the same, either constraining them to conform themselves, or to leave the county according to the laws of our kingdom, and canons of our church, and so to strike equally on both hands, against the contemners of our authority, and adversaries of our church. And as for our good people's lawful recreation, our pleasure likewise is, that after the end of divine service, our good people be not disturbed, letted,[5] or discouraged from any lawful recreation, such as dancing, either men or women, archery for men, leaping, vaulting, or any other such harmless recreation, nor from having of May games, Whitsun ales, and morris dances, and the setting up of maypoles and other sports therewith used, so as the same be had in due and convenient time, without impediment or neglect of divine service: and that women shall have leave to carry rushes to the church for the decoring of it, according to their old custom.

[3] **meaner sort:** of lower social station. [4] **Precisians:** people cut off from Communion in the Church of England. [5] **letted:** prevented.

But withal we do here account still as prohibited all unlawful games to be used upon Sundays only, as bear- and bull-baitings, interludes, and at all times in the meaner sort of people by law prohibited, bowling.

And likewise we bar from this benefit and liberty, all such known recusants, either men or women, as will abstain from coming to church or divine service, being therefore unworthy of any lawful recreation after the said service, that will not first come to the church, and serve God: prohibiting in like sort the said recreations to any that, though conform in religion, are not present in the church at the service of God, before their going to the said recreations. Our pleasure likewise is, that they to whom it belongeth in office, shall present and sharply punish all such as in abuse of this our liberty, will use these exercises before the ends of all divine services for that day. And we likewise straightly command, that every person shall resort to his own parish church to hear divine service, and each parish by itself to use the said recreation after divine service. Prohibiting likewise any offensive weapons to be carried or used in the said times of recreations. And our pleasure is, that this our declaration shall be published by order from the bishop of the diocese, through all the parish churches, and that both our judges and our circuit, and our justices of our peace be informed thereof.

Given at our manor of Greenwich the four and twentieth day of May, in the sixteenth year of our reign of England, France and Ireland, and of Scotland the one and fiftieth.

CHAPTER 7

Clowning and Laughter

Anyone who has ever tried to explain a joke can appreciate Quintilian's frustration in book 6 of his rhetorical manual *Institutio Oratoria.* Quintilian can tell a would-be orator how to manage his voice and how to order the evidence, but not how to be funny. Humor depends, after all, not on reason, but "on an emotion which it is difficult, if not impossible, to describe. For I do not think that anybody can give an adequate explanation, though many have attempted to do so, of the cause of laughter, which is excited not merely by words or deeds, but sometimes even by touch" (6.3.6–7). In tickling, literary theory finds a far greater challenge than in tragedy. Even words and deeds prove elusive, since what produces a belly laugh in one culture leaves observers from another culture scratching their heads. When it comes to comedy, Shakespeare is not above the problem of cross-cultural communication. Although stage productions of *Twelfth Night* continue to delight audiences today, the play has not exactly enjoyed a continuous production history across the past four hundred years. Although it was one of the first plays by Shakespeare to be revived when the theaters reopened in 1660, it was mounted only three times in the later seventeenth century. The diarist Samuel Pepys happens to have seen all three productions, but liked none of them. "One of the weakest plays that ever I saw on the stage" (9: 421), he pronounced the production of 1669.

Readers of the script, as opposed to watchers of the script in production, find themselves constantly compelled to look at the footnotes to catch the verbal jokes and to use their visual imaginations to conjure up the physical gags designed for the stage. Some of these jokes and gags will not strike us as funny, since ideas of decorum (and hence of *in*decorum) have changed over the past four hundred years no less than the English language has changed. At the same time, certain features of *Twelfth Night* do seem universal. As we saw in Chapter 4, the motif of twins mistaken for one another has its own entry in the Stith-Thompson *Motif-Index of Folk-Literature,* a compilation based on tales collected from all over the world. To inquire into the nature of clowning and laughter in *Twelfth Night* is, therefore, to pose questions that are both abstractly philosophical (what *is* funny?) and historically specific (what *was* funny to Shakespeare and his contemporaries?). After Quintilian's introduction to the issues, we shall proceed inductively, from the particulars of Feste's clowning to more general theories about the nature of comedy.

→ **QUINTILIAN**

From Institutio Oratoria

1st century C.E.

Let us begin with Quintilian, the first-century Roman instructor in rhetoric whose compendium of advice on the subject became the basis for humanist educational schemes in the fifteenth- and sixteenth-century Renaissance of classical culture. Always the practical teacher, Quintilian is interested in humor as a talent or power (*virtus*) that a successful speaker needs to have in order to sway the emotions of the judge who will be his primary auditor in a court of law. To that end, Quintilian investigates the examples of famous orators like Demosthenes and Cicero before deciding that humor is less a matter of art than of "nature and opportunity." In their looks or manners some people are just naturally funnier than others and have better timing when it comes to making others laugh. The excerpt that follows concludes with an attempt to divide humor into six distinct categories.

I do not think that anybody can give an adequate explanation, though many have attempted to do so, of the cause of laughter, which is excited not merely by words or deeds, but sometimes even by touch. Moreover, there is great variety in the things which raise a laugh, since we laugh not merely at

---

Quintilian, *Institutio Oratoria,* 6.3.1–21, trans. H. E. Butler, Loeb Classical Library (London: Heinemann, 1921), 2: 441–49.

those words or actions which are smart or witty, but also at those which reveal folly, anger or fear. Consequently, the cause of laughter is uncertain, since laughter is never far removed from derision. For, as Cicero[1] says, "Laughter has its basis in some kind or other of deformity or ugliness," and whereas, when we point to such a blemish in others, the result is known as wit, it is called folly when the same jest is turned against ourselves.

Now, though laughter may be regarded as a trivial matter, and an emotion frequently awakened by buffoons, actors or fools, it has a certain imperious force of its own which it is very hard to resist. It often breaks out against our will and extorts confession of its power, not merely from our face and voice, but convulses the whole body as well. Again, it frequently turns the scale in matters of great importance, as I have already observed: for instance, it often dispels hatred or anger. A proof of this is given by the story of the young men of Tarentum, who had made a number of scurrilous criticisms of Pyrrhus over the dinner table: they were called upon to answer for their statements, and, since the charge was one that admitted neither of denial nor of excuse, they succeeded in escaping, thanks to a happy jest which made the king laugh; for one of the accused said, "Yes, and if the bottle hadn't been empty, we should have killed you!" a jest which succeeded in dissipating the animosity which the charge had aroused.

Still, whatever the essence of humor may be, and although I would not venture to assert that it is altogether independent of art (for it involves a certain power of observation, and rules for its employment have been laid down by writers both of Greece and Rome), I will insist on this much, that it depends mainly on nature and opportunity. The influence of nature consists not merely in the fact that one man is quicker or cleverer than another in the invention of jests (for such a power can be increased by teaching), but also in the possession of some peculiar charm of look or manner, the effect of which is such that the same remarks would be less entertaining if uttered by another. Opportunity, on the other hand, is dependent on circumstances, and is of such importance that with its assistance not merely the unlearned, but even mere country bumpkins are capable of producing effective witticisms: while much again may depend on some previous remark made by another which will provide opportunity for repartee. For wit always appears to greater advantage in reply than in attack.

We are also confronted by the additional difficulty that there are no specific exercises for the development of humor nor professors to teach it. Consequently, while convivial gatherings and conversation give rise to frequent displays of wit, since daily practice develops the faculty, oratorical wit is rare,

[1] **Cicero:** Marcus Tullius Cicero (105 B.C.E.–43 C.E.), Roman philosopher and rhetorician.

for it has no fixed rules to guide it, but must adapt itself to the ways of the world. There has, however, never been anything to prevent the composition of themes such as will afford scope for humor, so that our controversial declamations may have an admixture of jests, while special topics may be set which will give the young student practice in the play of wit. Nay, even those pleasantries in which we indulge on certain occasions of festive licence (and to which we give the name of *mots,*[2] as indeed they are), if only a little more good sense were employed in their invention and they were seasoned by a slight admixture of seriousness might afford a most useful training. As it is, they serve merely to divert the young and merrymakers.

There are various names by which we describe wit, but we have only to consider them separately to perceive their specific meaning. First, there is *urbanitas,*[3] which I observe denotes language with a smack of the city in its words, accent and idiom, and further suggests a certain tincture of learning derived from associating with well-educated men; in a word, it represents the opposite of rusticity. The meaning of *venustus*[4] is obvious; it means that which is said with grace and charm. *Salsus*[5] is, as a rule, applied only to what is laughable: but this is not its natural application, although whatever is laughable should have the salt of wit in it. For Cicero, when he says that whatever has the salt of wit is Attic,[6] does not say this because persons of the Attic school are specially given to laughter; and again when Catullus says —

In all her body not a grain of salt!

he does not mean that there is nothing in her body to give cause for laughter. When, therefore, we speak of the salt of wit, we refer to wit about which there is nothing insipid, wit, that is to say, which serves as a simple seasoning of language, a condiment which is silently appreciated by our judgment, as food is appreciated by the palate, with the result that it stimulates our taste and saves a speech from becoming tedious. But just as salt, if sprinkled freely over food, gives a special relish of its own, so long as it is not used to excess, so in the case of those who have the salt of wit there is something about their language which arouses in us a thirst to hear. Again, I do not regard the epithet *facetus*[7] as applicable solely to that which raises a laugh. If that were so Horace[8] would never have said that nature had granted Vergil[9] the gift of being *facetus* in song. I think that the term is rather applied to a certain grace and polished elegance. This is the meaning which it bears in

[2] ***mots:*** quips. [3] ***urbanitas:*** sophistication (literally, "city-ness"). [4] ***venustus:*** charming. [5] ***Salsus:*** salty. [6] **Attic:** Athenian. [7] ***facetus:*** witty, amusing. [8] **Horace:** Quintus Horatius Flaccus (65–8 B.C.E.), Roman lyric poet. [9] **Vergil:** P. Virgilius Maro (70–19 B.C.E.), author of *The Aeneid.*

Cicero's letters, where he quotes the words of Brutus,[10] "In truth her feet are graceful and soft as she goes delicately on her way." This meaning suits the passage in Horace, to which I have already made reference, "To Vergil gave a soft and graceful wit." *Iocus*[11] is usually taken to mean the opposite of seriousness. This view is, however, somewhat too narrow. For to feign, to terrify, or to promise, are all at times forms of jesting. *Dicacitas* is no doubt derived from *dico,*[12] and is therefore common to all forms of wit, but is specially applied to the language of banter, which is a humorous form of attack. Therefore, while the critics allow that Demosthenes[13] was *urbanus,* they deny that he was *dicax.*[14]

[10] **Brutus:** Marcus Junius Brutus (c. 85–42 B.C.E.), one of Cicero's favorite literary and philosophical adversaries, and the prime assassin of Julius Caesar. [11] ***Iocus:*** jest. [12] ***Dicacitas . . . dico:*** raillery . . . "I speak." [13] **Demosthenes:** traditionally, the greatest Greek orator (c. 385–322 B.C.E.). [14] ***dicax:*** ready of speech, quick-witted.

Robert Armin's Career

The prominence of Feste's role in *Twelfth Night* has a lot to do with the arrival of a new professional clown in Shakespeare's acting company just the season before. Robert Armin (d. 1615) probably joined the Lord Chamberlain's Men in 1599 or 1600, when Will Kemp, the company's earlier clown, left the company for a self-promotional tour in which he *danced* the hundred miles from London to Norwich. Kemp wrote up a first-person account of the whole affair in *Kemp's Nine Days' Wonder . . . Written by Himself to Satisfy His Friends,* published as an illustrated pamphlet in 1600. Dancing was, indeed, Kemp's forte. In addition to creating the roles of Peter in *Romeo and Juliet,* Dogberry in *Much Ado About Nothing,* and probably of Falstaff in the two parts of *Henry IV* and *The Merry Wives of Windsor,* Kemp sent audiences on their merry way at the end of the company's performances by dancing the narrative jigs that concluded performances through the 1590s. Thomas Platter's account of *Julius Caesar* at the Globe in 1599 (see Chapter 4) makes it clear that jigs concluded tragedies as well as comedies. The fact that jigs seem to have been dropped by the Lord Chamberlain's Men after Kemp's departure (the only references to jigs after 1600 locate them in the downmarket playhouses north of the city) is one indication of changing ideas about clowning.

On the public stages of London, Kemp had two famous predecessors, Richard Tarlton and Robert Wilson, both of whom were noted for their extemporaneous wit, that is, for being inventive on their feet. In the case of Tarlton that nimbleness was physical as well. In addition to miming, he was a drummer, tumbler, and qualified Master of Fencing. John Manningham, as we saw in the Introduction, noted in his diary one of the many jests attributed to Tarlton that went around in Elizabethan and Jacobean England. Kemp's successor, Robert Armin, was a less flamboyant figure than either Tarlton or Kemp. In Andrew Gurr's account, the movement from Tarlton to Kemp to Armin represents a successive diminution in the importance of the clown's role vis-à-vis serious actors like Richard Burbage (Gurr 86–88). It was in 1600, the very year Armin joined the Lord Chamberlain's Men, that Shakespeare had Hamlet warn the visiting players,

> let those that play your clowns speak no more than is set down for them; for there be of them that will themselves laugh, to set on some quantity of barren spectators to laugh too, though in the meantime some necessary question of the play be then to be considered. That's villainous, and shows a most pitiful ambition in the fool that uses it (3.2.38–45).

From Armin, Shakespeare seems to have had nothing to fear. As Hamlet remembers him, Yorick, the Danish court's jester, may have been an extroverted physical comedian who carried the young Hamlet around on his back and set the table roaring with his gibes, gambols, songs, and flashes of merriment (*Hamlet* 5.1.185–191). But Armin was a different sort of clown. Armin's Feste is a sardonic wordsmith who also happens to sing.

In addition to his singing talents, Armin brought to all the roles he likely played for Shakespeare's company — Touchstone in *As You Like It,* Feste in *Twelfth Night,* Thersites in *Troilus and Cressida,* Lavatch in *All's Well That Ends Well,* the Fool in *King Lear* — a knack for taking other people's remarks and, as we might say today, deconstructing them.[1] Take, for example, the encounter of "Cesario" and Feste in act 3, scene 1. When the two enter, presumably at separate doors, the fool is tapping on a tabor, or small drum, and probably also blowing on the small pipe that made the player of pipe-and-tabor a one-man band favored for accompanying morris dancing. A standard figure in morris dancing was a Fool who not only interacted with the crowd of on-lookers but tried to trip up the dancers. In effect, that is just what Feste attempts with his fellow actors in *Twelfth Night.*

> VIOLA: Save thee, friend, and thy music. Dost thou live by thy tabor?
> FESTE: No, I live by the church.
> VIOLA: Art thou a churchman?
> FESTE: No such matter, sir. I do live by the church, for I do live at my house, and my house doth stand by the church.

[1] On Armin's clowning career, see Wiles, 144–58.

VIOLA: So thou mayst say the king lies by a beggar if a beggar dwell near him, or the church stands by thy tabor if thy tabor stand by the church.

FESTE: You have said, sir. To see this age! A sentence is but a cheveril glove to a good wit. How quickly the wrong side may be turned outward! (3.1.1–9)

Not for nothing does Feste refuse the fixed title of "fool." When Viola asks, "Art not thou the Lady Olivia's fool?", Feste replies, "I am indeed not her fool but her corrupter of words" (3.1.24, 27–28). To "live by," as Feste corrupts the phrase, can be a matter of geography as well as economics. It is ironic that he should refuse to take "live by" in its economic sense, since moments later he is asking "Cesario" to double his tip. Feste's frequent appeals for money in the course of *Twelfth Night* serve as a constant reminder that playing the fool is not something that comes naturally; it is a business. Like Will Kemp turning his London-to-Norwich jig into a printed text, Robert Armin authored a series of four jest books as well as two playscripts, *The Two Maids of Moreclack* and *The Valiant Welshman.* From one of the playscripts comes the woodcut portrait of Armin that appears as Figure 4 (see p. 23); from two of the jest books come the excerpts that follow.

Armin's clowning career came at a crucial moment in the social history of laughter. In the 1580s no less a personage than Sir Philip Sidney was happy to stand as godfather to Tarlton's son; by the 1640s and 1650s a gentlemen was expected to have nothing to do with open, loud laughter. Keith Thomas has sketched in the broad outlines of the place of laughter in English culture from the sixteenth century to the eighteenth. A number of factors — the shift from Catholic sanction of humor to Protestant suspicion, the increasing divide in communal life between common people and the elite, increasing centralization of state authority, expectations that individuals would exert greater control over their physical bodies, more compassionate attitudes to physical deformity and undeserved misfortune — converged to circumscribe the comic more and more in the course of the two hundred years from 1550 to 1750 (Thomas 77–81). Robert Armin's performance as Feste comes squarely in the middle of that great shift. In the person of Malvolio, "a kind of puritan," are represented some of the forces that across the next century would foreclose the scope of comic exuberance. In *Twelfth Night,* for the time being at least, "Festival" gets the best of "Ill Wishing" (*malvoglia* in Italian).

ROBERT ARMIN

From Fool upon Fool, or Six Sorts of Sots *1600*

The full title to Armin's jest book reveals a mock-scholarly intent: *Fool upon Fool, or Six Sorts of Sots: A Flat Fool and A Fat Fool, A Lean Fool and a Clean Fool, a Merry Fool and a Very Fool, Showing Their Lives, Humors, and Behaviors, with Their Want of Wit in Their Show of Wisdom. Not So Strange as True.* The random rhymes of the words here ("flat" and "fat," "lean" and "clean," "merry" and "very") suggest that these six categories are not to be taken too literally. A specification of the author's name in Latin — *"Clonnico de Curtanio Snuffe,"* "Snuff, Clown of the Curtain" — establishes Armin's mock-scholarly credentials of the Fool writing upon fools at the same time it identifies Armin in one of his guises as Snuff at the Curtain theater, where he played before joining the Lord Chamberlain's Men at the newly built Globe. The six sorts of "sots" (or "blockheads") in *Fool upon Fool* were more usually divided into just two: "natural" fools and "artificial" fools. Jack Oates, the "flat fool natural" in the anecdotes that follow, exemplifies the former category. As the authoritative Fool in *Fool upon Fool,* Armin establishes himself as an "artificial" fool, as an actor playing a role. In *Twelfth Night* Feste is recognized as just such an entertainer. Amazed (and perhaps jealous) that Olivia pays so much attention to Feste, Malvolio confides, "I saw him put down the other day with an ordinary fool that has no more brain than a stone." Feste, by contrast, is one of "these set kind of fools" who purport, at least, to have a brain and use it (1.5.65–69).

In the woodcut portrait that graces the title page to Armin's play *The Two Maids of Moreclack* (see Figure 4, p. 23), the clown — who may be Armin himself — wears the garb of a natural fool: hanging from his belt are a handkerchief to mop his dribble and a pen and inkhorn to indicate the mind of a schoolboy (Wiles 141–42). In the description of Jack Oates that follows, note that yellow — the color of Malvolio's stockings — is one of the natural fool's favorite colors. Hints in Shakespeare's scripts suggest that Armin did indeed look the part of a natural fool. Dressing himself as Sir Topas, for example, Armin as Feste alludes to his dwarfish stature and plumpness as he confesses, "I am not tall enough to become the function well, nor lean enough to be thought a good student." But Armin in all his roles deploys his verbal wit as an artificial fool who knows exactly what he is doing. Comparing his own qualities with the pretensions of the Puritan steward he is about to taunt, Armin as Feste continues: "but to be said an honest man and a good housekeeper goes as fairly as to say a careful man and a great scholar" (4.2.5–8). Here follows the artificial fool on the natural fool.

From *Fool upon Fool, or Six Sorts of Sots*[1]

The Description of Jack Oates, Being a Flat Fool Natural

He ware[2] a hat of straw common in view,
But it was dyed in colors red and blue:
Under which hat he lightly had a crown,
Commonly bald, for't was of no renown
Side locks of hair and something long before
Like Time[3] this idiot looked more and more.

Wrinkled his brow and brown as any berry,
Beetled his forehead, apt to make men merry:
Hair on his eyebrows that was something gray,
Hollow his eyes whose lids were dull to play.
His nose was something hooked and 'twas short,
His cheeks both hollow fit to make men sport.

His upper lip turned in, but [w]hat was stranger,
His under lip so big t'might sweep a manger:
Little his beard, like to a swallow's tail,
His chin grew upward to his own avail,
For when 'a drunk, still as 'a[4] laughed and jeered,
You would smile to see the fool suck in his beard.

His neck was swarty[5] overgrown with hair,
Which for his pleasure he would still have bare:
Big was his belly and he would carouse,
Bidding all welcome to his master's house,
And who so did deny to pledge him still,
With his jack[6] he would have brained him by his will.

Thick was his waist girt with a leather thong,
With which he would oft do a number wrong:
But for his hands both long, lean, fingered small,
Seldom the like in any natural,

[1] **sots:** fools, blockheads, dolts. [2] **ware:** wore. [3] **Like Time:** personified Time, which was imagined to approach from behind, was depicted with a forelock that had to be grabbed in order to seize opportunity. [4] **'a . . . 'a:** he . . . he. [5] **swarty:** swarthy, dark. [6] **jack:** leather jug or tankard.

Robert Armin, *Fool upon Fool, or Six Sorts of Sots* . . . (London: William Febrand, 1600), A3–B3v.

That lords and ladies still amazed stands,
That such a simple fool should have such hands.

A mighty wrist, an arm great, very strong,
A thigh but small yet it was something long:
A knee round lightly swelled and full of pain,
And that was all his grief he would complain.
His legs great, gouty,[7] and his small[8]
Of one self[9] bigness almost were they all.

His two feet broad and big, thus you before
Have heard his true description and no more.
Now backward you shall hear how he was made,
His heels both long and big as all men said.
His calves near like his smalls as big almost,
Made great but gouty, like a stake or post.

His hips too huge and that his chiefest fault,
On which his left hand still lay, and did halt:
His back was stooping and his shoulders high,
Over which still[10] the fool would have an eye,
Short neck behind, no band was ever worn,
His hair being long before, behind war shorn.

Motley his wearing, yellow or else green,
A colored coat on him was seldom seen.
No fool's cap with a bauble[11] and bell,
Swear he would not, for which all loved him well.
And he would feed the poor: few fools are such,
Which made him to be loved of poor and rich.

Thus you have heard Jack Oates his true description,
As my eyes witness and I can imagine:
He lived not long since and did pine away
After Sir Willy[12] died, as many say.
Such knights as he but few lives nowadays,
And such a fool had seldom times such a praise.

[7] **gouty:** afflicted with the gout, a disease proverbially thought to be brought on by too much drinking. [8] **small:** ankle. [9] **self:** same. [10] **still:** always. [11] **bauble:** baton mounted with a carved head with ass's ears. [12] **Sir Willy:** Jack Oates's master.

How Jack Oates Played at Cards All Alone

Jack Oates sitting at cards all alone was dealing to himself at Wide Ruff, for that was the game he joyed in, and as he spied a knave, "Ah knave, art there?" quoth he. When he spied a king, "King by your leave," quoth he. If he spied a queen, "Queen Richard, art come?" quoth he, and would kneel down and bid God bless her majesty, meaning indeed our queen, whom he heard Sir William Hollis his master so much to pray for. But here is the jest: Jack as I say being at cards all alone, spying a knave and saying, "Ah knave, art there?" a simple serving man being in the hall waiting his master's coming, walking by and hearing him say so, thought he had called him knave, took the matter in dudgeon,[13] and miscalled[14] the fool. Another serving man more foolish than both took Jack's part, so that in short time they two fell together by the ears. Who being parted, Jack Oates gives them each one a knave and so takes them into the buttery[15] to drink. The knight comes in, seeing the hall not yet quiet, asked the matter. Jack comes, "I'll tell thee Willy," quoth he, "as I was playing at cards, one seeing I won all I played for, would needs have the knave from me, which as very a knave as he seeing, would needs bear him knave for company. So to bid them both welcome to thy house, I have been to entreat the knave thy butler to make them drink." "Ay," says Sir William, "and you like a knave made them fall out." "Ay," answered Jack, "and your drink, Sir Knave, made them friends." Sir William laughing departed. . . .

How a Minstrel Became a Fool Artificial and Had Jack Oates His Reward for His Labor

At a Christmas time when great logs furnish the hall fire, when brawn[16] is in season, and indeed all reveling is regarded, this gallant knight kept open house for all comers, where beef, beer, and bread was no niggard.[17] Amongst all the pleasures provided, a noise[18] of minstrels and a Lincolnshire bagpipe was prepared, the minstrels for the great chamber, the bagpipe for the hall, the minstrel to serve by the knight's meat, and the bagpipe for the common dancing.[19] Jack could not endure to be in the common hall, for indeed the fool was a little proud-minded, and therefore was altogether in the great chamber at my lady's or Sir William's elbow. One time, being very melancholy, the knight to rouse him up said, "Hence, fool, hence I'll have another

[13] **in dudgeon:** offensively. [14] **miscalled:** maligned. [15] **buttery:** keeping room for beer and other provisions. [16] **brawn:** meat. [17] **niggard:** stingy person. [18] **noise:** band. [19] **knight's meat . . . common dancing:** the revels took place in two places, those of higher status being entertained in the great chamber, those of lower status in the great hall.

fool, thou shalt dwell no longer with me." Jack to this answered little, though indeed ye could not anger him worse. A gentleman at the board answers, "If it please you, sir, I'll bring ye another fool soon." "I pray ye do," quoth the knight, "and he shall be welcome." Jack fell acrying and departed mad and angry down into the great hall, and being strong-armed as before I described him, caught the bagpipes from the piper, knocked them about his pate,[20] that he laid the fellow for dead on the ground and all broken, carries the pipes up into the great chamber and lays them on the fire. The knight, knowing by Jack that something was amiss, sends down to see. News of this jest came, the knight angry (but to no purpose, for he loved the fool above all, and that the household knew, else Jack had payed for it, for the common people's dancing was spoiled) sent down Jack, and bade him out of his sight. Jack cries, "Hang Sir Willy, hang Sir Willy" and departs.

Sir William, not knowing how to amend the matter, caused the piper to be carried to bed who was very ill, and said, "I would now give a gold noble for a fool, indeed to anger him thoroughly." One of the minstrels whispered a gentleman in the ear and said, if it pleased him, he would, whereat the gentleman laughed. The knight demanded the reason of his laughing: "I pray you tell me," quoth he, "for laughing could never come in a better time; the fool hath madded me." "If it please you," says the gentleman, "here is a good fellow will go and attire him in one of his coats and can in all points behave himself naturally like such a one." "It is good," says the knight, "and I prithee, good fellow, about it, and one go call Jack Oates hither that we may hold him with talk in the meantime."

The simple minstrel, thinking to work wonders as one overjoyed at the good opportunity, threw his fiddle one way, his stick another, and his case the third way, and was in such a case of joy that it was no boot[21] to bid him make haste, but proud of the knight's favor away he flings as if he went to take possession of some great lordship. But what ere he got by it, I am sure his fiddle with the fall fell apieces, which grieved his master so that in love and pity he laughed till the water ran down his cheeks. Beside, this good knight was like to keep a bad Christmas, for the bagpipes and the music went to wreck, the one burnt, and the other broken.

In comes Jack Oates and being merry told the knight and the rest that a country wench in the hall had eaten garlic and there was seventeen men poisoned with kissing her, for it was use[22] to jest thus. By and by comes in a messenger (one of the knight's men) to tell him that such a gentleman had sent his fool to dwell with him. "He is welcome," says the knight, "for I am

[20] **pate:** head. [21] **no boot:** no use. [22] **use:** usual.

weary of this fool. Go bid him come in; Jack, bid him welcome." They all laughed to see Jack's color come and go, like a wise man ready to make a good end. "What say you to this?" says the knight. Not one word says Jack. Th[e]y tingled with a knife at the bottom of a glass, as tolling the bell for the fool, who was speechless and would die, than which, nothing could more anger him. But now the thought of the newcome fool so much moved him that he was as dead as a door nail, standing on tip-toe looking towards the door to behold his arrival, that he would put his nose out of joint.

By and by enters my artificial fool in his old clothes making wry mouths, dancing, looking asquint, who when Jack beheld, suddenly he flew at him, and so violently beat him that all the table rose, but could scarce get him off. Well, off he was at length, the knight caused the broken ones to be by themselves. My poor minstrel with a fall had his head broke to the skull against the ground, his face scratched, that which was worst of all his left eye put out, and withal so sore bruised that he could neither stand nor go.[23] The knight caused him to be laid with the piper, who was also hurt in the like conflict, who lacked no good looking to, because they miscarried in the knight's service. But ever after Jack Oates could not endure to hear any talk of another fool to be there, and the knight durst not make such a motion. The piper and the minstrel being in bed together, one cried O, his back and face, the other O, his face and eye; the one cried O, his pipe, the other O, his fiddle. Good music or broken consorts[24] they agree well together. But when they were well, they were contented; for their pains they had both money and the knight's favor. Here you have heard the difference 'twixt a flat fool natural and a flat fool artificial, one that had his kind,[25] and the other who foolishly followed his own mind, on which two is written this rhyme.

Natural fools are prone to self conceit,
Fools artificial, with their wits lay wait
To make themselves fools, liking the disguise,
To feed their own minds and the gazer's eyes.
He that attempts danger and is free,
Hurting himself, being well cannot see
Must with the fiddler here wear the fool's coats
And bide his penance 'signed[26] him by Jack Oates.
All such say I that use flat foolery,
Bear this, bear more, this flat fool's company.

[23] **go:** walk. [24] **broken consorts:** ensembles made up of instruments from different families, with a pun on "broken." [25] **had his kind:** followed his nature. [26] **'signed:** assigned.

→ ROBERT ARMIN

From Quips upon Questions, or A Clown's Conceit on Occasion Offered *1600*

The verbal mastery that made Armin famous is put on conspicuous display in another of his jest books, *Quips upon Questions, or A Clown's Conceit on Occasion Offered,* published the same year as *Fool upon Fool* by the same publisher, with the same attribution to "*Clonnico de Curtanio Snuff.*" This time, the title page continues, the collection of jests is set up as "A Moralified Metamorphoses of Changes upon Interrogatories." Each joke comes in three parts: first a question or a remark from a bystander, then Snuff's improvised verses on the subject at hand, followed by a one- or two-line moralization. "Metamorphoses" seems to be precisely chosen to recall Ovid's long poem, which was often published during the sixteenth and early seventeenth centuries with the kind of moralizing commentary we sampled from George Sandys's edition in Chapter 2.

The whole of *Quips upon Questions* presents itself as a transcript of extemporaneous performance in the theater, even if individual jokes reveal their origins in the world outside. Common to all the jests is Armin's virtuosity in using multiple voices: he is the questioner, the improvising clown, and the quipping moralist. In some of the jests he adopts even more voices. In response to the question "What's near her?" for example, he speaks a dialogue-within-the-dialogue as he argues back and forth for two possible answers: her smock and her skin. Similar ventriloquizing skills are on display in *Twelfth Night* as Feste plays Sir Topas. His great moment comes when he plays himself and Sir Topas at the same time:

> MALVOLIO: Sir Topas!
>
> FESTE: [*in Sir Topas' voice*] Maintain no words with him, good fellow. [*In his own voice*] Who, I, sir? Not I, sir, God b' wi' you, good Sir Topas. [*In Sir Topas' voice*] Marry, amen. [*In his own voice*] I will, sir, I will.
>
> MALVOLIO: Fool! Fool! Fool, I say!
>
> FESTE: Alas, sir, be patient. What say you, sir? I am shent for speaking to you. (4.2.78–84)

Several of the "interrogatories" in *Quips upon Questions* touch on matters likewise addressed in *Twelfth Night:* who plays the fool — the clown who plays or the man who pays the clown who plays? what wished the widow? why is this man drunk? what wit succeeds?

From *Quips upon Questions, or A Clown's Conceit on Occasion Offered*

Who Began to Live in the World?

Adam was he, that first lived in the world
And Eve was next. Who knows not this is true?
But at the last he was from all grace hurled,
And she for company, the like did rue.
Was he the first? Ay, and was thus disgraced,
Better for him, that he had been the last.

Quip. *Thou art a fool. Why? For reasoning so,*
But not the first, nor last, by many mo'.[1]

. . . .

He Plays the Fool

True it is, he plays the fool indeed,
But in the play he plays it as he must.
Yet when the play is ended, then his speed
Is better than the pleasure of thy trust,
For he shall have what thou that time hast spent,
Playing the fool, thy folly to content.

He plays the wise man then, and not the fool,
That wisely for his living so can do.
So doth the carpenter with his sharp tool,
Cut his own finger off, yet lives by it too.
He is a fool to cut his limbs say I,
But not so, with his tool[2] to live thereby,

Then 'tis his case[3] that makes him seem a fool,
It is indeed, for it is antic made.
Thus men wax wise when they do go to school,
Then for our sport we thank the tailor's trade,[4]

[1] **mo'**: more. [2] **tool:** with a pun on penis. [3] **case:** (1) situation, (2) motley garment, (3) codpiece. [4] **tailor's trade:** tailors were proverbial for lechery.

Robert Armin, *Quips upon Questions, or A Clown's Conceit on Occasion Offered* (London: William Febrand, 1600), A1, B4v–C1, D1v–D2, E2v–E3, F2v–F3.

And him within the case the most of all,
That seems wise foolish, who a fool you call.

Meet him abroad, and he is wise, methinks,
In courtesy, behavior, talk, or going,[5]
Of garment: eke[6] when he with any drinks,
Then are men wise, their money so bestowing,
To learn by him one time, a fool to seem,
and twenty times for once, in good esteem.

Say I should meet him, and not know his name,
What should I say, "Yonder goes such a fool"?
Ay, fools will say so, but the wise will aim
At better thoughts, whom reason still doth rule:
"Yonder's the merry man, it joys me much,
To see him civil, when his part is such."

Quip. A merry man is often thought unwise.
Yet mirth in modesty's 'lowed[7] of the wise.
They say, should he for a fool go
When he's a more fool that accounts him so?
Many men descant[8] on another's wit,
When they have less themselves in doing it.

. . . .

What Wished She?

A widow[9] wished, hark and I'll tell thee what.
Choice of a thousand things. What things, I pray?
Content thyself, man, and imagine that,
Think what she wished, and hit it if thou may.
What, was she rich? Ay, so a number say.
'Tis hard to jump with thee in what she would,
For women often wish not what they should,

She wished a husband that was rich like her.
That wealth to wealth were joined, was it not so?
Although in heart she could hit nothing near.

[5] **going:** walking. [6] **eke:** also. [7] ***'lowed:*** allowed. [8] ***descant:*** comment. [9] **widow:** proverbial for lust.

Then she wished wit, to govern it? Fie, no.
Then she wished health, to enjoy it? Yet ye go
    Far from her meaning, yet you came[10] so near,
    As you will hit it by and by I fear.

Oh, then I have it: women covet honor.
Honor is glorious, yet you want her mind.
Now fortune yield her wish so light upon her,
For I am senseless in her wish, and blind.
I cannot think her thought, how she's inclined:
    So wild are women in their thoughts and deeds,
    As no wise man knows where their humor breeds.

Now I will answer thee what wish she craved.
Not gold, she had enough, nor wit to keep it,
For when some thought she spent, she nearly saved,
And covetously together would she sweep it.
Let them alone, too well can women heap it.
    All wishes set apart, her eye being pleased,
    Her wish is granted and her heart is eased.

Quip. *Her eye to please is endless, not to do,*
    Whose scope, no power can compass thereunto.
    Well, let her wish but ne'er relieved thereby,
    Whose belly's sooner pleased, than is her eye.

. . . .

Why Is He Drunk?

I know not why, unless I knew his mind,
But many besides him is thus inclined.
Perchance for company he is disguised,
Or 'tis his nature to be thus sufficed,
    Or tasting good beer never found before,
    Against his will is drunk of his own score.

It may be his weak brain can bear no drink.
I am not of your mind, so well to think.
Then knowing his own weakness, he should shun,
Thus to be loathsome, as he has begun.

[10] **came:** with a pun on ejaculation.

How e'er it is I know not, but these people,
Are all brained with a brewer's washing beetle.[11]

Quip. *Company causeth cuckolds,*[12] *most men say,*
But shall this proverb bear it so away?
Ay, it must needs, for it is held least jeopardy,
When men go to the devil for company.

. . . .

He Had Much Wit

He had much wit, else had he ne'er been rich,
For what he hath, he had it through the fire.
He had much wit, and there are but few such,
That with their wit can purchase their desire.
A number live that wisely would be thought,
When their wit fails them, and doth come to nought.

Houses he hath a number, and much land,
His purse is stuffed, and he hath a full hand,
But of his store, what gives he to the needy?
Nothing at all, in that he is not speedy.
His purse is tied fast, and his mind is sparing,
And for the poorer sort hath little caring.

Had he much wit to get this world's increase
And hath he no wit left rightly to use it?
He hath no wit then now, and therefore peace,
Such as have God's true blessing, and abuse it,
Had better be still poor, for fellow credit me,
He hath but little wit, and far less honesty.

Quip. *He that gets much and little gives,*
He seems a living man, but little lives.
He that had wit himself to thrall,
Better say I, he had no wit at all.

[11] **washing beetle:** wooden bat for beating clothes during washing. [12] ***cuckolds:*** husbands whose wives have had sex with other men.

Theories of Laughter: Superiority

As Quintilian notes, the difficulty of defining just what it is that makes people laugh has not stopped theorists from trying. John Morreall's survey of those attempts in *Taking Laughter Seriously* distinguishes three types: theories based on superiority, on incongruity, and on relief (4–37). In this section of the chapter we shall sample texts arguing all three viewpoints before considering Sir Philip Sidney's argument for a fourth possibility. The oldest group of theories, those based on superiority, goes back to Plato (427?–347 B.C.E.) and Aristotle (384–322 B.C.E.). In the *Poetics,* Aristotle offers an account of the origins of tragedy and comedy that depends on distinctions that are both social and ethical. Poetry, he explains, broke up into two kinds, according to the character of the poets themselves: "for the graver among them would represent noble actions, and those of noble personages; and the meaner sort the actions of the ignoble." Poets of the first sort produced panegyrics, or poems of praise; poets of the second sort produced invectives (1448b). The idea that comedy is all about the reproving of vices in other people — especially one's social inferiors — was congenial to the Greek and Roman rhetoricians, to Christian writers of the Middle Ages, and to humanist writers in the fifteenth and sixteenth centuries.

The superiority theory remained the dominant theory of laughter in Shakespeare's day, as witness Thomas Heywood's explanation of comedy in his *Apology for Actors.* Of anti-theatricalists like Philip Stubbes, Heywood asks,

> What is then the subject of this harmless mirth? Either in the shape of a clown to show others their slovenly and unhandsome behavior, that they may reform that simplicity in themselves which others make their sport, lest they happen to become the like subject of general scorn to an auditory, else it intreats of love, deriding foolish inamorates who spend their ages, their spirits, nay themselves in the servile and ridiculous employments of their mistresses. (F4)

By this account, *Twelfth Night* is a warning against Feste's slovenly and unhandsome behavior and Orsino's love-longing. The shortsightedness of such an approach is easy to see. Feste the clown presents himself as the moralizer of other people's follies, not as the possessor of follies himself. Ridicule, nonetheless, is Feste's stock in trade. As a writer, Armin seems to have the superiority theory in mind when he offers *Quips upon Questions* as *moralized* metamorphoses, always ending in a gnomic tag. The emblem of a fool in George Wither's *A Collection of Emblems* (1635) likewise drives home a moral message: "The world is much for shows, and few there are / So diligent to *be* as to *appear.*" (See Figure 29.) According to the verses, those who strive to seem rich, wise, and holy are playing the parts of fools. (Take note, Malvolio.) The Fool in the emblem meets the gazer's eye and establishes a solidarity that allies a knowing *us* against the foolish likes of *them.*

PLATO

From Philebus

5th/4th centuries B.C.E.

In Plato's dialogues laughter is always assumed to be a form of derision in which the laugher measures his elevation — intellectual, ethical, and social — above an object of ridicule. In *Philebus,* for example, ridicule is taken up in connection with a discussion of pleasure. Ridicule belongs with those pleasures pertinent, not to the body, or to body and soul in combination, but to the soul alone. A consideration of the soul's experience of anger, sorrow, envy, and the mixed feelings engaged by watching tragedy and comedy, leads Socrates to the soul's experience of ridicule at other people's self-deceptions. Social distinctions come into play as Socrates distinguishes powerful people from powerless people. Only the latter can properly be objects of ridicule, since the self-deceptions of the former can lead to grave consequences. The excerpt concludes with Socrates' consideration of combinations of pleasure and pain, not only on the stage, but in life.

SOCRATES: I have just mentioned envy; would you not call that a pain of the soul?

PROTARCHUS: Yes.

SOCRATES: And yet the envious man finds something in the misfortunes of his neighbors at which he is pleased?

PROTARCHUS: Certainly.

SOCRATES: And ignorance, and what is termed clownishness, are surely an evil?

PROTARCHUS: To be sure.

SOCRATES: From these considerations learn to know the nature of the ridiculous.

PROTARCHUS: Explain.

Plato, *Philebus,* in *The Dialogues of Plato,* trans. Benjamin Jowett, 4th ed. rev. (Oxford: Oxford University Press, 1969), 3:606–09.

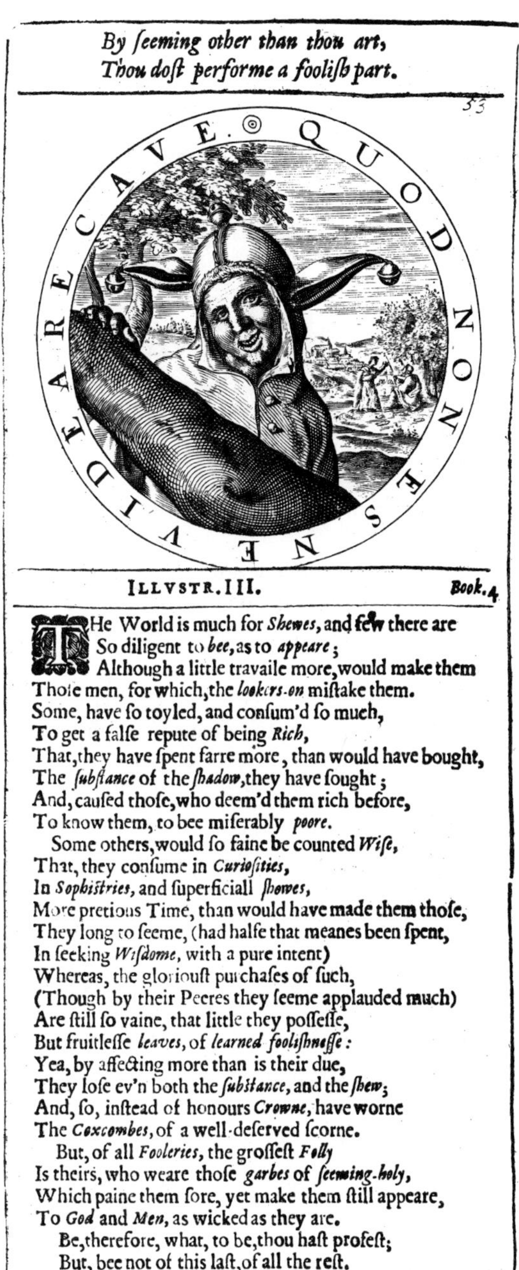
By ſeeming other than thou art,
Thou doſt performe a fooliſh part.

ILLVSTR. III. **Book. 4**

THe World is much for *Shewes*, and few there are
So diligent to *bee*, as to *appeare*;
Although a little travaile more, would make them
Thoſe men, for which, the *lookers-on* miſtake them.
Some, have ſo toyled, and conſum'd ſo much,
To get a falſe repute of being *Rich*,
That, they have ſpent farre more, than would have bought,
The *ſubſtance* of the *ſhadow*, they have ſought;
And, cauſed thoſe, who deem'd them rich before,
To know them, to bee miſerably *poore*.
Some others, would ſo faine be counted *Wiſe*,
That, they conſume in *Curioſities*,
In *Sophiſtries*, and ſuperficiall *ſhowes*,
More pretious Time, than would have made them thoſe,
They long to ſeeme, (had halfe that meanes been ſpent,
In ſeeking *Wiſdome*, with a pure intent)
Whereas, the glorious purchaſes of ſuch,
(Though by their Peeres they ſeeme applauded much)
Are ſtill ſo vaine, that little they poſſeſſe,
But fruitleſſe *leaves*, of *learned fooliſhneſſe*:
Yea, by affecting more than is their due,
They loſe ev'n both the *ſubſtance*, and the *ſhew*;
And, ſo, inſtead of honours *Crowne*, have worne
The *Coxcombes*, of a well-deſerved ſcorne.
But, of all *Fooleries*, the groſſeſt *Folly*
Is theirs, who weare thoſe *garbes* of *ſeeming-holy*,
Which paine them ſore, yet make them ſtill appeare,
To *God* and *Men*, as wicked as they are.
Be, therefore, what, to be, thou haſt profeſt;
But, bee not of this laſt, of all the reſt.

Ff 2 *Purſue*

FIGURE 29 *Who Is the True Fool? from George Wither,* A Collection of Emblems *(1635).*

SOCRATES: The ridiculous is in short the specific name which is used to describe the vicious form of a certain habit; and of vice in general it is that kind which is most at variance with the inscription at Delphi.

PROTARCHUS: You mean, Socrates, "Know thyself."

SOCRATES: I do; and the opposite would be, "Know not thyself."

PROTARCHUS: Certainly.

SOCRATES: And now, O Protarchus, try to divide this into three.

PROTARCHUS: Indeed I am afraid that I cannot.

SOCRATES: Do you mean to say that I must make the division for you?

PROTARCHUS: Yes, and what is more, I beg that you will.

SOCRATES: Are there not three ways in which ignorance of self may be shown?

PROTARCHUS: What are they?

SOCRATES: In the first place, about money; the ignorant may fancy himself richer than he is.

PROTARCHUS: Yes, that is a very common error.

SOCRATES: And still more often he will fancy that he is taller or fairer than he is, or that he has some other advantage of person which he really has not.

PROTARCHUS: Of course.

SOCRATES: And yet surely by far the greatest number err about the goods of the mind; they imagine themselves to be much better men than they are.

PROTARCHUS: Yes, that is by far the commonest delusion.

SOCRATES: And of all the virtues, is not wisdom the one which the mass of mankind are always claiming, and which most arouses in them a spirit of contention and lying conceit of wisdom?

PROTARCHUS: Certainly.

SOCRATES: And may not all this be truly called an evil condition?

PROTARCHUS: Very evil.

SOCRATES: But we must pursue the division a step further, Protarchus, if we would see in envy of the childish sort a singular mixture of pleasure and pain.

PROTARCHUS: How can we make the further division which you suggest?

SOCRATES: All who are silly enough to entertain this lying conceit of themselves may of course be divided, like the rest of mankind, into two classes — one having power and might; and the other the reverse.

PROTARCHUS: Certainly.

SOCRATES: Let this, then, be the principle of division; those of them who are weak and unable to revenge themselves, when they are laughed at, may be truly called ridiculous, but those who can defend themselves may be more truly described as strong and formidable; for ignorance in the powerful is hateful and horrible, because hurtful to others both in reality and in fiction, but powerless ignorance may be reckoned, and in truth is, ridiculous.

PROTARCHUS: That is very true, but I do not as yet see where is the admixture of pleasures and pains.

SOCRATES: Well, then, let us examine the nature of envy.

PROTARCHUS: Proceed.

SOCRATES: Is not envy an unrighteous pleasure, and also an unrighteous pain?

PROTARCHUS: Most true.

SOCRATES: There is nothing envious or wrong in rejoicing at the misfortunes of enemies?

PROTARCHUS: Certainly not.

SOCRATES: But to feel joy instead of sorrow at the sight of our friends' misfortunes — is not that wrong?

PROTARCHUS: Undoubtedly.

SOCRATES: Did we not say that ignorance was always an evil?

PROTARCHUS: True.

SOCRATES: And the three kinds of vain conceit in our friends which we enumerated — the vain conceit of beauty, of wisdom, and of wealth, are ridiculous if they are weak, and detestable when they are powerful: May we not say, as I was saying before, that our friends who are in this state of mind, when harmless to others, are simply ridiculous?

PROTARCHUS: They are ridiculous.

SOCRATES: And do we not acknowledge this ignorance of theirs to be a misfortune?

PROTARCHUS: Certainly.

SOCRATES: And do we feel pain or pleasure in laughing at it?

PROTARCHUS: Clearly we feel pleasure.

SOCRATES: And was not envy the source of this pleasure which we feel at the misfortunes of friends?

PROTARCHUS: Certainly.

SOCRATES: Then the argument shows that when we laugh at the folly of our friends, pleasure, in mingling with envy, mingles with pain, for envy has been acknowledged by us to be mental pain, and laughter is pleasant; and so we envy and laugh at the same instant.

PROTARCHUS: True.

SOCRATES: And the argument implies that there are combinations of pleasure and pain in lamentations, and in tragedy and comedy, not only on the stage, but on the greater stage of human life; and so in endless other cases.

PROTARCHUS: I do not see how any one can deny what you say, Socrates, however eager he may be to assert the opposite opinion.

PLATO

From Republic

5th/4th centuries B.C.E.

The social and ethical concerns of superiority theories of laughter mean that laughter itself is suspect, even when the laugher is above the vices he laughs at. To laugh is, in some degree, to lose the rational control that makes the laugher superior to start with. Hence the need for an ethics of humor. The idea that laughter is unbecoming to a person of intellectual substance can be traced back to Plato's *Republic* and Socrates' argument that poets like Homer ought not be allowed to depict gods and heroes in ridiculous situations. The risk is that ordinary mortals use their superiors' follies to excuse their own failings. Laughter, claims Socrates, is particularly reprehensible in the political guardians of the state. Whether or not Malvolio had read Plato is open to debate, but in his confrontation with Sir Toby, Sir Andrew, Maria, and Feste he argues for a sobriety of behavior that is expected in persons of their social station. "Is there," he asks, "no respect of place, persons, nor time in you?" (2.3.76–77). The more loquacious speaker in the excerpt that follows is, of course, Socrates. His interlocutor is Adeimantus.

We will once more entreat Homer and the other poets not to depict Achilles, who is the son of a goddess, first lying on his side, then on his back, and then on his face; then starting up and sailing in a frenzy along the shores of the barren sea; now taking the sooty ashes in both his hands and pouring them over his head, or weeping and wailing in the various modes which Homer has delineated. Nor should he describe Priam the kinsman of the gods as praying and beseeching,

> Rolling in the dirt, calling each man loudly by his name.[1]

[1] **Rolling . . . name:** This and the following quotations are from Homer's *Iliad.*

Plato, *Republic,* in *The Dialogues of Plato,* trans. Benjamin Jowett, 4th ed. rev. (Oxford: Oxford University Press, 1969), 2:232–33.

Still more earnestly will we beg of him at all events not to introduce the gods lamenting and saying,

> Alas! my misery! Alas! that I bore the bravest to my sorrow.

But if he must introduce the gods, at any rate let him not dare so completely to misrepresent the greatest of the gods, as to make him say —

> O heavens! with my eyes verily I behold a dear friend of mine chased round and round the city, and my heart is sorrowful.

Or again: —

> Woe is me that I am fated to have Sarpedon, dearest of men to me, subdued at the hands of Patroclus the son of Menoetius.

For if, my sweet Adeimantus, our youth seriously listen to such unworthy representations of the gods, instead of laughing at them as they ought, hardly will any of them deem that he himself, being but a man, can be dishonoured by similar actions; neither will he rebuke any inclination which may arise in his mind to say and do the like. And instead of having any shame or self-control, he will be always whining and lamenting on slight occasions.

Yes, he said, that is most true.

Yes, I replied; but that surely is what ought not to be, as the argument has just proved to us; and by that proof we must abide until it is disproved by a better.

It ought not to be.

Neither ought our guardians to be given to laughter. For a fit of laughter which has been indulged to excess almost always produces a violent reaction.

So I believe.

Then persons of worth, even if only mortal men, must not be represented as overcome by laughter, and still less must such a representation of the gods be allowed.

Still less of the gods, as you say, he replied.

Then we shall not suffer such an expression to be used about the gods as that of Homer when he describes how

> Inextinguishable laughter arose among the blessed gods, when they saw Hephaestus bustling about the mansion.

On your views, we must not admit them.

On my views, if you like to father them on me; that we must not admit them is certain.

ARISTOTLE

From Nicomachean Ethics

4th century B.C.E.

After having been the chief authority for medieval philosophers in the tradition of Thomas Aquinas, Aristotle continued to enjoy influence in the Renaissance because his ideas had been taken up by admired Roman thinkers like Cicero. Most assumptions about human society in the sixteenth and seventeenth centuries can be traced ultimately to Aristotle's *Nicomachean Ethics,* a treatise in which Aristotle trains his characteristically objective mind on the patterns of behavior that men adopt toward one another — and *should* adopt toward one another. In the course of considering the "excellencies" to which a man ought to aspire — courage, temperance, liberality, magnificence, pride, honor, good temper — Aristotle constantly stresses the importance of avoiding extremes. The ideal of moderation also governs his account of leisure and amusement. The principles that Aristotle delineates in the next-to-last chapter of book 4 are the ultimate source of the advice that modern writers like Castiglione, Guazzo, della Casa, Peacham, Brathwait, and their successors conveyed to gentlemen and would-be gentlemen of the sixteenth, seventeenth, and eighteenth centuries. A good and well-bred man should laugh, but not too much, and not at indecencies. Richard Brathwait, writing a generation after *Twelfth Night,* advises the English gentleman to countenance "no carnal but cordial joy, no laughter of the body but of the heart" (456).

Since life includes rest as well, and in this is included leisure and amusement, there seems here also to be a kind of intercourse which is tasteful; there is such a thing as saying — and again listening to — what one should and as one should. The kind of people one is speaking or listening to will also make a difference. Evidently here also there is both an excess and a deficiency as compared with the mean. Those who carry humor to excess are thought to be vulgar buffoons, striving after humor at all costs, and aiming rather at raising a laugh than at saying what is becoming and at avoiding pain to the object of their fun; while those who can neither make a joke themselves nor put up with those who do are thought to be boorish and unpolished. But those who joke in a tasteful way are called ready-witted, which implies a sort of readiness to turn this way and that; for such sallies are thought to be movements of the character, and as bodies are discriminated by their movements, so too are characters. The ridiculous side of

---

Aristotle, *Nicomachean Ethics,* in *Complete Works,* ed. Jonathan Barnes (Princeton: Princeton University Press, 1984), 2: 1780–81.

things is not far to seek, however, and most people delight more than they should in amusement and in jesting, and so even buffoons are called ready-witted because they are found attractive; but that they differ from the ready-witted man, and to no small extent, is clear from what has been said.

To the middle state belongs also tact; it is the mark of a tactful man to say and listen to such things as befit a good and well-bred man; for there are some things that it befits such a man to say and to hear by way of jest, and the well-bred man's jesting differs from that of a vulgar man, and the joking of an educated man from that of an uneducated. One may see this even from the old and the new comedies;[1] to the authors of the former indecency of language was amusing, to those of the laffer innuendo is more so; and these differ in no small degree in respect of propriety. Now should we define the man who jokes well by his saying what is not unbecoming to a well-bred man, or by his not giving pain, or even giving delight, to the hearer? Or is the latter, at any rate, itself indefinite, since different things are hateful or pleasant to different people'? The kind of jokes he will listen to will be the same; for the kind he can put up with are also the kind he seems to make. There are, then, jokes he will not make; for the jest is a sort of abuse, and there are things that lawgivers forbid us to abuse; and they should, perhaps, have forbidden us even to make a jest of such. The refined and well-bred man, therefore, will be as we have described, being as it were a law to himself.

Such, then, is the man who observes the mean, whether he be called tactful or ready-witted. The buffoon, on the other hand, is the slave of his sense of humor, and spares neither himself nor others if he can raise a laugh, and says things none of which a man of refinement would say, and to some of which he would not even listen. The boor, again, is useless for such social intercourse; for he contributes nothing and finds fault with everything. But relaxation and amusement are thought to be a necessary element in life.

The means in life that have been described, then, are three in number, and are all concerned with an interchange of words and deeds of some kind. They differ, however, in that one is concerned with truth, and the other two with pleasantness. Of those concerned with pleasure, one is displayed in jests, the other in the general social intercourse of life.

[1] **old . . . comedies:** "old" comedies by Aristophanes (c. 450–c. 380 B.C.E.) and other writers ridiculed specific individuals with scurrilous directness; "new" comedies by Menander (342–c. 290 B.C.E.) and other writers satirized general types, and in more polite terms.

GIOVANNI DELLA CASA

From Galateo . . . or rather A Treatise of the Manners and Behaviors It Behooveth a Man to Use and Eschew

1576

Translated by Robert Peterson

Aristotle's precepts are given an interesting turn in the following passage from Giovanni della Casa's conduct book *Galateo,* translated by Robert Peterson as *A Treatise of the Manners and Behaviors It Behooveth a Man to Use and Eschew in His Familiar Conversation, A Work Very Necessary and Profitable for All Gentlemen or Other.* To Aristotle's list of things a man of substance ought not to laugh at, della Casa adds physical deformities. Robert Armin's shortness and plumpness would put della Casa's "honest gentleman" on the spot. Della Casa goes on to formulate a distinction between "scorns" and "mocks" that likewise bears on *Twelfth Night.* A scorn involves pleasure in humiliating someone else and is thus not proper for a gentleman; a mock is done for merriment alone, in a sociable spirit, and hence is acceptable. The gulling of Malvolio presents a test case. In tricking Malvolio into presenting himself cross-gartered in yellow stockings, Maria, Sir Toby, and Sir Andrew are clearly delivering a mock. When they imprison Malvolio and try to convince him he is mad, does the mock become a scorn? Certainly Malvolio sees it as that in the play's last scene. "Madam," he complains to Olivia, "you have done me wrong, / Notorious wrong" (5.1.307–08). Where, in ethical terms, does that leave the audience who has shared the conspirators' pleasure? Feste tries to justify their actions by quoting from the forged letter the line that most incited Malvolio's ambition and self-love: "Some are born great, some achieve greatness, and some have greatness thrown upon them" (5.1.349–50). Malvolio's response is to leave the stage in a huff. The tone of his exit line — "I'll be revenged on the whole pack of you!" (5.1.355) — has presented a delicate problem to actors since the eighteenth century, if not also in 1602.

Do not allow that a man should scorn or scoff at any man, whatsoever he be. No not his very enemy, what displeasure soever he bear him, for it is a greater sign of contempt and disdain, to scorn a man, than to do him an open wrong, forasmuch as wrongs may be done, either of choler, or of some covetous mind or other. And there is no man will take a displeasure with that, or for that, he doth not set by,[1] nor yet covet that thing he doth alto-

[1] **set by:** value.

Giovanni della Casa, *Galateo,* trans. Robert Peterson as *Galateo . . . or rather a Treatise of Manners and Behaviors It Behooveth a Man to Use and Eschew . . .* (London: Ralph Newberry, 1576), 62–64, 120–21.

gether condemn. So that, a man doth make some account of him he doth wrong. But of him that he scoffs and scorns, he makes no reckoning at all, or as little as may be.

And the nature and effect of a scorn is properly to take a contentation[2] and pleasure to do another man shame and villainy, though it do ourselves no good in the world. So that, good manner and honesty would us beware we scorn no man in any case, wherein they be much to be blamed, that reprove men those blemishes they have in their person, either in words, as Master Horese da Rabatta did, laughing at the countenance of Master Giotta, or in deeds, as many do, counterfeiting those that stutter, halt, or be crooked-shouldered. And likewise, they that scoff at any man, that is deformed, ill shapen, lean, little, or a dwarf, are much to be blamed for it, or that make a jibbing and jesting at such follies as another man speaketh, or the words that escape him by chance, and withal have a sport and a pleasure to make a man blush. All these spiteful behaviors and fashions worthily deserve to be hated, and make them that use them unworthy to bear the name of an honest gentlemen.

And such as use to jest at a man, be very like unto these. I mean them that have a good sport to mock and beguile me, not in spite or scorn, but on a merriment alone. And you shall understand, there is no difference between a scorn and a mock but the purpose alone and intent a man hath in the meaning the one the other. For a man mocks and laughs otherwhile,[3] in a sport and a pastime, but his scorn is ever in a rage and disdain, although in common speech and writing, we take the one word sometime for the other. But he that doth scorn a man, feeleth a contentation in the shame he hath done him. And he that doth mock or but laugh taketh no contentation in that he hath done, but a sport to be merry and pass the time away, where it would be both a grief and a sorrow, per chance, unto him to see that man receive any shame, by anything he said or did unto him. . . .

A man must leave those foolish manner of laughings, gross and uncomely. And let men laugh upon occasion, and not upon custom. But a man must beware he does not laugh at his own jests and his doings. For that makes men ween[4] he would fain[5] praise himself. It is for other men to laugh that hear, and not for him that tells the tale.

[2] **contentation:** contentment. [3] **otherwhile:** now and again. [4] **ween:** surmise. [5] **fain:** desire to.

Theories of Laughter: Incongruity

If the superiority theory of laughter is social and ethical in nature, the incongruity theory is intellectual and cognitive. For something to be funny, so the theory goes, we have to expect one thing but get something else. In John Morreall's formulation, "While amusement for the superiority theory is primarily affective — it is self-glory or the feeling of triumph — for the incongruity theory amusement is an intellectual reaction to something that is unexpected, illogical, or inappropriate in some other way" (15). Ordinarily we trust the world to be an orderly place in which certain things happen over and over again in certain ways. When on occasion that turns out not to be the case, and the results are felicitous, we are surprised — and express that surprise in laughter. The separated twins who find each other at last, the dour Puritan who puts on yellow stockings, the boy who turns out to be a girl: *Twelfth Night* is full of felicitous incongruities of just this sort.

It was not until the eighteenth and nineteenth centuries that the incongruity theory received sustained philosophical attention, in the work of Kant and Schopenhauer, but the kernel of the idea is present in Aristotle's writings. In the *Poetics,* as we have seen, Aristotle seems to entertain the superiority theory of laughter, but in the *Rhetoric* he is forced to take a narrower, more practical view of the matter as he gives advice to would-be orators. Laughter in this account is a function of metaphor, of the joining together of two logically unlike things. "Liveliness," Aristotle advises, "is specially conveyed by metaphor, and by the further power of surprising the hearer; because the hearer expected something different, his acquisition of the new idea impresses him all the more. His mind seems to say, 'Yes, to be sure; I never thought of that.'" Epigrams and riddles provide good examples. So do "burlesque words" in stage comedies. As an example Aristotle cites the line "Onward he came, and his feet were shod with — chilblains," where the listener expects to hear "sandals" (1412a). Feste, Lady Olivia's "corrupter of words," has taken more than a page out of Aristotle's book.

QUINTILIAN

From Institutio Oratoria

1st century C.E.

The most extended discussion of incongruity as the source of laughter occurs in Quintilian's *Institutio Oratoria,* in the section that follows the philosophical framing of laughter that we have already read (see pp. 358–61). The passage below takes up just after Quintilian has divided wit into six types: *urbanitas, venustus, salsus, facetus, iocus,* and *dicacitas.* Toward the end of the passage he takes up questions of decorum not unlike those addressed by Plato (see p. 380) and Aristotle (see p. 382).

The essence, however, of the subject which we are now discussing is the excitement of laughter, and consequently the whole of this topic is entitled περὶ γελοὶου[1] by the Greeks. It has the same primary division as other departments of oratory, that is to say, it is concerned with things and words. The application of humor to oratory may be divided into three heads: for there are three things out of which we may seek to raise a laugh, to wit, others, ourselves, or things intermediate. In the first case we either reprove or refute or make light of or retort or deride the arguments of others. In the second we speak of things which concern ourselves in a humorous manner and, to quote the words of Cicero, say things which have a suggestion of absurdity. For there are certain sayings which are regarded as folly if they slip from us unawares, but as witty if uttered ironically. The third kind consists, as Cicero also tells us, in cheating expectations, in taking words in a different sense from what was intended, and in other things which affect neither party to the suit, and which I have, therefore, styled intermediate. Further, things designed to raise a laugh may either be said or done. In the latter case laughter is sometimes caused by an act possessing a certain element of seriousness as well, as in the case of Marcus Caelius the praetor, who, when the consul Isauricus broke his curule chair,[2] had another put in its place, the seat of which was made of leather thongs, by way of allusion to the story that the consul had once been scourged by his father: sometimes, again, it is aroused by an act which passes the grounds of decency, as in the case of Caelius' box,[3] a jest which was not fit for an orator or any respectable man to make. On the other hand the joke may lie in some remark about a

[1] περὶ γελοὶου: derision. [2] **curule chair:** chair in the form of a modern campstool. [3] **Caelius' box:** If there is a joke in Cicero's speech *Pro Caelio,* 100.25–29, modern commentators have not found it.

Quintilian, *Institutio Oratoria,* trans. H. E. Butler, Loeb Classical Library (London: Heinemann, 1921), 2: 449–57.

ridiculous look or gesture; such jests are very attractive, more especially when delivered with every appearance of seriousness; for there are no jests so insipid as those which parade the fact that they are intended to be witty. Still, although the gravity with which a jest is uttered increases its attraction, and the mere fact that the speaker does not laugh himself makes his words laughable, there is also such a thing as a humorous look, manner or gesture, provided always that they observe the happy mean. Further, a jest will either be free and lively, like the majority of those uttered by Aulus Galba, or abusive, like those with which Junius Bassus recently made us familiar, or bitter, like those of Cassius Severus, or gentle, like those of Domitius Afer. Much depends on the occasion on which a jest is uttered. For in social gatherings and the intercourse of every day a certain freedom is not unseemly in persons of humble rank, while liveliness is becoming to all. Our jests should never be designed to wound, and we should never make it our ideal to lose a friend sooner than lose a jest.

Where the battles of the courts are concerned I am always better pleased when it is possible to indulge in gentle raillery, although it is, of course, permissible to be abusive or bitter in the words we use against our opponents, just as it is permissible to accuse them openly of crime, and to demand the last penalty of the law. But in the courts as elsewhere it is regarded as inhuman to hit a man when he is down, either because he is the innocent victim of misfortune or because such attacks may recoil on those who make them. Consequently, the first points to be taken into consideration are who the speaker is, what is the nature of the case, who is the judge, who is the victim, and what is the character of the remarks that are made. It is most unbecoming for an orator to distort his features or use uncouth gestures, tricks that arouse such merriment in farce. No less unbecoming are ribald jests, and such as are employed upon the stage. As for obscenity, it should not merely be banished from his language, but should not even be suggested. For even if our opponent has rendered himself liable to such a charge, our denunciation should not take the form of a jest.

Further, although I want my orator to speak with wit, he must not give the impression of striving after it. Consequently he must not display his wit on every possible occasion, but must sacrifice a jest sooner than sacrifice his dignity. Again, no one will endure an accuser who employs jests to season a really horrible case, nor an advocate for the defense who makes merry over one that calls for pity. Moreover, there is a type of judge whose temperament is too serious to allow him to tolerate laughter. It may also happen that a jest directed against an opponent may apply to the judge or to our own client, although there are some orators who do not refrain even from jests that may recoil upon themselves. This was the case with Sulpicius

Longus, who, despite the fact that he was himself surpassingly hideous, asserted of a man against whom he was appearing in a case involving his status as a free man, that even his face was the face of a slave. To this Domitius Afer replied, "Is it your profound conviction, Longus, that an ugly man must be a slave?"

Insolence and arrogance are likewise to be avoided, nor must our jests seem unsuitable to the time or place, or give the appearance of studied premeditation, or smell of the lamp, while those directed against the unfortunate are, as I have already said, inhuman. Again, some advocates are men of such established authority and such known respectability, that any insolence shown them would only hurt the assailant.

As regards the way in which we should deal with friends I have already given instructions. It is the duty not merely of an orator, but of any reasonable human being, when attacking one whom it is dangerous to offend to take care that his remarks do not end in exciting serious enmity, or the necessity for a grovelling apology. Sarcasm that applies to a number of persons is injudicious: I refer to cases where it is directed against whole nations or classes of society, or against rank and pursuits which are common to many. A good man will see that everything he says is consistent with his dignity and the respectability of his character; for we pay too dear for the laugh we raise if it is at the cost of our own integrity.

Theories of Laughter: Relief

Thanks largely to Freud, the notion that laughter results from a release of repressed energy is probably the most common theory of laughter today. The explanation offered by Freud in *Jokes and Their Relation to the Unconscious* (1905, English translation 1916) assumes that the energy being released in laughter is surplus energy, energy that ordinarily would have been used to repress the violent, sexual, socially prohibited impulses that the joke lets us own and express. In the case of *Twelfth Night* those prohibited impulses are, in part, the polymorphous erotic desires that we addressed in Chapter 3. Freud's vocabulary of energy, repression, and release implies a physics-based model that informs a great deal of nineteenth-century thinking. According to this model, energy in a person's psyche is a quantifiable force that must be managed. It can be transferred from one part of the psyche to another, but if the quantity exceeds the system's capacity, some sort of release is required. Applied to the body, these physics-based abstractions become physiological realities in the form of erotic surfaces, fetishized body parts, convulsing lungs, shaking torso, and crying eyes.

Such a concept of laughter goes back, in fact, to Aristotle's treatise "On Parts of Animals." There tickling becomes the basis for Aristotle's characterization of man as "the laughing animal." With respect to laughter, the part in question is not the head but the midriff. In Aristotle's understanding of the human body the organs that respond most to sensation — the heart, the liver, the stomach, the spleen — are all located in the torso. Because these vital organs lie just below the surface, even the slightest heating of the midriff produces an immediate sensation there, quite overpowering the functions of the mind. Witness what happens in laughing:

> For when men are tickled they are quickly set a-laughing, because the motion quickly reaches this part, and being heated but slightly it nevertheless manifestly so disturbs the mental action as to occasion movements that are contrary to the man's intention. That man alone is affected by tickling is due firstly to the delicacy of his skin, and secondly to his being the only animal that laughs. For to be tickled is to be set in laughter. (*Complete Works* 1: 1049.)

Notable here is the idea that laughter is a "hot" sensation, associated with the hot, moist qualities of blood. In Galenic medicine, melancholy is a "cold" sensation, associated with the cold, dry qualities of black bile. Melancholy occurs when the spleen has no way of ridding itself of excess bile. One cure, then, for a melancholy disposition like Orsino's is a hearty laugh that will not only generate blood but relieve the spleen (Lemnius 143). *Twelfth Night* can be understood as performing just that function for all the onlookers in Middle Temple Hall, seated amid the dark February cold. It warms the blood.

→ **LAURENT JOUBERT**

From Treatise on Laughter

1579

Laughter might be therapeutic, but many of Shakespeare's contemporaries persisted in associating it with social ranks lower than themselves precisely because it was such a bodily phenomenom. Mikhail Bakhtin's study of the scatological humor of François Rabelais (1494?–1553) has sensitized us to the political implications of laughter's association with fleshly excess, with irrational abandon, with unguarded boundaries between the body and the world. In Bakhtin's analysis, Rabelais's laughter is a celebration of "the grotesque": "The very material bodily lower stratum of the grotesque image (food, wine, the genital force, the organs of the body) bears a deeply positive character. This principle is victorious for the final result is always abundance, increase" (62). Rabelais had a more theoretically minded successor in Laurent Joubert (1529–1582), royal physician to Henri III and author of a series of widely regarded medical books, as well as a collection of *Erreurs Populaires* not unlike Henry Bourne's *Antiquities of the Common People* (see Chapter 1). Joubert's *Traité du Ris* (1579) locates the cause of laughter in contrary actions about the heart. Perception of something funny causes the heart simultaneously to expand in pleasure and to contract in caution, causing spasms in the diaphram or belly. One chapter in Joubert's thesis explains "Whence it comes that one pisses, shits, and sweats by dint of laughing." Very much in the spirit of Aristotle's "On Parts of Animals," Joubert finds the cause in the physiology of contraction and release.

From *Treatise on Laughter*

CHAPTER 26

Whence It Comes That One Pisses, Shits, and Sweats by Dint of Laughing

At the neck of the bladder there is a round muscle which girds it all around like a ring, closing the passageway to the urine when it is contracted, and for which reason it is called the sphincter.[1] The anal bowel has a similar one with the same name forbidding issue of the fecal matter so long as we wish to retain it. In order to void these excrements, it is necessary to make such muscles open by means of others which are stronger and which obey our will. These are the epigastrics, eight in number[2] not counting the diaphragm, which press in from all sides all together and push against the bowels and the bladder with such violence that the sphincters give way, no longer able through their contraction to prevent those vessels, ordained to receive and keep for a time these superfluities, from discharging them (if we wish to consent to it) as soon as they become disgusted with them.[3] For it lies within our will to make the sphincters stop their contraction, which is their unique function, instituted for retention; and expulsion of the excrement is accomplished by the natural forcing of the bladder and bowels, aided nonetheless by the constriction which the epigastric muscles effect, with the diaphragm.

[1] **sphincter:** Sphincter signifies compressing, tightening, and restraining [Joubert's note]. [2] **eight in number:** Sometimes ten, counting the two small ones called the appendages of the uprights [Joubert's note]. [3] **disgusted . . . them:** They become disgusted with them when the excrements begin to displease, by their quality, quantity, or both [Joubert's note].

Laurent Joubert, *Treatise on Laughter,* trans. Gregory David de Rocher (Tuscaloosa: University of Alabama Press, 1980), 59–60.

It is, then, likely that when these muscles press a long time and with much violence, soliciting the bowels and the bladder to give up their contents (as it happens in laughter), if there is a quantity of liquid matter, all escapes us indecorously. For the agitation and jouncing is so strong that the sphincters are unable to resist, especially when after a long duration they become loose and weak, like the rest of the body, losing all strength.

As for the sweat (the third type of excrement which laughter forces to come out), it is easier to provoke it than those mentioned above; yet I put it last in order to proceed by degrees down to the weakness of fainting, and to death, if it can come from laughing. For these accidents commonly follow a notorious evacuation. Now perspiration comes after a long laugh, either out of the entire body or out of the face alone, in some people easily and quickly, in others later and more slowly. It is caused by the agitation and general commotion, which excite the humors and dilate the pores of the skin, neither more nor less than does hard labor. But the face especially sweats[4] profusely from a big laugh because of the moisture of this part of the body, which is adjacent to the brain, and because of the softness and sparseness of its skin, with the affluence of the spirits and sanguine vapors that rise up into it and are able to make a lot of water, either on their own or with the humors.

[4] **sweats:** Why one sweats more from the face even though it is a thin and unfleshy part is debated by Aristotle in the second problem of Book 36 [Joubert's note].

Theories of Laughter: Rejoicing

Each of the traditional three theories of laughter has its limitations. Each attends to just one or two aspects of laughter: the social and ethical (the superiority theory), the intellectual and cognitive (the incongruity theory), and the physiological (the relief theory). When applied to a particular case like *Twelfth Night,* each leaves something out. The superiority theory would have us believe that *Twelfth Night* is all about ridicule at the expense of lovers and fools — people who are not our type. The incongruity theory would stress the unexpected circumstances and turns of plot. The relief theory would explain our laughter at the play as a release of the energy that ordinarily represses desires like Orsino's and Olivia's for "Cesario," or indulgence in drink like Sir Toby's and Sir Andrew's, perhaps even violent revenge on the likes of pompous asses like Malvolio. What is missing in these accounts is a sense of amusement, mirth, merriment. John Morreall's survey of the three traditional theories ends with his proposal of a fourth theory that captures this missing something for which there seems to be no single word in English. Morreall's own explanation for this unnamed mood or affect is this: "Laughter results from a pleasant psychological shift." Laughter, in this view, is not the psychological shift itself (that much could be a matter of superiority or incongruity) nor the pleasant feeling itself but rather "the physical activity which is caused by, and which expresses the feeling produced by the shift" (39). Morreall presents his formulation as a new breakthrough, but it is anticipated in some respects by at least two Renaissance writers — Laurent Joubert and Sir Philip Sidney.

LAURENT JOUBERT

From Treatise on Laughter

1579

Several chapters before his disquisition on pissing, shitting, and sweating (see p. 391), Joubert proposes that it is not a single emotion that causes laughter but a confluence of emotions. Laughter cannot be simply the result of joy, because it is possible to be joyous without laughing, even though laughter cannot happen without joy. Joubert attempts to position the two phenomena vis-à-vis each other as two different versions of "rejoicing" (*rejouissance*) (E5). Joy, he decides, is rejoicing at serious things; laughter, rejoicing at foolish things. In effect, Joubert supplies us with the missing word we need for Morreall's pleasant psychological shift.

Chapter 10

That the Emotion Causing Laughter Is Not Simply One of Joy

Our argument begins to delve into what is the most useful, touching the best of the matter. The past has taught us what laughing matter is, provoking[1] in the soul a certain faculty which is responsible for laughter. We also said that this faculty resides in the heart as do the other emotions. There remains only to know what it is, and how it is to be named. I do not doubt

[1] **provoking:** To provoke means to move, to excite, and, as it were, to needle. We therefore say that objects move the faculty (Joubert's note).

Laurent Joubert, *Treatise on Laughter,* trans. Gregory David de Rocher (Tuscaloosa: University of Alabama Press, 1980), 38–39.

that it will be one of those that we have already mentioned: joy, sadness, hope, fear, love, hate, anger, pity, shame, boldness, zeal, envy, or malice (for that is all of them), or that it will be included under one of these, or that it draws upon several. It is not simply joy, as we shall deduce later, although it is closer to it than any other. For one does not laugh out of sadness, hope, fear, love, and so forth; but facetious things, which seem joyous, pleasant, and enjoyable — be they seen or heard — in delighting us, make us laugh. So much so that the risible emotion could well be a kind of joy; one would even say that it is one and the same, since the matter is so similar.

Seeing, however, that one can be joyous without laughing, and the laugher cannot be without joy, these must be different emotions, or one must extend further than the other. It is impossible that they be contraries, since their effects are similar. It is better to say that joy has the greater extension[2] and that the object or matter of the two, with the emotion wrought in the heart, is similar generally, but, particularly, has its object and proper movement, which will be easily understood if we compare them. The object or matter of rejoicing is a serious thing that brings pleasure, gain, profit, usefulness, or some other true contentment. The matter of the emotion causing laughter is only foolish, playful, empty, and often deceiving, turning around things of no importance. He who will want to consider this closely will see this difference; furthermore, they are sometimes so mixed and confused that the two matters will be in one object, without one's being able to discern them, unless it be the more or less serious rejoicing. From this one can understand their great affinity, since they differ only in that joy is over a more serious and grave matter, and laughter, over a lighter and more foolish. So much so that we shall be able to set up two kinds of rejoicing in order to facilitate our argument: one will be over serious things, the effect of which is named joy, just like the emotion; and the other over foolishness, whence comes laughter. The latter has no name of its own, the former is simple rejoicing, which has considerable modesty in all its movements. For the foolish type is dissolute,[3] debauched, and lascivious. So much so that, besides the difference in objects, there is also diversity in the emotions of the heart; and in this are these two emotions particularly dissimilar, as we said above.

Also, inasmuch as laughter is caused by something ugly, it does not proceed from pure joy, but has some small part of sadness, in such a way that it follows two contraries, one of which is superior to the other in its efficacy. In

[2] **joy . . . extension:** Joy has the greater extension, for under it is contained laughter, and the container must be greater than the thing contained [Joubert's note]. [3] **dissolute:** It is dissolute and immodest in Cachin laughter, from which the wisest and most experienced often cannot abstain [Joubert's note].

order to make my idea, foundation of this whole argument, better understood, it will be necessary to state separately what the role of joy is, and what comes about through sadness, and finally the effects of the risible faculty, which we believe to participate in both, for the simple must be sifted before their mixture[4] and compounding.

[4] **mixture:** This is the doctrinal order, which is called composite order [Joubert's note].

SIR PHILIP SIDNEY

From A Defense of Poesy *1579–80*

Joubert's notion of "rejoicing" finds confirmation of sorts in Sir Philip Sidney's *A Defense of Poesy,* written in 1579–80 to answer Stephen Gosson's anti-poetic diatribe *The School of Abuse.* (For biographical information on Sidney see Chapter 1.) Against Gosson's charge that poetry is no more than a form of lying, Sidney rejoins that poets, far from presenting their fictions as truths, affirm nothing. Instead, they seek to combine the general precepts of philosophy with the particularities of history. "Poesy" is Sidney's term for the resulting product. In the final section of the treatise, devoted to an evaluative survey of contemporary English writing, Sidney first berates contemporary dramatists for betraying classical principles of decorum by commingling clowns and kings within the same fiction, on the same stage. He goes on, however, to broach a theory of comedy that is far more inclusive than anything in Plato, Aristotle, or the literary theorists of his own time.

Anxious to rebut critics like Gosson, who see nothing but scurrility in comedy, Sidney proposes that there are two kinds of comedy: the comedy of laughter and the comedy of delight. The first takes as its object "things most disproportioned to ourselves and nature" — a version of the superiority theory. The second takes as its object "things that have a conveniency to ourselves or to the general nature" — something akin to Joubert's "joy." The ultimate source for both writers is probably Plato's description of the unmixed pleasure that lies beyond the pleasure-mixed-with-envy occasioned by comedy. Where Plato limits unmixed pleasure to abstract qualities that are "eternally and absolutely beautiful" (*Philebus* 51), Joubert and Sidney are quite willing to countenance things actually seen and heard. Sidney's "comedy of delight" qualifies each of the traditional theories of laughter: social distance in the superiority theory becomes imaginative sympathy; disparity in the incongruity theory becomes "conveniency"; relief becomes repose. Like Joubert, Sidney contends that the two kinds of comedy can occur together as well as separately. With its invitation to fall in love and to laugh at folly, all at the same time, *Twelfth Night* presents an occasion for both laughing and rejoicing.

From *A Defense of Poesy*

But besides these gross absurdities, how all their plays[1] be neither right tragedies, nor right comedies, mingling kings and clowns, not because the matter so carrieth it, but thrust in the clown by head and shoulders to play a part in majestical matters with neither decency nor discretion, so as neither the admiration and commiseration, nor the right sportfulness, is by their mongrel tragicomedy obtained. I know Apuleius[2] did somewhat so, but that is a thing recounted with space ot time, not represented in one moment; and I know the ancients have one or two examples of tragi-comedies, as Plautus hath *Amphitryo;*[3] but, if we mark them well, we shall find that they never, or very daintily, match hornpipes and funerals. So falleth it out that, having indeed no right comedy, in that comical part of our tragedy, we have nothing but scurrility, unworthy of any chaste ears, or some extreme show of doltishness, indeed fit to lift up a loud laughter, and nothing else: where the whole tract of a comedy should be full of delight, as the tragedy should be still maintained in a well-raised admiration.

But our comedians think there is no delight without laughter; which is very wrong, for though laughter may come with delight, yet cometh it not of delight, as though delight should be the cause of laughter; but well may one thing breed both together. Nay, rather in themselves they have, as it were, a kind of contrariety: for delight we scarcely do but in things that have a conveniency to ourselves or to the general nature; laughter almost ever cometh of things most disproportioned to ourselves and nature. Delight hath a joy in it, either permanent or present. Laughter hath only a scornful tickling.

For example, we are ravished with delight to see a fair woman, and yet are far from being moved to laughter; we laugh at deformed creatures, wherein certainly we cannot delight. We delight in good chances, we laugh at mischances: we delight to hear the happiness of our friends, or country, at which he were worthy to be laughed at that would laugh; we shall, contrarily, laugh sometimes to find a matter quite mistaken and go down the hill against the bias in the mouth of some such men — as for the respect of them one shall be heartily sorry, he cannot choose but laugh, and so is rather pained than delighted with laughter.

[1] **their plays:** plays by English writers. [2] **Apuleius:** first-century author who wrote the satirical romance *The Golden Ass.* [3] **Plautus . . . *Amphitryo:*** seduced by Jupiter in disguise as her husband, Alcmena is rewarded by giving birth to twins, one mortal and one immortal.

Philip Sidney, *A Defense of Poesy,* ed. Jan van Dorsten as *A Defence of Poetry* (Oxford: Oxford University Press, 1966), 67–68.

Yet deny I not but that they may go well together. For as in Alexander's picture[4] well set out we delight without laughter, and in twenty mad antics we laugh without delight; so in Hercules, painted with his great beard and furious countenance, in a woman's attire, spinning at Omphale's commandment, it breedeth both delight and laughter: for the representing of so strange a power in love procureth delight, and the scornfulness of the action stirreth laughter. But I speak to this purpose, that all the end of the comical part be not upon such scornful matters as stir laughter only, but, mixed with it, that delightful teaching which is the end of poesy. And the great fault even in that point of laughter, and forbidden plainly by Aristotle, is that they stir laughter in sinful things, which are rather execrable than ridiculous, or in miserable, which are rather to be pitied than scorned. For what is it to make folks gape at a wretched beggar and a beggarly clown; or, against law of hospitality, to jest at strangers, because they speak not English so well as we do? What do we learn, since it is certain

Nil habet infelix paupertas durius in se,
Quam quod ridiculos hommes facit?[5]

But rather, a busy loving courtier and a heartless threatening Thraso;[6] a self-wise-seeming schoolmaster; an awry-transformed traveller. These if we saw walk in stage names, which we play naturally, therein were delightful laughter, and teaching delightfulness — as in the other, the tragedies of Buchanan[7] do justly bring forth a divine admiration.

[4] **Alexander's picture:** famous portrait by the Greek artist Apelles (fl. fourth century B.C.E.). [5] **Nil . . . facit:** "Nothing is harder to bear in unfortunate poverty than the fact it makes men ridiculous" (Juvenal, *Satires* 3.152–53). [6] **Thraso:** braggart soldier in Terence's comedy *Eunuchus*. [7] **Buchanan:** George Buchanan (1506–1582), tutor to James VI in Scotland and to Montaigne in France and author of four tragedies based on classical models.

Bibliography

Primary Sources

Alleyn, Edward, and Philip Henslowe. An inventory of costumes belonging to the Lord Admiral's Men. C. 1600. *Henslowe's Diary.* Ed. R. A. Foakes and R. T. Rickert. Cambridge: Cambridge UP, 1961.

Aristotle. *Nicomachean Ethics. Complete Works.* Ed. Jonathan Barnes. Princeton: Princeton UP, 1984.

——. [attributed]. *The Problems of Aristotle, with Other Philosophers and Physicians.* London: Arnold Hatfield, 1597.

Armin, Robert. *Fool upon Fool, or Six Sorts of Sots. . . .* London: William Febrand, 1600.

——. *Quips upon Questions, or A Clown's Conceit on Occasion Offered.* London: William Febrand, 1600.

Ascham, Roger. *The Schoolmaster.* 1570. Ed. Lawrence V. Ryan. Ithaca: Cornell UP for the Folger Shakespeare Library, 1967.

Bancroft, Richard. *A Survey of the Pretended Holy Discipline.* London: John Wolfe, 1593.

Beaumont, Francis. *Salmacis and Hermaphroditus.* London: John Hodgets, 1602.

Bourne, Henry. *Antiquitates Vulgares, or The Antiquities of the Common People. . . .* Newcastle: J. White for the Author, 1725.

Bradshaw, William. *English Puritanism.* 1605. *Images of English Puritanism.* Ed. Lawrence A. Sasek. Baton Rouge: Louisiana State UP, 1989.

Case, John [attributed]. *The Praise of Music: Wherein besides the Antiquity, Dignity, Delectation and Use Thereof in Civil Matters Is also Declared the Sober and Lawful Use of the Same in the Congregation and Church of God.* Oxford: Joseph Barnes, 1586.

Cleaver, Robert, and John Dod. *A Godly Form of Household Government: For the Ordering of Private Families According to the Direction of God's Word.* London: Thomas Man, 1614.

Coke, Edward. *The Third Part of the Institutes of the Laws of England,* 1644. London: W. Lee and D. Pakeman, 1660.

Coryate, Thomas. *Coryate's Crudities.* London: William Stansby, 1611.

Crooke, Helkiah. *Microcosmographia: A Description of the Body of Man.* 1615. London: William Jaggard, 1631.

della Casa, Giovanni. *Galateo . . . or Rather a Treatise of Manners and Behaviors It Behooveth a Man to Use and Eschew. . . .* Trans. Robert Peterson. London: Ralph Newberry, 1576.

Donne, John. "Sappho to Philaenis." *Poems by J. D., with Elegies on the Author's Death.* London: M. Fleshner for J. Marriott, 1633.

The 1559 Book of Common Prayer. Ed. John E. Booty. Charlottesville: U of Virginia P for the Folger Shakespeare Library, 1976.

Gibson, Anthony. *A Woman's Worth Defended Against All the Men in the World.* London: John Wolfe, 1599.

Greene, Robert. *A Quip for an Upstart Courtier.* London: John Wolfe, 1602.

Grievous Groans for the Poor. London: Michael Sparke, 1621.

Guazzo, Stephano. *Civil Conversation.* Trans. George Pettie. London: T. Dawson for Richard Watkins, 1581.

Haec-Vir, or The Womanish Man. London: John Trundle, 1620.

Heywood, Thomas. *An Apology for Actors.* London: Nicholas Okes, 1612.

Hic Mulier, or The Man-Woman. London: John Trundle, 1620.

I. T. [or J. T.]. *The Haven of Pleasure, Containing a Free Man's Felicity and a True Direction How to Live Well.* London: P. Short, 1596.

Jackson, Henry. Account of *Othello* at Oxford 1610. Geoffrey Tillotson, "*Othello* and *The Alchemist* at Oxford in 1610," *The Times Literary Supplement,* 20 July 1933: 494.

Jonson, Ben. "To Penshurst." Before 1612. *The Works of Benjamin Jonson.* London: Will Stansby, 1616.

Joubert, Laurent. *Treatise on Laughter.* Trans. Gregory David de Rocher. Tuscaloosa: U of Alabama P, 1980.

The King's Majesty's Declaration to His Subjects Concerning Lawful Sports to Be Used. London: Robert Barker, 1633.

Lupton, Donald. *London and the Country Cardonadoed and Quartered into Several Characters.* London: Nicholas Oakes, 1632.

Lyly, John. *Gallathea.* 1592. Ed. Anne Begor Lancashire. Lincoln: U of Nebraska P, 1969.

Montaigne, Michel de. *Essays.* Trans. John Florio. London: V. Sims for E. Blount, 1603.

Overbury, Thomas [attributed]. *A Wife . . . Whereunto Are Added Many Witty Characters.* London: Lawrence Lisle, 1614.

Ovid. *The Heroical Epistles of Publius Ovidius Naso in English Verse.* Trans. George Turberville. London: H. Denham, 1567.

——. *Ovid's Festivals or Roman Calendar.* Trans. John Gower. Cambridge: Roger Daniel, 1640.

——. *Ovid's Metamorphosis Englished, Mythologized, and Represented in Figures.* Trans. George Sandys. Oxford: J. Lichfield, 1632.

Perkins, William. *Christian Economy.* 1608. *Collected Works.* Cambridge: Legge, 1618.

Phillips, Augustine. Last Will and Testament. 1605. *Playhouse Wills, 1558–1642.* Ed. E. A. J. Honigmann and Susan Brock. Manchester: Manchester UP, 1993.

Plato. *Philebus. The Dialogues of Plato.* Trans. Benjamin Jowett. Vol. 3. Oxford: Oxford UP, 1969.

——. *Republic. The Dialogues of Plato.* Trans. Benjamin Jowett. Vol. 2. Oxford: Oxford UP, 1969.

Platter, Thomas. *Travels in England 1599.* Trans. Clare Williams. London: Jonathan Cape, 1937.

Plutarch. *Lives of the Noble Grecians and Romans Compared Together.* Trans. Sir Thomas North. London: Thomas Vautrouillier and John Wright, 1579.

A Proclamation Enforcing Statutes and Proclamations of Apparel. London: Christopher Barker, 1597.

Prynne, William. *Histrio-Mastix, The Players' Scourge or Actors' Tragedy. . . .* London: Michael Sparke, 1633.

Quintilian. *Institutio Oratoria.* Trans. H. E. Butler. Loeb Classical Library. London: Heinemann, 1921.

Rainolds, John. *The Overthrow of Stage Plays.* Middelburg: R. Schilders, 1599.

Rich, Barnaby. *Barnaby Rich His Farewell to the Military Profession.* 1581. Ed. Donald Beecher. Ottawa: Doverhouse Editions, 1992.

Rudyerd, Benjamin. *Le Prince d'Amour, or The Prince of Love.* London: William Leake, 1660.

Sandys, George. *A Relation of a Journey Begun Anno Domini 1610.* 2nd ed. London: W. Barrett, 1615.

The Second Tome of Homilies. London: R. Jugge and J. Cawood, 1563.

Shakespeare, William. *Shake-spear's Sonnets, Never Before Imprinted.* London: Thomas Thorpe, 1609.

——. *Twelfth Night, or What You Will. Complete Works.* Ed. David Bevington. New York: Longman, 1997.

Sidney, Philip. *The Countess of Pembroke's Arcadia* (*The Old Arcadia*). Ed. Jean Robertson. [Orig. *Arcadia.* 1581.] Oxford: Clarendon Press, 1973.

——. *A Defence of Poetry.* Ed. Jan van Dorsten. [Orig. *A Defense of Poesy.*] Oxford: Oxford UP, 1966.

Stubbes, Phillip. *The Anatomy of Abuses in Ailgna.* 1583. Ed. F. J. Furnivall. London: New Shakespeare Society, 1877–79.

Vaughan, William. *The Golden Grove Moralized in Three Books.* London: Simon Stafford, 1600.

The Whole Volume of Statutes at Large. London: Christopher Barker, 1587.

Wright, Thomas. *The Passions of the Mind in General.* 1604. Ed. William Webster Newbold. New York: Garland, 1986.

Wroth, Mary. *The First Part of the Countess of Montgomery's Urania.* Ed. Josephine A. Roberts. Binghamton, NY: Medieval and Renaissance Texts and Studies, 1995.

——. *The Second Part of the Countess of Montgomery's Urania.* Ed. Josephine A. Roberts. Tempe, AZ: Renaissance English Text Society, 1999.

Secondary Sources

Andreadis, Harriette. "Sappho in Early Modern England: A Study in Sexual Reputation." *Re-Reading Sappho: Reception and Transmission.* Ed. Ellen Greene. Berkeley: U of California P, 1997.

Aristotle. *The Complete Works.* Ed. Jonathan Barnes. 2 vols. Princeton: Princeton UP, 1984.

Arlidge, Anthony. *Shakespeare and the Prince of Love.* London: Giles de la Mare, 2000.

Bakhtin, Mikhail. *Rabelais and His World.* Trans. Helene Iswolsky. Bloomington: Indiana UP, 1984.

Bamborough, J. B. *The Little World of Man.* London: Longmans, 1932.

Ben-Amos, Ilana. *Adolescence and Youth in Early Modern England.* New Haven: Yale UP, 1994.

Beveridge, William Henry. *Prices and Wages in England from the Twelfth to the Nineteenth Century.* London: Longmans, 1939.

Brathwait, Richard. *The English Gentleman, Containing Sundry Excellent Rules or Exquisite Observations Tending to Direction of Every Gentleman of Selecter Rank and Quality.* London: John Haviland for Robert Bostock, 1630.

Bray, Alan. "Homosexuality and the Signs of Male Friendship in Elizabethan England." *Queering the Renaissance.* Ed. Jonathan Goldberg. Durham: Duke UP, 1994.

——. *Homosexuality in Renaissance England.* London: Gay Men's Press, 1982.

Bredbeck, Gregory W. *Sodomy and Interpretation.* Ithaca: Cornell UP, 1991.

Breton, Nicholas. *The Good and the Bad. English Character Writings of the Seventeenth Century.* Ed. Henry Morley. London: Routledge, 1891.

Bullough, Geoffrey. *The Narrative and Dramatic Sources of Shakespeare.* 8 vols. New York: Columbia UP, 1957–75.

Burke, Peter. *Popular Culture in Early Modern Europe.* New York: Harper and Row, 1978.

Burt, Richard, and John Michael Archer, eds. *Enclosure Acts: Sexuality, Property, and Culture in Early Modern England.* Ithaca: Cornell UP, 1994.

Castiglione, Baldassare. *The Book of the Courtier.* Trans. Thomas Hoby. London: Dent, 1928.

Elton, G. R. *Reform and Reformation.* Cambridge: Harvard UP, 1973.

Feuillerat, Albert. *Documents Relating to the Office of the Revels in the Time of Queen Elizabeth.* Louvain: Uystpruyst, 1908.

Foakes, R. A., and R. T. Rickert, eds. *Henslowe's Diary.* Cambridge: Cambridge UP, 1961.

Garber, Marjorie. *Vested Interests: Cross-Dressing and Cultural Anxiety.* London: Routledge, 1992.

The Geneva Bible. Facsim. ed. Madison: U of Wisconsin P, 1969.

Gesner, Carol. *Shakespeare and the Greek Romance: A Study of Origins.* Lexington: U of Kentucky P, 1970.

Gesta Grayorum, or The History of the Prince of Purpool. Ed. Desmond Bland. Liverpool: Liverpool UP, 1968.

Gibbs, A. C. *Middle English Romances.* London: Edward Arnold, 1966.

Girouard, Mark. *Life in the English Country House: A Social and Architectural History.* New Haven: Yale UP, 1978.

Gosson, Stephen. *The School of Abuse.* London: Thomas Woodcock, 1579.

Gras, Henk. "*Twelfth Night, Every Man out of His Humour,* and the Middle Temple Revels of 1597–98." *Modern Language Review* 84.3 (1989): 545–64.

Greenblatt, Stephen. "Fiction and Friction." *Reconstructing Individualism: Autonomy, Individuality, and the Self in Western Thought.* Ed. Thomas C. Heller, Morton Sosna, and David E. Wellberg. Stanford: Stanford UP, 1986.

Greene, Robert. *Greene's Groatsworth of Wit, Bought with a Million of Repentance.* London: John Wolfe for William Wright, 1592.

Gurr, Andrew. *The Shakespearean Stage 1574–1642.* 3rd ed. Cambridge: Cambridge UP, 1992.

Haller, William. *The Rise of Puritanism.* New York: Columbia UP, 1938.

Harrison, William. *The Description of England.* Ed. George Edelen. Ithaca: Cornell UP, 1968.

Henderson, Robert W. "The King's Book of Sports in England and America." *Bulletin of the New York Public Library* 52 (1948): 539–53.

Heywood, Thomas. *An Apology for Actors.* London: Nicholas Oakes, 1612.

Hill, Christopher. *Puritanism and Revolution.* London: Secker & Warburg, 1958.

Hooper, Wilfrid. "The Tudor Sumptuary Laws." *English Historical Review* 30 (1915): 433–49.

Howard, Jean E. "Crossdressing, the Theatre, and Gender Struggle in Early Modern England." *Shakespeare Quarterly* 39 (1988): 418–29.

Hutton, Ronald. *The Rise and Fall of Merry England.* Oxford: Oxford UP, 1994.

——. *The Stations of the Sun: A History of the Ritual Year in Britain.* Oxford: Oxford UP, 1996.

Iamblichus. *Life of Pythagoras.* Trans. Thomas Taylor. London: Watkins, 1926.

James, Susan. *Passion and Action: The Emotions in Seventeenth-Century Philosophy.* Oxford: Oxford UP, 1997.

Jankowski, Theodora A. *Pure Resistance: Queer Virginity in Early Modern English Drama.* Philadelphia: U of Pennsylvania P, 2000.

Jardine, Lisa. *Still Harping on Daughters: Women and Drama in the Age of Shakespeare.* Brighton: Harvester, 1983.

Jones, Ann Rosalind, and Peter Stallybrass. *Renaissance Clothing and the Materials of Memory.* Cambridge: Cambridge UP, 2000.

Jonson, Ben. *The Complete Plays.* Ed. G. A. Wilkes. 4 vols. Oxford: Clarendon Press, 1982.

Joubert, Laurent. *Traité du Ris.* Paris: Nicolas Chesenau, 1579.

Knutson, Roslyn Lander. *The Repertory of Shakespeare's Company 1594–1613.* Fayetteville: U of Arkansas P, 1991.

Laqueur, Thomas. *Making Sex: Body and Gender from the Greeks to Freud.* Cambridge: Harvard UP, 1990.

Lemnius, Levinus. *The Touchstone of Complexions.* Trans. Thomas Newton. London: Thomas Marsh, 1576.

Levine, Laura. *Men in Women's Clothes: Anti-Theatricality and Effeminization 1579–1652.* Cambridge: Cambridge UP, 1994.

Long, John H. *Shakespeare's Use of Music.* 3 vols. Gainesville: U of Florida P, 1961–71.

Mallette, Richard. *Spenser and the Discourses of Reformation England.* Lincoln: U of Nebraska P, 1997.

Manningham, John. *The Diary of John Manningham of the Middle Temple 1602–1603.* Ed. Robert Parker Sorlien. Hanover, NH: U of New England P, 1976.

Marcus, Leah. *The Politics of Mirth.* Chicago: U of Chicago P, 1978.

Marotti, Arthur F. *John Donne: Coterie Poet.* Madison: U of Wisconsin P, 1986.

——. *Manuscript, Print, and the English Renaissance Lyric.* Ithaca: Cornell UP, 1995.

Masten, Jeffrey. *Textual Intercourse: Collaboration, Authorship, and Sexualities in Renaissance Drama.* Cambridge: Cambridge UP, 1997.

Montrose, Louis. *The Purpose of Playing: Shakespeare and the Cultural Politics of the Elizabethan Theater.* Chicago: U of Chicago P, 1996.

Morley, Thomas. *A Plain and Easy Introduction to Practical Music.* 1597. Oxford: Oxford UP, 1937.

Morreall, John. *Taking Laughter Seriously.* Albany: State U of New York P, 1983.

Muir, Kenneth. *The Sources of Shakespeare's Plays.* London: Methuen, 1977.

Orgel, Stephen. *Impersonations: The Performance of Gender in Shakespeare's England.* Cambridge: Cambridge UP, 1996.

Palmer, Daryl W. *Hospitable Performances: Dramatic Genre and Cultural Practices in Early Modern England.* West Lafayette, IN: Purdue UP, 1992.

Park, Katherine. "The Organic Soul." *The Cambridge History of Renaissance Philosophy.* Ed. Charles B. Schmitt. Cambridge: Cambridge UP, 1988.

——. "The Rediscovery of the Clitoris." *The Body in Parts: Fantasies of Corporeality in Early Modern Europe.* Ed. David Hillman and Carla Mazzio. London: Routledge, 1997.

Pepys, Samuel. *The Diary of Samuel Pepys.* Ed. Robert Latham and William Matthews. Vol. 9. Berkeley: U of California P, 1976.

Pequigney, Joseph. *Such Is My Love: A Study of Shakespeare's Sonnets.* Chicago: U of Chicago P, 1988.

Plato. *The Dialogues of Plato.* Trans. Benjamin Jowett. 4th ed. Oxford: Oxford UP, 1969.

Potter, Lois. *Twelfth Night: Text and Performance.* Basingstoke: Macmillan, 1985.

Poulton, Diana. *John Dowland.* Berkeley: U of California P, 1982.

Rayler, Timothy. *Cavaliers, Clubs, and Literary Culture.* Newark: U of Delaware P, 1994.

Shapiro, Michael. "Lady Mary Wroth Describes a 'Boy Actress.'" *Medieval and Renaissance Drama in England* 4 (1987): 187–94.

Simmons, J. L. "A Source for Shakespeare's Malvolio: The Elizabethan Controversy with the Puritans." *Huntington Library Quarterly* 36 (1973): 181–201.

Singer, Irving O. *The Nature of Love.* Vol. 1. Chicago: U of Chicago P, 1984.

Siraisi, Nancy G. *Medieval and Early Renaissance Medicine: An Introduction to Knowledge and Practice.* Chicago: U of Chicago P, 1990.

Smith, Bruce R. *The Acoustic World of Early Modern England.* Chicago: U of Chicago P, 1999.

——. *Ancient Scripts and Modern Experience on the English Stage 1500–1600.* Princeton: Princeton UP, 1988.

——. *Homosexual Desire in Shakespeare's England: A Cultural Poetics.* Chicago: U of Chicago P, 1991.

Strunk, Oliver, ed. *Source Readings in Music History.* Rev. ed. Gen. ed. Leo Treitler. New York: Norton, 1998.

Taylor, Charles. *The Sources of the Self: The Making of Modern Identity.* Cambridge: Harvard UP, 1989.

Thomas, Keith. "The Place of Laughter in Tudor and Stuart England." *The Times Literary Supplement,* 21 January 1977: 77–81.

Thompson, Stith. *Motif-Index of Folk-Literature.* 6 vols. Bloomington: U of Indiana P, 1955–58.

Tillyard, E. M. W. *The Elizabethan World Picture.* New York: Random House, 1959.

Todd, Margo. *Christian Humanism and the Puritan Social Order.* Cambridge: Cambridge UP, 1987.

Traub, Valerie. "The (In)Significance of Lesbian Desire." *Queering the Renaissance.* Ed. Jonathan Goldberg. Durham: Duke UP, 1994.

Wiles, David. *Shakespeare's Clown: Actor and Text in the Elizabethan Playhouse.* Cambridge: Cambridge UP, 1987.

Wolff, Samuel Lee. *The Greek Romances in Elizabethan Prose Fiction.* New York: Columbia UP, 1912.

Wrightson, Keith. *English Society 1580–1680.* New Brunswick: Rutgers UP, 1982.
Young, F. A., Jr. *The Proclamations of the Tudor Queens.* Cambridge: Cambridge UP, 1976.

Suggestions for Further Reading

Alexander, Bill. *Approaches to* Twelfth Night. London: Hern, 1990.
Astington, John. "Malvolio and the Eunuchs: Texts and Revels in *Twelfth Night.*" *Shakespeare Survey* 46 (1993): 23–34.
Barber, C. L. *Shakespeare's Festive Comedy.* Princeton: Princeton UP, 1959.
Barton, Anne. "*As You Like It* and *Twelfth Night:* Shakespeare's Sense of an Ending." *Shakespearian Comedy.* Stratford-upon-Avon Studies 14. Ed. Malcolm Bradbury and David Palmer. New York: Crane, Russak, 1972.
Berry, Edward. *Shakespeare's Comic Rites.* Cambridge: Cambridge UP, 1984.
Berry, Ralph. "The Season of *Twelfth Night.*" *New York Literary Forum* 1 (1978): 139–49.
Booth, Stephen. *Precious Nonsense: The Gettysburg Address, Ben Jonson's Epitaphs on His Children, and* Twelfth Night. Berkeley: U of California P, 1998.
——. "*Twelfth Night* 1.1: The Audience as Malvolio." *Shakespeare's "Rough Magic": Renaissance Essays in Honor of C. L. Barber.* Ed. Peter Erickson and Coppélia Kahn. Newark: U of Delaware P, 1985.
Brissenden, Alan. "The Dance in *As You Like It* and *Twelfth Night.*" *Cahiers Elisabethains* 13 (1978): 25–34.
Brown, John Russell. *Shakespeare and His Comedies.* 2nd ed. London: Methuen, 1962.
Callaghan, Dympna. "'And All Is Semblative a Woman's Part': Body Politics and *Twelfth Night.*" *Textual Practice* 7.3 (1993): 428–52.
———. "The Castrator's Song: Female Impersonation on the Early Modern Stage." *Journal of Medieval and Renaissance Studies* 26.2 (1996): 321–53.
Carroll, William C. *The Metamorphosis of Shakespearean Comedy.* Princeton: Princeton UP, 1985.
Charles, Casey. "Gender Trouble in *Twelfth Night.*" *Theatre Journal* 49.2 (1997): 121–41.
Charney, Maurice. "Comic Premises of *Twelfth Night.*" *New York Literary Forum* 1 (1978): 151–65.
——. "*Twelfth Night* and the 'Natural Perspective' of Comedy." *De Shakespeare à T. S. Eliot.* Ed. Marie-Jeanne Durry, Robert Ellrodt, Marie-Thérèse Jones-Davies, and André Roussin. Paris: Didier, 1976.
Coddon, Karin. "'Slander in an Allow'd Fool': *Twelfth Night*'s Crisis of the Aristocracy." *Studies in English Literature 1500–1900* 33.2 (1993): 309–25.
Crew, Jonathan. "In the Field of Dreams: Transvestism in *Twelfth Night* and *The Crying Game.*" *Representations* 50 (1995): 101–21.
D'Amico, Jack. "The Treatment of Space in Italian and English Renaissance Theater: The Example of *Gl'Ingannati* and *Twelfth Night.*" *Comparative Drama* 23.3 (1989): 265–83.

Davies, Stevie. *William Shakespeare, Twelfth Night.* London: Penguin, 1993.

Dodd, William. "'So Full of Shapes Is Fancy': Gender and Point of View in *Twelfth Night.*" *English Studies in Transition.* Ed. Robert Clark and Piero Boitani. London: Routledge, 1993.

Draper, John. *The* Twelfth Night *of Shakespeare's Audience.* Stanford: Stanford UP, 1950.

Eagleton, Terry. "Language and Reality in *Twelfth Night.*" *Critical Quarterly* 9 (1967): 217–28.

Elam, Keir. "The Fertile Eunuch: *Twelfth Night,* Early Modern Intercourse, and the Fruits of Castration." *Shakespeare Quarterly* 47.1 (1996): 1–36.

——. *Shakespeare's Universe of Discourse: Language-Games in the Comedies.* Cambridge: Cambridge UP, 1984.

Evans, Bertrand. *Shakespeare's Comedies.* Oxford: Clarendon Press, 1960.

Everett, Barbara. "Or What You Will." *Essays in Criticism* 35.4 (1985): 294–314.

Forrest, James F. "Malvolio and Puritan 'Singularity.'" *English Language Notes* 11 (1974): 259–64.

Freedman, Barbara. *Staging the Gaze: Postmodernism, Psychoanalysis, and Shakespearean Comedy.* Ithaca: Cornell UP, 1991.

Frye, Northrop. *A Natural Perspective: The Development of Shakespearean Comedy and Romance.* New York: Columbia UP, 1965.

Girard, Réné. "'Tis Not So Sweet as It Was Before': Orsino and Olivia in *Twelfth Night.*" *Stanford Literature Review* 7.1–2 (1990): 123–32.

Green, Douglas. "Shakespeare's Violation: 'One Face, One Voice, One Habit, and Two Persons.'" *Reconsidering the Renaissance.* Ed. Mario di Cesare. Binghamton, NY: Medieval and Renaissance Texts and Studies, 1992.

Gregson, J. M. *Shakespeare,* Twelfth Night. London: Edward Arnold, 1980.

Hart, John A. *Dramatic Structure in Shakespeare's Romantic Comedies.* Pittsburgh: Carnegie-Mellon UP, 1980.

Hartman, Geoffrey H. "Shakespeare's Poetical Character in *Twelfth Night.*" *Shakespeare and the Question of Theory.* Ed. Patricia Parker and Geoffrey Hartman. London: Methuen, 1985.

Hartwig, Joan. "Feste's 'Whirligig' and the Comic Providence of *Twelfth Night.*" *English Literary History* 40 (1973): 501–13.

Hassel, R. Chris, Jr. *Faith and Folly in Shakespeare's Romantic Comedies.* Athens: U of Georgia P, 1980.

——. "Malvolio's Dark Concupiscence." *Cahiers Elisabethains* 43 (1993): 1–11.

Hawkes, Terence. "Comedy, Orality, and Duplicity: *A Midsummer Night's Dream* and *Twelfth Night.*" *New York Literary Forum* 5–6 (1980): 155–63.

Hayles, Nancy K. "Sexual Disguise in *As You Like It* and *Twelfth Night.*" *Shakespeare Survey* 32 (1979): 63–72.

Hotson, Leslie. *The First Night of* Twelfth Night. New York: Macmillan, 1954.

Hunt, Maurice. "Malvolio, Viola, and the Question of Instrumentality: Defining Providence in *Twelfth Night.*" *Studies in Philology* 90.3 (1993): 277–97.

Huston, J. Dennis. "'When I Came to Man's Estate': *Twelfth Night* and Problems of Identity." *Modern Language Quarterly* 33 (1972): 274–88.

Hutson, Lorna. "On Not Being Deceived: Rhetoric and the Body in *Twelfth Night.*" *Texas Studies in Literature and Language* 38.2 (1996): 140–74.

Jardine, Lisa. "Twins and Travesties: Gender, Dependency, and Sexual Availability in *Twelfth Night.*" *Erotic Politics.* Ed. Susan Zimmerman. London: Routledge, 1992.

Jensen, Ejner J. *Shakespeare and the Ends of Comedy.* Bloomington: Indiana UP, 1991.

Jones, Ann Rosalind. "Revenge Comedy: Writing, Law, and the Punishing Heroine in *Twelfth Night, The Merry Wives of Windsor,* and *Swetnam the Woman-Hater.*" *Shakespearean Power and Punishment.* Ed. Gillian Murray Kendall. Madison, NJ: Fairleigh Dickinson UP, 1998.

Kerrigan, John. "Secrecy and Gossip in *Twelfth Night.*" *Shakespeare Survey* 50 (1997): 65–80.

King, Walter N. "Shakespeare and Parmenides: The Metaphysics of *Twelfth Night.*" *Studies in English Literature 1500–1900* 8 (1968): 283–306.

——. *Twentieth-Century Interpretations of* Twelfth Night: *A Collection of Critical Essays.* Englewood Cliffs, NJ: Prentice-Hall, 1968.

Ko, Yu Jin. "The Comic Close of *Twelfth Night* and Viola's *Noli Me Tangere.*" *Shakespeare Quarterly* 48.4 (1997): 391–405.

Kranidas, Thomas. "Malvolio on Decorum." *Shakespeare Quarterly* 15 (1964): 450–51.

Labriola, Albert C. "*Twelfth Night* and the Comedy of Festive Abuse." *Modern Language Studies* 5.2 (1975): 5–20.

Lamb, Mary Ellen. "Ovid's *Metamorphosis* and Shakespeare's *Twelfth Night.*" *New York Literary Forum* 5–6 (1980): 63–77.

——. "Tracing a Heterosexual Erotics of Service in *Twelfth Night* and the Autobiographical Writings of Thomas Whythorne and Anne Clifford." *Criticism* 40.1 (1998): 1–25.

Langman, F. H. "Comedy and Saturnalia: The Case of *Twelfth Night.*" *Southern Review* (Australia) 7 (1974): 102–22.

Leech, Clifford. Twelfth Night *and Shakespearean Comedy.* Toronto: U of Toronto P, 1965.

Leggatt, Alexander. *Shakespeare's Comedy of Love.* London: Methuen, 1973.

Lents, Cheryl Blain. "Shakespeare's *Twelfth Night, or What You Will:* A Bibliography of Editions, Books, Articles, Reviews, and Bibliographies, 1900–1972." *Bulletin of Bibliography* 31 (1974): 152–64, 180.

Levin, Harry. "The Underplot of *Twelfth Night.*" *De Shakespeare à T. S. Eliot.* Ed. Marie-Jeanne Durry, Robert Ellrodt, Marie-Thérèse Jones-Davies, and André Roussin. Paris: Didier, 1976.

Lewalski, Barbara. "Thematic Patterns in *Twelfth Night.*" *Shakespeare Studies* 1 (1965): 168–81.

Lewis, Cynthia. "'A Fustian Riddle?' Anagrammatic Names in *Twelfth Night.*" *English Language Notes* 22.4 (1985): 32–37.

——. *Particular Saints: Shakespeare's Four Antonios, Their Contexts, and Their Plays.* Newark: U of Delaware P, 1997.

Logan, Thad Jenkins. "*Twelfth Night:* The Limits of Festivity." *Studies in English Literature 1500–1900* 22.2 (1982): 223–38.
Malcolmson, Cristina. "'What You Will': Social Mobility and Gender in *Twelfth Night." The Matter of Difference: Materialist Feminist Criticism of Shakespeare.* Ed. Valerie Wayne. Ithaca: Cornell UP, 1991.
McKim, William M. "Viola's 'Many Sorts of Music' in *Twelfth Night." Kentucky Philological Review* 7 (1992): 22–26.
Nathan, Norman. "Cesario, Sebastian, Olivia, Viola, and Illyria in *Twelfth Night." Names: A Journal of Onomastics* 37.3 (1989): 281–84.
Nevo, Ruth. *Comic Transformations in Shakespeare.* London: Methuen, 1980.
Osborne, Laurie E. *The Trick of Singularity:* Twelfth Night *and the Performance Editions.* Iowa City: U of Iowa P, 1996.
Palmer, D. J. *Shakespeare:* Twelfth Night, *A Casebook.* London: Macmillan, 1972.
——. "*Twelfth Night* and the Myth of Echo and Narcissus." *Shakespeare Survey* 32 (1979): 73–78.
Pequigney, Joseph. "The Two Antonios and Same-Sex Love in *Twelfth Night* and *The Merchant of Venice." English Literary Renaissance* 22.2 (1992): 201–21.
Petronella, Vincent F. "Anamorphic Naming in Shakespeare's *Twelfth Night." Names: A Journal of Onomastics* 35.3–4 (1987): 139–46.
Relihan, Constance C. "Erasing the East from *Twelfth Night." Race, Ethnicity, and Power in the Renaissance."* Ed. Joyce Green MacDonald. Madison, NJ: Fairleigh Dickinson UP, 1997.
Riemer, A. P. *Antic Fables: Patterns of Evasion in Shakespeare's Comedies.* London: St. Martin's Press, 1980.
Roll, Michaela. "'Three'-Floating Sexuality: Viola's Identity in Shakespeare's *Twelfth Night." Upstart Crow* 18 (1998): 39–55.
Salinger, J. L. *Shakespeare and the Traditions of Comedy.* Cambridge: Cambridge UP, 1976.
Schleiner, Winfried. "The Feste-Malvolio Scene in *Twelfth Night* against the Background of Renaissance Ideas about Madness and Possession." *Deutsche Shakespeare-Gesellschaft West: Jahrbuch* (1990): 48–57.
——. "Orsino and Viola: Are the Names of Serious Characters in *Twelfth Night* Meaningful?" *Shakespeare Studies* 16 (1983): 135–41.
Siegel, Paul N. "Malvolio: Comic Puritan Automaton." *New York Literary Forum* 5–6 (1980): 217–30.
Thomson, Peter. "*Twelfth Night:* The Music of Time." *Essays on Shakespeare in Honor of A. A. Ansari.* Ed. T. R. Sharma. Meerut, India: Shalabh Book House, 1986.
Tvordi, Jessica. "Female Alliance and the Construction of Homoeroticism in *As You Like It* and *Twelfth Night." Maids and Mistresses, Cousins and Queens: Women's Alliances in Early Modern England.* Ed. Susan Frye and Karen Robertson. New York: Oxford UP, 1999.
Weaver, John J. W. "The Other Twin: Sebastian's Relationship to Viola and the Theme of *Twelfth Night." Essays in Honor of Esmond Linworth Marilla.* Ed.

Thomas A. Kirby and William J. Olive. Baton Rouge: Louisiana State UP, 1970.

Wells, Stanley, and Joseph Price, eds. *Twelfth Night: Critical Essays.* New York: Garland, 1986.

Wilson, John Dover. *Shakespeare's Happy Comedies.* London: Faber, 1962.

Woodbridge, Linda. "'Fire in Your Heart and Brimstone in Your Liver': Towards an Unsaturnalian *Twelfth Night.*" *Southern Review* (Australia) 17.3 (1984): 270–91.

Acknowledgments

Figure 1. Middle Temple Hall. By permission of the Honorable Society of the Middle Temple.

Figure 2. Sailing eastward, from Anthony Nixon, *The Three English Brothers* (London, 1607). By permission of the Folger Shakespeare Library.

Figure 3. Concocting the food of love, from Adrien LeRoy, *A Brief and Easy Instruction to Learn the Tablature . . . unto the Lute* (London, 1568). By permission of the Bodleian Library, Oxford.

Figure 4. A natural fool, from Robert Armin, *The Two Maids of Moreclack* (London, 1609). By permission of the Folger Shakespeare Library.

Figure 5. Landing in Ilyria, from *Mr. William Shakespeare's Comedies, Histories, and Tragedies, Published According to the True Original Copies* (London, 1623), p. 255. By permission of the Folger Shakespeare Library.

Twelfth Night, or What You Will from *The Complete Works of Shakespeare,* 4th ed. Ed. David Bevington. Copyright © 1997 by HarperCollins, Inc. Reprinted by permission of Addison-Wesley Educational Publishers, Inc.

CHAPTER 1

Figure 6. Locating Illyria, from George Sandys, *A Relation of a Journey Begun Anno Domini 1610* (1615). By permission of the Folger Shakespeare Library.

Roger Ascham, *The Schoolmaster* (1570), ed. Lawrence V. Ryan (Ithaca: Cornell University Press for the Folger Shakespeare Library, 1967), pp. 59–72. By permission of the Folger Shakespeare Library.

Figures 7, 8. Looking east in the Piazza San Marco, Venice, from Georg Braun and Franz Hogenberg, *Civitates Orbis Terrarum* (1606–08). By permission of the Folger Shakespeare Library.

Figure 9. Eastern apparel, from Abraham de Bruyn, *Omnium Gentium Habitus* (1581). By permission of the Folger Shakespeare Library.

Barnaby Rich, *Barnaby Rich His Farewell to the Military Profession* (1581), ed. Donald Beecher (Ottawa, Canada: Doverhouse Editions, 1992), pp. 180–201. By permission of Doverhouse Editions.

Figure 10. Calendar for January, from *The Bishops' Bible* (1575). By permission of the New York Public Library.

The 1559 Book of Common Prayer, ed. John E. Booty (Charlottesville: University of Virginia Press for the Folger Shakespeare Library, 1976), pp. 92–94. By permission of the Folger Shakespeare Library.

CHAPTER 2

Figure 11. Sirens, from Geoffrey Whitney, *A Choice of Emblems* (1586). By permission of the Folger Shakespeare Library.

Figure 12. Hearing, women, the power of music, and a prayer against despair, from Richard Day, *A Book of Christian Prayers* (1578). By permission of the Folger Shakespeare Library.

Figure 13. Apollo flaying Marsyas, from George Sandys, *Ovid's Metamorphosis Englished, Mythologized, and Represented in Figures* (1632). By permission of the Folger Shakespeare Library.

Figure 14. The tuning of the spheres, from Robert Fludd, *Utriusque Cosmi Maioris Scilicet et Minoris Metaphysica, Physica, atque Technica Historia* (1617). By permission of the Folger Shakespeare Library.

Thomas Wright, *The Passions of the Mind in General* (1604), ed. William Webster Newbold (New York: Garland, 1986), pp. 208–10. By permission of William Webster Newbold.

CHAPTER 3

Thomas Wright, *The Passions of the Mind in General* (1604), ed. William Webster Newbold (New York: Garland, 1986), pp. 94–96, 103–05. By permission of William Webster Newbold.

Figures 15, 16. Female reproductive organs, from Helkiah Crooke, *Microcosmographia: A Description of the Body of Man* (1625). By permission of the Folger Shakespeare Library.

John Lyly, *Galathea* (pub. 1592), ed. Anne Begor Lancashire (Lincoln: University of Nebraska Press, 1969), pp. 36–39. By permission of the University of Nebraska Press.

Figure 17. Acquaintance, from Richard Brathwait, *The English Gentleman* (1630). By permission of the Folger Shakespeare Library.

Figure 18. Salmacis and Hermaphroditus, from G. A. Bredero, *Thronus Cupidinis* (1620). By permission of the Universiteits-Bibliotheek, Amsterdam.

CHAPTER 4

Edward Alleyn and Philip Henslowe, An inventory of costumes, c. 1600, transcribed in R. A. Foakes and R. T. Rickert, eds., *Henslowe's Diary* (Cambridge: Cambridge University Press, 1961), pp. 291–94. By permission of Cambridge University Press and R. A. Foakes.

Figure 19. English apparel, from Abraham de Bruyn, *Omnium Gentium Habitus* (1581). By permission of the Folger Shakespeare Library.

Figure 20. Who can legally wear what, from *A Proclamation Enforcing Statutes and Proclamations of Apparel* (1597). By permission of the Folger Shakespeare Library.

Figure 21. Velvet Britches and Cloth Britches, from Robert Greene, *A Quip for an Upstart Courtier* (1592). By permission of the Folger Shakespeare Library.

Figure 22. Cross-gartering, from Abraham de Bruyn, *Omnium Gentium Habitus* (1581). By permission of the Folger Shakespeare Library.

Sir Philip Sidney, *Arcadia* (1581), ed. Jean Robertson as *The Countess of Pembroke's Arcadia (The Old Arcadia)* (Oxford: Clarendon Press, 1973), pp. 25–28. By permission of Oxford University Press.

Figure 23. The man-woman at his/her toilette, from *Hic Mulier, or The Man-Woman* (1620). By permission of the Huntington Library.

Figure 24. The man-woman and the womanish man in dialogue, from *Haec-Vir, or The Womanish Man* (1620). By permission of the Folger Shakespeare Library.

Mary Wroth, *The First Part of the Countess of Montgomery's Urania*, ed. Josephine A. Roberts (Binghampton, NY: Medieval and Renaissance Texts and Studies, 1995), 73. By permission of the Arizona Board of Regents for Arizona State University.

Mary Wroth, *The Second Part of the Countess of Montgomery's Urania*, ed. Josephine A. Roberts, Suzanne Gossett, and Janel Mueller (Tempe, AZ: Renaissance English Text Society, 1999), pp. 41, 159–60. By permission of the Arizona Board of Regents for Arizona State University.

CHAPTER 5

Figure 25. The rich of this world, and figure 26. How youth shall obey their elders, from Anthony Skoloker, *The Ordinary for All Faithful Christians* (1549?). By permission of the Folger Shakespeare Library.

Augustine Phillips, Last Will and Testament (1605), in E. A. J. Honigmann and Susan Brock, eds., *Playhouse Wills, 1558–1642* (Manchester: Manchester University Press, 1993), pp. 72–74. By permission of E. A. J. Honigmann and Susan Brock.

CHAPTER 6

William Bradshaw, *English Puritanism* (1605), ed. Lawrence A. Sasek in *Images of English Puritanism* (Baton Rouge: Louisiana State University Press, 1989), pp. 81–94. By permission of Louisiana State University Press.

Figure 27. "Good Fellows Must Go Learn to Dance" (1569). By permission of the British Library.

Figure 28. Gaming, bereavement, debauchery, from Geoffrey Whitney, *A Choice of Emblems* (1586). By permission of the Folger Shakespeare Library.

CHAPTER 7

Quintilian, *Institutio Oratoria,* trans. H. E. Butler, Loeb Classical Library (London: Heinemann, 1921), 2:441–57. By permission of Harvard University Press.

Plato, *Philebus,* in *The Dialogues of Plato,* trans. Benjamin Jowett, 4th ed. rev. (Oxford: Oxford University Press, 1969), 3:606–09. By permission of Oxford University Press.

Figure 29. Who is the true fool?, from George Wither, *A Collection of Emblems* (1635). By permission of the Folger Shakespeare Library.

Plato, *Republic,* in *The Dialogues of Plato,* trans. Benjamin Jowett, 4th ed. rev. (Oxford: Oxford University Press, 1969), 2:232–35. By permission of Oxford University Press.

Aristotle, *Nicomachean Ethics,* in *Complete Works,* ed. Jonathan Barnes (Princeton: Princeton University Press, 1984), 2:1780–81. By permission of Princeton University Press.

Laurent Joubert, *Treatise on Laughter,* trans. Gregory David de Rocher (Tuscaloosa: University of Alabama Press, 1980), pp. 38–39, 59–60. By permission of the University of Alabama Press.

Index